Performing Poetry

ARCADIA UNIVERSITY LIBRARY

Thamyris/
Intersecting: Place, Sex, and Race

Series Editor
Ernst van Alphen

Editorial Team
Murat Aydemir, Maaike Bleeker, Yasco Horsman,
Isabel Hoving, Esther Peeren

Performing Poetry:
Body, Place and Rhythm
in the Poetry Performance

Editors
Cornelia Gräbner
Arturo Casas

Colophon

Design
Mart. Warmerdam, Haarlem, The Netherlands
www.warmerdamdesign.nl

Printing
The paper on which this book is printed meets the requirements of "ISO 9706:1994, Information and documentation – Paper for documents – Requirements for permanence".

ISSN: 1570-7253
E-Book ISSN: 1879-5846

ISBN: 978-90-420-3329-0
E-Book ISBN: 978-94-012-0025-7

© Editions Rodopi B.V.,Amsterdam – New York, NY 2011
Printed in The Netherlands

Mission Statement

Intersecting: Place, Sex, and Race

Intersecting is a new series of edited volumes with a critical, interdisciplinary focus.

Intersecting's mission is to rigorously bring into encounter the crucial insights of black and ethnic studies, gender studies, and queer studies, and facilitate dialogue and confrontations between them. *Intersecting* shares this focus with *Thamyris*, the socially committed international journal which was established by Jan Best en Nanny de Vries, in 1994, out of which *Intersecting* has evolved. The sharpness and urgency of these issues is our point of departure, and our title reflects our decision to work on the cutting edge.

We envision these confrontations and dialogues through three recurring categories: place, sex, and race. To us they are three of the most decisive categories that order society, locate power, and inflict pain and/or pleasure. Gender and class will necessarily figure prominently in our engagement with the above. *Race*, for we will keep analyzing this ugly, much-debated concept, instead of turning to more civil concepts (ethnicity, culture) that do not address the full disgrace of racism. *Sex*, for sexuality has to be addressed as an always active social strategy of locating, controlling, and mobilizing people, and as an all-important, not necessarily obvious, cultural practice. And *place*, for we agree with other cultural analysts that this is a most productive framework for the analysis of situated identities and acts that allow us to move beyond narrow identitarian theories.

The title of the new book series points at what we, its editors, want to do: *think together*. Our series will not satisfy itself with merely demonstrating the complexity of our times, or with analyzing the shaping factors of that complexity. We know how to theorize the intertwining of, for example, sexuality and race, but pushing these intersections one step further is what we aim for: How can this complexity be understood in practice? That is, in concrete forms of political agency, and the efforts of self-reflexive, contextualized interpretation. How can different socially and theoretically relevant issues be *thought together*? And: how can scholars (of different backgrounds) and activists think together, and realize productive alliances in a radical, transnational community?

We invite proposals for edited volumes that take the issues that *Intersecting* addresses seriously. These contributions should combine an activist-oriented perspective with intellectual rigor and theoretical insights, interdisciplinary and transnational perspectives. The editors seek cultural criticism that is daring, invigorating and self-reflexive; that shares our commitment to thinking together.

Contact us at intersecting@let.leidenuniv.nl.

Contents

9	Introduction	**Cornelia Gräbner and Arturo Casas**
21	**I. Theorizing Performance Poetry: Critical and Analytical Views**	
23	Allen Ginsberg, "Howl," and the 6 Gallery Poetry Performance	**Jonah Raskin**
33	Stage Fever and Text Anxiety: The Staging of Poeticity in Dutch Performance Poetry since the Sixties	**Gaston Franssen**
53	Artimanha, the Precise Moment of Being: Performance and Carnival in the Poetry of Brazil's Nuvem Cigana	**Jeffrey Manoel Pijpers**
71	"The Hurricane Doesn't Roar in Pentameters": Rhythmanalysis in Performed Poetry	**Cornelia Gräbner**
89	**II. Registers of Performance**	
91	The Body's Territories: Performance Poetry in Contemporary Puerto Rico	**Urayoán Noel**
111	Politics of Sound: Body, Emotion, and Sound in the Contemporary Galician Poetry Performance	**María do Cebreiro Rábade Villar**
133	Producing World and Remnant: Dialogue with Chus Pato	**Arturo Casas**
151	Poetry and Autofiction in the Performative "Field of Action": Angélica Liddell's Theater of Passion	**Anxo Abuín González**
173	Roberto Echavarren's *Atlantic Casino* and *Oír no es ver*: The "Neobarocker" Body in Performance	**Irina Garbatzky**
191	My Life and Performances	**Roberto Echavarren**
195	**III. Locations of Performance**	
197	"Set in Stone": Lemn Sissay's and SuAndi's Landmark Poetics	**Deirdre Osborne**
219	Eartha Kitt Once Told Me	**SuAndi**
229	Heterotopical Routes through Barcelona: The Reshaping of Public Space in the "Galactic" Poetry of Jaume Sisa	**Mercè Picornell Belenguer**
247	Absent Cities: Text, Performance, and Heterotopia	**Zoë Skoulding**

263	New *Loci* in Contemporary Catalan Art and Poetry: Perejaume's Performance of/on the Rural	**Margalida Pons**
279	The Contributors	
283	Index	

Introduction

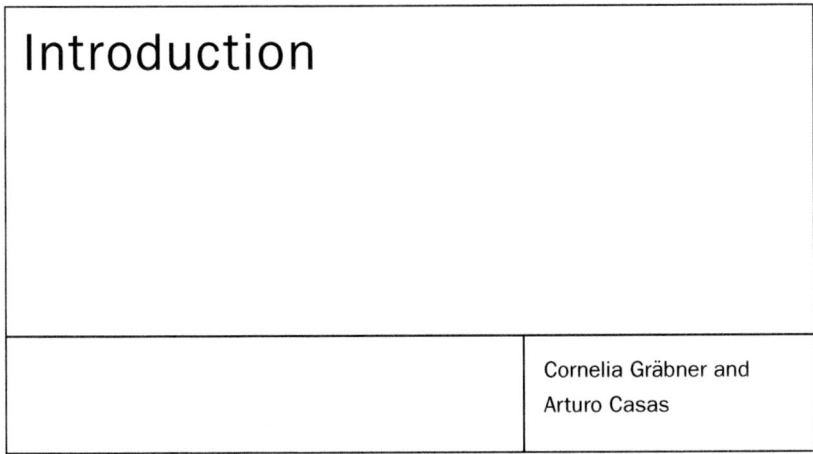

Cornelia Gräbner and
Arturo Casas

Performing Poetry: Body, Place and Rhythm in the Poetry Performance comprises fifteen essays from international scholars and poets on the performance of poetry in a variety of linguistic and cultural – sometimes migratory – contexts. The case studies presented in these essays encompass performed poems in Brazilian Portuguese, Dutch, Catalan, English, French, Galician and Spanish. Many of the poets whose work is discussed here have received very little – if any – attention from scholars who write in English; and the work of several of the contributors to this volume is not usually available in English and has been translated specifically for this publication.

As far as theoretical approaches to the poetry performance are concerned, the essays presented here pursue, develop, and revisit lines of analysis that have been opened up by two previously published essay collections, Charles Bernstein's *Close Listening: Poetry and the Performed Word* and Adelaide Morris's *Sound States: Innovative Poetics and Acoustical Technologies*. The preference for close analysis and the keen interest in sound and poetic form that characterize the contributions to these volumes also informs most of the essays in *Performing Poetry*. However, *Close Listening* and *Sound States* focused on sound and on performed poetry in the English language, and on the formal and text-internal elements of the poem; *Performing Poetry* adds the intercultural dimension and shifts the focus of analysis towards the relationship between text-internal and text-external elements of the performance. This relationship is explored in light of its ramifications for the triangular relationship between performed poem, author or performer, and the audience. Text-external elements figure here not primarily as categories that are developed elsewhere and applied to the poem by way of analysis, as characteristics that are bestowed on the poem by its context, or as supplementary to the poetic text; they are considered intrinsic to poetry in its performed form and, as such, *produce* theoretical approaches instead of applying already extant ones. Performed poems are discussed as theatrical, visual, sonic, and spatial interventions, and the contributors draw on analytical frameworks that are oriented along the lines of the three concepts suggested by the subtitle of this volume: body, place, and rhythm.

Similarities between the case studies presented here criss-cross languages and cultural contexts: the Galician Chus Pato and the Uruguayan Roberto Echavarren both explore social constraints on gender roles and sexuality through the interaction of poetry and visual performances; Echavarren and the Brazilian group Nuvem Cigana engage in poetic practices that take recourse to the carnivalesque as one element of countercultural practices; Chus Pato and the British poet SuAndi address the feeling of emotional precariousness that comes from being a woman *and* a public poet; SuAndi, her fellow-Brit Lemn Sissay and the Catalan poet Jaume Sisa intervene in the spatial organization of their respective cities; Sisa, his compatriot Perejaume and Chus Pato explore notions of "home" and "territory" that are also central to the poetry of Nuyorican and Puerto Rican poets like Pedro Pietri, "Gallego" and Guillermo Rebollo-Gil; Sisa and the British poets Hazel Marsh and Fiona Templeton explore urban space as heterotopic entities, to give only a few examples.

Similarly, several theoretical issues keep recurring throughout the essays, with reference to the work of different poets. The first of these concerns the performance of authorship and the presence of the author at the site of the performance, and the ways in which this influences reception. Secondly, most essays comment on the genealogy of the poetry performance. Views on the origins of the poetry performance differ according to the cultural context of the poem; while some contributors identify continuities with older, marginalized or oppressed poetic traditions, others see a countercultural rupture with the establishment. Importantly, all contributors seem to agree in that the performance of poetry embraces a critical, marginal or even outsider position towards the poetic establishment. The mediatic and cultural hybridity of the poetry performance emerges as the third major theme, which challenges scholars to develop analytical categories and concepts that allow an in-depth critical engagement with performed poems. Fourthly, the ways in which performed poems emerge from and engage with their social environment and how they deal with place and space is a crucial concern. Finally, the discussion of most of the above-mentioned issues is informed by contributors' mindfulness of the political commitment of the poet and the political context of the poetry performance, which often manifests itself in the poets' position on the margins of society.

We have attempted to structure this volume along the lines of a debate between poets and scholars, rather than as a statement of academic expertise. The contributions of María Rábade and Chus Pato, of Irina Garbatzky and Roberto Echavarren, of Deirdre Osborne and SuAndi, of Gaston Franssen and Jonah Raskin, can be read together as dialogues between poets and academics. Zoë Skoulding's decision to include an analysis of her own poetry in her essay, moreover, makes academic discourse permeable to poetic language and highlights the self-reflexive component of performed poetry. We hope that, in this way, the volume can contribute to a productive dialogue between poets and scholars from different areas of the Western world.

Authorship
The poetry performance almost by default obliges poets to address the question of authorship: the enunciation of the poem by the poet him- or herself and the poet's presence at the site of enunciation emphasize the poet's position as an author who accepts responsibility for his or her work. Poets use this in a variety of different ways. On the one hand, the performance can frame individual authorship within a context of community or collectivity, as in the performances of Chus Pato, Willie Perdomo, or Roberto Echavarren who articulate the concerns of sidelined communities; at the same time, the enunciation of the poem can draw on the perlocutionary and illocutionary force of spoken poetry to create community. Alternatively, if the performance takes place in a context that alienates the identity proposed by the poet, it can emphasize the poet's sense of not-belonging, of rebellion, or of isolation. This is the case in Johnny the Selfkicker's performance during *Poëzie in Carré* as discussed by Gaston Franssen, where the poet intentionally violates those conventions of performance that define this particular performance space and, as a result, causes discomfort to the audience and attracts the outrage and disdain of audience and critics; or in a performance by Linton Kwesi Johnson in a university lecture theater at the University of Stirling which Gräbner attended, and throughout which the contrast between Johnson's heavily rhythmed dub poetry on the one hand, and the sonic isolation of the lecture theater and the surrounding rural campus created a productively disconcerting atmosphere. In other cases, poets mobilize devices specific to the performance in order to problematize the constraints of identity and test the limits of belonging and community, as Saul Williams does through the use of socially and politically coded rhythms in his studio recording of "Twice the First Time". Anxo Abuín takes a different approach to a related subject and discusses the staging of authorship and its implications in terms of "auto-fiction"; his analysis can be brought to interact productively with many case studies discussed in other essays, for example with Johnny the Selfkicker's invention of various public personas for himself in the chapter by Franssen, Perdomo's use of the character of Papo as *alter ego* as discussed by Gräbner, or Echavarren's experimentations with the identities made possible by glam rock. In all cases, the performance provides poets with an opportunity to experiment with different, often dissident or marginalized forms of identity. The explicitness of these experiments is the result of a self-reflexive attitude towards authorship and identity promoted by the poetry performance.

Genealogy of the Poetry Performance

The concern with the origin and genealogy of the poetry performance links in with a wider scholarly debate on this question, as already indicated above. On the one hand, scholars like John Miles Foley or Peter Middleton take the poetry performance as a continuation of oral traditions and as a challenge to academic theory, which needs to change in order to accommodate it; on the other hand, the inheritors of counterculture and the proponents of slam poetry argue that the performance of poetry is a radical alternative to poetry as endorsed by academic theory.

In *How to Read an Oral Poem* (2002), John Miles Foley takes as his four introductory examples a Tibetan paper-singer, a North American slam poet, a South African praise-poet, and an ancient Greek bard. Foley focuses on the critical instrumentarium for analyzing oral performances of poetry, and for this reason looks at shared characteristics of the performances. If one takes a less pragmatic approach and prefers a focus on the social and political context of the poem, one might very well question whether it is meaningful across the board to place – for example – a slam poem in the same category as a South African praise-poem. Neither of the two practices is ideologically neutral; slam has been defended as a "democratization" of poetry but also embraces competitiveness in a way that resonates strongly with neoliberal ideology, whereas South African praise-poems are a traditional, non-competitive form of collective remembering. To place them in the same category would call for a very careful substantiation of such an argument, for which a pragmatic approach leaves little room.

Nevertheless, the approach through orality has been important for poets who do draw on oral traditions and who have been confronted with the prejudice that poetry needs to be written in order to allow for silent contemplation and lyricism. Studies like Gregory Nagy's *Poetry as Performance: Homer and Beyond* (1996) and Viv Edwards and Thomas J. Sienkewicz's *Oral Cultures Past and Present: Rappin' and Homer* (1990) emphasize the oral roots of Western literature and lyric poetry. In *Orality and Literacy* (1982), Walter Ong addresses and deconstructs the dominance of writing. His argument is fundamental to the appreciation of the complex staging of the encounter between oral and written literature that is carried out in the work of many African, African-American and Caribbean poets. Deirdre Osborne's analysis of the works of Lemn Sissay and SuAndi emphasizes the significance of oral traditions as "resistant" to dominant cultural models and thus as foundational to a position from which Black British poets can articulate their identity. Gräbner's discussion of Edward Kamau Brathwaite's conceptualization of poetic rhythm also highlights the importance of the oral tradition for contemporary performed poetry.

A second point of origin for the poetry performance is U.S. American counterculture. References to Charles Olson, the Beat poets, and the countercultural movements of the 1960s recur throughout many of the essays in this collection. Irina

Garbatzky and Urayoán Noel explicitly cite elements of U.S. American counterculture as points of reference and influences for the poets whose work they discuss, and Gräbner takes Charles Olson's essay "Projective Verse" as one of two central pieces of writing by performance poets on rhythm. Jonah Raskin and Gaston Franssen address counterculture in most detail. Raskin, biographer of Allen Ginsberg and himself a performance poet, discusses the reading at the 6th Gallery in San Francisco and its significance for Beat Poetry. Franssen takes one of the first poetry performances in the Netherlands – *Poëzie in Carré* – as his case study, and identifies two contrasting styles of reciting poetry. He argues that one of these strands, represented by poets such as Johnny the Selfkicker or Simon Vinkenoog, explicitly took U.S. American counterculture as its model; and that the poetic practice of these poets was an expression of rebellion against the literary establishment. The second strand, represented by poets like Gerrit Kouwenaar, draws on what Franssen calls the "declamatory tradition" in The Netherlands. In an argument similar to the one pursued by Peter Middleton in his essay "A History of the Poetry Reading," published in *Close Listening*, Franssen traces the "declamatory tradition" back to the eighteenth and nineteenth centuries. However, whereas Middleton argues for continuity between the declamatory tradition and the contemporary poetry performance as such, Franssen's analysis of Johnny the Selfkicker's countercultural performance brings him to a different conclusion: he comes to distinguish between two different types of poetry performances and argues that the countercultural poetry performance marks a clear rupture with the declamatory tradition, and not its continuation.

A third current in the genealogy of the performance of poetry is related to the political context in which the practice of performing poetry emerged. Jeffrey Pijpers, María Rábade and Mercè Picornell point out that in the Brazilian, Galician and Catalan contexts the performance of poetry was one way of circumventing censorship imposed by the Brazilian military dictatorship and General Franco, respectively. Similarly, Roberto Echavarren and other poets of the Southern Cone used the performance space opened up by rock music to experiment with gender identities in ways that, at the time, were not accepted in the cultural field; for them, the performance literally opened up alternative spaces in a prohibitive and confining environment. Echavarren's performances, like those of the poets discussed by Franssen, Pijpers and Raskin, and some of those discussed by Gräbner, took their inspiration from countercultural movements. A comparative reading of the approaches presented here highlights two poles of "the political" as manifest in the poetry performance. On the one hand, "the political" is expressed in the radical rupture with traditional forms and through the construction of alternative spaces of performance; on the other hand, "the political" is expressed in a recovery of oppressed traditions by means of the performance and in the re-appropriation of existing performance spaces. Most poems discussed here explore the territory between these two extreme poles, and political position is articulated through the relationship between marginality and mainstream, as discussed further below.

Mediatic and Cultural Hybridity

The mediatic and cultural hybridity of the poetry performance emerges as one of the main challenges to artistic practice and also to academic analysis. In different ways, all the essays in this volume struggle with this challenge and elaborate categories and concepts that enable an in-depth critical and theoretical engagement with the poetry performance as a practice and, implicitly, with performance poetry as a genre. The performances discussed here mobilize stagecraft, film, visual arts, the audio recording, digital technology, print technology, monuments, built environments, and musical instruments. Theater, performance art, and music are among the art forms with which the performance of poetry seems to share the strongest affinities. Anxo Abuín places the performance of poetry within the performative "field of action," on the intersections of poetic language, theater, and the happening. Pijpers's analysis of Nuvem Cigana focuses on the ways in which the interaction of music, spoken word poetry, and visual arts expresses a group identity on the margins of a repressive and constrained society. María Rábade investigates how sound in spoken language is foregrounded by the use of performance strategies that draw on visual and musical performance, and how this sonic dimension of spoken poetic language appeals to affect. Her analysis brings her to differentiate between "timbral" and "accentual" performances. Gräbner conceptualizes the interaction of several layers of signification with reference to poetic rhythm through the concept of "polysensual layering." Garbatzky analyzes the ways in which two of Echavarren's works use film and visual arts in order to integrate the style and cultural connotations of rock music – and of glam rock in particular – into the performance of poetry. In his own contribution to this volume, Echavarren further emphasizes that he used film in order to reflect his own experience of physical and linguistic dislocation in the form of the performance. Moreover, Echavarren turned to rock music and glam rock in order to integrate transculturality and the blurring of clear-cut sexualities into his performance style. Thus, mediatic hybridity accomodates his identity within the formalistic aspects of the performance. Margalida Pons studies the representation of nature in the poetic, photographic, plastic and graphic work of Perejaume, with particular reference to the aesthetic and political dimensions of language, and Deirdre Osborne contrasts the ephemerality of the performance with the same performed poems being literally "set in stone" through their inscription in monuments and plaques in London and Salford.

Location or Dislocation?

Aficionados of the poetry performance have long argued that the poetry performance is by default located in the moment and the place of the performance, and that it emphasizes the cultural, social, and political position of the poet. In "History of the Poetry Reading," Middleton identifies the interaction between place, venue, and poem as one of the three defining characteristics of the poetry reading, and Paul Beasley makes a similar argument in his article "Vive la différance!" This argument posits that the poet, by way of the performance, draws on and contextualizes his poem within an environment that is characteristic of the place in which the poem is performed. It suggests a harmonious and mutually supportive relationship between performing poet, poetry performance, place and community. While this point holds for some of the poets whose work is discussed here, it might have to be revisited in light of the work of others, who explore the relationship between locatedness and dislocatedness, or who highlight their sense of non-belonging.

Noel brings out the tension between locatedness and deterritorialization in the poetry of Puerto Rican and Nuyorican performance poets. He argues that the traffic of influences between Puerto Rican and Nuyorican performance poetry leads to the emergence of a deterritorialized poetic practice and cultural politics, which manifests through the "eccentric" or "unremitting" body. Deirdre Osborne, Zoë Skoulding, and Mercè Picornell focus on practices of performance poetry that engage with city environments. Osborne analyzes the "landmark poetics" of Lemn Sissay and SuAndi, whose poetry is inscribed onto sculptures and plaques in London and Salford to mark areas linked to the slave trade. The physical intervention of both poets in the physical space of these cities is complemented by the mobile engagement with cities that is foregrounded in the contributions by Skoulding and Picornell. Both scholars draw on Foucault's conceptualization of heterotopia within two very different contexts. Picornell focuses on the poetry of Jaume Sisa, which is closely interlinked with Sisa's musical work and which addresses the relationship between the imaginary and the everyday experience of Barcelona in the 1970s. Skoulding compares performances by Hazel Marsh, Geraldine Monk, and Fiona Templeton, who explore different elements of mobility in Northern English cities, the relationship between the body and built environments, and who develop performance strategies that involve the reader in the production of space. On the conceptual level, Foucault's approach to heterotopia proves productive for Picornell's analysis of Sisa's work, whereas Skoulding comes to problematize heterotopia through Lefebvre's critique of it.

Margalida Pons's essay sets a counterpoint to the interest in urban culture that informs most other essays presented here. Her analysis focuses on the ways in which contemporary Catalan poetry draws on rural spaces for the performative exploration of Catalan identity. Rural landscapes and metaphors that draw on them are used to revisit concepts such as tradition and textuality, and notions of land and territory. This last point connects Pons's essay back to that of Noel and his revisiting of the concepts of territory, land, and nation in the Puerto Rican and Nuyorican context. These same concepts are also discussed in Arturo Casas's interview with Chus Pato and in the articles of Rábade and Picornell. They intersect with debates on language and cultural identity in plurinational states and problematize the hybridization and even the neutralization of identities in areas that are characterized by the coexistence of several cultures and languages. Skoulding addresses this latter point when she reflects on the role of Welsh in her work and on the ways in which languages affect her experience of cities. A comparative reading of these articles suggests that the medial hybridity of the poetry performance and the possibility of the simultaneous interaction of several layers of signification (see the conceptualization of these practices as "polysensual layering" by Gräbner) lends this art form to an articulation of identities and experiences which are, in one way or another, multiple.

Marginality or Mainstream: Articulations of the "Political"
The question of the positioning of performed poetry on the intersection between the social, the political, and the poetic is addressed in different ways and with reference to different contexts throughout this volume. Some poets, like Chus Pato, Roberto Echavarren or Saul Williams, take very clear political positions, are engaged in political activism, and have developed their poetry at least partially within this context: Pato's first poetry reading took place at an anti-NATO protest, Echavarren created much of his poetry in dialogue with the Gay Rights movement, and Williams is well known for his vocal opposition of the invasion of Iraq and his participation in the "Not in Our Name" campaign.

Most of the essays presented here do not directly address the question of political commitment, but there is a widely shared interest in the embrace of marginality as resistance to the mainstream. Pijpers elaborates on the notion of "marginality" as driving force for the work of Nuvem Cigana. Similarly, one could read Echavarren's work as an attempt to create, through poetry, a space of enunciation for a culturally and politically marginal position. Johnny the Selfkicker, who is the main case study for Franssen's article, mobilizes and embraces his own marginality as an alternative to a corrupt and corrupted mainstream. SuAndi's marginal position as a woman of mixed African and English origin is constituent of her poetic voice and practice. It manifests itself in what Osborne calls SuAndi's "marginalia poems," which are written on the edges of newspaper articles, on napkins, or whatever materials the poet has at her disposal at the moment of writing. SuAndi's compassionate attention to others who are in a marginal position, together with her continuous poetic search for self-knowledge, makes her poetry a performance of a type of empathy and relationality that becomes possible because of her own marginal position.

The poet Chus Pato reflects on the relationship between marginality and mainstream from yet another point of view. She is interested in the dialectics between dominant culture and poetic practices of resistance and emancipation, from an activist viewpoint. Her reflections revolve around the effectiveness of practices that aim at occupying as large a part of public space as possible, and that question through their presence and materiality the cultural, political, and national hegemony against which these practices intervene. Picornell's analysis captures Jaume Sisa's artistic development at a point when his work, as an expression of Catalan identity, could have turned mainstream, after being marginal and explicitly resistant to the dominant paradigm. Through her analysis of Sisa's own displacement of himself into a different cultural context from Barcelona to Madrid, Picornell addresses the problematic implications of becoming mainstream in a politically more favorable environment. Skoulding discusses Lefebvre's critique of Foucault's concept of heterotopia, which is predicated upon Lefebvre's skepticism towards the marginal. She resolves the tension between the two by focusing her analysis on the presence of otherness in lived space.

Gräbner's analysis of rhythm in poems by Willie Perdomo and Saul Williams shows how Perdomo uses rhythm to locate his poetry within a marginalized community which is reaffirmed as a constructive locus of enunciation, whereas Williams uses rhythms to doubly marginalize himself. Williams problematizes Hip Hop becoming increasingly mainstream; this process removes it from the combative political project it originally espoused, and from the cultural identity that is expressed in this political project. Franssen and Noel address the question of marginality or mainstream with reference to cultural politics and slam poetry. They emphasize the constructive role of slams as opportunities of encounter and debate between poets and audience, and acknowledge that slam has played an important role in providing spaces for the performance of poetry. Yet, Noel problematizes slam poetry and its spin-off Def Poetry Jam, most explicitly in his analysis of the anti-consumerist stance of a performance by Karina Claudio. Throughout his essay he endorses a marginal deterritorialized national identity, the artistic and utopian potential of which is safeguarded precisely because it does not seek to become mainstream. Franssen's field work into the reception of slam poetry suggests that word craft is superseded by the theatrical and "show" elements of slam. Overall, relatively little attention is paid to slam poetry throughout this volume. This might be due to it being popular mainly in the Anglo-Saxon context but also to slam becoming increasingly mainstream and thus falling outside the interest for the marginal. The articles collected here seem to endorse marginality as a source of empowerment, critique, and as an ethically and aesthetically more productive position than the mainstream.

In the face of the crossovers indicated above, the organization of the essays in this volume according to the three subject areas of "Theorizing Performance Poetry: Critical and Analytical Views," "Registers of Performance," and "Locations of Performance" has mostly a practical purpose. The subheadings in this introduction suggest an alternative mode of organizing them and there are many more shared concerns that we could make reference to. As it stands, we hope that the comparative focus of this volume contributes to the formation of a theoretical framework and a public and academic debate that appreciate the multi-faceted challenge of the performance of poetry. Maybe most importantly, the essays presented here identify cultural and mediatic hybridity as a foundational and shared feature of a wide array of practices. The poetry performance explores the implications of this hybridity and develops the creative possibilities that it opens up, especially for those who find themselves in marginal positions or who experience their identity as multiple. Moreover, the contingency of form and content allows for the conclusion that the performance of poetry as a practice and "performance poetry" as a genre highlight the significance of the cultural for the social and the political, and that it provides artists with a powerful mode of critiquing and challenging mainstream cultures.

Acknowledgments

We would like to thank all contributors for their outstanding contributions and for their dedication to the project, and Antón Lopo for generously granting permission to use an image from his performance "Dentro" for the cover of this book. We are grateful to the editors of *Thamyris/Intersecting: Place, Sex, and Race* for their assistance, especially to Esther Peeren for her patient advice on countless editorial questions. Finally, we would like to acknowledge that some of the research presented in this volume is linked with the research project "Non-lyric discourse in contemporary poetry: Spaces, Subjects, enunciative Hybridity, Mediality," which is funded by the Ministry of Science and Innovation of the Spanish government (FFI2009-12746).

Bibliography

Bernstein, Charles. *Close Listening: Poetry and the Performed Word*. Oxford and New York: Oxford University Press, 1998.

Edwards, Viv, and Thomas J. Sienkewicz. *Oral Cultures Past and Present: Rappin' and Homer*. Oxford: Basil Blackwell, 1990.

Foley, John Miles. *How to Read an Oral Poem*. Urbana and Chicago: University of Illinois Press, 2002.

Middleton, Peter. "A History of the Poetry Reading." *Close Listening: Poetry and the Performed Word*. Ed. Charles Bernstein. Oxford and New York: Oxford University Press, 1998, 262–99.

———. "How to Read a Reading of a Written Poem." *Oral Tradition* 20.1 (2005): 7–34.

———. *Distant Reading: Performance, Readership and Consumption in Contemporary Poetry*. Tuscaloosa: University of Alabama Press, 2005.

Morris, Adelaide. *Sound States: Innovative Poetics and Acoustical Technologies*. Chapel Hill: The University of North Carolina Press, 1998.

Nagy, Gregory. *Poetry as Performance: Homer and Beyond*. Cambridge: Cambridge University Press, 1996.

Ong, Walter. *Orality and Literacy: The Technologizing of the Word*. London and New York: Methuen, 1982.

I. Theorizing Performance Poetry: Critical and Analytical Views

Allen Ginsberg, "Howl," and the 6 Gallery Poetry Performance

Jonah Raskin

A few dates in American literary history stand above all the others as landmarks in the transformation of poetry and poetics in the United States. The first is the publication on Independence Day – July 4, 1855 – of Walt Whitman's *Leaves of Grass*, the single-most important, and innovative, American book of poetry published in the nineteenth century, though most of Whitman's contemporaries never realized its originality.[1] The second decisive date in the annals of American poetry took place one hundred years after the publication of Whitman's book, on October 7, 1955. On that day, Allen Ginsberg, a 29-year-old, mostly unknown, and largely unpublished American poet, performed a poem that would soon be published as "Howl" but that existed then only in a rough draft. Though Ginsberg did not outdo Whitman – no one really can – that was his stated aim. He wanted to be more "naked" on the page and in person than he thought Whitman had ever been, and he put his heart into his own personal struggle to be candid. American poetry has not been the same since his initial performance of a poem that went on to be read around the world.

Ginsberg had never before performed his poem in public and he was understandably anxious on October 7. At 11 PM that night he stood before a live audience that included a handful of his oldest, closest friends, in an art gallery in San Francisco. The place – the 6 Gallery – was significant for its insignificance, though the work of notable contemporary California artists such as Jay DeFeo was exhibited there. Still, no major cultural or social event had ever taken place there, and never would again. Ginsberg's performance put both Ginsberg and the 6 Gallery on the literary map of San Francisco. It also altered the course of American poetry and popularized the performance of poetry. Though the 6 Gallery no longer exists as a physical space, it long ago attained literary immortality when it entered the pages of fiction – in Jack

Kerouac's novel *The Dharma Bums* – as the birthplace of the Beat Generation. If there are poetry events every week of the year in nearly every major American city today, it is in large measure due to Ginsberg, the poets who shared the stage with him, and the audience at the 6 Gallery on October 7, 1955.[2]

Ginsberg, of course, was not the first American poet to present poetry to a live audience. Twentieth-century American poets frequently read their work in public, often at formal occasions, and by invitation only. But not just anyone could attend; poetry readings tended to be for the elite. The site could be the Library of Congress, in Washington, D.C., or the Museum of Modern Art in New York, where Ginsberg heard William Carlos Williams – one of his mentors – read his poems in the early 1950s.

A poetry performance in Ginsberg's style was different than a poetry reading. At a reading, the poet held a book in his or her hands, and stood at a podium in front of an audience, usually seated in chairs. There was a formal start to the program and a formal conclusion. At the 6 Gallery the audience sat on the floor and drank wine. Ginsberg finished the performance of his poem not long before midnight; at the very end of his performance he was in tears. Afterwards he and friends went out for Chinese food and then an orgy, or so legend has it. There were other significant ways in which his performance was different from traditional readings. The "charming event," as he called it in the publicity he generated, was free and nothing was for sale either; not even the poem Ginsberg performed, because it was still unfinished and unpublished. The only money that was visible was in the donations for the wine that Jack Kerouac bought.

In the 1940s and 1950s, poets in San Francisco, in Berkeley, and in Oakland across San Francisco Bay, had been in the habit of reading their poems to one another in the privacy of their own homes and at literary salons that took place behind closed doors. Robin Blaser, Robert Duncan, and Jack Spicer gathered in apartments to read to one another. San Francisco was fertile ground for poetry in part because there was a tradition of poetry that went back a hundred years; as early as the Gold Rush days European and English writers like Oscar Wilde performed for appreciative miners.

American authors like Mark Twain, Bret Harte, Jack London, and Ina Coolbrith, California's first poet laureate, gave San Francisco a crash-course in literary culture. Literary magazines appeared out of nowhere, lectures and readings flowered. In 1949, San Francisco State University created a thriving Poetry Center. A local, listener-sponsored radio station, KPFA, broadcast a weekly literary program by the poet Kenneth Rexroth, who served as the Master of Ceremonies at the 6 Gallery and who introduced Ginsberg to the audience. Thanks largely to Rexroth's efforts as poet, critic, and teacher, audiences were already listening to poetry in the fall of 1955; they were primed for new poetry when Ginsberg arrived on the scene. Poets felt free to experiment with form, voice, and theme because San Francisco was on the other side of the continent from New York, the nation's literary capital. The geographical distance made a difference to Ginsberg, too: far from home, parents, and professors he grew less constrained and in San Francisco he felt liberated. His poetry blossomed and he discovered his own voice.

The performance he gave on October 7 thus built on local traditions, but it also signaled a break from the local by incorporating the feeling and mood of a European, avant-garde event. It took place in an art gallery rather than a private home. Ginsberg designed attractive posters and displayed them. He mailed postcards that announced the "reading," as he initially described it. Ginsberg was, of course, not the only poet on the program at the 6 Gallery, though he garnered most of the attention. Two poets from the Pacific North West – Gary Snyder and Philip Whalen – joined him, along with one poet from Kansas – Michael McClure – and one San Francisco native – Philip Lamantia. Gary Snyder, who would be the last poet to read that night, had promoted the event, and in letters to friends predicted that it would turn out to be what he called a "poeticall Bomshell" – intentionally altering the spelling for effect. Indeed, it was an explosive event that sent shock waves across the country, far beyond poetical circles. Before the event Ginsberg was still thinking in traditional ways about the presentation of his poem to the audience: the event was to be a reading. He was going to read his new, unfinished poem. It was only at the 6 Gallery itself that the *reading* turned into a *performance*, in part because he was inspired and also because members of the audience – some of whom were intoxicated – pushed him to experiment. Kerouac, who was in the audience drinking red wine, urged him on by shouting, "Go, Go, Go," and indeed, as a performer Ginsberg went further than he had ever gone before.

The original title for the work was "Strophes" and it was an experiment in the form of poetry itself. It would take another year for Ginsberg to complete the poem. He would rearrange whole sections and make the whole poem much longer than it was on October 7. From about 2,000 words it grew to about 3,000. Ginsberg changed the title from "Strophes" to "Howl" because he envisioned it as a raw, unpolished work, a kind of animal scream meant to wake up a society that, in his view, had been anaesthetized by the mass media. Still, for all its raw power and energy "Howl" was carefully crafted.

Over the course of a year – from the fall of 1955 to the spring of 1956 – Ginsberg moved from apartment to apartment and from San Francisco to Berkeley, finally settling in a cottage near the campus of the University of California that he shared with Kerouac. He continued to revise the poem while Kerouac insisted that he ought not to change a single word. While he wrote, he listened to Ella Fitzgerald and Bach on a record player, and not surprisingly described his long poem as a "jazz mass." With revision, "Howl" became richer, denser, with three separate sections divided by Roman numerals: I, II, and III. The poem's long lines sprawled across the pages.

There was nothing box-like or tidy about them. When Ginsberg wrote Part I of "Howl," he was performing on the page for readers and for himself, too. In some of the poem's most colorful phrases, like "drunken taxicabs of Absolute Reality" and "angel headed hipsters burning for the ancient heavenly connection" – which did not appear in the first draft and was only added with revision – he meant to show off his verbal skills and dexterity with language. In fact, Part I is so densely packed with images, one on top of the other, that the first listeners missed much of it; what they caught was a feeling, a tone, and a voice. The message of the poem was the messenger himself – the "I" who explains in the first line, "I saw the best minds of my generation destroyed by madness." Early critics of "Howl" noted that only the author himself could perform the poem and do it justice. Indeed, rarely have a poem and a poet been so inextricably connected.

As it evolved, "Howl" became more musical and more suited for public performances. The enthusiastic response by audiences to Part I of the poem, which Ginsberg read at the 6 Gallery and at other locations, persuaded him to give Parts II and III more verbal flourishes and to include more repetition of words and phrases. Part II, which is sometimes referred to as the "Moloch Section," repeats the word Moloch – the name for an Old Testament deity that devoured children – more than fifty times. Part III repeats the refrain, "I am with you in Rockland," nearly two dozen times. Ginsberg revised "Howl" at least a dozen times, changing specific words, phrases, and images; though he would later insist in essays he wrote about the composition of the poem and in interviews with reporters that he never changed a word.[3]

After finishing "Howl," Ginsberg wrote what he called a "Footnote to Howl" – a short poem that begins with the word "Holy," and that is repeated fifteen times. This poem was a kind of private joke; T.S. Eliot's *The Waste Land* had footnotes. For Ginsberg, who admired Eliot and his masterpiece, "Footnote to Howl" was a way of acknowledging his debt to Eliot. For a year before he wrote "Howl" he was reading Eliot's poetry and literary criticism, and he aimed to achieve what Eliot called the "telescoping of images," which would link seemingly unrelated things and ideas. In "Howl" he accomplished what he set out to do and some of the poem's most striking images, such as "crack of down on the hydrogen jukebox," do indeed telescope images and yoke dissimilar objects and things. They also reflect Ginsberg's apocalyptic imagination, which echoed Eliot's voice of doom and disaster.

In 1956 the entire poem was printed in England in a paperback edition of 1,000 copies entitled *Howl and Other Poems*. Ferlinghetti had sent the manuscript there because he was afraid that no American printers would be willing to typeset and then print a book with so many obscenities. Later editions were published in the U.S. and no printer grumbled or refused to print it. "Howl" itself took up most of the volume. There were ten other poems, such as "America," which Ginsberg frequently performed in public and which contains two of the most memorable lines in twentieth-century

American poetry: "America when will we end the human war?" and "Go fuck yourself with your atom bomb." The book was shipped from England to the port of San Francisco where customs officials seized all copies, pending an investigation by the U.S. district attorney, who declined to prosecute for obscenity. Yes, the poem had four-letter words, but it also seemed to have redeeming social value and the U.S. Supreme Court had ruled that works with redeeming social value could not be deemed obscene. However, the city of San Francisco still prosecuted Ferlinghetti for obscenity; at the trial, lawyers for the defense read from "Howl" and performed passages for the judge. The national news media attended and the attendant publicity, wittingly or unwittingly, created an audience and a market for the book.

Before long, customers were lining up outside City Lights to buy *Howl and Other Poems*, which had a black and white cover, sold for 75 cents, and was small enough to fit into the back pocket of a pair of trousers or a jacket. It was eminently portable; fans carried it around, brought it out, and read from it on the spur of the moment. Word of the four-letter words and sexual imagery spread rapidly and Ginsberg publicized his own work by giving performances from Berkeley to Los Angeles and New York. His friends talked about the reading at the 6 Gallery and helped to make it and him both famous and infamous.

Ginsberg's San Francisco publisher Lawrence Ferlinghetti – a poet and ex-New Yorker who had studied at the Sorbonne – owned City Lights, a bookstore in North Beach that only carried paperback books; it was the first all-paperback bookstore in the United States. Ferlinghetti was present – along with about 150 other audience members – at the 6 Gallery and knew instantly that he wanted to publish Ginsberg's poem in what he called "The Pocket Poet's Series." He liked the sound of the poem, its cadence and rhythm, and he was also struck by Ginsberg's intense and lucid performance. Though he did not see the text, he sent a telegram to Ginsberg on October 8 in which he said, "I greet you at the beginning of a great career. When do I get the manuscript."

Ferlinghetti was consciously and deliberately echoing the words of Ralph Waldo Emerson, the nineteenth-century American transcendentalist who was an admirer of Whitman and *Leaves of Grass*. In July 1855, the same month that *Leaves of Grass* was published, Emerson wrote to Whitman: "I greet you at the beginning of a great career, which yet must have had a long foreground somewhere" (Allen 60). Ferlinghetti regarded Ginsberg as a latter-day Whitman and indeed Ginsberg admired Whitman and used two lines from *Leaves of Grass* – "Unscrew the locks from the doors! Unscrew the doors themselves from their jambs!" – as the epigraph for "Howl." However, Ginsberg had been profoundly conflicted about Whitman for years, in part because he was conflicted about his own sexual identity and because he was drawn to and under the influence of very different and often antithetical poets such as T.S. Eliot and W. H. Auden, who he heard at the Poetry Center of San Francisco State University. As an apprentice poet, he imitated John Donne and T.S. Eliot, and his own early poetry was influenced by a diverse group of poets that included Hart Crane, William Butler Yeats, Arthur Rimbaud, and William Blake. His own father Louis was a published poet and a teacher of poetry who read aloud at home to his two sons from the works of John Milton and the American poets Vachel Lindsay and Carl Sandburg. That experience of his father catching fire as he read poetry played a decisive role in Allen Ginsberg's boyhood.

By the time Ginsberg performed the first part of "Howl" at the 6 Gallery he was beginning to appreciate Whitman once again after turning his back on him and his work for years. The long lines of "Howl" and its musical quality reflect the influence of Whitman, and Ginsberg cobbled together a multicultural tradition of poetry that included English, French, Spanish, and Russian as well as American authors. There were several other influences on Ginsberg's writing and his performance of poetry that ought to be mentioned. He read Dylan Thomas and heard him read when he came to the United States in the early 1950s, astounding listening audiences. There was more than a little of Thomas in Ginsberg's work, though he did not like to admit it.

Ginsberg's poetry was also influenced by jazz, as played and interpreted by musicians in the 1940s and 1950s, a golden age of saxophonists. Ginsberg learned much of what he knew about jazz from his closest friend in New York, Jack Kerouac, who was profoundly influenced by the jazz of African-American musicians such as Charlie Parker. In New York in the 1940s, Ginsberg became an aficionado of jazz; he listened to recordings and live performances, and in "Howl" he describes the poem itself as a "saxophone/cry that shivered the cities down to the last radio."

Ginsberg and Kerouac idealized jazz musicians and assumed that saxophonists and trumpeters played spontaneously, without rehearsing. Their view was inaccurate. Jazz virtuosi such as Charlie Parker, John Coltrane, and the jazz pianist Thelonious Monk – another influence on Ginsberg – rehearsed their work before they performed it, though on stage they took musical themes and played variations on them. Ginsberg and Kerouac admired the art of improvisation, by which they meant the ability to create music and words on the spur of the moment, refraining from rehearsing, revising, memorizing, and repeating in a mechanical way. That was their avowed aesthetic. In practice they both revised and rehearsed, though they also aimed to break down barriers between rehearsal and performance. From the start, Ginsberg's poetry was shaped by the technology of the tape recorder, namely the ability to press the stop button, rewind, replay, and listen again to his own voice. In the 1940s, he recorded his poems on a tape recorder and played the recordings for himself and his friends. By the time he was nineteen – nearly a decade before he arrived in San Francisco – he was writing poetry with an eye and an ear on listening audiences, and with the notion that he might perform poems in public. For forty years, from 1956 to 1996, he performed his own poetry as well as the poetry of William Blake, which he set to music. He learned to play the harmonium and traveled ceaselessly around the United States and the world. In this way, he became a master of performance poetry and a role model for others to follow. His work influenced John Lennon of the Beatles and Bob Dylan, who noted in a blurb on the back cover of Ginsberg's *Collected Poems* that Ginsberg was "a lyrical genius," and "probably the single greatest influence on American poetical voice since Whitman."

Though he never wrote a guidebook for performance poetry, he established practices and standards that others followed. Beginning in 1956 in Berkeley, he recorded himself reading "Howl" as well as many other poems; the recordings made their way onto 33 1/3 long-playing records, and later CDs, including a box set entitled *Holy Soul, Jelly Roll*. To Ginsberg, performing a poem, as opposed to reading it, meant injecting a sense of theater. The poet on stage before an audience used body language and facial expressions, changed tone of voice, made eye contact, and acknowledged the presence of the audience. For Ginsberg performance poetry was liberated poetry and he often liberated his own work from itself. No two readings of "Howl" were exactly the same; the pace, the rhythm, and even the words changed. When he performed the poem at the San Francisco Poetry Center in 1955, he changed the phrase "who let themselves be fucked up the ass" to "who let themselves be censored up the censored." Performing "Howl" could be physically exhausting and as he aged, it also took longer and longer to move from the first line to the last.

The original performance of "Howl" at the 6 Gallery was a personal triumph for Ginsberg. He found his voice, his public persona as a poet, and launched his career. He was soon famous across America and after the poem was translated into nearly thirty languages, he and it became famous globally. The media helped to spread his fame; the *New York Times* sent the reporter and poet Richard Eberhart to San Francisco to interview Ginsberg and write about him as a performance poet. Eberhart's article, "West Coast Rhythms," appeared in the *New York Times* on September 2, 1956 and contributed to the growing legend of "Howl" and its author. "West Coast Rhythms" was probably the first and the last time that the *Times* published an article about a poem that had not yet been published and only existed as a performance piece.

Performing "Howl" was also a therapeutic experience for Ginsberg. When he arrived in San Francisco the year before he began to write his poem, he was conflicted about his own poetry, his place in the pantheon of poets, both living and dead, and his identity. To resolve his personal issues and overcome anxieties and a writing block, he went into psychotherapy with Dr. Philip Hicks. He brought his own poems, including drafts of "Howl," to sessions with Dr. Hicks and emerged from them feeling self-confident and ready to perform in public. It was one thing, however, to tell Dr. Hicks, as he did, that he was a homosexual (or at least thought he was). It was quite another to write lines about homosexuality and then utter them, scream them, in public. There was little if any ambiguity in lines like "who let themselves be fucked up the ass by saintly motorcyclists, and/screamed with joy." Puritanically inclined readers were shocked and wanted far less transparency.

After a year of writing and rewriting, "Howl" evolved into a poem about coming out: sexually, politically, and poetically. It became a poem about the act of writing and the act of performing poetry. The last section of Part I culminates in a description of the creation of "Howl," a process in which the author says that he "joined the elemental verbs and set the noun and dash of/consciousness together." After therapy with Dr. Hicks, there was little or no room for secrecy, silence, or the muffling of feelings. The point was to confess loudly and clearly, to express experiences, dreams, and fears that had been bottled up inside him since childhood.

The October 7 event at the 6 Gallery also marked the beginning of the Beat Generation – though its roots extended much further into the past – and the start of a literary outpouring that would come to be known as the "San Francisco Poetry Renaissance." Soon after "Howl" was published, Jack Kerouac's novel *On the Road* appeared in print and became a bestseller. Kerouac appeared on television and read from his work with live music in the background: TV personality Steve Allen played the piano. The avant-garde performance artist became mainstream and reached a national audience; soon thereafter, poetry events, often with live jazz, mushroomed across the United States in coffee houses and cafés.

Even though all the poets who participated in the 6 Gallery program were white males, performance poetry spread beyond white male enclaves. Women poets like Diane di Prima and African-American poets like Le Roi Jones (later Amiri Baraka) joined the movement, performed their poems in public, and published their own literary magazines. By the mid-1960s, the cultural wave that the Beats and the Beatniks had started morphed into the counterculture, and Ginsberg and Snyder performed their work before large, open-air gatherings of hippies. In 1969, Ginsberg testified at the "conspiracy trial" of the Chicago Eight defendants, who were charged with rioting in the streets at the Democratic National Convention the previous year. On the witness stand, he read parts of "Howl," which had become a kind of national anthem for the counterculture; hearing Ginsberg perform it live or listening to a tape or a record of him performing "Howl" was a rite of passage for a generation.

In the last decade of the twentieth and at the start of the twenty-first century, performance poetry came into its own all over again all across the United States. Poets like David Meltzer – whose work was published in Donald Allen's *The New American Poetry* (1960), the first anthology to include all poets from the 6 Gallery and others such as Le Roi Jones and Jack Kerouac – continued the Beat tradition of performing poetry on stage and with music. Clubs and venues in New York, such as the Nuyorican Poets Café, the St. Mark's Poetry Center, and the Bowery Poetry Club, which was founded in 2002 by Bob Holman, provided new opportunities for young poets and performers to share their work with lively audiences.

The kind of inspired performance that Ginsberg gave at the 6 Gallery continued, albeit with variations such as the poetry slam, which introduced a competitive edge missing from the 6 Gallery, where Ginsberg and company did not feel moved to rival or up-stage one another. Holman, who was influenced by Ginsberg and who was a longtime admirer of "Howl," defended the slam and the open mike, though his approach came under attack for being too informal and too much like an athletic contest. Holman wanted democratic, egalitarian, and anti-elitist readings and performances where anyone in the audience could perform or read, as well as readings in languages other than English, and music and dance along with poetry, too.

In homage to the Beat tradition of renewing the past, Holman's Bowery Poetry Club celebrated the fiftieth anniversary of the 6 Gallery event in 2005 with dramatic performances of "Howl" by a dozen or so poets and actors. Anne Waldman performed "Footnote to Howl" perhaps more dynamically than anyone had performed it before. From the back of the room, she bounded through the audience and began to cry out "holy, holy, holy," repeating the word until she arrived on stage – a performance that Ginsberg surely would have loved. Ginsberg's message was that poetry was holy and the performance of poetry was holy, too. This message reverberated long after the voices at the 6 Gallery were just a memory. Ironically, however, in 2007, on the fiftieth anniversary of the obscenity trial of "Howl" that Ferlinghetti won, no American radio station had the courage to broadcast Ginsberg performing "Howl." New regulations by the Federal Communications Commission leveled hefty fines on stations for airing material with four-letter words. "Howl" was, in the eyes of the U.S. government, obscene once again and unfit for listeners' ears.

Notes

1. Emily Dickinson's work was innovative, too, but it would have to wait until the twentieth century to be published in book form.

2. Anyone who wants to hear Ginsberg perform "Howl" can do so. Recordings are available on a variety of CDs. One can also find the complete text of the poem by googling it.

3. In this essay all the direct quotations from "Howl" are from *Allen Ginsberg: Collected Poems* published by Harper & Row in 1984. The breaks in the lines are different in the *Collected Poems* than in the City Lights edition of *Howl and Other Poems*, and readers can put the texts side-by-side and trace the differences. Moreover, to see the extensive revisions that Ginsberg made in the text – a major topic in *my American Scream* – readers can turn to *Howl: Original Draft Facsimile, Transcript & Variant Versions*, edited by Barry Miles. That book and my own ought to put to rest forever Ginsberg's absurd claim that he did not revised the text.

Bibliography

Allen, Gay Wilson. *Walt Whitman*. New York: Grove Press, 1961.

Eberhart, Richard. "West Coast Rhythms." *The New York Times Book Review*, 2 September 1956. Rpt. *On the Poetry of Allen Ginsberg*. Ed. Lewis Hyde. Ann Arbor: University of Michigan Press, 1974. 24–25.

Ginsberg, Allen. *Collected Poems: 1947–1980*. New York: Harper & Row, 1984. Rpt. New York: Perennial Library, 1988.

Miles, Barry, ed. *Howl: Original Draft Facsimile, Transcript & Variant Versions*. New York: Harper & Row, 1986. Rpt. New York: HarperPerennial, 1995.

Raskin, Jonah. *American Scream: Allen Ginsberg's "Howl" and the Making of the Beat Generation*. Berkeley: University of California Press, 2004.

Stage Fever and Text Anxiety: The Staging of Poeticity in Dutch Performance Poetry since the Sixties

Gaston Franssen

The increasing visibility of performance poetry in the literary field of the Netherlands since the 1960s has led to a deadlock in Dutch literary criticism. Literary reviewers shy away from reviewing performance poetry and on the rare occasion that they do reflect on a publication by a poet of stage or slam fame, they generally do so in disapproving terms. Writing on a collection of poems by Tjitske Jansen, known for her stage personality, the critic Koen Vergeer, for example, criticizes the "aiming at effect that always works well on stage, but results in weakness when put to paper" ("In stilte").[1] Likewise, Piet Gerbrandy, poetry critic for *De Volkskrant*, doubts whether the "lyrics" of the performance poet Serge van Duijnhoven "will hold on paper." His final judgment is merciless: "The problem with [Van Duijnhoven's poetry] is the almost total lack of catchy images, while only very rarely is the language handled efficiently."[2] In his review of Ingmar Heytze's *Aan de bruid* 'To the Bride' (2000) Jos Joosten, poetry critic for *De Standaard*, analyzes the "problem" of performance poetry in a comparable manner: "The comprehensibility and the much-needed punch lines, which are part and parcel of a stage performance, inevitably diminish the effect of written poetry."[3] In this context, it is significant that the yearly Dutch Championship Poetry Slam has not been seriously reviewed by any major poetry critic since it was organized for the first time in 1998. Dutch critics evidently suffer from stage fever: though they acknowledge that they cannot appreciate performance poetry when it is set down on paper, they continue to display a dogged preference for a formalist, strictly "textual" type of literature and refrain from writing on the actual practice of performance poetry.

At the same time, performance poets turn their back on traditional (literary magazine and newspaper) criticism. "It seems to me that the previous generation of poets, critics and connoisseurs can be blamed for locking up poetry in an ivory tower," according to Heytze: "Academic drivel is still the norm; poetry that any normal human being would fling into the corner, crying from boredom" (qtd. in Vergeer, "Poëzie" 325).[4] He is not alone in his rejection of traditional criticism: Tom Lanoye also criticizes what he calls the "hegemony of the scriptural" (qtd. in Vergeer, "Poëzie" 325).[5] And in the introduction to the collection *Sprong naar de sterren* 'Leap for the Stars' (1999), containing work by poets who explicitly associate themselves with a performance tradition (such as Heytze, Arjan Witte, Bart F.M. Droog, and others), editor Ruben van Gogh claims that a "new dimension" has been added to poetry, "a dimension that has be located outside the literary world" (5). He continues: "In Dutch newspapers and magazines one reads hardly anything about this, since these review poetry according traditional literary ways of thinking. Consequently, new developments are not noticed."[6] Quite a number of performance poets back up this rejection of textual forms of academic reviewing as well as newspaper and literary magazine criticism with a cultivation of the oral roots of their work. Van Duijnhoven's performance collective De Sprooksprekers 'The Tale-tellers', for example, claims to revitalize the medieval tradition of storytelling, and Lanoye insists that he is an actor in the body of an author (Brems 649–52; Vergeer, "In stilte" 328).

As a consequence of their unfavorable disposition towards literary criticism, performance poets have developed a preference for a different, more elusive mode of evaluation. In the Dutch slam circuit, evaluative practices are either completely democratized by the use of a clapometer or "performed" by an elected jury during or immediately after the slam. An analysis of about sixty written accounts of poetry slams, all of which took place in Festina Lente, an Amsterdam pub that forms the stage for a highly regarded monthly slam, revealed that the latter form of criticism is based on criteria such as the looks of the performer, his or her authenticity, and his or her diversity in performance style (Franssen, "Hopend" 238–42). Needless to say, these criteria would be difficult to apply to written poetry.

Thus, performance poets show themselves to be fundamentally distrustful of the written word. This distrust manifests itself on several levels of their literary praxis, as has become clear: they distance themselves from the formal practice and aesthetic preferences of the traditional literary critics; they emphasize the oral roots of their work; and they develop their own, instantaneous practices of evaluation on the basis of criteria that are for the most part incompatible with written poetry criticism. When one takes into account that some Dutch performance poets even refrain from publishing their poetry in print altogether, it becomes possible to conclude that this reserved attitude towards written poetry amounts to a genuine "text anxiety."

The mutual incomprehension between performance poets and poetry critics in the Dutch literary domain has been explained in several ways. Thomas Vaessens maintains that these poets cannot be understood by the critics because the former "do not operate according to the classic avant-garde scenario, which requires that the young revolutionary first has to relate to the previous generation of poetic innovators" (72).[7] Because Dutch performance poets, according to Vaessens, refrain from defining their position in relation to the literature of preceding generations, the work of these performers lacks the "literary frame of reference" that most critics rely on. Vaessens believes that this is a major source of misunderstanding: while the critics look for "literary references" and a "complex interweaving" with literary history, which would be "characteristic for paper poetry in the tradition of the avant-garde," the performers opt for "the immediacy of the performance" (72).[8] Bertram Mourits, on the other hand, is less concerned with the supposed lack of literary references in performance poetry, but argues that the poetics of modernism, which have long dominated Dutch criticism, lie at the heart of the problem. Modernism's preference for ambiguity and poly-interpretability has blocked the critical view on performance poetry, according to Mourits (338).

Vaessens's and Mourits's explanations, however, are not satisfactory, for it has been pointed out that performing poets do enter into a discussion with literary traditions and do embrace literary experiments. Dirk de Geest reminds us that performance poets expressly associate themselves with a "centuries-old oral tradition," including "the troubadours, medieval literature, the primitive story-tellers and the shaman" (870).[9] And, writing on contemporary slam poetry, Brems observes that there is "an undeniable historical line, originating in Dada," linking "the happenings" of the sixties and "performers in the seventies" to a new generation of "recitation poets and poetry slam poets" (651).[10]

In this essay I attempt to come to a clearer understanding of the deadlock between Dutch performance poetry and literary criticism. I focus on an event that, according to many performance poets, marked the break-through of *podiumpoëzie* (stage poetry) in the Netherlands, namely the *Poëzie in Carré* 'Poetry in the Carré Theater' event in 1966. A comparison of the different poetry readings given on that occasion suggests the existence of two performance traditions: on the one hand, a tradition that goes back to the classic eighteenth- and nineteenth-century conventions of poetry declamation or recitation; on the other hand, a tradition based on the performance experiments carried out by the avant-garde movements of the first half of the twentieth century. While the former tradition harmonizes with a widespread set of expectations about the qualities of poetry and its evaluation, the latter contradicts these expectations and even deconstructs them. It is therefore possible to view performance poetry's clash with Dutch literary criticism as a "staging of poeticity."

The term "poeticity" is here understood as the potentiality of a linguistic event to be experienced as poetic. This understanding of poeticity is analogues to the approach of Roman Jakobson,[11] provided that such a poetic potentiality in my view cannot be understood properly without also taking into account the complex of aesthetic assumptions, interpretive conventions, and other socio-cultural conditions that allow us to experience an artifact or performance as poetic. With the concept of "staging," I refer to a linguistic process during which, due to a clash of expectations, such assumptions, conventions, and conditions are brought to light and put into play.

This staging of poeticity, I argue, calls for a different critical approach. Such an approach, a "performative" reading of performance poetry, is demonstrated in the following section, which proposes a closer analysis of the work of one particular participant in *Poëzie in Carré*, Johnny van Doorn, also known as Johnny the SelfKicker (1944–1991). In the final section of this contribution, I conceptualize performative reading in more detail.

Performing Poetry in the Sixties and the Conflict between Two Traditions
Many Dutch poets and literary scholars consider *Poëzie in Carré* the breakthrough of performance poetry in the Dutch context. The event was organized by the poet Simon Vinkenoog, who had attended *The International Poetry Incarnation*, a large happening in the Royal Albert Hall (London), on 11 June 1965. At this event, Vinkenoog and 8,000 others had witnessed performances by famous Beat poets such as Gregory Corso and Allen Ginsberg. Vinkenoog was determined to organize a similar event in Amsterdam and succeeded quickly: on 28 February 1966 he gathered twenty-five Dutch poets in the Carré Theater for an evening of poetry readings and performances.

The success of the event was undeniable: the two thousand tickets sold out quickly, the event was broadcast on radio and television, and the newspaper commented extensively on the performances (Vinkenoog 252–276). Furthermore, it inspired Guido Lauwaert to organize a similar festival in Flanders, resulting in the successive *Nachten van de Poëzie* 'Nights of Poetry' in 1973, 1975, 1980 and 1984. During these infamous Nights, "the audience, which came in large numbers, could actively participate in a true poetry celebration, where poets read their own work or tried to amuse or provoke the audience with their act," according to De Geest (869).[12] The lasting impact of *Poëzie in Carré* is also documented by several modern Dutch overviews of literary history, in which the event is mentioned as an important date (Goedegebuure 777; Brems 459). Today, some critics even acclaim that particular evening in 1966 as "the birth of the culture of the literary stage" (Rijghard and Wijndelts 21).[13]

At the Carré Theater, the poets who contributed to the evening were united in their aspiration to intensify the communication between the poet and his audience. Yet the individual performances of the contributors differed significantly from each other. Poets such as A. Roland Holst or Gerrit Kouwenaar faithfully recited their poems from a piece of paper or a collection of their poetry, whereas Ewald Vanvugt and Johnny van Doorn introduced elements of improvisation, experiment, and interaction in their performances. Vanvugt, according to one particular critic, put on an "exuberant" show: he read poems containing lines such as "Blits!! Paaaauw!! Zzzzzoemmmmm... Kjing-kjing-kjinggg... Tsak! Tsak!!" with his fellow poets Van Doorn and Hans Verhagen humming in the background (Vinkenoog 210–212). Van Doorn performed what he called an "electric act": the poet screamed his poems in a high-pitched voice, wildly waving his arms, and imitating with his voice the sounds of fireworks and jazz drum solos. His performance ended (unexpectedly) in a "grand finale" when the wife of the political cartoonist Opland, pen name of Rob Wout, ran onstage and started to bash the poet with a bouquet of flowers (Goedegebuure 782). The audience was partly amused, partly annoyed. Critics found it difficult to grasp what these poets were attempting to do. One critic dryly remarked that Vanvugt "did not rave any better or worse than he normally does" (Vinkenoog 212).[14] Van Doorn was said to revert to "bizarre shouting," "incoherent, sometimes rather candid exclamations," and "quasi-psychopathic showing off" (Vinkenoog 128–30).[15] "What is he talking about?" one journalist wondered. Another stated: "[Van Doorn's] words perhaps did not make everyone stop and think" (Vinkenoog 212, 128).[16]

At the time, Vanvugt's and Van Doorn's acts at Poëzie in Carré may have seemed minor disturbances, but in hindsight they have a far greater significance: they mark the clash between two different performance traditions. Most of the poets who contributed to the event were influenced by the declamatory tradition. This tradition emerged in the eighteenth and nineteenth centuries, when the popularity of recitals, literary contests, and public orations caused a genuine "cult of the oral" to emerge (Couttenier and Van den Berg 45).[17] During this time period, declamatory handbooks written by rhetoricians, literary scholars, and skilled actors formalized the enunciation of verse (Couttenier and Van den Berg 197). In the Dutch context two publications were particularly influential: B.H. Lulofs's *De declamatie; of de kunst van declaméren of recitéren en van de mondelinge voordragt of uiterlijke welsprekendheid in het algemeen* 'Declamation; or, The Art of Declamation or Recitation and of Oral Delivery or Outward Eloquence in General' (1848) and J.M. Larive's *Cours de Déclamation* (1804–1810), which was translated into Dutch in 1856 by G.T.N. Suringar as *De kunst van het declameren* 'The Art of Declamation' (Van den Berg 473). The authors described (and prescribed) in great detail the poses, use of intonation, and movements that were most appropriate for the recitation of poems. The recitation of a love poem, for example, had to fulfill different conditions than the reading of an epic work. Yet two rules seemed to apply to every recitation and were even deemed essential for a good performance.

The first rule was that the text had to be recited exactly as it was written by the poet; no changes or improvisations were allowed. In his revised handbook *De kunst der mondelingen voordracht of uiterlijke welsprekendheid* 'The Art of Oral Delivery or Outward Eloquence' (1877) Lulofs stated that the recitation should "conform to all the divisions and parts of that which is recited; to every sentence, constituent, word, syllable, even to the letter" (138).[18] In his *Cours de Déclamation*, Larive pushed the argument further and argued that "one of the major obstacles" to the "perfection of the art" of declamation was the tendency "to ignore or to neglect punctuation" (23).[19] He even expressed the wish to use "half a comma" – or even "a quarter of a comma" – to indicate the subtle pauses that were needed to convey the full import of the poem (23).

The second rule concerned self-mastery and restraint: no matter how strong the emotions one had to convey, the verse speaker had to control himself at all times. Only "he who has power over himself will soon rule over his listeners as well," Larive reminded his readers (8).[20] This rule was commonly accepted, as shown in a poem entitled "Reciteeren" 'To Recite' by the nineteenth-century Dutch poet Nicolaas Beets. Beets advised all those who wished to recite a poem:

> Let beautiful verses flow evenly from smooth lips,
> But do not scream, nor boom, nor quack, nor roar, wildly and loud;
> . . . .
> Keep your composure, maintain your strength and mastery,
> And when you shock another, do not even seem moved yourself. (2: 391)[21]

Writing more generally on nineteenth-century recitation practice, Van den Berg concludes: "Declamation is an art that is not based on excess or exaggeration, but that can convince only by restraint" (475).[22]

Even though this tradition of poetry performance was past its prime by the second half of the nineteenth century, and even though it was followed by a radical shift towards a notion of experiencing poetry as an individual and introspective event (Couttenier and Van den Berg 487; Mourits 331; Pfeiler 28), it has continued to influence the performance practice up to the present time. At *Poëzie in Carré* the declamatory tradition was influential: most poets read their own poetry, kept to the letter of the written texts, and kept their composure. They gave a classic poetry reading, just as many of the performance poets in the contemporary Dutch poetry scene do (Franssen, "De dood" 263). Therefore, Middleton's observation that contemporary poetry readings in the U.K. "draw upon a long history of training and practice of formal oral performance," the history of which is often "ignored" (*Distant* 85), can be said to apply to the Dutch situation as well.

The difference between performers likes Vanvugt and Van Doorn on the one hand, and poets like Kouwenaar on the other, becomes clear when one considers this lasting impact of the declamatory tradition. Vanvugt and Van Doorn draw their inspiration from avant-garde movements such as Dadaism, Expressionism, and Surrealism. Van Doorn acknowledged his affinity with avant-garde performances when he said that he was influenced by the Swiss Dadaist Kurt Schwitters, the Flemish poet Paul van Ostaijen, "several Dada-poets" (Dütting 16, 77), and the French playwright Antonin Artaud (Van Doorn 173). In contradistinction to the classic style of poetry reading, this performance tradition, which has its roots in the historical avant-garde and the countercultural experiments of the post-war period, foregrounds improvisation, experiment, interaction, and a conscious effort to lose control of the performance. Unlike the practice of declamation, the avant-garde performance has never been formalized in handbooks or a generally acknowledged system of rules. Still, one can distinguish several structural tendencies within the avant-garde performance tradition. These will be discussed in more detail in the following section.

Poëzie in Carré, then, not only marked the breakthrough of performing poets in the Netherlands, but the Carré Theater also realized a space in which an intriguing clash occurred between two contrary performance traditions: a tradition based on classic declamation and one inspired by the experiments of the avant-gardes. The performances of Vanvugt and Van Doorn conflicted with – and thereby revealed – widespread notions on what it means to bring poetry to the stage. In other words, these performers *staged* poeticity: they dramatized the presumptions and conventions that enable one to experience a specific linguistic event as something poetic. The question, then, becomes: what exactly were these presumptions and conventions with regard to poetry and its performance, and how were they staged?

Performance, Poetry, and the Limits of Criticism

The similarities between Dutch poetry readings in the 1960s and the experimental practices of the avant-garde movements invite a consideration of the problematic relationship between performance poetry and literary criticism. The avant-garde is often thought of as being anti-traditional, nihilistic or anarchistic (Poggioli ch. 4). However, several studies suggest that the crisis caused by avant-garde performance art creates an opportunity to rethink traditional notions on art and literature (Goldberg 1988; Clemons 2003; Sell 2005). Sell, for instance, draws a distinction between an institutionalized, critically appropriated avant-garde performance and a radical, "countercultural" avant-garde performance (48). He goes on to define countercultural performances in the 1950s and 1960s as events that "challenge the basic assumptions, methods, and institutional bases of criticism and scholarship" (8). He stresses that these assumptions, methods, and institutional bases pertain not only to the domain of art reviewing or academic criticism, but also to a wider "cultural politics," to wit the bourgeois-liberal discourse governing the production, distribution, and consumption of culture. Countercultural performance challenges this discourse and creates a crisis, according to Sell, who underlines the virtuous and productive aspects of such a crisis:

> countercultural performance addressed the need (1) to identify and disrupt existing social, cultural, and economic boundaries, (2) to systematically challenge existing discourses of experience, everyday life, and the politics of culture, (3) to produce new ways of thinking and acting that effectively valued aspects of

experience, everyday life, and culture systematically excluded from the mainstream, and (4) to ground all of this in specific social and cultural situations. (16)

Sell's observations on the ability of avant-garde performances to "identify and disrupt" existing "cultural . . . boundaries" and to challenge the "politics of culture" apply to the performance of poetry and its reception as well. For, Sell reminds his readers that all "culture is composed of various kinds of institutionalized and socialized hermeneutic strategies" (33). With respect to literature, such strategies can be defined either as a form of "literary competence," as Culler (113–130) would argue, or as a set of rules governing an "interpretive community," as Fish (171) would say. However, the main point is that the interpretation and evaluation of poetry is shaped and colored by a cluster of conventions determining how a work of literature should be read. These conventions become part of the institution of literature when they are put to practice in textbooks, works of criticism, or literary theory. They are internalized by most professional poetry readers. The result of this process of internalization is an "implicit theory of the lyric," as Culler puts it in *Structuralist Poetics* (162). Culler distinguishes three expectations that guide most interpretations. The first concerns the enunciator of the poem. Readers assume that the poem is uttered by a "poetic personae" that "fulfils the unifying role of the individual subject" (170). The poem is understood as the message of a single subject to whom all utterances can be traced back. The second expectation pertains to the belief that a poem is a "harmonious totality" (171). All of its elements are expected to relate to each other in a meaningful way. The third and last expectation is that the poem has significance:

> To write a poem is to claim significance of some sort for the verbal construct one produces, and the reader approaches a poem with the assumption that however brief it may appear it must contain, at least implicitly, potential riches which make it worthy of his attention. (175)

This last expectation also establishes a connection to the poetics or the literary program of the author of the work. The reader tacitly assumes that the poet takes his own writing seriously and operates in a well-considered manner: the poet is assumed to formulate a consistent and coherent poetics and is expected to act accordingly.

The three conventions discerned by Culler are, of course, historically and culturally fixed. They are part and parcel of an implicit theory of poetry that dominated Anglo-Saxon critical and academic discourse on literature from the New Critics to the Structuralists. In their 2006 study Joosten and Vaessens demonstrate that these conventions have had a lasting impact on criticism in the Netherlands. Taking their lead from Dorleijn, who demonstrated that Dutch poetry textbooks can be seen as "mirrors" that reflect common assumptions about poetry from a certain era (115–128), Joosten and Vaessens analyze post-war textbooks "as they have been used in the Dutch and Flemish classrooms" in order to reconstruct "the dominant presuppositions governing the reading of poetry" (20). They identify three 'classic' interpretive premises. The first premise is that "the text represents a subject, it allows us to hear an authentic 'voice'"; a second basic assumption entails that "even when [the poem] initially strikes the reader as chaotic, [it] will show its inner coherence on a higher level"; and the third premise states that "the poem is an 'organic' whole and is valued as 'natural' and as a source of exceptional knowledge" (21–22).[23] These three premises correspond to the conventions of the poetic personae, of the expectation of coherence, and of significance, as identified by Culler. This merits the conclusion that the main New Critical and Structuralist assumptions on poetry continue to dominate critical discourse in The Netherlands.

Moreover, these general assumptions fit in very well with the characteristics of the declamatory tradition in Dutch performance poetry. Poets read their own poetry, maintain self-control, and in doing so, satisfy the expectation of a single speaking subject and an authentic voice. They are faithful to the written texts and therefore, respond to the convention of coherence: the text is enunciated as an organic whole that should not be altered when performing it. Finally, the fact that these poets perfect their enunciation and keep their composure is in line with the convention of significance as well: they thereby demonstrate that they take their work seriously and that it is worthy of the listener's attention.

The correspondences between the conventions of poetry and the tradition of declamation came to the fore on the Carré stage in 1966. Most poets performing at *Poëzie in Carré* adhered to the principles of declamation and, in doing so, fulfilled the dominant expectations of poetry. However, Vanvugt and Van Doorn did not respond to these expectations. The criticism raised against them is quite revealing in that sense. Descriptions of their performances using pejorative terms such as "raving," "bizarre shouting," and "quasi-psychopathic showing off," indicate that their critics had expected to encounter an authentic voice and a central and more or less composed persona. They had expected (self) mastery, not what they considered the antics of two madmen. Furthermore, the above-cited critic who dismissed Van Doorn's act as "incoherent" unintentionally proves that a convention of coherence was operative in the evaluative discourse; another critic, who criticized that Van Doorn's poetry "did not make everyone stop and think," was applying the convention of significance: in his opinion poetry *should* make one stop and think (Vinkenoog 128–130, 212).

Thus, Vanvugt's and Van Doorn's performances effectively staged the then-dominant conventions of poetry. In their performances the traditional preconceptions about what it means to write and perform poetry were thwarted and, consequently, exposed. In the following, an analysis of the poetry of one of the performers, Johnny van Doorn, will bring out the connection between the strategies of performance and the staging of literary conventions.

The Holy Hypocrite: Johnny van Doorn as Case Study

During his lifetime Van Doorn published two poetry collections: *Een nieuwe mongool (Post-Sexuele ZondagsPoëzie)* 'A New Mongol (Post-Sexual Sunday Poetry)' (1966) and *De heilige huichelaar* 'The Holy Hypocrite' (1968). His *Verzamelde gedichten* 'Collected Poems' were published in 1994, three years after his death. Studying the work of a performance poet by analyzing his written poetry is not unproblematic, as it does not take into account the actual physical realization of the poems (Middleton "How to Read" 13; Pfeiler 29). Van Doorn himself questioned the validity of such an approach: "My own poetry on paper, put into words, has always struck me as something very unpleasant; I have always related [my poems] to my *acts*" (qtd. in Dütting 15).[24] Nonetheless, it is possible and useful to analyze Van Doorn's work as a form of "new oral poetry," which Economou defines as follows:

> By "new oral poetry" I mean poetic work made specifically, but obviously in varying degrees, with an awareness of a live audience to whom the work could be read aloud, or of a reader-audience who could interpret that poetry in print in such a way as to approximate in the mind's ear an oral performance of it in any voice the reader-audience chooses but ideally in the voice of the poet him/herself. (654)

Admittedly, an interpretation of Van Doorn's work as new oral poetry may not take fully into account that any poetry reading is "irreducibly singular and historical" (Middleton, "How to Read" 17), yet such an approach can shed light on the performance strategies implicit in his work and explain why it should be analyzed in terms of a staging of traditional poetry conventions.

Van Doorn structurally frustrates the expectations of his readers and audience in his poetry and performances. At first glance he does not seem to deviate from the conventional assumption that a central and centered poetic persona is speaking in the poem. Almost without exception his poems consist of a single long sentence, divided over many extremely short verse lines. The imagery is immediately recognizable as his, since Van Doorn has a preference for the grotesque, combining explicitly sexual and violent images with religious and sentimental motives. Furthermore, he constantly stresses the uniqueness and the strength of his voice: he presents himself as "The Big Voice of Arnhem," "the greatest singer of my time," "accurately [firing]" his "blood-curdling scream," and sending his "hypnotic commands into stereophonic space" (Van Doorn 36, 89, 50, 91).[25] Finally, the distinctiveness of his oeuvre is paralleled by his incomparable diction, at first slow and solemn, towards the end of a performance fast, wheezy, and stuttering. In short, both on paper and on stage, Van Doorn appears to put forward a well-defined poetic persona with an authentic voice.

Upon closer analysis, however, the identity of the central persona turns out to be impossible to ascertain. Not only did Van Doorn admit to operating under a variety of pen names, including Johnny the SelfKicker, Electric Goebbels, Electric Jesus,

Electricity Jesus, and John Jesus Electric. Van Doorn also aimed at a transgression of the limits of the self and craved an "ecstatic bliss" and an "absence of ego" (16, 197).[26] In addition, he created confusion by introducing various points of view in his poems. The central character and speaker in *Een nieuwe mongool* is identified with the poet himself. In *De heilige huichelaar*, the main character of the "Holy Hypocrite" is identified as "Johnny the SelfKicker" (173), but he is portrayed in the third person by an unnamed "I" or "we" – and in an interview, Van Doorn claimed to be "the disciple" of the Holy Hypocrite (Herbergs). The pen name "The SelfKicker" in itself is revealing in this context, even more so when it is used, as in *De heilige huichelaar*, to refer to someone other than the speaker. Furthermore, Van Doorn's obsession with other forms of transgression such as eroticism, violence, drug abuse, and ecstasy reveals a longing for self-annihilation as well. During his performances, he would often scream himself into a trance-like state, with or without the help of drugs. One person present at a performance in 1962 described this process in detail:

> He coils up on the table, says in a disgusting way aaah to the unlucky artist in front of the table . . ., carries out daredevil feats, while he is anxiously supported by the helping hands of his followers; . . . in between there are some carefully memorized refrains, which do contain some beautifully recited phrases, and sometimes very erotic and anti-erotic exclamations too. (Dütting 22)[27]

Reflecting on his performance in *Poëzie in Carré*, Van Doorn writes: "At such a moment you are a different being, something that separates itself from your own person" (Dütting 68).[28]

When Van Doorn frustrates the reader's expectation to encounter a well-defined subject in a poem, he breaks with one of the central laws of the tradition of declamation: the need for self-mastery. In fact, Van Doorn is aiming for the opposite. He describes his infamous "self kick" as "the moment that I control what is not controlled" and adds: "Yet in a completely different manner than an actor or theater performer would envision that" (Dütting 15).[29] He sees himself as the "personification" of "Anti-Theater" and models his performance style on "Artaud's Thea-/Tre of Cruelness" (Van Doorn 77, 173).[30] This explains why he continuously criticizes Dutch drama schools, for declamation and traditionalist, bourgeois dramaturgy were still the norm at such institutes during the first half of the sixties (Van Engen 752–59). In one particular poem, he vehemently criticizes the "caste of artists" consisting of the "conventional/Actors (for whom still exist/To my greatest surprise/Academies)" (Van Doorn 87), while another poem ends as follows:

> With a horrible
> Raising of my voice
> I demand the ex-
> Tradition of a number of

> Prominent
> Theater educators
> (The main target
> Being the principal): (49)[31]

In relation to this it is significant that Van Doorn came to perform his electric acts at the Carré Theater. Carré is one of the most important stages in Dutch theater, where many popular cabaret, theater, and revues in the 1960s premiered. This added a new layer of meaning to Van Doorn's performance, for by participating in *Poëzie in Carré* he braved the lion of traditional bourgeois entertainment in its den. The flower bashing that he had to suffer at the end of his performance is therefore quite ironic: the bouquet, which traditionally expressed the gratitude of the audience for the actor's controlled display of mastership, now became a means to signify the audience's disapproval of Van Doorn's ecstatic improvisations. The location, the flowers, and the bashing, in other words, turned out to be meaningful elements of the performance, which contributed significantly to the staging of poeticity.

Thus, the poetic persona in Van Doorn's poetry is shifting, unreliable, and problematic. On the one hand, a single subject with an authentic voice seems to manifest itself; on the other hand, the poet thwarts identification, undermines the stability of the self, and distances himself from the rigid and restraining skillfulness of declamatory (theater) performances.

Van Doorn also opposes the idea that a poem should be an organic whole, a well-thought out structure in which every element is meaningful. This is very obvious in his written poetry, in which he favors random line breaks, nonsensical punctuation, and open endings. Typical line breaks for Van Doorn are, for example, "concentra-/Tioncamp," "ru-/Ral," "cine-/Mas" (15, 28, 144).[32] No metric, syllabic or logical reason for these line breaks can be discerned. Furthermore, Van Doorn indulges in idiosyncratic punctuation: numerous lines end with '&' or ': –'. One poem even ends with the lines: "Dream freely . . . /Of kidney level-/Ing &//&?" The title of the next poem is "&?" and continues the narrative (52–53).[33] In the poem quoted earlier, Van Doorn undercuts the self-sufficiency of the poem by radically cutting off the thread of the narrative: after the lines "With a horrible/Raising of my voice" the poem ends with a colon, but the following poem is no way related to it. Van Doorn's verse technique thus blurs the traditional boundaries of the (single) poem.

On a more thematic level, the disrespect for the convention of coherence is abundantly demonstrated and sometimes even explicitly addressed. This is foregrounded by two particularly interesting poems. The first, "Misunderstanding about scene such and such," starts with the description of an orgy (54–55).[34] Next, the poet breaks into a torrent of words, followed by the information that two "Calvinists downstairs" are planning a murder. The poem ends with a scene in which a landlady stumbles onto the orgy. The connection between these thematic lines is hard to identify and the title of the poem ("scene such and such") implies that it consists of random scenes. In another poem, entitled "Result of a working day," Van Doorn ridicules the expectation of coherence by explicitly underlining that even the poet himself does not know whether there is a meaningful connection between the elements of his poem:

> *Result of a working day*
>
> Busy with
> Talking a TV pastor
> Who speaks the epilogue
> three times a week
> Into a suicide attempt &
> Dutch viewers look
> Surprised when
> After a murmured Amen
> He shoots a bullet
> Into his throat
> With a double-barreled gun:
> Short-winded I receive
> During the arisen fit of laughter
> A masturbatory vision
> Of a highly-strung
> Rubber planter in the
> Matto Grosso &
> Nervously I search
> For the connection… (64)[35]

Admittedly, it is possible to perceive a certain "connection" between the scenes that is established through Van Doorn's mixture of religion, violence, sex, and absurdity. Nonetheless, it remains telling that the "I" himself is unsure about the relationship between the events he describes. As a consequence, the reader will doubt whether there is any connection at all. Clearly, coherence is far from self-evident in Van Doorn's work.

The third and final expectation of poetry identified above is that of significance: it is assumed that the poet is serious about his work and that his poems contain some form of exceptional knowledge. Van Doorn also refuses to meet this expectation. He poses as a prophet, even as a messiah, yet at the same time as the "ParanoiaMan" with a "psychopathic mask," or as "a quite common poetry manufacturer/That hacks away at it with a bloody axe/Unsubtle and full of ran-/Cour." Van Doorn warns his readers: "Our poet is a miraculous/Mixture of/Crisscrossing/*Inconsequences*,/

Worlds,/Opinions &/Unshakable/Facts" (Van Doorn 81, 175, 197, 201).[36] The figure of the "Holy Hypocrite" unites these characteristics. The holy hypocrite reveals the truth; however, being hypocritical, he distorts it at the same time. "I am a poseur and an imposter. And I know it," Van Doorn confessed in an interview, and on several other occasions he claimed that he had "nothing to do with literature" (Herbergs; Dütting 39).[37] In light of such statements the reader will no doubt find it difficult to take Van Doorn seriously. After all, how trustworthy is a poet who starts one of his poems with the German lines "Wir Sind Serioes Nicht-Serioes In/Unseren Manifestationen Und/Das Ist Richtig" 'We Are Seriously Not-Serious In/Our Manifestations And/That is Right' (171)?

The embrace of insincerity is an important strategy for Van Doorn. He makes use of it in his poetics as well. His comments on his work and his literary opinions are often contradictory and it is nearly impossible to pin him down on a statement. In an interview, for example, he stated: "You could say that my work is pervaded with a latently present moralistic spirit . . . I really do propagate a message. It's a form of protest poetry, really." Two years later, he seemed to have changed his mind: "Protest. Disgusting. I am not doing anything, really. I am just an imposter" (Dütting 24, 32).[38] Van Doorn displayed the same obstructive attitude when one critic called him a "pop or a performance poet": "Wait a minute, listen," he responded, "I am just an old-fashioned declamatory artist, a declaimer. Not a performer, because that always makes me think of something American that is by now out-dated" (Dütting 106).[39] It is of course possible to assume that Van Doorn simply had an unsettled personality, but one could also argue that he is playing with the traditional notion that a poet ought to have a clear-cut and consistent literary program. Unlike many of his fellow poets, this performer does not want to use language seriously, sincerely, and efficiently to convey a profound insight. Quite on the contrary: he flouts the convention of significance, both in his "seriously unserious" poetry and in his apparently incoherent poetics.

We have seen that Van Doorn's work conflicts with all three main critical assumptions concerning poetry: the poetic persona is dismantled, the need for coherence is disregarded, and the poet explicitly states that he does not have a serious message to convey. Moreover, he not only breaks with these conventions, but tauntingly appropriates them. He is, in his own words, "overdoing" them:

> The form that I am using is always overdone. I am always too much of a good thing. That is precisely what I like, transgressing things, making mistakes, to make sure that things misfire constantly. (Dütting 32–33)[40]

Van Doorn's "overdoing" of traditional poetic conceptions turns his poetry into a "performance" of them. His poems and acts "stage" the limits of literary criticism. Attridge argues that such a staging occurs when a literary work "fails to answer to our habitual needs in processing language." Consequently, it presents itself as "simultaneously familiar and other" and puts us under the obligation "to attend scrupulously, to suspend as far as we can our usual assumptions and practices, to translate the work into our terms while remaining aware of the necessary betrayal that this involves" (Attridge 120). Middleton stresses that a performance, too, can

> sometimes exceed existing explanations of its functioning and significance, and this excess provides one of the main reasons for the continuing success of readings: the performance of the poem compels recognition of the limits of our understanding of language. (Distant 72)

Van Doorn's performances exceed the "limits of our understanding" of poetry, which stipulated the poetic persona, coherence, and significance as the conditions to be met for a text to be experienced as "poetic." The poetry of Van Doorn explicitly and implicitly engages with these conventional assumptions about poetry and its performance, exploits them, and explores new poetic possibilities. As a consequence, it poses a challenge to critics and literary scholars; it compels them to reflect on, and depart from, their critical premises.

Conclusion: A Performative Reading of Performance Poetry

This analysis of Van Doorn's work has several implications for the study of performance poetry in general. It sheds new light on the critical deadlock between Dutch literary criticism and performance poetry which has been in place since the sixties, because it demonstrates that performers like Van Doorn reveal and enact a specific cultural politics. Unlike Vaessens's suggestion cited above, they do enter into discussion with literary traditions. They appropriate those traditions that are generally appreciated and draw attention to those forms of art which *cannot* be appreciated by literary critics, due to the limits of their mode of criticism. Nonetheless, these performers do appeal to conventions and strategies that ought to be very familiar to most professional critics. Their performance practice can form a fruitful point of departure for critical analysis, provided that the reviewer or scholar is willing to reflect on his aesthetic assumptions and critical limits. In short, a critical debate between performers and critics becomes possible. This is of great importance for the contemporary Dutch performance scene, for there is a range of, until now, critically unnoticed performers that operate in the wake of Van Doorn's experiments, among them Sieger Baljon, Didi de Paris, ACG Vianen and Peter Holvoet Hanssen (Franssen, "De dood" 263–67).

This case study of Van Doorn's poetry practice also refutes Mourits's wholesale suggestion that performance poetry stays clear of ambiguity (338). While many contemporary performing poets do strive for a largely unproblematic intelligibility (such as Hagar Peeters, Ingmar Heytze or Bart F.M. Droog), Van Doorn's subversive relation to the literary tradition and his ambivalent stance towards his own poetics prove that not all poets have this aim. Today, performers like Bernhard Christiansen, Tsead Bruinja or Jaap Blonk continue in his footsteps: they embrace experiments and favor ambiguity.

Also, the case of Van Doorn shows that performance poetry can be understood as a staging of poeticity. As a poetic phenomenon it reveals and transgresses the interpretive and aesthetic limits of literary criticism. This explains why Van Doorn's critics found it difficult to evaluate his work. The same holds true for contemporary critics, such as the above cited Vergeer and Gerbrandy. Their rejection of certain performance poets because they are "aiming at effect" or because they do not handle language "efficiently" indicates that these critics adhere to a critical tradition that prefers reticence and efficiency to exaggeration and transgression.

The analysis of Van Doorn's acts and poems that is put forward in this essay explores a form of literary analysis that acknowledges the limits of traditional criticism and can perhaps overcome the deadlock between performance poetry and literary criticism. This mode of literary analysis has been described as a "performative" or "creative" reading. It is a "singular putting into play of – while also testing and transforming – the set of codes and conventions that make up the institution of poetry and the wider cultural formation of which it is part" (Attridge 105–106). Such an interpretive mode is a performance in itself. Performative reading can cure the poetry critic of his stage fever, for it invites him to come to terms with his limited focus on formalist, textual forms of literature; and it can release the performer of his text anxiety, for it acknowledges the singular and transgressive nature of his work.

A performative approach to performance poetry is all the more needed, since the latter seems to be a form of literature that constitutes a structural transgression. The staging of poeticity that occurred at *Poëzie in Carré* was not a one-time event, a non-reproducible reaction against one particular instant of cultural politics: as the institution of literature changes, performance, continually transgressing its limits, changes with it. An intriguing illustration of this ongoing dynamic is that the new mode of performance criticism that has been developed within the Dutch slam scene appears now to be challenged by the recent work of a number of Dutch performers. Simon Mulder, for one, has made a name for himself at several poetry slams by traditionally declaiming dark romantic sonnets and has aroused much discussion on where the limits of performance poetry and its criticism are to be drawn (Franssen, "Hopend" 241). It seems that he and others practise a new staging of poeticity that questions the currently dominant views on performance poetry.

Notes

1. "al te gewild effectbejag dat het op het podium altijd goed doet, maar in bundels leidt tot slapte."

2. "Maar het probleem met *Bloedtest* is de vrijwel totale afwezigheid van pakkende beelden, terwijl er maar heel zelden effectief met de taal wordt omgegaan."

3. "De verstaanbaarheid en de broodnodige punchlines die een podiumoptreden vereist, doen onontkoombaar af aan het effect van geschreven poëzie."

4. "Ik vind dat vorige generaties dichters, critici en kenners kan worden verweten dat ze de poëzie in een ivoren toren hebben opgesloten. Academisch geneuzel is nog altijd de norm; poëzie die een normaal mens huilend van verveling in een hoek gooit."

5. "hegemonie van het schriftuurlijke."

6. "een dimensie die buiten de literaire wereld gezocht moet worden. In de Nederlandse kranten en tijdschriften lees je daar nog weinig over, daar wordt de poëzie voornamelijk besproken volgens traditioneel literaire zienswijzen. Nieuwe ontwikkelingen worden op deze manier nauwelijks opgemerkt."

7. "handelen niet meer volgens het klassieke avant-gardescenario dat voorschrijft dat de jonge hemelbestormer om te beginnen maar eens zijn of haar positie moet bepalen tegenover de vorige lichting poëzievernieuwers."

8. "Voor de literaire referenties en de complexe verwevenheid met de traditie die papieren poëzie uit de traditie van de avant-garde kenmerken, komt de onmiddellijkheid van de *performance* in de plaats."

9. "de eeuwenoude traditie die hij wil voortzetten – de troubadours, de middeleeuwse literatuur, de primitieve vertellers en de sjamaan."

10. "Er loopt een onmiskenbare historische lijn, met oorsprong in dada, van de Vijftigers over de happenings, via de performers uit de jaren zeventig en de Maximalen, naar deze nieuwe generatie al dan niet rappende podiumdichters en poetryslampoëten."

11. Jakobson states that "poeticity is present when the word is felt as a word and not a mere representation of the object being named or an outburst of emotion, when words and their composition, their meaning, their external and inner form, acquire a weight and value of their own instead of referring indifferently to reality" (378).

12. "het in groten getale opgekomen publiek actief participeren aan een waar poëziefeest, met dichters die voorlazen uit eigen werk of met hun act het publiek beurtelings trachtten te amuseren of te provoceren."

13. "Maar 'Carré' was vooral de geboorte van de literaire podiumcultuur."

14. "Ewald Vanvugt raaskalde niet beter of slechter dan hij normaal al doet."

15. "bizarre kreten"; "onsamenhangende, soms nogal vrijmoedige exclamaties"; "kwasi-psychopathische aanstellerij."

16. "Waar heeft hij het over?" "Zijn woorden hebben misschien niet iedereen tot nadenken gestemd."

17. "orale cultus."

18. "dat zij voorts voegt bij al de deelen en onderdeelen van dat voorgedragene, tot bij ieder zin, zinsnede, woord, lettergreep, ja, letter toe."

19. "Een algemeen gebrek, hetwelk aan de volmaking der kunst het meest in den weg staat, is gelegen in het verkeerd lezen, in het niet inachtnemen der zinsverdeeling, in het voorbijzien of verwaarlozen der scheidteekens."

20. "hij, die magt heeft over zichzelven, ook spoedig zal kunnen heerschen over zijne toehoorders."

21. "Laat schoone verzen glad van effen lippen vloeien,/Maar gil, noch galm, nock kwaak, noch

bulder woest en luid; / . . . / Gij, blijf uw kalmte, uw kracht, uw meesterschap bewaren,/En daar ge een ander schokt, schijn zelf niet eens ontroerd."

22. "Declameren is een kunst, die het niet van overdaad of overdrijving moet hebben, maar slechts overtuigt door terughoudendheid."

23. Joosten and Vaessens elaborate their argument in the first part of *Postmoderne poëzie in Nederland en Vlaanderen* (15–30).

24. "M'n eigen poëzie, op papier, in woorden overgebracht, doet mij bizonder onprettig aan, ik heb ze altijd in verband gebracht met mijn *acts*."

25. "grootste zanger/Van mijn tijd"; "Akkuraat vuur ik/Een ijselijke gil"; "Met mijn hypnotiserende/Bevelen stereofonisch/De ruimte in."

26. "Extatische/Verrukking"; "de/Afwezigheid van ego."

27. "Hij kruipt ineen op de tafel, zegt op een walgelijke manier 'aaaa' tegen de ongelukkige kunstenaar die vlak voor de tafel zit . . . , voert halsbrekende stuiptrekkingen uit, hierbij angstvallig ondersteund door de behulpzame handen zijner volgelingen; . . . met daartussen enkele zorgvuldig gememoriseerde refreinen, waarin wel enkele mooi voorgedragen frasen, en soms ook wel erg erotische tot anti-erotische uitroepingen."

28. "Op zo'n moment ben je een ander wezen, een afsplitsing van je eigen persoon."

29. "Het moment dat ik de niet-beheersing beheers. Maar dan geheel anders dan een acteur of toneelspeler zich dat voorstelt."

30. "the Anti-Theatre (waarvan hij al/Jarenlang de personificatie is)"; "Gelijk Artauds Thea-/Ter Van De Wreedheid."

31. "de achtergebleven / Kunstenaarskaste:/ De conventionele/Akteurs (waarvoor tot/Mijn grote verbazing/Nog steeds Akademies/ Bestaan)"; "Met gruwelijke/Stemverheffing/ Eis ik de uit-/Levering van enkele/ Vooraanstaande/Toneelpedagogen/(Met als hoofddoel/De direkteur):"

32. "concentra-/Tiekamp"; "Ian-/Delijk"; "cine-/Maas."

33. "Droom vrijuit/. . . /Over nierspiege-/ Lingen & // &?"

34. 'Misvatting omtrent scene zoveel'

35. "*Resultaat van een werkdag*//Druk in de weer met/Het inpraten van een/ Zelfmoordpoging aan/Een 3maal in de week/ TVdagsluitende dominee & /Kijkend Nederland kijkt/Verrast op als hij/Na een gepreveld Amen/Met een dubbelloops/Pistool een kogel/ Z'n keel inschiet:/Aamborstig krijg ik/In de ontstane lachstuip/Een onanatievisioen/Van een fijnbesnaarde/Rubberplanter in de/Matto Grosso door & /Zenuwachtig zoek ik/Naar het verband . . ."

36. "ParanoiaMan"; "Psychopatisch masker"; "doodgewoon een werkman, / Een potsierlijke poëziefabrikant / Die ongenuanceerd en ranku- / Neus er met bebloede / Bijl op inhakt"; "Dat onze dichter / Een wonderlijk / Mengsel is van / Kriskras door- / Elkaarlopende / *Inkonsekwenties, / Werelden, / Meningen & / Onwrikbare / Feiten.*"

37. "Ik ben een aansteller en een oplichter. En ik weet het"; "dat ik . . . niets met literatuur te maken heb."

38. "Je zou kunnen zeggen, dat mijn werk een latent moralistische geest ademt, zoals ook satire en de sick joke in feite moralistisch zijn. Ik draag wel degelijk een boodschap uit. Het is eigenlijk een soort protestpoëzie"; "Protest. Weerzinwekkend. Ik doe gewoon nergens aan. Ik ben gewoon een oplichter."

39. "Ja, hoor eens . . . , ik ben gewoon een oud- erwets voordrachtskunstenaar. Een declamator. Geen performer, want daarbij moet ik altijd denken aan iets Amerikaans dat al lang gedateerd is."

40. "De vorm die ik gebruik, is altijd *overdone*. Ik ben voortdurend te veel van het goede. Ik hou juist van dingen overtreden, fouten maken, zodat dingen, voortdurend de mist ingaan."

Bibliography

Attridge, Derek. *The Singularity of Literature.* London: Routledge, 2004.

Beets, Nicolaas. *Dichtwerken van Nicolaas Beets.* 3 vols. Amsterdam: W.H. Kirberger, 1876.

Berg, Wim van den. "1848: B.H. Lulofs publiceert *De declamatie; of de kunst van declaméren of recitéren.* Op gehoorafstand." *Nederlandse literatuur, een geschiedenis.* Ed. M.A. Schenkeveld-Van der Dussen. Groningen: Martinus Nijhoff Uitgevers, 1993. 473–78.

Brems, Hugo. *Altijd weer vogels die nesten beginnen. Geschiedenis van de Nederlandse literatuur 1945–2005.* Amsterdam: Uitgeverij Bert Bakker, 2006.

Clemons, Leigh. "Serious Fun: Berlin Dada's Tactical Engagement with German National Narration." *Theatre Research International* 28.2 (2003): 143–56.

Couttenier, Piet, and Wim van den Berg. *Alles is taal geworden. Geschiedenis van de Nederlandse literatuur 1800–1900.* Amsterdam: Uitgeverij Bert Bakker, 2009.

Culler, Jonathan. *Structuralist Poetics: Structuralism, Linguistics and the Study of Literature.* London: Routledge, 1997.

Dorleijn, Gillis. "Spiegel en doorgeefluik: schoolpoëtica's in de twintigste eeuw." *Poëtica-onderzoek in de praktijk.* Ed. F.A.H. Berndsen. Groningen: Passage, 1993. 115–28.

Doorn, Johnny van. *Verzamelde gedichten.* Amsterdam: De Bezige Bij, 1994.

Dütting, Hans, ed. *Archief Johnny van Doorn: beschouwingen en interviews.* Baarn: De Prom, 1994.

Economou, George. "Some Notes Towards Finding a View of the New Oral Poetry." *Boundary 2* 3.3 (Spring 1975): 653–63.

Engen, Max van. "9 oktober 1969: begin van Aktie Tomaat. De crisis in het theater leidt tot openlijk protest en acties van het publiek." *Een theatergeschiedenis der Nederlanden: tien eeuwen drama en theater in Nederland en Vlaanderen.* Ed. R.L. Erenstein. Amsterdam: Amsterdam University Press, 1996. 752–59.

Fish, Stanley. *Is There A Text in This Class? The Authority of Interpretive Communities.* Cambridge: Harvard University Press, 1982.

Franssen, Gaston. "De dood van de podiumdichter? Over voordrachtskunst en poëzieperformance." *Spiegel der Letteren* 50.2 (2008): 255–68.

———. "Hopend op een plek in de finale: een kleine antropologie van de podiumpoëziekritiek." *Dietsche Warande & Belfort* 154.2 (2009): 234–45.

Geest, Dirk de. "5 april 1989: Hugo Claus viert zijn zestigste verjaardag. Poëzie, poëzie-opvattingen en publieke belangstelling in Vlaanderen." *Nederlandse literatuur, een geschiedenis.* Ed. M.A. Schenkeveld-Van der Dussen. Groningen: Martinus Nijhoff Uitgevers, 1993. 867–71.

Gerbrandy, Piet. "Het leven gaat gewoon zijn gang." *De Volkskrant* 9 May 2003.

Goedegebuure, Jaap. "28 februari 1966: Poëzie in Carré. De literaire lezing." *Nederlandse literatuur, een geschiedenis.* Ed. M.A. Schenkeveld-Van der Dussen. Groningen: Martinus Nijhoff Uitgevers, 1993. 777–82.

Gogh, Ruben van, ed. *Sprong naar de sterren: de laatste generatie dichters van de twintigste eeuw.* Utrecht: Kwadraat, 1999.

Goldberg, RoseLee. *Performance Art: From Futurism to the Present.* London: Thames and Hudson, 1990.

Herbergs, Ben. "Johnny the Selfkicker: de discipel van de Heilige Huichelaar." *Het Vrije Volk* 8 March 1968.

Jakobson, Roman. "What is Poetry?" *Language and Literature.* Eds. Krystyna Pomorska and

Stephen Rudy. Cambridge, MA: Belknap Press of Harvard University Press, 1987. 368–78.

Joosten, Jos. "Hipper bestaat niet." *De Standaard* 21 December 2000.

Joosten, Jos, and Thomas Vaessens. "Postmodern Poetry Meets Modernist Discourse." *Postmodern Writing and Cultural Identity*. Ed. Th. D'haen and P. Vermeulen. Amsterdam: Rodopi, 2006. 15–53.

Larive, J.M. *De kunst van het declameren*. Trans. G.T.N. Suringar. Leeuwarden: Suringarm, 1856.

Lulofs, B.H. *De declamatie; of de kunst van declaméren of reciténen en van de mondelinge voordragt of uiterlijke welsprekendheid in het algemeen*. Groningen: Van Bolhuis Hoitsema, 1848.

———. *De kunst der mondelinge voordracht of uiterlijke welsprekendheid (voor studenten, rederijkers, en verdere beoefenaars)*. Amsterdam: Brinkman, 1877.

Middleton, Peter. *Distant Reading: Performance, Readership, and Consumption in Contemporary Poetry*. Tuscaloosa: University of Alabama Press, 2005.

———. "How to Read a Reading of a Written Poem." *Oral tradition* 20.1 (2005): 7–34.

Mourits, Bertram. "Een totale show: over poëzie en voordracht." *Nederlandse letterkunde* 7.4 (December 2002): 322–42.

Pfeiler, Martina. *Sounds of Poetry: Contemporary American Performance Poets*. Tübingen: Gunter Narr Verlag, 2003.

Poggioli, Renato. *The Theory of the Avant-Garde*. Cambridge: Belknap Press of Harvard University Press, 1968.

Rijghard, Ron, and Ward Wijndelts. "Waar moet dat heen met de poëzie? Poëzie in Carré 1966: de geboorte van de literaire podiumcultuur in Nederland." *Meer Poëzie in Carré, 1966 & 2006*. Amsterdam: Van Gennep, 2006. 21–5.

Sell, Mike. *Avant-Garde Performance and the Limits of Criticism: Approaching the Living Theater, Happenings/Fluxus, and the Black Arts Movement*. Ann Arbor: The University of Michigan Press, 2005.

Vaessens, Thomas. *Ongerijmd succes: poëzie in een onpoëtische tijd*. Nijmegen: Vantilt, 2006.

Vaessens, Thomas, and Jos Joosten. *Postmoderne poëzie in Nederland en Vlaanderen*. Nijmegen: Vantilt, 2003.

Vergeer, Koen. "In stilte en luidkeels: Marjoleine de Vos en Tjitske Jansen." *De Morgen* 19 November 2003.

———. "Poëzie buiten de bladspiegel." *Ons Erfdeel* 43.3 (May-June 2000): 322–29.

Vinkenoog, Simon, ed. *Poëzie in Carré op 28 februari 1966 in Theater Carré, Amsterdam*. Amsterdam: De Bezige Bij, 1966.

Artimanha, the Precise Moment of Being: Performance and Carnival in the Poetry of Brazil's Nuvem Cigana

Jeffrey Manoel Pijpers

a palavra precisa lança o som
à velocidade da luz
onde nós e você dominamos o espaço
a imagem fala por si
e por mim
. . . .
é fundamental que o texto entre
olhos e ouvidos
se envolva nos pêlos do cérebro
revelando-se a cada repetição
a quantas repetições por segundo?
o eco sonoro se instala
guarda a direção da força
a trajetória interna da palavra
o momento de ser
o é
preciso
claro
suaveamargo
artimanha[1]

(Bernardo Vilhena, "o é preciso")

Introduction

The first Artimanha in Brazil took place in the basement of a small bookstore in Ipanema, Rio de Janeiro. This poetic event combined poetry readings with music, dance, and other performance elements. Organized in October 1975 by the group of marginal poets Nuvem Cigana, what would later become the first Artimanha was originally meant to be an exposition of independently published mimeograph books and journals where music, audiovisual projections, and dance performances would be additional elements to create the ambiance.

Nuvem Cigana ("Gipsy Cloud") started off as a group of young poets who, under the military repression and censorship of the early 1970s, had to look for alternative ways of disseminating their poetry. Because the emerging artistic underground scene at the time in Rio was very small, interaction between artists from different disciplines was frequent and intense: this exchange was born out of the intimacy of shared subversive activities. By the time Nuvem Cigana was officially inaugurated as a group, their activities included the design and independent production of mimeographed poetry books and journals, short movies, theater plays, song compositions, carnival *blocos*[2] and soccer matches.

As the artists themselves refer to the first Artimanha in interviews by Sergio Cohn in *Nuvem Cigana – Poesia e Delírio no Rio dos anos 70*, the actual reading of poetry was not planned as an integral part of the event, because the poets themselves did not consider the act of reciting to be a welcome addition to the created festive atmosphere. Poetry readings were not a popular phenomenon at the time and the interactive poetry-music performances in the style of the North-American Beat Poets had not yet left their mark on Brazilian poetry. However, something that was not planned happened during the presentation of an audiovisual documentary, entitled *Cacique de Ramos*, on the carnival *bloco*, which shows how its members set out to revive carnival as it had been before the politically tainted or tourist-oriented mass events. During the presentation, Bernardo Vilhena, the poet who had co-written the documentary, climbed the stage and started to rhythmically recite the title words of the presentation: "Lê lê o, Cacique é bom." He and the other Nuvem Cigana members discovered that the audience responded well to this, and directly afterwards the poet Chacal went on stage and recited one of his poems. Subsequently, all poets took turns to improvise words or existing poems to the background of the presented images, adding a new dimension of signification to the images and words that interacted with each other. The Artimanha as an event that brought poetry into interaction with samba, images and performance, was born (Cohn 82–90).

The act of reciting their work in Artimanhas influenced the way in which the Nuvem Cigana members structured their stanzas and styled the language they used. Whereas the poems that were read out loud at the first Artimanha had been originally created in writing, the work produced by the Nuvem Cigana members after 1979 is characterized by longer sentences and flowing structures, as the material was often written and rewritten by recording it and listening to how it actually sounded in its pronounced form. Bernardo Vilhena states that the very sound of his own voice has influenced the form of his poems and he mentions the poem "o é preciso," cited in the epigraph of this essay, as the best example of this process (Cohn 107). Chacal expresses the word's necessity to be spoken as follows: "*uma/palavra/escrita é uma/palavra não dita é uma/palavra maldita*" 'a written word is a non-spoken word is a damned word' (recollected in Cohn 169).

The Nuvem Cigana members not only stress the sonic dimension of the word. They also insist on the importance of the visual element that is being added to the written word when evoked in the Artimanha. The intricate connection between word and image in an act of performance is expressed in the cited poem by Vilhena when he says that the word can "*lança o som/à velocidade da luz*" 'launch its sound at light-speed' because it is being transmitted visually. It is for this reason that the lyrical subject says: "*é fundamental que o texto entre/olhos e ouvidos*" 'it is fundamental that the text penetrates eyes and ears.' Towards the end of this essay, I will return to this visual dimension of the Artimanha and the effect it has on the interaction between performer and audience.

The sonic and the visual are only two important elements of the performance. A third, physical/corporeal dimension is crucial to the Artimanha. In an Artimanha held in January 1976, this dimension responds directly to the contemporary socio-political environment in Brazil. The poets of Nuvem Cigana presented their newly launched underground magazine *Almanaque* in Rio's Museum of Modern Arts (MAM). The status of the venue contrasted with the intimate and underground character of the Artimanhas held in the bookstore basement up until then. This sudden possibility of public exposure, which is surprising for a group of poets that was marginalized under the existing censorship, was made possible for two reasons: first of all, the established plastic artists of that moment had an interest in the performance of art such as the poetry of Nuvem Cigana, which is why they offered them this space to expose their books and perform their poetry. Secondly, the fact that Artimanhas were organized independently and without funding from the state made them non-official events that did not need to pass censorship in order to be granted permission to take place. However, because this Artimanha in the MAM was freely accessible and openly visible to the public in the middle of the military dictatorship, it became a potential threat to the established order. The result was that, by the end of the event, the military police had lined up with their dogs in front of the museum to block the exit of everyone inside. In a spontaneous and desperate plan for peaceful evacuation, the people inside decided to leave the museum in a carnival procession that went out into the streets singing and dancing, thus putting the spirit of the Artimanha into practice.

The astonished policemen could do nothing but watch the carnival procession go by (Cohn, 94–98).

These introductory descriptions bring up a number of questions about the interaction of Artimanha poetry with its social and political environment. First of all, one can ask to what extent the added sonic, visual, and even corporeal dimensions of the poem mediate between poet and audience, between the artistic subject and the object. Secondly, the Artimanha, even though it is considered part of marginalized counterculture, includes in its repertoire elements that were associated with the forced folklorization of Brazilian cultural identity by the authoritarian regime, such as samba and carnival. This apparent paradox calls for an analysis of the ways in which these images were incorporated into the act of (poetic) performance and of whether it consequently brings about a transformation in the reception and social function of these folkloric elements. Finally, the question arises whether this type of performance makes it possible to resist or even invert the established power relations in a military dictatorship such as Brazil in the 1960s and 1970s.

In order to answer these questions, I will address a number of concepts and contextual situations that are crucial to a better understanding of the Artimanha as an event. Through an analysis of the musical movement *Tropicalismo* I will introduce the concept of hybridity, which is also manifest in the very performance of Nuvem Cigana poetry. Through the example of contemporary plastic art I will establish a link between performance and resistance, which I will then relate to the theory of the carnivalesque. Finally, the concept of the "pure present" will be introduced to propose the a-historical character of the (poetry) performance. Firstly, however, the way in which the Nuvem Cigana poets moved in an underground scene and managed to find a certain freedom of expression within this realm of the non-official calls for further information on the contemporary phenomenon of the *marginália* artists and their strategy of resistance to hegemonic power through active auto-marginalization.

Marginália

Rio de Janeiro's cultural scene after 1968 has often been referred to as the period of *"vazio cultural"* 'cultural emptiness', due to the harsh political censorship imposed through the Institutional Act n°5 (AI-5) under general Costa e Silva, which led to the imprisonment or forced exile of the country's most famous artists. During the wave of repression that marked this "coup within the coup" the authorities were given permission to use violent methods to maintain military control, after a period of relative *laissez faire* towards artistic or political activities linked to the political left or other subversive groups. Although the music industry, cinema, theater, and literary activity were not prohibited as such, strict control was exercised over every single music album, theater play or novel that was about to appear (Treece 307–12; Coelho 163). In order to circumvent the censors, the artists had to come up with inventive tricks that went beyond the mere use of metaphors. Chico Buarque, for example, who was often suspected of sending critical messages through his metaphorical lyrics, had to invent an alter ego, Julinho da Adelaide, in order to be able to have some of his songs produced. The young singer Milton Nascimento, after the production of his album *Milagre dos Peixes* was prohibited, recorded the entire album again, replacing most of the lyrics with purely improvised mumbled sounds that could not be censored.

Meanwhile, on the streets of Rio, on Ipanema beach and at the entrance of theaters, young poets were to be found selling their poetry. They were accustomed to the marginalized role they fulfilled in society as artists, and in order to counter repression they came up with ways of printing their work and selling it themselves without having to request permission from the censors. Leftist student groups used the technique of mimeograph printing on privately owned machines to disseminate information and pamphlets. When the young poets started to employ this same technique in order to publish their work, a new underground genre of poetry emerged. Later on, this mimeographed poetry would be one of the main characteristics of the Nuvem Cigana group. Ronaldo Santos, member of Nuvem Cigana, states that their independent way of publishing poetry has allowed them to "be as radical as [they] were" at a time when censorship was harsh and it was hard for artists to be allowed any form of public exposure (Cohn 22, 40).

The plastic artist Hélio Oiticica put into words and images the conceptualization of marginality in arts as a way to resist censorship. In a letter that was published by Luciano Figueiredo and of which a fragment is cited in Frederico Coelho's Master's thesis "Eu, Brasileiro, confesso minha culpa e meu pecado" 'I, Brazilian, confess my guilt and my sin,' Oiticica explains:

> Today I am marginal in a marginal way, not marginal aspiring to be part of the petty bourgeoisie or the conformist groups, which is the case for the majority, but really marginal: at the margins of everything, which will give me incredible freedom to act. (Coelho 119, my translation)[3]

However, more than just a way of avoiding artistic censorship, marginality was a way of refusing to compromise with what was officially "legitimate" in the type of Brazilian society the military government during the 1970s wished to create. Oiticica provided this strategy of resistance with its iconic image: a picture of his friend, the outlaw Cara de Cavalo from the *favelas* (outskirts, suburbs) of Rio, lying on the floor after having been shot by the police. The story of Cara de Cavalo had become exemplary of the violent conflict between the police and the outlaws from the *favelas*. Responsible for the death of a policeman, Cara de Cavalo was chased down by an officially created death squad that is said to have fired more than a hundred shots when finding and liquidating him. Although this image reappeared several times in various creations by Oiticica dedicated to Cara de Cavalo in an almost cathartic way, the most famous frame was the picture of the corpse accompanied by the words: "*Seja marginal, seja herói*" 'Be marginal, be a hero.' In this work of art Oiticica shows how his idea of marginality as resistance, or "*marginália*," refers to the heroism of daring to trespass institutionalized borders, either at the level of social codes or aesthetic attitude (143). If one takes Oiticica's message more literally, the conclusion can be drawn that the presented heroism is also about daring to not-exist, or cease to exist as a consequence of self-chosen marginality. The death of Cara de Cavalo is the physical representation of this non-existence. If, then, marginal resistance has recourse to the ability of being invisible, the tools of repression that the authorities invoke when trying to force potentially dangerous groups into oblivion are turned against them. The death of the marginal subject, as presented by Oiticica, is therefore the ultimate victory of the subject, because it can no longer be controlled by the forces of authority.

When Giorgio Agamben addresses the construction and deconstruction of the subject in *Remnants of Auschwitz* he argues that the two essential modalities in the existence of a certain subject are possibility (of being) and contingency (possibility of being not-)[4], as they offer the possibility of choice and action where the subject becomes actively involved with his or her environment. The modalities that are in turn associated with the non-existence of the subject as an active player in the world that surrounds it are impossibility (no possibility of being) and necessity (no possibility of being not-) (153–54). In terms of social configuration, these contrasting modalities can be considered as representative of, respectively, the hegemony and the subaltern/marginal. However, as hegemonic agency in the case of 1970s Brazilian society lay almost exclusively with the military government, this should mean automatically that the active creation and delimitation of a national cultural identity (i.e., establishing what forms part of Brazilian culture and what is not) is only possible for this particular group. Marginalized social groups and artists would then only be characterized by their negativity and by what they are not, without having the ability of constituting and articulating their own imagined identity. The attitude of marginality that Oiticica suggests, however, turns this negativity into a possibility or potentiality: a strategy set out by the subject that actively chooses to situate itself on the outside of the limitations imposed by those in power. In the terminology suggested by Agamben, the modalities related to the existence of the active subject are in this case the driving force behind the marginalized subject's effort of achieving its apparent non-existence.

This concept of marginality as potentiality of action can be found in the way Nuvem Cigana, as a group, established itself in an underground artistic circuit and therefore managed to conquer a certain level of freedom of action and expression that was unthinkable in the "official" part of society. But Nuvem Cigana did not only outsmart censorship. Their poetry also entails elements of subversion that manifest themselves in the act of performance. The spontaneous and instantaneous transmission of poetry through sounds and images allows the Nuvem Cigana poets to look for in-between forms of artistic expression that also question the absoluteness of hegemony's defining borders. In order to understand how performance can be used as a weapon against censorship and hegemonic power, it is necessary to turn to an analysis of the *Tropicalismo* movement and its particular way of re-conceptualizing the images of Brazilian cultural identity that were being promoted. *Tropicalismo* has had a significant influence on most Brazilian (and foreign) art after the 1970s and has been a crucial antecedent in the development of Nuvem Cigana's particular style of poetry performance.

Tropicalismo and Hybridity

In their conversations with Sergio Cohn, Nuvem Cigana members make reference to the legacy of *Trópicalia* and to the musicians of the *Tropicalismo* movement when they talk about the time period in which they first started their artistic activity.[5] Chacal, for example, describes a sense of disorientation among the *carioca*[6] youth at the start of the 1970s, and links it directly to the absence of the main figures of the *Tropicália* since the start of 1969 (40). The *Tropicalistas* and their rebellious attitude had been a constant and important point of reference for the younger generations that found themselves entangled in the process of coming to artistic maturity. Military repression, however, made all central figures of *Tropicália* disappear from the Brazilian cultural scene in a relatively short period of time. The musicians Gilberto Gil and Caetano Veloso were imprisoned and later forced into exile. Following the footprints of other important figures of the *Tropicália* such as Hélio Oiticica they moved to London, where a small group of Brazilian artists had settled. The poet Torquato Neto, who was one of the remaining examples of rebellious *marginália* left in Brazil, committed suicide after reiterated imprisonment and psychiatric treatments. As a result, the (artistic) youth in Brazil was left without clear guidance in a hostile society.

Surprisingly enough, when the AI-5 and its repressive censorship came into force, it was the *Tropicalismo* movement (whose members did not explicitly identify themselves with either left or right in the Brazilian political spectrum) that was more severely persecuted than the more pronounced left-wing and politically engaged *MPB, Musica Popular Brasileira*. The most obvious explanation for this is that the *Tropicalistas*, up until that moment, had managed to spread their music through the military controlled channels of mass media. The military government used these channels to propagate their version of a Brazilian national identity among the majority of the population. The fact that the *Tropicalistas* were allowed exposure through these channels had given them a lot of visibility in political, cultural, and "popular" society. The newly established authorities had promoted a consumerist lifestyle among the middle classes after the coup of 1964, in accordance with the ideals of a new impulse for economical growth through advanced national industrialization and the creation of a competitive export market. In order to provide an image for this initiative of modernization within the existing mix of ethnic and regional cultures in Brazilian culture, the military government turned towards the carnival tradition. This cultural expression was able to capture the multifaceted character of Brazilian culture where primitive cultures and modernity went hand in hand. The pop image of the *Tropicalismo* and its musical sound, which resembled international commercial rock and pop music mixed in a carnivalesque way with folkloric elements of Brazilian culture, made it a product that fitted the strategy of a mass-media based national identity construction (Treece 311–14). Then, when the *Tropicalistas*'s aesthetically and politically non-committed way of representing the Brazilian cultural spectrum turned out to undermine the propagandistic cultural strategies of the military authorities, *Tropicalismo*, precisely because of its high visibility, became a serious threat to the established order.

However, the situation was more complex than this, as the very artistic attitude of aesthetical non-commitment of the *Tropicalistas* also reflected a political attitude that was hard to place in a left-right dichotomy. *Tropicalismo* did not enjoy an undisputed popularity among the leftist groups that countered the right-wing authorities, but was also treated with growing suspicion by these same authorities on the right. For the traditionalist groups on the political left, the use of the electrical guitar and melodic/rhythmic structures in *Tropicalismo* music that showed influences of the Beatles or North-American pop music signified an intrusion of imperialist elements into the pureness of Brazilian culture. For the right-wing groups and the regime itself, the fact that *Tropicalismo* returned to elements of Brazilian cultural traditions that were not politically legitimized – like samba and carnival – and that were therefore considered primitive and taboo, conflicted with the image of modernity and progress that was being promoted. Also, the fact that *Tropicalistas* in some of their songs brought to light aspects of social struggle and poverty uncovered a part of Brazilian reality that was silenced by the authorities (Treece 315–16). This allows for the conclusion that the main characteristic of the *Tropicalista* music that caused the conflict with both extremes of the political spectrum was the hybrid way in which they represented stylistic and social elements of Brazilian culture.

A classical example of social hybridity is the song "Tropicália" by Caetano Veloso, named after an interactive ambience or "*Instalação*" created by Hélio Oiticica, and also the song that gave the movement its name. Throughout the song, the lyrical subject juxtaposes modern and primitive elements associated with Brazilian culture as a "disconcerting contiguity" (Veloso), which is the fundament of his perception of contemporary Brazilian music and culture:

> Above my head the airplanes/trucks beneath my feet/my nose is pointed towards the plateau/I organize the movement/I direct the carnival/I inaugurate the monument on the central highlands of the country/Long live the bossa/Long live the straw hut. (Veloso 186–87, my translation)[7]

In these stanzas, the lyrical subject unifies elements of modernity and nature, between which the subject itself functions as the unifying element. Apart from the action of "inaugurating the monument on the central highlands" – referring to the creation of the new capital Brasilia, which confirmed the entrance of Brazil into modernity – the lyrical subject "directs the carnival," which holds reference to the more "primitive" character of Brazilian culture. This blurring of limits leads to what Homi Bhabha calls a field of tension that is situated in the "in-between" of power relations. The lyrical subject claims a position of hybridity, which gives it the potency of subversion, confirming the Brazilian authorities' fear of the *Tropicalismo* movement. Bhabha captures the essence of this perception of hybridity by describing it as "a form of power that is exercised at the very limits of identity and authority" (89). The subversion is thus based on the fact that it does not combat another power-camp from its own fixed, opposed location, but dissolves the ideological borders that constitute the separation between the two.

Performance and Resistance
The previously mentioned artist Hélio Oiticica, who is now considered the key thinker behind the conceptualization of the *marginália* strategy, maintained close relations with the musicians of the *Tropicalismo*. During a concert by Veloso and Gil in November 1968, his frame *Seja Marginal, Seja Herói* formed part of the stage decoration and supposedly was the decisive provocation of the authorities that led to the arrest and forced exile of both singers a month later. It is also through the work of Oiticica's that the importance of performance in marginal resistance and thus in the poetry of Nuvem Cigana can be appreciated. Oiticica believed in organic and intimate art forms, in the integration between art and person, and in art as experience (Veloso 426). The *Parangolé* most powerfully expresses this fusion of subject and object. The *Parangolé* is an artistic concept rather than a specific object, developed in 1964 and related by Oiticica to a whole range of artistic and socio-political prepositions. A mantle made out of different pieces of colored cloth, the *Parangolé* only becomes a work of art in the act of being worn, when its "wearer" becomes observer, participant, and work of art at the same time. Wearing the *Parangolé* transforms it and brings it to life. Movement and dance reveal its different layers of colors and fuse visual impressions with rhythm and spatial interaction: it becomes performance. Oiticica explains how the multiplying function of being both object and subject of the work of art presupposes an experience where the individual commits with all its actions and movements to the purposes of the work of art itself. In this way, the work of art is not meant to condition any specific individual action, but rather sets out to cancel all conditioning factors and unleash the individual freedom that is at the base of artistic creation (Oiticica, *Revista Vozes*; Nagle 2–3).

Returning to Agamben's argument that the existence of the subject is measured by either its ability or inability to be actively involved with its (social) environment, the insertion of the artistic creation into an independent realm gives the (artistic) subject access to the fundamental modalities of its existence. Departing from this premise of individual freedom, the subject is offered the possibility of choice between being and being not-, and is therefore given access to the power of decisions over its actions that constitute the very process of creation. If the symbolism of this creative process is projected onto the role of the individual subject in Brazilian society, the importance of this freedom of action becomes clear when one realizes that it is this freedom that was denied to marginal groups in the process of constructing a national identity.

Because of the interaction with the subject that is required for the *Parangolé* to become more than merely a colorful piece of cloth, it is a form of art that only exists in the act of performance. It is therefore an intangible art form; ephemeral in its process of instant meaning production, and multiple in the artistic experience of reception, interaction, and creation. For this reason, the entire production of meaning and the reason for being of the work of art have come to depend on the individual subject and its performance.

Oiticica, in his effort to integrate the concept of marginality into artistic expression and performance, also filmed and photographed people from the *favelas* of Rio wearing a *Parangolé*. This was a very direct way of visualizing how the marginalized were given the possibility of creation, of existence as active subjects. Instead of inverting a binary power relation by putting the subaltern in a hegemonic position, the fleeting character of the *Parangolé* evokes the in-between character of hybridity as Bhabha described it earlier on. The subject becomes observer, participant, and creator, and now finds itself placed on the borderline between identity and authority: there lies its power of subversion. The hybridity that is referred to in this case is no longer the intertwinement of popular and erudite culture that is to be found at the core of the *Tropicália* aesthetics; instead of working at the level of the *effects* of power relations, blurring the established limits between the dominant and the subordinated, the performance proposed by Oiticica inverts the very *causes* of power relations and their articulation.

Although the *Parangolé* as such never formed part of the Nuvem Cigana performances, their artistic attitude strongly leans on the ideas proposed by thinkers of the *marginália*, one of whom was Oiticica. Linking the concept of marginality and performance of the *Parangolé* to the Artimanha poetry performances of Nuvem Cigana, one can observe a similar reclaiming of expressive freedom by a marginalized (artistic) subject. When the performance of poetry becomes a spontaneous act in which the direct, instantaneous interaction between poet and audience can transform the way in which a poem is being expressed, the improvisational character of the event blurs the clear separation between performing artist and observing audience. The core of the *marginália*'s power of resistance is located in the in-between space that is the result of this blurring. In it, artist and audience regain a potency of creation and action that is denied to them in official society.

The poet Torquato Neto had been part of the *Tropicália* and later became an important figure in the *marginália* movement and a key point of reference for the younger generation of poets from Nuvem Cigana. In his numerous texts, criticisms, and pamphlets he conceptualized the idea of marginality and the role of poetry in the process of resisting, through this marginal attitude, the imposed censorship. In his poem "Let's play that," which was put to music and performed by the marginal singer[8] Jards Macalé, the lyrical subject talks about an angel that is "not baroque," but "crazy, very crazy/with wings of an airplane" who comes to give the order: "*vai bicho, desafinar o coro dos contentes!*" 'go, animal, detune the choir of the satisfied.' The hybrid character of the angel – combined with elements of modernity – recalls the *Tropicália* and the blurring of oppositions between contrasting elements. The fact that this angel asks the listener to "detune the choir of the satisfied" clearly refers to the task of the marginal subject to dislocate the established power relations of Brazilian society from the inside. The craziness of the angel is a reference to the otherness of the young people that were characterized as the *desbunde* ("out of control")[9], whom most of the Nuvem Cigana poets considered themselves to be part of. It was the young *cariocas* that gathered at Ipanema beach for two consecutive summers at the start of the 1970s, behind big hills that had been formed due to the construction of a sewer system leading into the open water. Behind these dunes, the *cariocas* could not be seen from the boulevard, meaning that it was a place with a relative lack of (police) control where young people gathered to enjoy life according to the ideals of the hippie movement. This freedom included the use of drugs, open exhibition of (gay) sexuality, and even the very fact of gathering in groups larger than three persons. It was also one of the places where the first mimeographed books of poetry were sold (Cohn 17–25). Caetano Veloso describes in his autobiography/*Tropicália* testimony how the *desbunde* considered the fact of being crazy – either temporarily due to the use of drugs or clinically proven mentally ill – a privilege, as it implied independence from the rules of a dictatorial society and gave the sensation of a certain form of freedom (470–71). Therefore, as Torquato Neto suggests in the images of his poem, the craziness that leads to social marginalization is the very weapon that can be used to dislocate ("detune") the existing power structure. The Nuvem Cigana poet Ronaldo Santos, in one of the interviews with Cohn, stresses this active involvement of the *desbunde* groups with their social environment and states that their behavioral disconnection from society did not mean that they were unaware of what was happening around them (111).

Artimanha: The Carnivalesque Experience
In relation to the connection created above between *desbunde*, performance, and the subversion of power relations, the work of Mikhail Bakhtin on the carnivalesque and

the grotesque in the Middle Ages can shed light on the subversive character of festive rituals and corporeal expression. The Artimanha shares some of these carnivalesque characteristics.

One aspect of the Artimanha in the MAM that launched the *Almanaque*, which I already referred to at the start of this article, lends itself in particular to an analysis through the concept of the carnivalesque. At a certain point during the event a person impersonating a street vendor was amongst the crowd selling *Almanaques*, shouting and advertising his merchandise, when another person dressed up like a skeleton and holding a machine gun halted him and started to hit him with a police baton whilst shouting "give me the bread and the money that you don't have!" The people in the audience, who recognized in this performance a symbolic reference to the repression by the authorities in daily life outside of the museum, spontaneously attacked the skeleton in turn. Such was their level of immersion in the play that the Nuvem Cigana members had to step in and drag the actor out of the hands of the outraged crowd in order to prevent him from being killed. As Ronaldo Santos says, the performance became a catharsis for the frustrations that could not be expressed or processed in everyday life (95–96).

The description that Bakhtin gives of medieval popular carnivalesque festivities, which counterbalanced the seriousness and religiousness of the "official" culture, strongly resonates with this experience of catharsis. In analyzing carnivalesque traditions, Bakhtin points out how festivities in popular culture created a reality that functioned parallel to and independently of the social stratifications and systems of state organization that had gradually come to dominate "official" society. Social rules had put limits to what was permitted in public behavior and not all social groups had equal rights when it came to freedom to act. The carnival tradition, however, became a festivity where – in contrast to official society – the rules of *freedom* were supposed to be lived (and thus performed) by everyone involved. This led to the invention of a new set of informal codes of interaction that served to undo any form of inequality among people who in official society belonged to different social groups. Bakhtin also points out that these carnivalesque codes of interaction in medieval times had a direct link with theatrical behavior. However, carnival had no stage necessity and thus undid the separation between audience and performer: life itself became the realm of performance where everybody was actively involved (Bakhtin 9–12).

Again, the analysis of performance has led to a space of encounter between different cultural elements or subject positions from which the very act of (artistic or carnivalesque) expression is born. In the carnivalesque character that can be recognized in the Artimanha there is a blurring of limitations. The transcendence of the separation between actor and audience, artistic subject and object, official ("high") or non-official ("low"/"primitive") culture, is reminiscent of Bhabha's conceptualization of hybridity and Oiticica's reflections on the *Parangolé*. The medieval carnival tradition comes from an agricultural festivity that marks the closing of one period and the inauguration of another. Consequently, Bakhtin argues that carnival is situated in an in-between realm where an endless process of death and (re)birth is being celebrated (7–10). Thus, the cathartic function of the Artimanha can be interpreted as a rebirth of the assisting individual into a life that is independent of oppressive reality and that allows for freedom of action and behavior. The image of the skeleton in the Artimanha performance, which symbolized an authoritarian repressive intervention, becomes particularly meaningful here, as it indicates the insertion of this authoritative element into the continuous process of death and revitalization. The character of authority is not in itself complete or absolute, but can become part of the revitalizing process where death leads to new life, represented by the audience attacking the skeleton as a way of inaugurating a new vital cycle.

In contrast to the "official" medieval religious or state festivities, which looked back in time to fortify the existing social order as absolute and immutable, carnivalesque expressions emphasize the incompleteness and the continuous renewal that characterize the present (Bakhtin 11–12). The grotesque representation of the body exaggerates the dimensions of those organs that seem to expose the internal parts of the body – and its functions – to the outside world. For example, the emphasis placed by grotesque paintings of the Middle Ages on genitals, the intestines (big bellies), and other orifices (big noses and ears), indicates that these bodily parts symbolized the incompleteness of the body as not self-supportive, but as a system that is in constant exchange with the outside world through a revitalizing (eschatological) process of absorption and excretion. These organs that symbolize the – organic – connection of the body with the world that surrounds it therefore become symbols of carnivalesque regeneration, the celebration of the cyclic movement through death and rebirth (20–21). The bodily expression of poetry that in Nuvem Cigana was closely linked to rhythmical speech, carnival, and samba dancing or singing, therefore becomes a way of revitalizing traditional and folkloric elements in the present as a subversive act against political hegemony by refuting the supposed absolute value of its proposed images of cultural identity construction. A more explicit expression of protest against the repressive authority occurred when Tavinho Paes, during an Artimanha in the Teatro Municipal of São Paolo (where the performers had to be on a stage and thus relatively separated from the audience), urinated on stage in front of the audience (Cohn 109–10). The subversive character of the grotesque as Bakhtin characterized it could not have been demonstrated more clearly. Also, the reaction of disgust by the authorities and the ensuing repercussion for the Nuvem Cigana group, inevitably recall Torquato Neto's words: "*vai bicho, desafinar o coro dos contentes!*" 'Go, animal, detune the choir of the satisfied.'

The Present as *Pléroma*
As I stated earlier, the spontaneous character of performed poetry means that its performance takes place in a specific (physical/social) space and at an

ephemeral, instantaneous moment in time. This makes it necessary to look deeper into the a-historical character of performance poetry and how its entanglement with the present moment becomes an element of resistance against ideological censorship.

The name of the interactive happenings and poetry performances organized by Nuvem Cigana, Artimanha, was inspired by a poem by Torquato Neto. Artimanha, which refers to a cunning strategy of resistance, turned into a reference to "*arte*" as attitude (or "*manha*") and as a weapon assembled out of the sounds of Neto's poem: ". . . *manha/sdarm/asdho/jedha/manhã*" 'attitude/sofweap/onsofto/dayofto/morrow' (qtd. in Cohn 87–88). An important element in this poem is the connection of this strategy of rebellion with "today" and "tomorrow," introducing a sense of temporality into the act of resistance though poetry. The absence of "yesterday" as representing the past is notable, as is the absence of the word tomorrow: "*amanhã*" appears as "*hamanhã*," which could be interpreted as a playful way of inserting the prefix "*ha*" ("since"; "ago") to make a past tense out of the future/tomorrow, thereby turning it into a hybrid present tense.

The emphasis on the present moment in the Artimanha is also a key element in Bernardo Vilhena's poem, which I quoted at the beginning of this article. The title "*o é preciso,*" playfully duplicating the significance of "*preciso*" as both 'exact and necessary', expresses the search for "*o é*" 'the being,' or rather "the is," that indicates the pure present of the moment, which has already passed when it is mentioned. The visual experience of the poetry that is performed at the Artimanha is the spoken word that, according to Vilhena, emits its sound "at the speed of light." In the words of the lyrical subject, the importance of the visual dimension of the poem is based on the fact that the created image constitutes its own independent artistic space, where "it speaks for itself and for me." Therefore, the act of pronouncing and observing the "precise word" ("*a palavra precisa*") of a poem that is made up of sounds and images blurs the separation between the performer and the audience. The expression, in "*Nos e você*" 'We and you,' of a plural first person (who speaks) and a singular second person (who receives) confuses the roles that are traditionally assigned to poet and audience, creator and observer.

The carnivalesque element of the Artimanha manifests itself in the disappearance of the (traditional) distance between artistic subject and object, the lack of a stage that separates both entities in the process of artistic creation. Situated in the pure present, the multiple artistic subject finds itself at the limit between death and revitalization. His or her creative and subversive potential is a result of this situation because it creates the possibility of being (or becoming) in a realm that constitutes the in-between of power relations. Oiticia's comments on the Parangolé further illuminate this phenomenon. He emphasizes the "inherent collective condition of the Parangolé," which, just like the carnivalesque celebration of the present, creates a space for the re-invention of Brazilian culture. Oiticica argues that each individual becomes a "*célula-mater*" 'stem cell' of the world that surrounds him or her when he or she is empowered to assume the position of subject in artistic creation. Oiticica reacts against the "oppressive folklorization" of Brazilian culture, which glorifies a closed system of "non-creation" where "all that is ours" is already predetermined in the discourse of the hegemony (1). With "predetermination" I refer to the closed set of cultural clichés and the selective legitimization of historical chronology, defined by the military authorities, within which only a certain type of cultural production can have a right of existence.

The collective experience of the Artimanha presents a counterpoint to this. It is based on a process of creation that does not build on historical or discursive predetermination. The spontaneous character of the poetry performance, in which the work of art only exists in the very moment of its (collective) enunciation, emerges from the plenitude of the present moment. This instant – which Oiticica characterizes as the "exposed root of Brazilian culture" – guards the potentiality of a culture in formation. This culture can exist because it has the potential of choice between being or being not- (as Agamben would explain it. When Bernardo Vilhena mentions the "sounding echo" that "guards the direction of its force," he is referring to this moment of potentiality that exists just before the moment of determination. This very moment of contained energy is "*o momento de ser*," the purely present 'moment of being' that holds the *possibility* of creation. This creation, furthermore, is not inscribed in a chronological historical process, but springs from an active process of reconstruction based on the "exposed root of culture" that is being accessed in the precise present moment. The Italian poet Mario Perniola captured this idea in the concept of the *pléroma*, explained by Susana Scramim as the state of non-being beyond human perception; a plenitude from which all that exists is being created and to which it is also destined to return (3). This image of non-being describes the revitalizing potential of the carnivalesque present moment and explains why the idea of marginality sees in the death of the subject its full potency of resistance. In the intangible position of non-existence the marginal subject is capable of continuous renewal, endlessly (re-)creating its own cultural identity out of the *pléroma* of the pure present, independent from the folklorizing historical discourse of the authorities.

The spontaneous samba-procession at the end of the Artimanha in the MAM is an example of the re-invention of cultural identity from the plenitude of the present moment. The created collective subject position left unclear who was accountable for the poetry that had been performed or who actively took part in the *desbunde* of the procession and who did not. The latter soon came to include the policemen, who, by recognizing in the carnival procession their own cultural identity, became the involuntary co-authors of the performance they were witnessing and actively interpreting. In a truly contemporary carnivalesque experience, the members of Nuvem Cigana created a situation in which the festive atmosphere blurred the hierarchical stratifications of the "official" part of society. The act of performance reached its highest creative potential by involving both a marginal group of artists and the executive body of state authority in a shared process of active re-creation of the folklorized Brazilian carnival tradition. By bringing together in the same dynamic process two contrasting elements – repression and spontaneity, authority and marginality – a (hybrid or grotesque) limit situation was created in which Brazilian culture, instead of being a defined set of folkloric elements that link back to past times, regained its spontaneous character of incomplete creation through death and rebirth in the precise moment of being, *O é preciso:*

Suaveamargo, bittersoft
Artimanha

Notes

1. "The precise word launches the sound/At lightspeed/Where we and you dominate the space/The image speaks for itself/And for me . . . /it is fundamental that the text penetrates/eyes and ears/that it entangles itself in the cerebral hairs/Revealing itself in every repetition/At how many repetitions per second?/The resounding echo installs itself/Preserves the direction of its force/The internal trajectory of the word/The moment of being/The being/precise/clear/bittersoft/ Artimanha"

2. *Bloco*: a carnival group that prepares for the annual carnival processions around a central theme that characterizes its particular image and underlying philosophy.

3. ". . . *hoje sou marginal ao marginal, não marginal aspirando à pequena burguesia ou ao conformismo, o que acontece com a maioria, mas marginal mesmo: à margem de tudo, o que me dá surpreendente liberdade de ação.*"

4. Instead of using the conjugation of "not-being," which departs from a status quo, I use "being not-" in order to emphasize this negativity as an actively taken decision. This is more in line with the argument of the subjects' existence.

5. I will use the term "*Tropicalismo*" when referring specifically to the musical movement that was founded and headed by Caetano Veloso and Gilberto Gil, among others. However, as the artistic movement also included other forms of expression such as cinema and plastic arts, I will use the term "*Tropicália*" when referring to the movement in general (which includes names such as Hélio Oiticica and filmmaker Rogério Sganzerla). The term "*Tropicalistas*," as a way to refer to the movements' members, does not make this distinction between musicians and others. In most of the cases, however, the term "*Tropicalistas*" will refer to the musicians. This idea is developed by Frederico Coelho in his thesis *Eu, Brasileiro, confesso minha culpa e meu pecado* (73–77).

6. *Carioca*: an inhabitant of Rio de Janeiro.

7. "*Sobre a cabeça os aviões/Sob os meus pés os caminhões/Aponta contra os chapadões meu nariz,/Eu organizo o movimento/Eu oriento Carnaval/Eu inauguro o monumento no planalto central do pais/Viva bossa-sa-sa/Viva palhoça-ça-ça-ça-ça.*"

8. The more correct way of referring to the musicians that belonged to the *marginália* collective would be "*os malditos*" (the damned). I base this on the classification given by Coelho. However, in order not to complicate the text too much, I have presented the singer Macalé simply as a "marginal" musician.

9. *Desbunde* and its verbal use *desbundar* describe an uninhibited attitude that is closely related to the hippie lifestyle of the U.S.A. in the 1960s. It includes the African word "*bunda*," which stands for "bum." According to Caetano Veloso, the reference to the bum is a synecdoche for the entire body in an attitude of completely surrendering to one's bodily drives (469).

Bibliography

Agamben, Giorgio. *Remnants of Auschwitz: The Witness and the Archive*. Cambridge: The MIT Press, 2002.

Bakhtin, Mikhail. "Introducción: Planteamiento del problema." *La cultura popular en la Edad Media y en el renacimiento: El contexto de Francois Rabelais*. Madrid: Alianza Editorial, 2003. 4–51.

Bhabha, Homi. *The Location of Culture*. 1994. London/New York: Routledge, 2008.

Coelho, Frederico. "'Eu, brasileiro, confesso minha culpa e meu pecado': cultura marginal no Brasil dos anos 60 e 70." Diss. UFRJ Rio de Janeiro, 2002.

Cohn, Sergio. *Nuvem Cigana: poesia & delírio no Rio dos anos 70*. Rio de Janeiro: Beco do Azougue, 2007.

Nagle, Marilene. "Viva o Parangolé: experiência e performance em Hélio Oiticica." International Symposium Archivo y Experiencia, Department of Latin American Languages and Cultures, Faculty of Humanities, Leiden University, 23–24 Febr. 2007.

Oiticica, Hélio. "As possibilidades do Crelazer." *Revista Vozes* (1970): n. pag.

Treece, David, and Mike González. *The Gathering of Voices: The Twentieth Century Poetry of Latin America*. London/New York: Verso, 1992.

Scramim, Susana. "Literatura e Pós-Modernidade." *Revista de Estudos Universitários UNISO* 35 (2009): 1–6.

Veloso, Caetano. *Verdade tropical*. 1997. São Paulo: Companhia Das Letras, 2004.

"The Hurricane Doesn't Roar in Pentameters": Rhythmanalysis in Performed Poetry

Cornelia Gräbner

In the essays published in his posthumous collection *Rhythmanalysis*, Henri Lefebvre proposes a new approach to the analysis of everyday life, especially – but not only – in cities: through rhythm. The analysis of rhythms, carried out in a discipline which Lefebvre calls "rhythmanalysis," is crucial to the understanding of everyday life in a particular location and at a particular point in time because rhythms express and perform the relationship between time and practices. In order to analyze them, because rhythms cannot be captured through the written word, the rhythmanalyst needs to engage with them through all his senses:

> The rhythmanalyst calls on all his senses. He draws on his breathing, the circulation of his blood, the beatings of his heart and the delivery of his speech as landmarks. Without privileging any one of these sensations, raised by him in the perception of rhythms, to the detriment of any other. He thinks with his body, not in the abstract, but in lived temporality. (Lefebvre 21)

The product of such engagement relates its outcome to poetry:

> Does the rhythmanalyst thus come close to the **poet**? Yes, to a large extent . . . Like the poet, the rhythmanalyst performs a verbal action, which has an aesthetic import. The poet concerns himself above all with words, the verbal. Whereas the rhythmanalyst concerns himself with temporalities and their relations within wholes. (24)

Lefebvre suggests that the verbal and the temporal are separate from each other, and that in poetry and rhythmanalysis they remain separate: poetry is concerned with the verbal and takes place outside of temporality, whereas rhythmanalysis is concerned with producing a "verbal action" on and within temporality. In this article I will revisit these contentions through an analysis of performed poems. The poetry performance upsets the clear separation between poetry and rhythmanalysis for two reasons. Firstly, it situates the poem and its rhythms within temporality. Thus, it throws into relief the a-temporal character of poetry that Lefebvre cites as one of the defining differences between poetry and rhythmanalysis. The question I will explore here is whether the poetry performance's preoccupation with temporality changes the relationship between poetry and rhythmanalysis and, if so, how. Secondly, the poetry performance, just like rhythmanalysis, involves the listener and the poet on several levels of perception. In the poetry performance, rhythms simultaneously interact with body language, sound, music, tone of voice, tempo, pace, visual elements of the performance, the sound of words, and semantic meaning. I call this technique "polysensual layering."

Four features of the poetry performance make it particularly suitable for a staging of and reflection on rhythms.[1] The first is the presence of the poet at the site of the performance, as a representative of his – conceivably absent – community or as a member of the community that is constructed during the performance. The performer's presence highlights the importance of the cultural, social, political, and historical elements of his background, and the traditions that inform his work. The second characteristic is the importance of place. The impact of a performed poem is different at a community center, a political rally, a school, or a festival hall. A particular venue can make a poem vulnerable to external rhythms, or can exclude these. An example of the former is the intrusion of beats from other shows that are taking place in other rooms in the same venue. An example of the latter is the way in which silent venues can highlight the rhythms used in the poem, as in a recital I saw at the University of Stirling, where Linton Kwesi Johnson performed heavily rhythmed dub poetry in a completely silent university theater. Thirdly, performed poetry often uses the vernacular or dialect of the poet. It incorporates accents and, in doing so, emphasizes and validates class and group identities. Finally, the performed poem focuses on stylistic features that appeal to the oral (as in speaking) and the aural (as in hearing). This enables the simultaneous performance of various layers of signification, i.e. polysensual layering.[2]

All these characteristics make the performance of poetry permeable by its surroundings. Rhythms highlight this permeability and can only be understood within it because their social coding comes from their associations.[3] Lefebvre alludes to this when he writes that the rhythmanalist "separates out through a mental act that which gives itself as linked to a whole: namely rhythms and their associations" (87–88). Derek Attridge makes a similar point when he reflects on the significance of meter, which he subsumes under the category of poetic rhythms:

> The strength of these general associations of regular verse form is also witnessed by the need to combat them that is experienced in poetic revolutions: they bring a tradition forcefully to mind, and to reject them is to reject that tradition. This is

true of specific metres, too; the iambic pentameter is a legitimate target for populist poetic reformers not because of its inherent properties (its "hegemonic stance towards the ordinary language of men", say), but because of its traditional associations with "high art." (302)

In the first section of this article I will engage with the debate on rhythm versus meter through an analysis of two essays in which poets reflect on the use of rhythm in performed poetry. Charles Olson's "Projective Verse" (1950) and Edward Kamau Brathwaite's "A History of the Voice" (1980) are of seminal importance both for contemporary poetry in the English language and for performance poetry. Olson is considered a precursor of the Beat Poets and of U.S. American counterculture,[4] while Brathwaite approaches the performance of poetry within a postcolonial context, in which the languages of the Caribbean have to be rediscovered. Similarities and differences in their takes on rhythm in performed poetry are therefore important for the question of whether the performance of poetry connects practices from different cultural backgrounds within a hybrid and multicultural genre. I will then analyze performed poems by Nuyorican poet Willie Perdomo and African-American poet Saul Williams with a view to determining how they use rhythms to connect the poem with its surroundings. Both poets situate their poems within the context of an urban environment. Thus, their use of rhythms benefits from an engagement with Lefebvre's approach to rhythms.[5]

On a theoretical level, my argument seeks to contribute to the debate of whether "performance poetry" is a poetic genre in its own right. The argument presented here attempts to extricate this debate from its polemicized framework. Rather, my analysis will explore whether the use of rhythm in performed poems is so specific that it exceeds the possibilities of an analysis of the performance of poetry as one of many poetic practices. If this is the case, then it calls for theorists to look at performed poems as part of a genre called "performance poetry" or "spoken word poetry."

Conceptualizing Rhythm: Breath or Hurricane?
Brathwaite and Olson conceptualize rhythm through metaphors. Olson argues that poetry needs to be re-made in light of the possibilities of the poet's breath, through the process of "composition by field." Brathwaite argues that the emergent languages in the Caribbean need to engage with the forces of nature, which he symbolizes as a hurricane; the way in which poetry engages with the hurricane is through its rhythms. Both poets argue that rhythm is distinct to, and an alternative to, meter. Rhythm and meter, and consequently the choice for one over the other, are charged with cultural and political significance, and also make a statement towards poetic tradition.

Olson proposes that the flow of energy lies at the heart of projective verse and of "composition by field." This process is opposed "to inherited line, stanza, over-all form," which, in the past, determined all other elements of a poem. Composition by field breaks the dominance of inherited form through three crucial elements: kinetics, principle, and process. Kinetics conceptualizes the poem as "an energy-discharge": "A poem is energy transferred from where the poet got it . . . , by way of the poem itself to, all the way over to, the reader" (Olson 3). The principle of projective verse is that "FORM IS NEVER MORE THAN AN EXTENSION OF CONTENT" (Olson 4). Process refers to "how the principle can be made so to shape the energies that the form is accomplished" (4). This is accomplished through pace: "ONE PERCEPTION MUST IMMEDIATELY AND DIRECTLY LEAD TO A FURTHER PERCEPTION" (4). The combination of these three elements in composition by field creates the projective poem.

Composition by field encourages and requires a particular relationship between the poet and his poem on the one hand, and reality on the other:

> It comes to this: the use of a man, by himself and thus by others, lies in how he conceives his relation to nature, that force to which he owes his somewhat small existence. If he sprawl, he shall find little to sing but himself, and shall sing, nature has such paradoxical ways, by way of artificial forms outside himself. But if he stays inside himself, if he is contained within his nature as he is participant in the larger force, he will be able to listen, and his hearing through himself will give him secret objects to share. (Olson 10)

The poet has two options: he can turn inward, towards himself and as a result his poetry will take on forms that are imposed on poetry from the outside, forces of poetic tradition and social convention. Alternatively, the poet can interact with the forces of nature – apparently exterior to him – by conceiving of himself and his own voice as one part of this larger exteriority. The individuality of the poet will then flourish in interaction with his surroundings and the poem will take a shape that emerges out of this unique interaction. Nature now turns into the poem's driving energy, in contradistinction to earlier forms of poetry when nature was a poem's motive.

Breath mediates the interaction between poet and nature:

> But breath is man's special qualification as animal. Sound is a dimension he has extended. Language is one of his proudest acts. And when a poet rests in these as they are in himself (in his physiology, if you like, but the life in him, for all that) then he, if chooses to speak from these roots, works in that area where nature has given him size, projective size. (Olson 11)

"Breath" stands for that very moment in which the poet is simultaneously in touch with himself and his environment, and expresses this connection through the poem. Breathing in, the poet takes in and participates in what the environment gives him; holding his breath, the poet internalizes the exterior and puts it in touch with himself; breathing out, he returns his own inner life to his environment. As the poet breathes, he listens to himself and the listener listens to his breathing. The rhythm and pace of a poem emerge out of this interactive practice of breathing and listening.

Like Olson, Brathwaite struggles with the "inherited dominance of meter." He, too, posits that poets negotiate their encounter with nature through the poem and, consequently, that the poem expresses the poet's "stance towards reality." However, his argument is framed within the entirely different context of the de-colonizing of Caribbean culture and, more precisely, within a reflection on the role of poetry in the rediscovery or reconstruction of the emergent languages of the Caribbean. Brathwaite posits that this reconstruction needs to take place in close engagement with the natural environment of the Caribbean, metaphorized in the hurricane.[6] Meter conceptualized as opposed to rhythm is one of the main impediments for poetry's engagement with its surroundings:

> What is even more important, as we develop this business of emergent language in the Caribbean, is the actual rhythm and the syllables, the very software, in a way, of the language. What English has given us as a model for poetry, and to a lesser extent prose (but poetry is the basic tool here), is the pentameter: . . . There have, of course, been attempts to break it. . . . Over in the New World, the Americans – Walt Whitman – tried to bridge or to break the pentameter through a cosmic movement, a large movement of sound. cummings tried to fragment it. And Marianne Moore attacked it with syllabics. But basically the pentameter remained, and it carries with it a certain kind of experience, which is not the experience of the hurricane. The hurricane does not roar in pentameters. And that's the problem: how do you get a rhythm which approximates the natural experience, the environmental experience? (Brathwaite 9–10)

Brathwaite argues that rhythm is the crucial link between the poem on the one hand, and the poet's experience of nature on the other. Traditional meter has alienated poets from the Americas from the rhythms of their natural environment, which is symbolized by the hurricane. Thus, the emergent languages of the Caribbean have to find a poetic language that is based on the rhythm that has been denied to them in the past.

Both poets argue that rhythm is an expression of the poet's stance towards "the world" or "reality," and at the same time the vehicle for the reconfiguration of this stance through the poem. Each poet uses one central metaphor for poetic rhythm: in Olson's case, the metaphor is breath; in Brathwaite's case, it is the hurricane. These metaphors highlight the differences between their approaches to rhythm. The hurricane impacts on the poet from the outside. The energy flows from the environment to the poet and the poet has to work it into his poetry in such a way that the poem becomes imbibed with its environment. Olson's reflections on breath imply that the energy moves from inside the poet towards the outside. This movement of energy, which takes place during the enunciation of the poem, creates a space for the encounter of subjectivity with nature. Consequently, energy as expressed through rhythm is one important means by which poets reflect on and perform the relationship between the performed poem, its surroundings, and its context.

Brathwaite and Olson contend that meter channels poetic energy into socially accepted forms; since they are both politically positioned outside of the realm of the socially accepted, they reject meter and propose the internalization of external rhythms as an alternative poetic form. To read Brathwaite and Olson's critique of meter as a wholesale rejection of "high art" for the sake of poetic revolution would simplify their concerns. Both poets experience meter as prohibitive and as impeding them from making full use of the possibilities of poetic language and poetic rhythm for self-expression and the exploration of their relationship with their environment. At stake is not the institution of high art or of meter as such, but the constraints that they impose – precisely meter's "hegemonic stance towards ordinary language," to paraphrase Attridge. In response, Brathwaite and Olson look to create a new form of poetry that includes the poet's interaction with his environment among its core elements and the reflection on this interaction among its key principles.

"Strap in and hold on tight": Rhythm in "Writing about What you Know" by Willie Perdomo

The poetry of Nuyorican poet Willie Perdomo is deeply rooted within the culture of Spanish Harlem.[7] Through the recurring character of Papo, a young poet from this area, Perdomo formulates the poetics of a kind of poetry that can be written in an environment characterized by police violence, domestic violence, crime and poverty, but also by mutual support, community identity, love, and a deep affection for the area.[8] Here, I will focus on the first two segments of his poem "Writing about What You Know," as Perdomo performed it at the festival poesiaenvozalta.05 in Mexico City in November 2005. In these two segments of the poem, Perdomo explores the role of poetry in Papo's troubled youth and young adulthood. Perdomo uses polysensual layering to evoke the environment in which Papo grows up. Socially coded rhythms, which Perdomo places in relation to each other, form part of the texture created through polysensual layering.

In his analysis of city rhythms, Lefebvre argues that rhythms can interact in different ways and suggests the following categories for the analysis of the relations between different rhythms:

> Polyrhythmia? It suffices to consult one's body; thus the everyday reveals itself to be a polyrhythmia from the first listening. Eurhythmia? Rhythms unite with one another in the state of health, in normal (which is to say normed!) everydayness; when they are discordant, there is suffering, a pathological state (of which arrhythmia is generally, at the same time, symptom, cause and effect). (16)

Polyrhythmia, eurhythmia, and arrhythmia take on different meanings in each of the segments, depending on Papo's age. Lefebvre's positive or negative association with each of the stages of rhythm will be accordingly problematized.

The first segment of the poem recounts Papo's first encounter with poetry in the context of his childhood environment. Perdomo's performance conveys Papo's experience of his polyrhythmic *barrio*, which is characterized by a simultaneous and fast-paced interaction of rhythms, sounds, smells, images, and tastes. These are then contrasted with the slow-paced rhythms that dominate the public library, where Papo's class is taken by their schoolteacher:

> Up and down the block there are jingles for manteca, yucca, tamarindo, matadona, plátano maduro y pan caliente and Papo is listening to the Head Librarian lecture on the value of learning the Dewey Decimal System. "If you need something on Earth Science, you first go to the card catalog and" – but all Papo can hear is the wahwahwahwahwah of urgent police sirens speeding towards the projects. (Perdomo 64)

Perdomo's pace of enunciation emphasizes Papo's fast perception of many simultaneous exterior stimuli. The <t>, <k>, and <p> sounds and the plosives in the enumeration of different types of food in Spanish increase the tempo, making it difficult for the listeners to keep track of the different types of food and requiring their complete attention. The contrast between the quick rhythms of the outside world on the one hand, and the emphatic, slow-paced and monotonous lecture by the Head Librarian on the other hand, is emphasized by them being named in the same sentence and by an apparently sudden decrease in Perdomo's enunciative tempo. Papo's inability to pay attention to the librarian's lecture is rhythmically underlined by Perdomo's imitation of the police sirens. Through sound and rhythm Perdomo captures the clash between Papo's world and knowledge: Papo's world starts right outside the library and enters it by way of sounds, whereas knowledge is tucked away in the card catalog and bears no relation to Papo's world.

The monotony of the head librarian's lecture and the card catalog are contrasted by an exciting discovery of Papo's in another section of the library:

> He turns his head toward the one-week Express Book section. There's a book with a picture of his block on the cover. He can tell by the identification tags on the wall telling him who loved who and for how long. The book says that there is poetry inside. The title buzzes on Papo's tongue like a biscuit of neon announcing instant Lotto and liquor. The poet is standing in the reflection of a lamp post that beams on Puerto Rican flags dangling chest forward out of tenement windows. Cuchifrito stands blink their 24-hour fluorescent crowns for the late night tree blazers who end their cipher sessions with a taste for un relleno de papa and a large cup of sesame seed juice. (Perdomo 64)

Polysensual layering expresses Papo's excitement: the "Express Book section" evokes a faster pace than the search in the card catalog; the book "says" that there is poetry inside, the title "buzzes" on Papo's tongue like a biscuit in an appeal to hearing, tact, and taste, but in fact the metaphorical biscuit is made of neon and blinks an announcement, thus appealing to visuality. With the mention of liquor Perdomo appeals to taste, cuchifrito stands blink but they also smell, and the passage ends with a reference to the taste of "un relleno de papa and a large cup of sesame juice," a phrase which mixes two different languages.

Papo experiences the polyrhythmia of his environment as eurhythmic: to him, the rhythms form one coherent texture. Inside the library, the polyrhythmia of the *barrio* is excluded and even explicitly rejected, most vocally by the teacher who tells Papo off when he attempts to engage with the book that captures the polyrhythmia of the outside. This exclusion and rejection of the *barrio*'s polyrhythmic environment creates a feeling of arrhythmia for Papo; Perdomo makes this arrhythmia felt when he switches from one rhythm to another within one sentence, without engaging the two rhythms. So far, Perdomo's performance of the rhythms of Spanish Harlem coincides with Lefebvre's evaluations: polyrhythmia is exciting, arrhythmia is disconcerting.

In the next section of the poem, Perdomo undermines this evaluation of rhythms by re-contextualizing them. Papo, now a teenager, learns to write his own poetry. His creative writing teacher gives him the assignment to "Write about what you know. And remember: don't tell me, show me." The poem continues:

> That night he was hillin' in front of Caridad's Grocery with Baby Face Nelson and Green-Eye Raymond. A silver BMW drives by with a jukebox in the trunk. The Yellow-Top Crew just cracked their first bottle of champagne. The tempo for Papo's first assignment will be set by a round of Uzi shots ringing off the Wagner Project rooftops. The shots are supported by a heavy, deep, hip-hop jeep, bass line thump with a stream of furious congas keeping rhythm in the background, warning you to strap in and hold on tight. (Perdomo 65)

The teacher's grammatically neat and tonally pedagogical, encouraging and polite request echoes the librarian's lecture in the first section. Papo's reality, however, has changed from the exciting and rich environment of a child to the rhythmically defined and coded environment of an adolescent who lives just on, or over, the edge of legality. The tempo is set "by a round of Uzi shots," accompanied by a hip-hop bassline and congas. The hip-hop rhythm is echoed in Perdomo's enunciation of the line and the accelerated speed of enunciation conveys to the listener the tension felt in Papo's environment. The event of the shots is rhythmically embedded within the bass line beat and the conga rhythms. Thus, the Uzi shots, the bass line, and the conga rhythms are eurhythmic, as were the rhythms of the *barrio* in Papo's childhood. Yet, whereas the eurhythmia in Papo's childhood environment expressed a sense of stimulation and discovery, the eurhythmia of his adolescence is the result of a cohesive and closed-off environment of violence and crime.

Interestingly, the pace and rhythm of Papo's assignment do not fit into his eurhythmic environment; instead, his poem creates an arrhythmia:

> *To Live and Die in Spanish Harlem*
>
> *His name was Papo.*
> *We didn't know his real name.*
>
> *He was born with a plastic spoon*
> *melting in his mouth.*
>
> *His face was carved from marble.*
>
> *He had silver daggers for eyes.*
>
> *His heart shaped like a green toy soldier,*
> *ready to attack.*
>
> *He had hawk wings attached to his brains.*
>
> *He crawled to the corner and started running*
> *after death.*
>
> *He played follow the leader by himself.*
>
> *He lived and died in Spanish Harlem.* (Perdomo 66)

The even, regular pace of Papo's poem could be a response to the teacher's tone of voice and his implicit expectations. Such an interpretation suggests that the poem marks Papo's alienation from his environment because he complies with exterior expectations. However, it is also possible to read the poem as Papo's attempt to find his own voice, away from the dominant rhythms of his environment. Yet, as "Writing about What You Know" continues, we find out that he cannot separate himself from his environment. Thus, Papo can express himself only when he learns to creatively and constructively appropriate rhythms that mark a socially violent environment, and then reframes these rhythms within the positive aspects of his community. As the poem continues, Papo does acquire this ability. The result is a poetic practice that questions another one of Lefebvre's assertions about the rhythmanalyst:

> He changes that which he observes: he sets in motion, he recognizes its power. In this sense, he seems close to the poet, or the man of the theater. Art, poetry, music and theater have always brought something (but what?) to the everyday. They haven't reflected on it. The creator descended to the streets of the city-state; the portrayed inhabitants lived amongst the citizens. They assumed the city life. (25)

Lefebvre evokes the poet as creator who "descends" (one might wish to ask, from where?) to "the streets of the city-state," i.e. the mundane aspect of everyday life.

Once immersed in it, he "portrays" the rhythms of the city. Perdomo/Papo do not descend into the city streets. Neither is their analysis of rhythms carried out from a distance, as Lefebvre's own analysis in "Seen from A Window" or Michel de Certeau's view of the streets from the top of the Empire State Building. Perdomo/Papo's creativity is motivated and nurtured by the continued contact with the streets; yet, it is constructive only if it passes through the self-reflexive process that according to Lefebvre is not part of rhythmanalysis.

Offbeat Heartbeats

Perdomo/Papo constructs a position of enunciation through the constructive engagement with the rhythms of his environment. African-American poet Saul Williams pursues the opposite project in his poem "Twice the First Time": he "separates out through a mental act that which gives itself as linked to a whole: namely rhythms and their associations" (Lefebvre: 88). Williams extricates four different rhythms from their social context and explores the ways in which rhythms are socially coded and, through these codes, produce meaning and identity. This leads him to question whether it is at all possible to speak from a position that is overdetermined by socially coded rhythms.[9]

"Twice the First Time" is organized around three audible components and one invoked component. The audible components are the spoken word, Hip Hop beats, and a melody based on chain gang and work songs. The invoked component is the speaker's heartbeat. Williams puts the four components into a "triadic relationship" (Lefebvre 12). Lefebvre argues that the triadic structure of dialectics lends itself to rhythmanalysis because the latter is carried out "in the presence of the **world**" (12), and emphasizes relations between triads rather than static positions. As a result, it "does not isolate an object, or a subject, or a relation. It seeks to grasp a moving but determinate complexity . . . ." (11–12). Triadic analysis distinguishes itself from Hegelian dialectics in that "It doesn't lead to a *synthesis* in accordance with the Hegelian schema. Thus, the triad 'time-space-energy' links three distinct terms that it leaves distinct, without fusing them in a *synthesis*" (12). Williams establishes the triad of words-beat-melody. Yet, Williams's search for liberation problematizes Lefebvre's positive assessment of the triadic structure for rhythmanalysis: triadic analysis has no place for the fourth, potentially liberating element of the poem, the speaker's heartbeat.

The four components are organized into three stanzas and a chorus, which is based on the first stanza. The spoken word component of the poem is developed through a chorus and two long stanzas in which the speaker verbally articulates a reflection on the alienating and oppressive effect of the prescribed use of Hip Hop beats. The melody consists of a series of dissonant improvisations over the theme of traditional chain gang and work songs, by a cello and a violin. The melody's blues rhythm contrasts with the Hip Hop break beats underlying the spoken word sections of the poem. The beats are performed through the use of the body as instrument and the voice as beat box. The meaning produced by the poem originates from the tension between and the interaction of its four core elements. The poem reconfigures the relationships between these elements as, alternatively, supportive, contradictory, or mutually undermining. The first stanza/chorus begins and ends the poem. It outlines the speaker's position of enunciation in relation to the dominant rhythms of the poem. The second stanza addresses the conditions of the production of Hip Hop, and the third stanza suggests a possible alternative. The final stanza suggests a cyclical movement, as it draws on the motives and phrasing of the introduction but modifies it in light of the points made in the spoken word stanzas. As the poem progresses, the voice – which initially performs alone – is accompanied by a dissonant combination of beats and melody. The introduction/chorus is performed in a sing-song, by the voice alone:

> (sung)
> I will not rhyme on tracks
> niggas on a chain gang used to do that (Huh!) way back
> I will not rhyme over tracks
> niggas on a chain gang used to do that (Huh!) way back
> don't drop the beat on me
> don't drop the beat no
> ah
> (spoken)
>
> I am not the son of sha klak klak
> I am before that
> I am before
> I am before before before death is eternity after death is eternity
> there is no death there's only eternity
> and I be riding on the wings of eternity like
> CLA CLA CLA SHA KLACK KLACK
> GET ME THE FUCK OFF THIS TRACK

The metonymical connection between, on the one hand, the train tracks built by chain gangs and, on the other, the Hip Hop tracks provided by drum machines, encapsulates one of the central points made in the poem: the rhythms of the chain gang and Hip Hop beats are equally prescriptive and therefore confining and oppressive. Their presence by evocation – as opposed to explicit performance – highlights their powerful presence in the speaker's consciousness because the speaker has internalized them to the extent that they are present even when they cannot be heard. The speaker's request to not drop the beats shows that the beats not only oppress him, but define his enunciative position to such an extent that without them he cannot speak at all. In the second part of the stanza Williams refers to the possibility of an identity linked to an eternity that exists before and beyond death. However, the speaker's ride "on the wings of eternity" is interrupted by the "cla cla sha klack sha klack" of the chain gang and he ends the stanza with the line "Get me the fuck off this track." In response to this line, the Hip Hop beat kicks in and replaces the chain gang rhythm with the Hip Hop track. In interaction with the cello, the Hip Hop beat sets the pace for a forcefully and emphatically enunciated passage in which Williams reflects on the conditions under which the Hip Hop rhythms are produced and how these conditions impact on the identity they express:

> as if the heart beat wasn't enough
> they got us using drum machines now
> the hums of the machines
> tryin to make our drums humdrums
> tryin to fuck our magic
> instruments be political prisoners up inside computers
> as if the heart were not enough
> as if the heart were not enough
>
> and as heart beats bring percussions
> fallen trees bring repercussions
> cities play upon our souls like broken drums
> redrum the essence of creation from city slums
> but city slums mute our drums and our drums become humdrums
> cuz city slums have never been where our drums are from
> just the place where our daughters and sons become
> offbeat heartbeats
> slaves to city streets
> and hearts get broken and heartbeats stop
> broken heartbeats become breakbeats for niggas to rhyme on top, but...
>
> I won't rhyme on top of no tracks... etc.

The relationship between rhythms and alienation is key here. In the first place, African-Americans are alienated from themselves through the removal of "our sons and daughters" from free open space into city slums. The urban setting in which the creative process then takes place disconnects its inhabitants from the location where "our drums are from" and further alienates them from "our magic." In a second move, drum beats are alienated from instruments and the people who play those instruments by being locked up in drum machines. These drum machines are the means of production of rhythm. Their owners are only ever named as "them," which emphasizes their anonymity and power. The implications of these two combined processes of alienation are highlighted by the opposition of drum machines versus heart beats. As a result of both forms of alienation, the creative process becomes fundamentally damaging to the individuals who define themselves through it: "hearts get broken and heartbeats stop/broken heartbeats become breakbeats for niggas to rhyme on top." The analytical, verbally expressed element of the poem is at all times sonically contextualized within the performance of beats and melody, the other two elements of the triad. Thus, the analysis cannot be separated from a position of enunciation that is determined by the identity performed by these rhythms. This performs an apparently irresolvable tension between the speaker's search for liberation and the rhythms that determine and constrain his identity.

In the following stanza, the same rhythmic identity is contextualized by the spoken word within a different setting: nature. Williams takes the listener back to the roots of Hip Hop. He asks his listener to "extract the urban element which created it/and let an open wide countryside illustrate it." Hip Hop can only be experienced "riding in a freight train/in the freezing rain/listening to Coltrane." The new environment permits the speaker to engage with his environment and his community in different, more sensitive ways: "and my fingers run through grains of sand/like seeds of time/ the pains of man/the frames of mind/which built these frames/which is the structure of my urban superstructure/the trains and planes can corrupt and obstruct your plane of thought/so that you forget how to walk through the woods/which ain't good cuz you ain't never walked through the trees/listenin' to nobody beats the biz/and you ain't never heard hip hop." The rhythms and the melody that define the speaker's identity continue throughout the spoken word part that speaks of liberation, thus emphasizing that the identity expressed by rhythm and melody *could* be exercised in this different and liberatory context.

The poem closes on an iterated version of the chorus which exacerbates the contradiction between the need for the tracks vis-à-vis the need for the heartbeat:

> and you must stop that damn track from going…
> please don't drop the beat
> don't drop the beat nooo
> and…
> I will not rhyme on tracks
> niggas on a chain gang used to that (huh) way back
> (repeat)

>   don't drop the beat noooo
>   don't drop the beat no
>   don't drop the beat no
>   don't drop the beat
>   heartbeat
>   my heartbeat
>   goes on
>   and on
>   and on…
>   yeah

Even though the heartbeat prevails in this final stanza, it has no impact on the construction of African-American identity or on the power structures that determine the conditions of peoples' lives. As a result, the poem ends without resolution. The triad spoken word-beat-melody can be read as two types of dialectical arguments. In one reading, the chain gang song is the thesis and the break beat its antithesis. The synthesis is missing and the argument of the poem explores the reasons why thesis and antithesis do not lead to a synthesis. One can also read the break beat and the chain gang song as part of the same thesis. Its antithesis is the heartbeat. However, since the heartbeat is only ever evoked and therefore does not audibly contribute to the performed poem as a whole, the antithesis remains powerless and the situation continues cyclically instead of evolving into synthesis. The studio recording as opposed to the live performance emphasizes the cyclical movement, as no two live performances are ever the same but a studio recording enables potentially endless repetition. In "Twice the First Time" Williams rhythmically articulates a meta-theoretical dilemma. The poem emphasizes that a materialist critique of technology is indispensable to achieving liberation and avoiding co-option. At the same time, the poem explores the limitations of dialectical analysis, which does not give space to the potentially liberating fourth element, the heartbeat. This tension remains unresolved.[10]

Conclusion: The Search for the Hurricane

In the analysis presented in this essay I have addressed a number of ways in which rhythms can signify in performed poetry. In all cases, they are one dominant feature of the performance and are used to explore the relationship between the poet and their environment. Brathwaite and Olson theorize rhythms through the powerful metaphors of the breath and the hurricane. The implications of both metaphors highlight the different ways in which rhythms can function: they can internalize external rhythms and, in so doing, situate the poem within its environment; or they can emerge performatively through an engagement of the poet with his environment at the moment of enunciation and, in so doing, express the poet's relationship with his surroundings.

Perdomo and Williams explore the limitations of this clear separation between the poet's subjectivity and his surroundings as the sources of rhythm. In Perdomo's case, the urban environment can be metaphorized as a potentially destructive hurricane. The poet's position of enunciation is contingent on the constructive appropriation of the rhythms of his environment. Williams, on the other hand, articulates the desire to extricate oneself from this environment in order to find liberation – but this destroys his rhythmically defined positions of enunciation. Interestingly, the continuation of beats and rhythms in a context of nature suggests that liberation *is* possible and Williams's use of the body as instrument reclaims the breakbeat from the drum machines, for himself and his community. Both poets thematize the search for the origin of breath. In doing so, their poetry problematizes Olson's comfortable assumption that everyone within themselves carries the origin of their own breath. Williams's metaphor of the heartbeat goes so far as to imply that without hearing one's heartbeat, one cannot possibly pay attention to one's breath.

The engagement with Lefebvre's principles of rhythmanalysis is constructive and useful for the performance of poetry, because it responds to the temporality of the performance as different from the temporality of written poetry, and because it addresses one of the most important stylistic features that make poetry permeable to its environment: rhythms. However, the use of rhythms in performed poetry also confronts Lefebvre's analysis with practices that question many of his assumptions. Maybe most importantly, poets like Perdomo and Williams make a strong case for the inseparability between intervention and reflection. Both reflect on the social coding of rhythms and, at the same time, create a new object for rhythmanalysis by staging rhythms in their performance.

Notes

1. This definition of key characteristics of performance poetry draws on Beasley.

2. In *The Rhythms of English Poetry*, Derek Attridge argues that rhythms can be externally or internally oriented. In the first case, they "work by establishing relations between the linguistic artifact and the world beyond it other than those determined by the normal processes of signification." In the second case, they "work by highlighting or linking elements within the poem and thereby modifying its semantic texture" (287). Attridge's distinction is different from the notion of polysensual layering in that the latter refers not exclusively to rhythms but contextualizes rhythms within other elements of the poem and its surroundings, and in that the latter emphasizes the necessarily simultaneous interaction of several elements of signification. Nevertheless, Attridge's distinction between external and internal rhythms is useful for identifying different types of rhythms, and their effects, within a poem or within a polysensually layered passage.

3. Attridge analyzes how rhythms are given meaning by way of their associations in some detail.

4. For the influence of the Beat Poets and of U.S. American counterculture on the performance of poetry, see Raskin's and Franssen's articles in this volume.

5. In this essay I focus on Lefebvre's approach to rhythms in order to highlight the ways in which the performance of poetry locates the poem within its surroundings. Other approaches have focused specifically on poetic rhythm. The Russian Formalists, especially Osip Brik and after him Boris Tomaševskij, problematized the relationship between rhythm and meter along similar lines as Olson. For the original texts, see Todorov. For a summary and discussion of their approaches, see Steiner. Henri Meschonnic theorizes the politics of rhythm in general, and of poetic rhythm in particular, in his seminal studies *Critique du rhythme* (1990) and *Politique du rhythme* (1995), with a focus on the relationship between society, subjectivity, and poetic rhythm. He argues for the historic situatedness of rhythms. Ammittai Aviram takes the opposite approach and makes a case for rhythm as pleasure in poetry; he contends that meter is the carrier of rhythm-as-pleasure. For him, poetic rhythms transcend the historic moment and instead create the sublime moment of poetry. Charles Bernstein and Marjorie Perloff address prosody and free verse respectively with a focus on performed and recited poetry in their contributions to Bernstein's *Close Listening* (1998).

6. For a book-length study of the poetry performance in the Caribbean, see Cooper. Brathwaite's concept of Nation Language became a bone of contention in his debate with the poet Derek Walcott, also known as the Walcott-Brathwaite debate.

7. The poetry of Willie Perdomo is also discussed in Urayoán Noel's contribution to this volume. At poesiaenvozalta.05 Perdomo performed only the first two segments of the poem. The remaining sections of the poem (published in *Smoking Lovely*) recount Papo's trajectory through the cycle of drugs, crime, and prison, until he finds his own poetic voice and becomes a creative writing teacher for young persons from a background similar to his own.

8. See my analysis of Perdomo's poem "Where I'm from" in Timmer.

9. Williams has forcefully criticized the commercialization and co-option of Hip Hop and African-American identity throughout his career. His work sets a counterpoint to arguments like the one put forward by Marcus Reeves, where the recognition of African-American identity by U.S. American society is posited positively as contingent upon the development of a successfully marketable product by African-American culture, i.e. Hip Hop. The analysis I present here does not even begin to do justice to the poetic and theoretical complexity of Williams's work or even to "Twice the First Time." For the purpose of this publication, I have had to

limit my analysis strictly to some of the rhythmic dimensions of the poem, but "Twice the First Time" also articulates a dialogue with the heritage of the Black Arts Movement and Black Power. Amiri Baraka is one of several implicit interlocutors of Williams's complex and multi-layered enquiry into African-American identity and Hip Hop, and into the possibilities for art as political intervention. Baraka is also the most obvious connection between the Black Arts Movement and Olson and the Beat Poets; it was Baraka who recovered the almost-forgotten essay "Projective Verse" and re-published it in 1959 (see Thomas). The popular perception that Hip Hop is a continuation of Beat Poetry is articulated in Fernando Jr.'s *The New Beats*, among others.

10. Williams's critique of co-option through the ownership of the means of production resonates with two apparently very different influences on or precursors of the performance of poetry. In *Poetry at Stake*, Carrie Noland analyzes the ways in which poets use and reflect on technology. She draws a connection from nineteenth-century poets such as Rimbaud to contemporary poets like Patti Smith and Laurie Anderson. She argues that these poets "realize . . . that means of

production are embedded in a network of relations of productions and cannot easily be materially extracted – or conceptually abstracted – from these relations. Although the dream of many of the poets considered here is to employ technologies in a fashion *not* determined by their conditions of manufacture, they rarely blind themselves . . . to the link between industrial support and the possibilities offered for creative reappropriation" (8–9). One could easily argue that Williams and other poets influenced by Hip Hop draw on this tradition for the performance of poetry. Particularly useful for a reading of "Twice the First Time" in light of such an approach would be Noland's analysis of Adorno's conceptualization of lyricism in *Negative Dialectics*, though Williams's critique of Hip Hop also shows a strong affinity with Adorno and Horkheimer's critique of the culture industries in *Dialectic of Enlightenment*. Another influence on Performance Poetry is, obviously, Rap and Hip Hop. Williams's critique is a counterpoint to publications like Tricia Rose's *Noise: Rap Music and Black Culture in Contemporary America*, which confidently relies on the possibility to appropriate the products of the culture industries.

Bibliography

Adorno, Theodor. *Negative Dialectics*. Trans. E. B. Ashton. London: Routledge, 1973.

Adorno, Theodor, and Max Horkheimer. *Dialectic of Enlightenment*. Trans. John Cumming. London: Verso, 1997.

Attridge, Derek. *The Rhythms of English Poetry*. London and New York: Longman, 1982.

Aviram, Ammittai. *Telling Rhythms: Body and Meaning in Poetry*. Ann Arbor: University of Michigan Press, 1994.

Beasley, Paul. "Vive la différance!" *Critical Quarterly* 38.4 (1994): 28–38.

Bernstein, Charles. "Introduction." *Close Listening: Poetry and the Performed Word*.

Ed. Charles Bernstein. New York: Oxford University Press, 1998. 3–26.

Brathwaite, Edward Kamau. *History of the Voice: The Development of Nation Language in Anglophone Caribbean Poetry*. London, Port of Spain: New Beacon Books, 1984.

Cooper, Carolyn. *Noises in the Blood: Orality, Gender and the 'Vulgar Body' of Jamaican Popular Culture*. Oxford: Macmillan, 1993.

Fernando Jr., S.H. *The New Beats: Exploring the Music, Culture and Attitudes of Hip Hop*. London: New Beacon Books, 1994.

Gräbner, Cornelia. "Los ritmos de la megalópolis: La poesía en voz alta en la Ciudad de México y en Spanish Harlem, Nueva York." *La ciudad latinoaméricana y escrituras del siglo XXI. Ed. Nanne Timmer. Leiden: Leiden University Press, forthcoming.

Lefebvre, Henri. *Rhythmanalysis: Space, Time and Everyday Life*. London: Continuum, 2004.

Meschonnic, Henri. *Critique du rhythme. Anthropologie historique du langage*. Lagrasse: Verdier, 1990.

———. *Politique du rhythme. Politique du sujet*. Lagrasse: Verdier, 1990.

Noland, Carrie. *Poetry at Stake: Lyric Aesthetics and the Challenge of Technology*. Princeton: Princeton University Press, 1999.

Olson, Charles. *Projective Verse*. Ed. By Le Roi Jones. New York: Totem Press, 1959.

Perdomo, Willie. *Smoking Lovely*. New York: Rattapallax Press, 2005.

Perloff, Marjorie. "After Free Verse: The New Non-Linear Poetries." *Close Listening: Poetry and the Performed Word*. Ed. Charles Bernstein. New York: Oxford University Press, 1998. 86–110.

Reeves, Marcus. *Somebody Scream! Rap Music's Rise to Prominence in the Aftershock of Black Power*. New York: Faber and Faber, 2008.

Rose, Tricia. *Black Noise: Rap Music and Black Culture in Contemporary America*. Hanover: University Press of New England, 1994.

Steiner, Peter. *Russian Formalism: A Metapoetics*. Ithaca and London: Cornell University Press, 1984.

Thomas, Lorenzo. "Neon Griot: The Functional Role of Poetry Readings in the Black Arts Movement." *Close Listening: Poetry and the Performed Word*. Ed. Charles Bernstein. New York: Oxford University Press, 1998. 300–23.

Todorov, Tzvetan, ed. *Théorie de la littérature*. Paris: Éditions du Seuil, 1965.

Williams, Saul. "Twice the First Time." *Xen Cuts (Missed, Flipped and Skipped)*. Ninja Tunes, 2000. CD.

II. Registers of Performance

The Body's Territories: Performance Poetry in Contemporary Puerto Rico

Urayoán Noel

In an interview posted on YouTube, the Puerto Rican poet and spoken-word artist José Raúl González, better known as "Gallego," acknowledges as his mentors Nuyorican poets like Pedro Pietri, and goes on to express his desire to work with the poets laureate of reggaetón and salsa respectively: Tego Calderón and Rubén Blades (Gallego, "Entrevista"). Cognizant of the trendiness of what he calls "lo urbano," a hip-hop-inflected urban youth culture gone global, Gallego is quick to identify himself with a specific tradition, or counter-tradition, of politically conscious and transnational musical/verbal artists.

This insistence on a politically engaged (counter)tradition resistant to the facile commodification of "lo urbano" is at the heart of "Intro – Mi Historia – Acto 1," the spoken-word opening track from Gallego's debut full-length CD *Teatro del Barrio* (2007). In the spirit of the Nuyorican poets, Gallego here points to a non-juridical and self-reflexive conception of Puerto Rican "citizenship," one founded in and as performance, as the titular "barrio theater" that is the living embodiment of a shared history/story:

> eso mismo, mi pana
> la historia
> eso que nos hace país
> ese registro maravilloso,
> lo que somos,
> independientemente de nuestro estatus politico, bródel (Gallego, *Teatro*)

> that's it, my friend
> the history [or story]
> that which makes us a country

> that marvelous register,
> what we are
> independently of our political status, brother

In his recent book *The Diaspora Strikes Back: Caribeño Tales of Learning and Turning*, Juan Flores insightfully reads the emergence of a poet like Gallego, the leading figure of the performance poetry scene that has flourished on the island of Puerto Rico over the past ten years, as a key example of what he calls "cultural remittances" (186). Although he uses the term to analyze the expressive cultures of Hispanic Caribbean diasporas and their increasing impact on the home islands, Flores's conception of the term is broad, encompassing "the ensemble of ideas, values, and expressive forms introduced into societies of origin by remigrants and their families as they return 'home,' sometimes for the first time, for temporary visits or permanent re-settlement, and as transmitted through the increasingly pervasive means of telecommunications" (4).

In this essay, I want to expand upon and complicate Flores's formulation by highlighting what I will call the "unremitting body" of performance poetry. While I agree with Flores's consideration of Gallego, and of the recent spoken-word boom in Puerto Rico more generally, as "cultural remittances," I want to emphasize the complexities of personal and political articulation in spoken-word, a hybrid practice at the intersection of archive and repertoire, where the "live" performing body meets various more or less coercive media.[1]

Seen from this nuanced perspective, performance poetry[2] in contemporary Puerto Rico appears as a self-reflexive practice that rethinks, often translocally, the terms of community, belonging, and exclusion, questioning not only uncontested mass public discourses of nation (with their embedded anxieties regarding class, race, gender, and difference more generally), but also the language, strategies, and institutional place of poetry within the larger culture.[3] Key to this rethinking is, I suggest, the figuration of the Puerto Rican body as "unremitting," as one that cannot be resolved transactionally, that cannot be easily restored to a prior condition of meaning. Thus, the strategic turn towards Nuyorican poetry in the work of contemporary island performance poets is best understood neither as simply the assimilation of a heretofore excluded part of the Puerto Rican patrimony nor as a mere act of resistance to the longstanding hegemony of island cultural and literary elites. Rather than hewing to a programmatically celebratory or denunciatory or hortatory or confessional tone (as in much of HBO's *Def Poetry*), these poetries tend towards moments of self-consciousness and irony, as they reflect on the difficult task of opening up new expressive imaginaries while acknowledging the constraints of political and poetic articulation from the contested territories of the marked (raced, gendered, etc.) and marketable Puerto Rican body.

Recent scholarship in anthropology and cultural studies has looked to Deleuze and Guattari's concepts of "deterritorialization" and "reterritorialization" in an effort to productively engage with complex processes of cultural displacement. For my purposes, however, it is worth noting that Deleuze and Guattari see this de/re/territorialization in the context of the birth and evolution of "minor" (marginal? minority? revolutionary?) literatures. They contend that "minor or revolutionary literature begins by speaking and only sees and conceives afterward" (591), that it is "one with desire, above laws, states, governments" and "always historical in itself, political and social" (606).[4] While I do not have room here to explore the many resonances of such a provocative claim, let me suggest that island poets' renewed interest in Nuyorican poetry has everything to do with its deterritorializing/reterritorializing potential. These island poets understand the literature produced by a historically marginalized group of New York Puerto Rican poets beginning in the 1960s and 1970s as a "minor" one in Deleuze and Guattari's sense, inasmuch as it encodes a politics that "begins by speaking," where affect trumps strict juridical or territorial conceptions of belonging.

In the aforementioned interview, Gallego jokingly describes the origin of his stage moniker as a matter of "confusión territorial" (territorial confusion), since his father was not Galician, but rather from the Canary Islands. Gallego's remark, though little more than a throwaway punch line, in fact underscores the de/reterritorializing impulse of contemporary Puerto Rican performance poets, many of whom work from and against the limits of the page and the body, blurring poetry's territories in an attempt to remap cultural/national/communal imaginaries.

Ruptures and Continuities

In his *La memoria rota* (1993), Arcadio Díaz-Quiñones famously suggested that the success of the modern Puerto Rican commonwealth or "Estado Libre Asociado" (Associated Free State) required a sustained and systematic national forgetting of economic inequality, of military occupation, of diaspora (121). *La memoria rota* further argues that the new modes of historiography and literature that emerged in 1960s and 1970s Puerto Rico sought to confront, make sense of, and even reconfigure Puerto Rico's broken memory.

The incorporation of Nuyorican writers to island literary imaginaries would be crucial to any such attempt at reconfiguration, and in fact it would be possible to trace a diaspora-friendly counter-genealogy of this kind, stretching from the 1970s journal *Zona de carga y descarga*[5] to the various projects spearheaded by writer Mayra Santos Febres, including the early, Nuyorican-inspired 1990s poetry collective En la mirilla, where Gallego first came to prominence, her co-translation of Willie Perdomo's *Postcards of El Barrio* (2002), and *Grado cero*, a public-television show devoted to performance poetry, which she created and co-hosted.

It is precisely this sort of strategic incorporation of Nuyorican poetry into island imaginaries that Guillermo Rebollo-Gil attempts in his insightful M.A. dissertation (2004), which is cited, somewhat skeptically, by Flores. Rebollo-Gil argues for the "Nuyorican aesthetic . . . as a curative agent for Island culture" inasmuch as it makes possible a "people-centered approach to political and social change" ("The New Boogaloo" 51, 52). I will return to Rebollo-Gil's "people-centered" conception of poetry towards the end of this essay; what interests me at this point is how his study links the politics of the recent Nuyorican-inspired performance poetries on the island to the new modes of historiography and social analysis described by Díaz-Quiñones.

Performed poetry in Puerto Rico has a long and rich history, from the folk poetry of the *trovadores* and the hyper-rhythmic, Afro-centric *negrista* poetry inaugurated by Luis Palés Matos's seminal *Tuntún de pasa y grifería* (1937) to the poetry readings of such modern masters as Luis Lloréns Torres and Julia de Burgos. What is clear, though, is that the recent performance poetry boom in Puerto Rico must be understood as part of this larger effort to find a counter-tradition in and of rupture. Expanding upon Díaz-Quiñones, one might say that Gallego's key post-millennium contribution to this project of reconfiguration is to trace Puerto Rico's broken memory from and against the poet's body.

To be sure, Gallego's undertaking would be unthinkable without the inspiration and example afforded by earlier generations of performance poets on and off the island, many of whom he namechecks in "Intro – Mi Historia – Acto 1."[6] What is new in Gallego, however, is the extent to which he links the success or failure of his project to a shared culture of poetry off the page, at once local and globally circulating (both liberating and coercive), unimaginable before the 1990s and the rise of hip-hop and Nuyorican slam. While such a culture of poetry can in fact link poets in San Juan and New York, it cannot undo, at least in the short term, the fissures and fractures of memory that allowed for the forgetting of diaspora in the first place.[7]

In the context of Gallego's translocal barrio poetics, "territorial confusion" is both a constant pitfall and a condition of possibility, inasmuch as poetry can seemingly only name a succession of haunts and hauntings. In a broader sense, my insistence on the simultaneously liberating and coercive nature of this public culture of poetry is based on the realization that contemporary spoken-word must negotiate "good" and "bad" types of deterritorialization. There is the potentially revolutionary deterritorialization Deleuze and Guattari value in minor literatures, and then there is the deterritorialization of the global/neoliberal market, where minority spoken-word, with all its encoded political potential, is just another multicultural commodity, the key to a prized international "urban" demographic that has become all-important in an era when, as Arlene Dávila's work constantly reminds us, ethnicity and identity become crucial means of (local and global) niche marketing.

Punctuated by the refrain "que nos hace un país" 'that makes us a country,' "Intro – Mi Historia – Acto 1" reveals Gallego as constructing "un personaje" (a persona/

character) through his use of both the third person and the hip-hop trope of self-mythologizing autobiographical narrative. Soon enough, the track opens up to a first-person plural "nosotros" contiguous with his theater of the barrio, a transnational space that opens up a poetic counter-tradition linking the island and its diaspora, from name checking founding Nuyorican poet Pedro Pietri to reciting a few lines from Miguel Piñero's signature poem "Seekin' the Cause" to lovingly invoking two island poets (both women of color) widely regarded as forerunners of today's performance poetries: the late Angela María Dávila and the aforementioned Mayra Santos Febres. Later in the track, Gallego's counter-tradition opens up even further, so as to include artists and musicians, community arts organizations such as the Puerto Rican Traveling Theater, and eventually the transnational city itself: its single mothers, its children, its ghosts.

Gallego's self-mythologizing does not preclude moments of vulnerability and irony. In fact, while the track is mostly celebratory, in its unexpected pauses and silences Gallego's flow hints at the loneliness and fragility of the transnational body. Flores rightly notes that Gallego's poetry "bears the clear imprint of Pietri's unmistakable ironic twists and uncanny understatement" (186). While he does not elaborate the point, Flores is likely referring to Pietri's poetics of radical juxtaposition, most evident in run-on lines where one element cancels out, inverts, or compromises the one that immediately preceded it, such as these from "The Broken English Dream":

> Wall to wall bad news was playing
> over the radio that last week was stolen
> by dying dope addicts looking for a fix
> to forget that they were ever born
> The slumlord came with hand grenades
> in his bad breath to collect the rent
> we were unable to pay six months ago (Pietri 25)

Often the line break serves as a setup for an unexpected punch line, as in the last two of these lines from "Puerto Rican Obituary," Pietri's legendary, laugh-tracked late 1960s epic of New York Puerto Rican life and death: "All died/waiting for the garden of eden/to open up again/under a new management" (16).

The similarities between Gallego and Pietri extend off the page as well. Gallego's delivery recalls Pietri's trademark monotone, as does his frequent use of apostrophes: "Intro" is addressed by turns to a homosocial "bródel" (brother) or "pana" (friend) and to a utopically transnational Puerto Rican "nosotros" (we). In the constant shifts between a "you" and a "we," the "I" appears to blend into the barrio tableau, thereby highlighting the porousness and doubleness (stage/street; script/song; commodity/expressive culture; lyric/epic) of performance poetry's *embodied territory*, where the lowercase barrios of Puerto Rico meet the iconic uppercase Barrio, the Puerto Rican enclave of East Harlem.

Unfortunately, there is very little else in *Teatro del Barrio* that captures the nuance and complexity of Gallego the performance poet, as the CD trades his sophisticated rhymes for rote choruses, mostly content to reshuffle the conventions of commercial *reggaetón*. In songs like "Imagínate," the richness of his poetics is occluded by the plodding rhythm track, as lazy, loping horns preface some perfunctory scatting. Lost in the flashy trappings of the accompanying video is the staging of the relationship between poet and audience/community that is at the heart of Gallego's poetry and of his Puerto Rican and Nuyorican forebears.

Charles Bernstein has argued that in an increasingly spectaclized culture, poetry readings are comparatively lo-tech affairs, and perhaps part of their staying power and cultural resonance has to do with their simplicity, their rawness ("Introduction"), how they buttress what he elsewhere calls the "provisional institutions" of contemporary poetry ("Provisional"). Bernstein's point is not lost on those of us who have had the privilege of seeing Gallego perform unplugged, with little more than a feedbacking microphone or no mic at all. Perhaps Gallego's is, in Auslander's sense, a poetics of liveness; he is one of those performance poets who does not "archive" well. There is a disarming quality to Gallego's performances that has to do with his insistence on the provisionality of the poem read aloud, delivered without pretense yet endlessly resonant, marking the body as "unremitting," outside of the transactional economy of *Def Poetry* and corporate slam, its meaning inseparable from its live sharing.[8]

We are still awaiting a release (CD, DVD, etc.) fully representative of Gallego the performance poet, something that can only be partially gleaned by reading his books of poetry: *Barrunto* (2000) and *Residente del lupus* (2005). Like Pietri's, Gallego's poetry exceeds its scoring on the page; both poets summon the nervous energy and fragility of a body that is at once sited (community-specific, urban) and deterritorialized (transnational, subnational, paranational). Poet and audience meet and mesh in the territorial confusion of (provisionally) embodied language.

As I argue in my book manuscript, one way Pietri, in his later work, sidestepped the impasse between archive and repertoire, between the liveness of performance and the commodification of the spoken word, is by undertaking hybrid, open-ended projects (collaborations, installations, digital multimedia works) that pushed against the limits of both the textual and the performing "body," from unstageable plays to object poems to *ElPuertoRicanEmbassy.org*, an online installation in collaboration with the visual artist Adál Maldonado featuring passports, an anthem, and a manifesto for a "conceptual territory" called El Spirit Republic de Puerto Rico. In Pietri and Maldonado's conceptual territory, territorial confusion is embraced as a surrealist strategy, and the digital coordinates of the web become a site for the dissolution of all territories and for their utopian projection. Taking seriously both Pietri's conceptual territory and Gallego's translocal barrio, we can begin to understand territorial confusion not as something to be simply overcome (a symptom of a colonial condition), but as something to be strategically embraced, as a condition of meaning, in working through the body's difficult legibility.[9]

Eccentric Bodies

How can a Puerto Rican body be transnational when Puerto Rico is not a *de jure* nation, when the transit is between the barrios of San Juan and New York City, enclaves of the same empire? As I suggested earlier, contemporary Puerto Rican performance poets, like their Nuyorican counterparts, reject *de jure* conceptions of identity, embracing poetry as an eccentric movement on and off the page.

In thinking through the eccentric body, I am building on the work of Israel Reyes, especially his 2005 book *Humor and the Eccentric Text in Puerto Rican Literature*. Reyes reads the articulation of an "eccentric" Puerto Rican subject in and against the formal experiments and unconventional textual practices of a variety of (mostly recent or contemporary) Puerto Rican writers. Particularly helpful in this context is Reyes's analysis of the later works of Pedro Pietri, where he argues that

> Pietri's works participate as foundational texts in the articulation of a diasporic identity, yet their eccentric sensibility also critiques the very notion of cultural foundations, dislodging Nuyorican identity from its rootedness in geographic determinism. His various poetic practices reflect a shift from an island-oriented construction of identity to a more culturally open-ended negotiation of selfhood and otherness. (128)[10]

Given the diversity of performance poetries in Puerto Rico, it is hard to isolate a lingua franca or shared method. That said, the "eccentric" deterritorializing impulse in Pietri's texts that both Reyes and I highlight can, if extrapolated onto the performing body, lead us towards a critical frame, if not yet a working critical vocabulary. For, although very few of the many island poets that Gallego paved the way for share his personal connection to Pietri, and to Nuyorican poetry more generally, there is, in many of their performance works, a similar insistence on the body as an eccentric space that cannot be easily readable or mapped. At this point, I want to turn my attention to the work of two performance poets who continue this eccentric exploration of the body's territories: Karina Claudio and Hermes Ayala.

In a performance from the TV show *En la punta de la lengua*, Claudio reads from the page while standing on a box in the middle of a crowded *plaza del mercado* (market square). The performance cleverly underscores the tension between her own forceful body movements and the consumerist aloofness of the passersby, a tension reinforced by the piece's ominous refrain: "se procura desastre en este estanque venidero" 'disaster is sought out in this coming standstill.' Her self-contained delivery eschews the vocal histrionics of much slam-era work; instead, Claudio clips her phrases, often ending her lines on unstressed syllables, all of which lends the piece a mournful, angry yet wistful air not unlike Pietri's "Puerto Rican Obituary." (She even dresses in Pietri's trademark long-sleeved black.)

Far from Pietri's utopian or dada-surreal brand of deterritorialized nationalism, Claudio scores a dystopian landscape via tricky internal rhymes: "derretirnos en el lecho de la patria hecha hueco" 'let us melt in the bosom of a hollowed-out homeland.' Still, her litany of "excremento" 'excrement' reveals a Pietrian faith in the movement of autonomous, non-juridical Puerto Rican bodies, a repudiation of the police state captured in her line "no leyes ni mano dura" 'neither laws nor crackdown,' a reference to former governor Pedro Rosselló's infamous pro-police crime-fighting policy "Mano dura contra el crimen." Claudio's performance is populist, inasmuch as it places the poet in the town square, at the heart of civic deliberations, and it inveighs against the generalized lack of faith in "la tierra" and "el colectivo" (the land and the collective), but it also reveals an awareness, impressive for a young poet, of the constraints of populism, of the impasses that define attempts to shape a "cultural politics," reminding us that, for all of the performance poet's efforts to impact the space and terms of deliberation, the masses might just be too rapt in their shopping to stop and take notice.

Claudio's performance works from and beyond the page, as she reads some passages and recites others from memory; the complex relationship between page and body marks an eccentric doubleness: it is exalted literature and it is quotidian performance, it is both an antidote to and a function of the facile modes of publicness that have come to define contemporary Puerto Rican society. Framed by the idling movement of the shoppers, Claudio offers a self-reflexive poetics beyond slam theatrics, where collective deliberation and participation is not enough: at a more basic level, she suggests, any politics of performance poetry must begin by engaging with the body's often messy relationship to its milieu, making the most of the possibilities and the constraints of the spoken word and its complex circulation. Such a poetics understands the body, in Judith Butler's famous formulation, as "always an embodiment *of* possibilities both conditioned and circumscribed by historical convention" (404, emphasis in original).

The significance of such horizons of possibility should not be underestimated, as Jill Dolan reminds us in her *Utopia in Performance* (2005), where she provides an insightful analysis of Def Poetry Jam on Broadway in distinctly utopian and democratizing terms. Claudio, though, locates her eccentric, unhomely poetics in a "hollowed-out homeland" coextensive with neither the liberal state nor the global circulation of Def Poetry and slam. Such a poetics can split the difference between the documentary and the utopian, between articulating an ongoing reality and displacing politics onto an ideal future, between the sited body and its translocal re-siting/reciting/re-sighting.

An eccentric impulse of a different sort animates Hermes Ayala's performances. In his signature piece, "Chicky Starr es mi líder espiritual" 'Chicky Starr is my spiritual leader,' a playful paean to 1980s Puerto Rican professional wrestler and folk antihero Chicky Starr, Ayala postulates an eccentrically subcultural, mediatized yet affect-loaded Puerto Rican subject. Ayala invokes Starr's legendary rivalry with Puerto Rican champion and national hero Carlitos Colón, but, in proper hip-hop fashion, he sides with Starr's constructed bad boy cool – all flash, wit, and irreverence – over Colón's squeaky-clean image of patriotic uplift. Ayala's Puerto Rico is, while not quite jaded, still much savvier and edgier, much less mindlessly patriotic than nationalist ideology demands: "Por eso en Puerto Rico todo el mundo güele perico, / y la gente sabe que Chicky Starr le va a meter las cabras a Carlitos Colón siempre" 'That's why in Puerto Rico everyone sniffs coke, / and people know that Chicky Starr will sucker Carlitos Colón every time.' In privileging Starr's style over the "substance" of national pride, Ayala finds the outlines of a more honest Puerto Rican self-definition: "Chicky Starr hace ver a Carlitos Colón como el Estado Libre Asociado: mediocre, viejo y ciego ante lo que tiene alrededor." 'Chicky Starr makes Carlitos Colón look like the Associated Free State: mediocre, old, and blind to what's around him.'

As with much spoken-word, Ayala's piece builds upon anaphora, with the title phrase, repeated at irregular intervals, serving as hook for the performance. His delivery is by turns engagingly aloof and remorselessly rapid-fire, characterized by playful variations in speed and tone, as he juggles the personae of wrestler, fan, announcer, and cultural critic. Ayala's eccentric vocal style is matched throughout the piece by his body language: full of nervous energy, moving from side to side, addressing everyone and no one at once. A key to the piece's affective impact is the contrast between Ayala's vocal tone – forceful, over-modulated, yet with all the deliberateness of a reggaetón-era stoner – and the tonal shifts of the poem itself, as in an intimate moment of self-deprecation when Ayala wishes his son could be less like him and more like the effortlessly cool Chicky Starr. For a moment here, the homosocial front of the poet-rapper is turned against itself, revealing the performance poet's persona as always painfully, inevitably self-constructed, just as Ayala's bodily quirks underscore how far his own performance style is from Starr's easy cool. As in Claudio's performance, the spoken word here is both hyper-public and intimate, and the eccentric body of the poet is attuned to the complexities of representation.

Ayala manages the competing pulls of openness and intimacy through skillful deployment of the vernacular, a Puerto Rican Spanish that opens up to Spanglish and English by turns organically and performatively. Despite Puerto Rico's colonial status and its bustling diaspora, island Puerto Rican identity has traditionally been coded and idealized in terms a "proper" (formal, refined, standard) Spanish, even as the Spanish of even the most educated speakers, with its liberal adoption of English words and its performative use of Spanglish, often flies in the face of such conventions.

Since the 1970s, Puerto Rican writers such as Ana Lydia Vega and Joserramón Melendes have turned towards a more realistic depiction of Puerto Rican Spanish, strategically embracing slang, Spanglish, and even phonetic writing. In a performance context, the use of "real" (nonstandard) Puerto Rican Spanish allows Ayala to foreground the intimacy of the poem, to invoke a community of address, to imagine a Puerto Rican identity beyond linguistic, national, racial, or ideological purity. To see Ayala perform is to be reminded that, as linguist Gloria D. Prosper-Sánchez writes, "where Puerto Rican cultural identity is constantly tested on the basis of standard competence, the menace is not foreign penetration; the enemy is already inside" (188).

Problematically, Ayala's word choices often tend towards politically incorrect humor, as in "güelebichos" (literally "cocksniffers") and the portmanteau "mariconfudido" 'faggotconfused,' often with a presumably counter-institutional impulse: he argues that Chicky Starr "debe ser el fuckin' Papa" 'should be the fuckin' Pope' and praises him as "el verdadero hijoepauta" 'the true sonofabitch.' The "low" status of the language matches the low status of pro wrestling; together, they offer a more honest subcultural alternative to national discourses of belonging and exclusion, just as Starr's trash-talking (an unlegislated speech act) is ultimately more honest than Colón's flag-waving (an empty ideological gesture). Both waving a flag and unscripted trash-talking could be read as performances, but, whereas flag-waving immediately conjures up centuries of ritual and symbolism available to everyone (even "flag-less" Puerto Ricans), the meaning and import of Starr's clever trash-talking is contextual and relational, available to us only if we already are (or somehow, at the poetry reading, become) participants in the trashy subculture of Puerto Rican pro wrestling and the over-the-top national drama that it plays out. Ayala's/Starr's speech acts are doubly performative in that they do more than merely deliver an already encoded political valence (the way flag-waving instrumentalizes a normative and normalizing national ideology): the performing is the possibility of politics itself, not just its instrument.

It is significant that, unlike Gallego, Ayala has not preoccupied himself too much with publication, or with linking his performance project to a countercanon of Puerto Rican poetry; performance poetry as practiced by Ayala is, like punk or hip-hop, a hyper-rhythmic urban subculture with a practice-centered and communal ethos. Even as Puerto Ricans have, in their broken memory, embraced the ideal of a middle class suburban lifestyle that never was, Ayala insists on a low culture populism, immune to suburbanization. When he proclaims, towards the end of the piece, that "Chicky es Borikén" 'Chicky is Puerto Rico,' he has placed his bet on pop culture metonymy, on performance cool, on irreverent yet media-savvy speech acts as the only Puerto Rican identity. In Ayala's deterritorializing gesture, the discursive space that is Chicky Starr fully occupies the territorial space that is Puerto Rico: "Chicky es todo el que haya nacido en este puto 100 por 35/y se las sabe todas" 'Chicky is everyone born on this fuckin' 100 miles by 35 miles/and you can't fool him.'

Ayala's quirky style never quite reaches Starr's carefully constructed bad boy cool, but that is the problem with metonymies: whole bodies keep getting in the way – just as Miguel Piñero's "outlaw" performances ironically emphasized how the Nuyorican body's attempt at cool is compromised by its abject hyper-visibility. Can post-1960s youth cultures (punk, hip-hop, and now spoken-word) still deliver on their promise of subcultural belonging in the wake of their rapid globalization and commodification? What happens to the sited body when faced with such a violent deterritorialization? The work of Guillermo Rebollo-Gil, which I turn to now, can shed some light on these difficult questions.

I have argued that Hermes Ayala's performances eloquently articulate an increasing suspicion, also evident in the work of other contemporary Puerto Rican poets, that a populist poetics can only be non-coercive if understood subculturally, as a practice that assumes its own uneasy belonging to the larger culture. "Chicky Starr es mi líder espiritual" illustrates how, increasingly, a sense of community (as unread or misread poets, as misunderstood admirers of Chicky Starr) develops counterpublicly, defining itself in opposition, in exclusion, or, as Claudio puts it, in a homeland made hollow.[11]

Without a book or CD of Ayala's poetry to refer to, I have limited myself to a version of "Chicky Starr es mi líder espiritual" posted on YouTube, and to my recollection of seeing Ayala perform. The challenges involved in establishing a working archive and genealogy of contemporary performance poetry outside the global reach of HBO or MTV highlight a key aspect of the unremitting body: its provisionality, its eccentric circulation. (I came across the YouTube clip by accident, months after it was initially posted, while researching another project.) As a prized cultural good, spoken-word circulates easily and profitably, but the sited body is another (difficult) question. In their performances, Ayala and Claudio embody this difficulty, highlighting another sense of "unremitting": persistent, unwilling to remit to a prior standard, insisting on performance as the possibility of politics itself.

Forma/Performa (Form as Cultural Politics)

Readings of spoken-word have typically been the province of sociologists like Flores, and have, understandably, focused on its function as an expressive culture; literary scholars, in turn, have had little to say about the aesthetics of performed poetry.[12] Here, I turn my attention to Guillermo Rebollo-Gil's spoken-word versions of the poems from his book *La carencia*, in an effort to read how performance poetry's negotiation of form, on and off the page, opens up the possibility of a cultural politics.

Rebollo-Gil first burst onto the poetry scene with *Veinte* (2000), a satirical (auto) ethnography of the upper middle class *blanquito* ("whitey"), a raced term that denotes both race and class privilege. From the affluent San Juan suburb of Chaparral, the "I" here can address Puerto Rico's race and class problematic without fear of reprisal and in the comfortably English-laced Spanish that is afforded by his elite private school education. But it is not enough to diagnose from the suburbs, so in poems such as "you quire taco bell" Rebollo-Gil, in a clear homage to the Nuyorican tradition, turns to English to articulate a denunciatory poetics which might counterbalance his caricatures of *banquet* privilege. The allusions to *raze*, the cultural-revolutionary discourse, and the simultaneously angry, earnest, and somewhat self-ironizing take on capitalism, link such poems to the spoken word and slam poetics of the 1990s. (Rebollo-Gil has stated that he was inspired to write and perform by a high school reading of Willie Perdomo's *Where a Nickel Costs a Dime*, and Perdomo would go on to blurb his 2003 book *Sooner.*)

As I suggest in the prologue to Rebollo-Gil's 2005 collection, *Teoría de conspiración*, the importing of Nuyorican poetics by contemporary island-based poets is also a way of interrogating the institutional place of poetry on the island: in poems from *Teoría de conspiración* such as "pop poetry," "open mica," and "performance poetry," Rebollo-Gil engages self-reflexively with the newfound cachet of spoken-word in Puerto Rico – by then he had opened for rap and reggaetón acts, including Tego Calderón – in an ironic commentary on the commoditization of performance poetry very much in keeping with Perdomo's 2003 collection *Smoking Lovely*. "I" and "you" blur in these poems, as Rebollo-Gil describes a poetry milieu where the spoken word has generated its own caricature,[13] where everyone is always touring, always changing editors, always awaiting the next big break. His performance style, occasionally flattened and clearly informed by Perdomo's patented ironic understatement, underscores the tensions and contradictions of this poetry milieu.

Rebollo-Gil's most recent book, *La carencia* (2008), is a departure from the programmatically denunciatory social satires of his earlier work, seeking out a poetics that is more intimate, more inwardly oriented, less dependent upon political fiat. It is also the first of his books for which he has released a spoken-word accompaniment: a series of tracks, posted online, featuring electronic sounds capes. While at times the electronic background music overwhelms the voice, making it seem eerily disconnected, at other times it works to highlight a culture of inauthentic publicans, as in the image of "una modelo overdosing" 'an overdosing model' in the track "celebrity culture."

The utopian wager that animates Gallego's best work (and some of Rebollo-Gil's own earlier work as well) is bracketed off here, as Rebollo-Gil's tracks eschew the organic improvisational energy of a poetics of liveness in favor of a relationship with the spoken word that acknowledges its lack and feeds off its constraints: "tus tratados de redención se hacen más difíciles de creer/bienvenido a la carencia" 'your redemption treaties become harder to believe/welcome to the lack.' These lines from "narcoliteratura," delivered in Rebollo-Gil's flattened tones and backed by icy electronica, might not be entirely successful as spoken-word (the voice is lost in the cavernous, prefabricated soundscape), but, taken together with the print version, they outline a poetics of strategic incompleteness that finds its meaning somewhere between print lyric and conceptual performance. As such, Rebollo-Gil asks us to approach performance neither as a supplement to the print text nor as its negation, but rather as a tangle of articulations, an exploration of the hauntings of the word as printed and as spoken. Form thus becomes a vehicle for relation, between print and spoken-word, and between the poet and his shifting interlocutors.

In a recent essay, David Palumbo-Liu brings together Henry James, Tzvetan Todorov, and R.P. Blackmur so as to explore "Form" – his uppercasing – from a transnational perspective, as "an integral aspect of a meditation on the possibilities of being together" (224). While Palumbo-Liu is not too clear about what exactly counts as "Form," his seductive phrase is helpful in thinking through how a poet-performer such as Rebollo-Gil moves away from the genre conventions of spoken-word and slam, and towards an open-ended engagement with the multiple forms of poetry, "foreign" and "domestic," on and off the page, fusing lyric, narrative, satire, and various performance idioms. Put another way, Rebollo-Gil's work, while not always convincing from a pure formalist perspective (i.e. as print poetry), is successful as a cultural politics that takes as its starting point this complex sense of form: the blurring of print and performance idioms in the post-slam era.

Staking out poetry's territories here is, as in some of Victor Hernández Cruz's work, more about mindscape than about realistic depiction of externalities. Thus, a somewhat sophomoric equating of lover and terrorist becomes, for Rebollo-Gil, a subtle working through of the terms of straight male anxiety. Colonial politics is never out of the picture entirely; in the mental tourism or road trip of "la isla es mental" parodic allusions to drug-prevention campaigns and terrorist attacks serve to emphasize the contradictions of an island where tourists write on lovers'/islanders' backs.

The marriage between the obtrusive soundtracks and Rebollo-Gil's understated delivery is a forced one. Still, it sometimes works by shedding light on the tension between the poems' intimate tone and the strangely depersonalized lounge music. Such is the case of "sala de espera," a surrealist love poem reminiscent of Pietri's "Hangover" sequence in *Traffic Violations* that finds a poignancy in the struggle between the digital soundtrack and the analog voice.

In the most powerful tracks, such as "cultural tourism," busy electronic soundscapes underscore the voice's inability to deliver on poetry's plenitude. As a result, some tracks come across as oddly minimalist in their excess, in a way that points to a deeper shift on and off the page. Rebollo-Gil's early work operated more or less firmly within the tradition of 1990s Nuyorican slam: it was spoken-word as multicultural critique, as an opening of the canon. Unsurprisingly then, his performances were all about liveness, insisting on unmediated/immediate presence as a means of embodied critique of power. In this early work, Rebollo-Gil followed Gallego in celebrating

1970s salsa icons like Héctor Lavoe as larger-than-life figures whose voice and life story could bridge island and mainland; for both poets, Nuyorican salsa and spoken-word were source points for an embodied poetics of transnational opening. While Gallego has continued the difficult task of negotiating a poetics of opening, Rebollo-Gil's recent work suggests a growing suspicion, evident in the titles *Teoría de conspiración* ("conspiracy theory") and *La carencia* ("the lack," "the shortage," "the absence") of the public culture of poetry. As the shrill soundtracks – often reminiscent of new age, club techno, and other "occasional" or niche musics far removed from the public square – overwhelm Rebollo-Gil's voice, the idea of a translocal performance poetics that could map the body's territories seems quaintly nostalgic, like the yearning for counterculture in the age of global commodity.

Far from Gallego's difficult but restorative embodiment, in "cultural tourism" the poet remains outside the community (even the imagined community of the transnational Barrio theater), condemned to a failed or insincere brand of tourism. Obviously, tourism is still a privilege, and there is an obvious class distinction to be made between Gallego's barrio poetics and Rebollo-Gil's bemused poet-tourist. Beyond class symptomatology, though, and given his increasing suspicion of 1990s-style spoken-word's political claims, Rebollo-Gil's soundtracks insist on a new kind of relation, a new way of thinking through one's place in the city, the island, the social body.

A new, perhaps unexpected, influence in Rebollo-Gil's recent work is the poetry of Frank O'Hara, evident in the allusions to O'Hara in the pointedly titled "new york school," a piece he recites over appropriately understated bongo sounds. Like O'Hara in his essay/manifesto "Personism," Rebollo-Gil works against the distinction between a purely lyric poetry and a socially invested one, positing instead a personal/social poetics of self-criticality and intersubjectivity, one that re-sites as its recites, cognizant of its place in the complex economy of bodies that is post-millennium Puerto Rico. Such an economy of bodies cannot necessarily be addressed by national, or even transnational, approaches to questions of identity and belonging; a "people-centered approach to political and social change," Rebollo-Gil suggests, would need to begin intersubjectively, considering poetry's competing and overlapping modes of address, and its travels across and along various markets, canons, audiences, and horizons of meaning, on and off the page. Whereas his early, slam-inspired work used address as a means of multicultural advocacy and education (similar to what Dolan finds in Def Poetry on Broadway), his poetry and performances increasingly mine address as a means of seduction. His claim that the island is "mental" chimes with Pietri's insistence on a deterritorialized Puerto Rican identity, but it also suggests something else, at once problematic and hopeful: that there is no Puerto Rico – not even in the transnational sense – only networks of fumbling laugh-tracked lovers and terrorists and tourists. Rebollo-Gil's turn away from national or transnational frames, and towards an intersubjective embodied cultural politics, is very much of a piece with O'Hara's attempts to develop a poetics that explores, in the words of Lytle Shaw, "alternative models of kinship, both social and literary" (6).

Perhaps performance poetry in contemporary Puerto Rico is best understood thusly, as a kinship structure that brings together social and literary practice in and against the body, keeping in mind that the body is always somewhere between the political (the promise of "liveness," of a poetics of translocal opening) and the metapolitical (the messy working through the institutional and market constraints of archive). From a sociological perspective, it still seems necessary to defend performance poetry – from those who would dismiss it as mere spectacle or as "poetry lite"[14] – by insisting, as Flores does, on its expressive force, shaped by its complex cultural crossings. What, then, can a close reading (or listening, to pick up on Bernstein's pun) of performance poetry contribute? To begin with, a focus on the unremitting body: on the difficulties involved in poetry's circulation, distribution, consumption, and valuation on and off the page. Poetry scholars would do well to pay attention to this history of crossings, in an effort to approach poetry, in its various manifestations, as the poets I have examined here do: less as a fixed form, and more as an arena of aesthetic and political choices, a laboratory for new positionings, a new way to map poetry's territories self-reflexively, as commodity and as community.[15]

Notes

1. I am using "archive" and "repertoire" roughly in keeping with Diana Taylor's *The Archive and the Repertoire: Performing Cultural Memory in the Americas*. Pragmatically, if at the risk of simplifying Taylor's nuanced formulation, I take "repertoire" to refer to the performing body itself and its varied verbal and nonverbal vocabularies, whereas I use "archive" to designate both the necessarily provisional and insufficient technologies by means of which the repertoire circulates (e.g. audio, video, print) and the larger power dynamics and institutional and market forces that regulate the performing body's "proper" circulation. Of course, there is an important sense in which contemporary spoken-word continues an oral tradition unbeholden to the trappings of the culture industry; still, unlike the indigenous performance that Taylor is concerned with, Nuyorican spoken-word is by now a hybrid form that must self-reflexively leverage the resistant potential of the sited body against its concomitant commodification and global circulation. It is in this sense that I refer to performance poetry in contemporary Puerto Rico, using Philip Auslander's term, as a poetics of "liveness." Auslander's "liveness" points to the generative potential of the tensions and productive contradictions of the performing body in a mediatized culture.

2. Throughout, I use "performance poetry" to refer to the object of study. I use "spoken-word" as a broad category that includes the various manifestations of poetry off the page that have flourished in the hip-hop era (*Def Poetry*, Nuyorican slam, fusion poetry, etc.). I am aware that "spoken-word" is an older and somewhat problematic non-poetry-specific term, but it has come to be used in something like the way I am using it, so I have chosen to retain it here for pragmatic reasons. It should be noted that in Puerto Rico there are also print poets who do creative readings but are not typically considered "performance poets" (Mara Pastor, Yara Liceaga), as well as nonpoets who experiment with performance art sometimes verging on poetry (director and performer Aravind Adyanthaya, and Dominican-born, Puerto Rico-based fiction writers Rey Andújar and Rita Indiana Hernández). I am not certain that a term like "performance poetry" does justice to these sorts of nonpoetry experiments, so I do not consider them here. For a colloquial yet sophisticated reflection on spoken-word and its relation to hip-hop culture on the one hand and to various poetry (counter) traditions on the other, see Joseph. For a genealogy of Nuyorican slam along similar lines, see the opening chapters of Aptowicz.

3. For a sense of the complexity of Puerto Rico's cultural landscape, see Dávila's *Sponsored Identities*, an important, if somewhat overreaching, analysis of how government and business elites used the arts and expressive cultures as a means of marketing national consensus in 1990s Puerto Rico. It is worth keeping in mind that one of the key spaces for the circulation of these eccentric bodies of Puerto Rican performance poetry in the past decade has been local public television, especially shows such as *En la punta de la lengua* and *Grado cero*. A key question would be: How can contemporary Puerto Rican performance poetry reconcile its countercultural politics (inspired, Flores reminds us, by the voices of a Nuyorican diaspora "from below") with the privilege afforded to it in the post-millennium lettered city, where, in enlightened circles at least, spoken-word is just one more strand of the national cultural patrimony?

4. For an effective recent application of Deleuze and Guattari's term to literary studies, see Giles. Of course, my own use of the term seeks to unsettle normative conceptions of the literary so as to highlight poetry's life off the page. Still, I share Giles's preoccupation with the institutional and disciplinary limits of literary studies.

5. As Suzanne Hintz notes, *Zona de carga y descarga* was a student-run journal with an anti-War, pro-independence orientation that was (for its time) pro-feminist and pro-gay, published Nuyorican writers, and leaned towards an internationalist surrealism with an anti-colonialist (and not just anti-Americanist) sensibility.

6. For Gallego's candid thoughts on the Puerto Rican poetic tradition, and for a further sense of the counter-tradition he is claiming, see Flores's interview (126–28). Gallego appears under the pseudonym "Samuel."

7. It is more or less along these lines that Flores frames his skepticism towards Rebollo-Gil's "curative" project.

8. I am grateful to Rebollo-Gil for sharing his insights on what he terms the "ternura" or tenderness at the heart of Gallego's work. Following Rebollo-Gil, I think the theorization of affect would be very helpful in understanding the personal and political imaginaries of Puerto Rican performance poetry. Hopefully, my reflections on the unremitting body will serve as a starting point for future scholarship along these lines.

9. For an analysis of the (racialized) Puerto Rican body that takes seriously the difficulties involved in navigating institutional and market constraints, see Negrón-Muntaner, particularly her reading of Jean-Michel Basquiat.

10. I devote further attention to Reyes's reading of Pietri in my book manuscript, *Nuyorican Movements: Poetry and Counterpolitics from the Sixties to Slam*, where I also explore in depth many of the questions I can only point to here (the relationship between poetry and community, etc.). Of course, performance poetries on the island cannot always be smoothly equated to their diasporic "counterparts."

11. See, for example, Warner. I offer a counterpublic reading of Nuyorican slam in my book manuscript.

12. Noteworthy in this context is Bernstein's edited volume *Close Listening: Poetry and the Performed Word*, as it includes contributions, by Maria Damon and Lorenzo Thomas respectively, on the scoring of poetry for performance in Nuyorican and Black Arts poetry. Flores, to his credit, points to important aesthetic affinities between Gallego and his Nuyorican mentors.

13. For a sense of how familiar the caricature of the self-important spoken-word poet or "poeta urbano" 'urban poet' has become, note that performer Lucienne Hernández has developed a character called "Guanina, la poeta urbana" 'Guanina, the urban poet,' a parody complete with political and erotic themes. In an interview, Hernández states: "Me inspiré en algunas de las personas que realizan 'spoken word' que son súper parodiables. Ella es seria, muy crítica, erótica y egocéntrica" 'I was inspired by some people who do spoken word who are very easy to parody. She [Guanina] is serious, very critical, erotic and egocentric.'

14. For a lucid critique of Puerto Rican performance poetry along these lines, see Áurea María Sotomayor's "Cuerpo Caribe: entre el performance, la poesía (y el tono … su esplendor)," a substantive critical consideration of the performance politics of Pietri, Santos Febres, and others. Following Debord, Sotomayor worries that performance poetry in Puerto Rico might, for all its political pretensions, be little more than a new society of spectacle. I engage with and respond to Sotomayor's concerns in detail in my book manuscript.

15. I should note that my ability to generate such a history of crossings directly correlates to my experience as a Puerto Rican poet and performer, and a contemporary (and, to varying extents, also a friend) of Gallego and Rebollo-Gil. In the U.S., this sort of first-hand connection is common, and seemingly taken for granted, in various relevant fields (experimental poetics, performance studies). Given my focus on kinship structures, institutional politics, and the terms of belonging, it seems to me, however, that I should at least address my own relationship with the poets at hand. In fact, my own poetry and performance work informs, to a significant extent, my theorization of archive, institutional spaces, the market, and the possibilities of embodied poetics. As a way of making sense of my messy, imbricated relationship to the material I consider here, I refer to Bonin-Rodriguez, Dolan, and Pryor's recent theorization of what they call "colleague-criticism." They write: "As colleague-critics, we write about performance as artists, as colleagues, as friends, and as scholars; we speak to our knowledge of both the work at hand and the experience and context of making work; we keep our theory and practice in

a state of present dialogue; and we work to expand the role of the artist in local, public arts discourse" (1). I take seriously the authors' questions: "What does it mean to engage critically and publicly with the work of a queer artist and/or artist of color who privately is a friend, colleague, and/or collaborator? How might foregrounding one's relationship as critic to the artist produce an alternative model of critical exchange in which theory and practice productively collide, collapse, and melt?" (1).

It seems to me that answering these difficult questions, however provisionally, would be an important corollary to the de/reterritorializing project I outline here, since any thorough questioning of poetry's territories would necessarily entail questioning the role, status, and allegiances of the poetry critic and the act of critical intervention itself. It seems worth emphasizing that mine is a practice-centered conception of both creative and critical work that actively seeks out the overlaps between the two.

Bibliography

Álvarez Valle, Alana. "Improvisación, comedia y crítica social en 'El Show de Luci.'" *El vocero*. 30 Jan. 2009. Web. 8 June 2009.

Aptowicz, Cristin O'Keefe. *Words in Your Face: A Guided Tour Through Twenty Years of the New York City Poetry Slam*. New York: Soft Skull, 2008.

Auslander, Philip. *Liveness: Performance in a Mediatized Culture*. London: Routledge, 1999.

Ayala, Hermes. "Chicky Starr es mi líder espiritual." Performance. Café Teatro Araba, San Juan. May 2008. *YouTube*. Web. 8 June 2009.

Bernstein, Charles, ed. *Close Listening: Poetry and the Performed Word*. New York: Oxford University Press, 1998.

———. "Introduction." Bernstein, *Close Listening* 3–26.

———. "Provisional Institutions: Alternative Presses and Poetic Innovation." *My Way: Speeches and Poems*. Chicago: University of Chicago Press, 1999. 145–54.

Bonin-Rodriguez, Paul, Jill Dolan and Jaclyn Pryor. "Colleague-Criticism: Performance, Writing, and Queer Collegiality." *Liminalities: A Journal of Performance Studies* 5:1 (April 2009). Web. 1 Aug. 2009.

Butler, Judith. "Performative Acts and Gender Constitution: An Essay in Phenomenology and Feminist Theory." *Writing on the Body: Female Embodiment and Feminist Theory*. Ed. Katie Conboy, Nadia Medina and Sarah Stanbury. New York: Columbia University Press, 1997. 401–17.

Claudio, Karina. "Desastre." Performance. *En la punta de la lengua*. WIPR, 2007. Television. *YouTube*. Web. 8 June 2009.

Dávila, Arlene M. *Sponsored Identities: Cultural Politics in Puerto Rico*. Philadelphia: Temple University Press, 1997.

Deleuze, Gilles, and Felix Guattari. "Kafka: Toward a Minor Literature: The Components of Expression." Trans. Marie Maclean. *New Literary History* 16:3 (Spring 1985): 591–608.

Díaz-Quiñones, Arcadio. *La memoria rota. Ensayos sobre cultura y política*. Río Piedras, PR: Huracán, 1993.

Dolan, Jill. *Utopia in Performance: Finding Hope at the Theater*. Ann Arbor: University of Michigan Press, 2005.

Flores, Juan. *The Diaspora Strikes Back, Caribeño Tales of Learning and Turning*. London: Routledge, 2008.

Gallego. "Entrevista a Gallego." Alto K-libre TV. 2006. *YouTube*. Web. 8 June 2009. *Teatro del Barrio*. Machete Music 2007. CD.

Giles, Paul. "The Deterritorialization of American Literature." *Shades of the Planet: American Literature as World Literature*. Ed. Wai Chee

Dimock and Lawrence Buell. Princeton: Princeton University Press. 2007. 39–61.

Hintz, Suzanne S. "*Zona de carga y descarga*: Nascent Postmodernism in Puerto Rican Letters." *LANIC*. Web. 8 June 2009.

Joseph, Marc Bamuthi. "(Yet Another) Letter to a Young Poet." *Total Chaos: The Art and Aesthetics of Hip-Hop*. Ed. Jeff Chang. New York: BasicCivitas, 2006. 11–17.

Negrón-Muntaner, Frances. *Boricua Pop: Puerto Ricans and the Latinization of American Culture*. New York: New York University Press, 2004.

Noel, Urayoán. "Will the real street poets please stand up?" Prologue. *Teoría de conspiración*. By Guillermo Rebollo-Gil. San Juan: Isla negra, 2005. 7–11.

Palumbo-Liu, David. "Atlantic to Pacific: James, Todorov, Blackmur, and Intercontinental Form." *Shades of the Planet: American Literature as World Literature*. Ed. Wai Chee Dimock and Lawrence Buell. Princeton: Princeton University Press. 2007. 196–226.

Pietri, Pedro. *Puerto Rican Obituary/Obituario Puertorriqueño*. San Juan: Isla negra, 2000.

Pietri, Pedro, and Adál Maldonado. ElPuertoRicanEmbassy.org. Web. 1 Aug. 2009.

Rebollo-Gil, Guillermo. *La carencia*. Performance. Blakevox. Web. 8 June 2009.

———. *La carencia*. San Juan: Terranova, 2008.

———. "The New Boogaloo: Nuyorican Poetry and the Coming Puerto Rican Identities." Diss. University of Florida, 2004. Web. 20 June 2008.

———. *Teoría de conspiración*. San Juan: Isla negra, 2005.

———. *Veinte*. San Juan: Isla negra, 2000.

Reyes, Israel. *Humor and the Eccentric Text in Puerto Rican Literature*. Gainesville: University of Florida Press, 2005.

Shaw, Lytle. *Frank O'Hara: The Poetics of Coterie*. Iowa City: University of Iowa Press, 2006.

Sotomayor, Áurea María. "Cuerpo Caribe: entre el performance, la poesía (y el tono su esplendor)." *Femina Faber: letras, música, ley*. San Juan: Callejón, 2004. 217–31.

Warner, Michael. *Publics and Counterpublics*. New York: Zone, 2002.

Politics of Sound: Body, Emotion, and Sound in the Contemporary Galician Poetry Performance

María do Cebreiro
Rábade Villar

The Middle Ages were considered to be the golden age of Galician literature. After this, literary production in Galician was for centuries predominantly oral. During the second half of the nineteenth century the cultural and political movement known as the *Rexurdimento* (Renaissance) led to a radical transformation of this situation. Authors such as Rosalía de Castro, Manuel Curros Enríquez, and Eduardo Pondal – the canonical trio of the *Rexurdimento* – began to forge a new linguistic and literary model. The recognition of Galicia as a political entity was fostered, in large part, by Romantic sensibilities towards oral and popular cultural traditions. Throughout the first half of the twentieth century, several groups and poetic waves would follow – some of these notably influenced by the historic avant-garde. The generational succession was severed by the outbreak of the Spanish Civil War (1936–1939). Like Basque and Catalan literatures, Galician culture also faced harsh repression during the reign of Franco and it was only with the arrival of democracy that something approaching cultural normality could be reestablished.[1] In the 1980s the inclusion of the Galician language into the teaching system ushered in a new era for the Galician culture. From the 1980s, Galician poetry begins to move through new avenues such as poetry performance. The poetic discourse and generational controversy that find their precedents in the avant-garde run parallel to this. The clash between the "poets of the eighties" and the "poets of the nineties" has been much remarked upon, even though the most recent critical approaches tend to relativize the opposition between the two groups.[2]

This essay aims to explore what the commitment to orality of Galician poets and performers since the 1990s has meant for both Galicia's poetry and the performance of poetry in general. Even though Galician poetry can claim some isolated examples of video-art and its entrance into digital technologies is more and more evident, perhaps the most surprising phenomenon from a historical point of view has been the return to the oral. A symptom of this change was the proliferation of poetic readings during the second half of the nineties. Since the year 2000, the presence of the voice in performance has acquired a poetic and political relevance which I will address later on.

In focusing on contemporary poetry performance, I would also like to test the extent to which this practice succeeds in modifying certain ideological presuppositions held by Galician cultural agents. Since the *Rexurdimento*, and as a product of the influence of Herderian romanticism, Galician poetry and the nationalist project have been interlinked, a connection which continues to this day. In this context, it is useful to determine whether poetry performance increases or decreases the strength of this bond.

In this analysis of Galician poetry performance I will prioritize the relationship between body, voice, and affect. In what way do these align themselves in order to enable specific performances? Does their presence or absence in a performance enable different political and poetic projects? In the past, concepts of body, voice, and affect established singular approaches to performance; perhaps their usefulness can be exponentially multiplied when one observes their interaction as a whole. One example of the possibilities that open up when assessing this triad of body, voice, and affect is the recognition of two distinct types of poetry performance, which I shall denominate as either timbral or accentual.

Timbral performances I conceive as actions based on the relevant weight given to the emotional substratum of the poetic presentation. These emotions not only affect the performers carrying them out, but rather (and especially) the public that receives them. To a large extent, the efficiency of timbral performances lies in their flight from narrative codes. This non-narrativity also supposes the rejection of metanarratives,[3] sacrificed in favor of a multidirectional expansion of affects. By virtue of their potential impact in the social sphere, timbral performances allow for the transfer of politically subversive contents and ideas. In more precise terms: because they are rooted in markers of an affective nature which are not ideologically predetermined, an evaluation of the political effectiveness of a timbral performance calls for a reinvention and expansion of the meanings given to the very notion of politics.

Accentual performances, on the other hand, are often defined by their performers as sociopolitical interventions connected to the defense of minority cultural identities – in this case, the Galician. Authors in this context tend to commit themselves to narrative linearity, which is seen as a way of strengthening the effectiveness of their communication. Timbral perfomances work to generate an affective delocalization which manages to spread emotions without connecting them to individuals. As will be pointed out, an important aspect of accentual performances is the high standing granted to the localization of the voice. This essay explores two methodological approaches. On the one hand, I will attempt to examine the oral and performative practices in Galician poetry through the use of critical tools. On the other, I intend to formulate hypotheses related to the functioning of poetry performance in general. The validity of these hypotheses must await confrontation with other poetic formats, which will then allow them to be corroborated or clarified.

The Politics of Sound: The Voice-Object

Poetic performance is one of the spaces in which body, affect, and voice neatly intersect, these elements being understood here as vectors of intervention in the social space. Beyond their most immediate meaning – in which they are often incorrectly seen as self-evident – these categories acquire connotations of the highest theoretical relevance. In reference to the body and emotions, it is enough to think of Judith Butler's book *Precarious Life: The Powers of Mourning and Violence* (2004), where the emotional experience of struggle and corporeal vulnerability is outlined as a vehicle for the understanding of political violence in the contemporary world. In establishing a link between reflection on affect and what was happening in the military prisons of Guantanamo, Butler showed the potential of the study of emotions such as melancholy or fear for opening paths of research capable of connecting the social and subjective spheres.

The voice must also be taken as a point of departure for a poetic analysis sensitive to new enunciative practices in contemporary cultural spaces, and not solely as the acoustic emanation of a previous text or as a more or less useful label for ascribing a subject to a statement from an immanent perspective. The poetic tradition has seen much exploration of the possibilities of converting sound into an instrument of socio-literary communication, although few scholars have theorized these practices without being either descriptive or celebratory. The historical and repertorial variability of these manifestations can be seen in the proliferation of terms such as phonetic poetry, acoustic poetry, oral poetry, talk-poetry, sound-poetry, or poetry slam. However, the richness of these practices does not always find the necessary correspondence in the processes of poetic theorization of the socio-political implications of concepts such as "voice." Labels like the aforementioned are usually used in a descriptive rather than a heuristic sense.

The term *voice* itself, apparently not problematic, has been the object of quite distinctive approaches throughout the history of poetic thought. Reconstructing the conceptual history of the voice would require taking account of traditions of thought as heterogeneous as the theory of orality and grammatology. Furthermore, when it is necessary to pinpoint social and political values granted to this notion by literary communities, attention must be given to disciplines somewhat removed from the field of literary studies, such as Marxist or psychoanalytic theory. Thus, Slavoj Zizek, in *The Parallax View*, explores the potential of the Lacanian concept of voice-object for analyzing the moment when the vagabond of Charlie Chaplin's *City Lights* swallows a whistle and produces

> a spectral sound emanating from within his body, sound as an autonomous "organ without a body," located in the very heart of the body and at the same time uncontrollable, like a kind of parasite, a foreign intruder – in short, what Lacan called the voice-object, one of the incarnations of objet petit a, that which is "in me more than myself." (19)

The advantage of the Lacanian concept of voice-object is that it recognizes the tight interpenetration of voice and body. In the following section I will outline the impact of somatic cultures in Galician poetry through the presence and absence of the voice. I will begin with an examination of two performances by Antón Lopo. In the first, the author does without the voice in order to let the body talk. In the second, he uses the voice in one of its most meaningful modulations – the whisper – in order to question capitalist consumer society.

Somatic Cultures: How Bodies Lend New Readings of the City
Brigitte E. Jirku, Cecilia López Roig, and Herta Schulze Schwarz seem to gloss the Lacanian conception of voice-object when, in their introduction to a volume dedicated to the body in German language and literature, they argue that there is no possible escape from the body (5). The authors recognize the conversion of somatic cultures into one of the objects of inescapable attention in the area of linguistic and literary studies – a verifiable process underway for at least thirty years, and one which appears to have attained new nuances over the last decade.[4] I will try to show the scope of some of these approaches by way of a performance taken from the practical repertoire of the poet, journalist, playwright, actor, and performer Antón Lopo, who has been making the body into the nucleus of his artistic project.[5] This centrality is perceptible with great clarity in its theatrical and performative facets, as can be seen in *Lob*s* 'S/he-wolves' (1998), a show conceived in cooperation with Ana Romaní (to whom I shall return later), and in *Prestidixitador* 'Conjurer' (2001), presented to the press as "oral poetry close to *body art* and theater." Here, however, I will focus on one of his performances most closely related to the interaction between *body art* and the construction and destruction of urban space.[6] On June 15, 2006, the author, working with Iván Prado, staged a happening in Santiago de Compostela titled *Co ceo a costas* 'Carrying the Sky,' which consisted in them walking through the Compostelan historical quarter carrying mirrors on their backs. The authors considered the performance to be an investigation into the limits of resistance, "ironic in its conception and powerful in its physical development . . . a metaphor about reality and the limits of liberty, about social traditions and the particles of emotional resignation."[7] The performance,

conceived as part of a cycle in conjunction with Antón Lopo's exposition *Dentro* 'Inside,' succeeded in expanding the limits of the poetic, much as other works by the author have done. The performance leads us to ask what the underlying means for the poeticity of a mute and perambulatory act such as the one carried out by Prado and Lopo are. Lopo's use of the concept of metaphor in his description of the happening functions as an invitation to explore the gradual process of poetic dis-verbalization, verifiable since the first third of the twentieth century. This process affects visual poetry as well as other modalities of relation between poetry and image, such as holopoetry.

As far as all poetic performance is a stage practice, its analysis requires an analytical approach that moves away from the exclusive focus on the verbal level towards an analysis of the visual sign in artistic communication. Authors such as Roman Jakobson, Jacques Lacan, and Ernesto Laclau have shown the possibilities of extending the opposition between metaphor and metonym, going beyond rhetorical trope theory. In the same fashion, analyses of poetic performance could benefit from organizational mechanisms of their imaginary content, partially reformulating the tradition of the psychoanalytical interpretation of dreams. Essentially this means replacing the individualist conception of traditional psychoanalysis with an exploration of that which Jameson (1981) would term the "political unconscious," understanding poetic performance as an inscription of the word into social space and an active questioning of the norms that regulate it under ordinary conditions. The performance of Prado and Lopo is effective because it is not normal for two transients to cross an entire city with a mirror on their backs. The poeticity of the performance rests on the activation of subjective mechanisms – unconnected, in this case, to the verbal sign – even if in the past these mechanisms have been restricted to this sphere. In addition to condensation (relatable to the metaphor, and here linked to a simultaneous physical and non-physical understanding of the notion of resistance) and displacement (ascribable to the realm of metonym, and attentive to the continuity between body and city), the role of processes such as symbolization or dramatization must be taken into account. In the happening conducted by Lopo and Prado, the symbol of the mirror (pointing to the apparent splitting of the real and, above all, the possibility of seeing the real from a completely new perspective; it is an instrument of illumination, as well as a weight that forces the body to bend) carries the maximum signifying charge. Dramatization, understood as the temporal development of a sensory motor activity governed by certain previous conventions, supposes the radical opening up of the poetic to interpretive coordinates which transcend the limits traditionally assigned to poetry.

On the other hand, and as illustrated in the celebrated urinal by Marcel Duchamp, which uncovers much more than a descriptive statement in the ironic heading *FOUNTAIN*, the closing and opening title of the happening, *O ceo a costas*, becomes the framework and catalyst for a series of complex semantic operations that beckon us to interpret the performance in light of cultural referents as disparate as mythology (Atlas), film (*Lisbon Story* by Wim Wenders), or the artistic post-vanguardism of the twentieth century (situationism). The mirror that Prado and Lopo carry on their backs encourages an unprecedented interpretation of a city increasingly integrated into the tourist circuit and forces the strolling people to question the itineraries that attempt to direct their perception of the city. In this and other cases, poetic performance proposes new ways of reading urban space. This is inevitably attained through the use of the body, which is conceived as an instrument that appropriates the collective space. In the words of Carlos A. Jáuregui: "El cuerpo constituye un depósito de metáforas. En su economía con el mundo, sus límites, fragilidad y destrucción, el cuerpo sirve para dramatizar y, de alguna manera, escribir el texto social" (13).[8]

These words foreshadow Lopo's latest performance, which introduces the voice as a powerful effect in his poetic practice. This show was conceived within the framework of the festival "A revolta das letras" 'Literary revolution,' organized by the City Council of Santiago de Compostela in May 2009. Lopo participated in a session titled "A rebelión dos poetas" 'The poets' rebellion,' and the multinational store Zara, located in the center of town on the Praza de Galicia, was chosen to be the stage. While shoppers selected the items of clothing they wished to try on, Lopo would approach them, whispering into their ears comments about the clothes or about their bodies. "Are you sure this will look good on you?" was one of the most-repeated phrases. Here, by means of the whispered word, the spoken performance partakes of the social rituals surrounding the secret. In addition, it makes the cultural correlation between the body and taboo explicit through its setting in one of the temples of capitalist consumer society.

One paradox must not be overlooked, however: even though Zara is a business with its origins in Galicia, the fact that it hosted a performance carried out in the native language was seen as quite an unexpected event. Following a period of suppression during Franquism, the Galician language now claims many uses and social functions, though the diglossic situation continues to be striking. If there is one thing that Galician is not, it is a language associated with consumerism. More than simply testing the power of the whisper in poetic actions, therefore, Lopo's performance made it clear that Galician continues to be a disruptive language in certain social contexts.

Theories of Affect: The Historization of the Emotional in Performance Poetry
Over the last twenty five years, the history of emotions has experienced a remarkable surge, something that is especially perceptible if we look to the abundant wave of publications dealing with the relationship between historical change and feelings. The foundational nature of the work of Stearns (1985) or, more recently, Reddy (2001), Rosenwein (2002), and Konstan (2004), is apparent in their elaboration of a terminological and conceptual apparatus in a field traditionally hindered by either

biological essentialism or intuitive psychologism. In the face of a mechanical and ahistorical comprehension of the emotional world, cultural-based references imbue the study of emotions with a sociopolitical dimension and in so doing emphasize its constructed character and its dependence on contextual conditionings. Notions such as emotional mechanism, of Foucauldian provenance; historiographical problems such as the relationship between emotion and agency; and questions surrounding gender roles and markers of sexual codification or the performative dimension of emotion, are some of the aspects pertinent to this bibliographic corpus, which can all be relevant to the study of performance poetry in Galicia.

The emotional continuum body-gender-sex is central to the poetic work of the journalist, poet, and performer Ana Romaní.[9] Her poetic performance most connected to the sociopolitical and therefore historical quality of emotions is that which accompanied the presentation of her book *Love me tender. 24 pezas mínimas para unha caixa de música* 'Love me tender: 24 tiny pieces for a music box' (2005). In a reading during the book launch at the café *Casino* in Santiago de Compostela, Romaní used a tiny music box that played the famous song by Vera Matson and Ken Darby, made popular by Elvis Presley and representative of the sentimental codes exported by U.S. pop culture from the 1950s onward. The strong contrast created between the sounds of the music box and the content of the poems, which explicitly address gender-based violence, is accentuated by the almost inaudible quality of the melody. The music box, the centerpiece of this poetic performance, thus becomes both the medium for messages connected to sentimentalism (and therefore complicit in a certain sexist codification of the emotional experience) and the metaphorical carrier of the fragility of the subjects affected by violence.

Feminism, understood as a political practice which enables gender and body to be seen from new coordinates, has been the basis for many of Chus Pato's (Ourense, 1955) contributions to poetic performance. Together with contemporary artist María Ruído and photographer María Estelrán, Pato participated in the performance-installation *Mateino porque era meu* 'I killed him because he was mine' (1993), the performance *A Sereíña* 'The little mermaid' (1997), the party-performance *Ethics of the care* (1999), as well as the video-performance *Carbone A. C.* (2001), which debuted in Frankfurt. The author has also participated in recital-performances, such as those celebrated in the Fine Arts Faculties in Pontevedra in 1994, with Ignacio Vilariño, and those forming part of the presentation of her book *Nínive* in Vigo in 1996. On the latter occasion the poet made use of the heart of a cow, piercing it with violet irises. The strong stage presence of the heart-object (reminiscent of Christian imagery and the metaphorical system that makes this organ the center of the emotional life, and, as a cow's heart, one of central reference points of the Galician cultural imagination) succeeds in bringing to the stage, and thereby making socially visible, complex ideas on the constructed (and destructible) quality of affect. This does not refer merely to any possible significance attached to the heart-object (the visual correlate of the heart symbol), but rather to its power to unleash effects on the spectators of the performance. These effects are often favored or fostered by what we might call "statements of emotional value" (in this context, the verses of the poet).

One of the first authors to recognize the subjectifying quality of emotional value statements was the anthropologist Vincent Crapranzano, who has expressed it in the following terms:

> I do not claim that such utterances as "I love you" or "I am angry at you" are explicit performatives but they do have considerable illocutionary force. They do bring about through their very utterance a change in the context of that utterance. Their very utterance is taken as a manifestation, a symptom, of the condition – the emotion – they are said to be describing, in a way which is simply not true of the third person propositions. It is as though their referentiality looped over onto itself and became at once its own object and yet, through some sort of topological contortion, other than itself. (234–35)

Continuing from where Crapranzano left off, the historian Reddy (2001) introduced the term "emotives," a semantic replica of the acclaimed "performatives." As is well known, the term "performatives" refers to statements which are not merely descriptive, but which possess illocutive power, or, in non-technical terms, and borrowing the title of an already classic book by J.L. Austin (1962), that which is capable of "doing things with words." Crapranzano himself recognized that it is not easy to see a performative statement in a declaration of love. "I love you," as Jacques Derrida demonstrated on several occasions, is an enigmatic speech act, and is, at the same time, foundational. In an insightful commentary on Derrida, Hillis Miller points out the following[10]:

> Like the Declaration of Independence, "Je t'aime" creates the event it names. What Derrida means here sounds scandalous; you do not fall in love until you say "Je t'aime". The question of the relation of language to passion, affect or pain has an important place in twentieth-century thought, even in Anglo-American philosophy. The question is seen as in one way or another exemplary of the opposition between constative and performative language. When I express one passion or another, love or anger, or articulate my pain, do my words do no more than name something that already exists, or do my words create what they name, performatively? (137)

Derrida sees the statement "I love you" as an inaugural act that creates the very situation it founds. What this implies is that performativity does not fall on the emotional content of the statement – insofar as that referred to the subject of the speech – but rather on the effect produced by its expression. Thus it would seem preferable to replace the technical term "emotives" with "emotional statements of performative value."

At any rate, comprehending emotions in the light of speech acts emphasizes the importance of understanding feelings in the context of human communication theories. Aristotle's *Rhetoric*, brilliantly interpreted by Konstan, tried to do no more than this in its time: emotions were thought of as the cornerstone for convincing. When Reddy applies the concept of "emotional translation" in order to put into perspective the fact that any exchange of feelings implies a process of mediation, he finds in language the possibility of conferring a historical, cultural, and social basis to the study of emotions.

Within this field of research on emotions, it is worth referring to a series of studies that part from an explicit or implicit contraposition between the pulsional and the affective.[11] As opposed to "pulsions" – oriented, lineal, and characteristic of gender identities – "affects" move about in a diffuse spectrum without a stable subjectivity that sustains them. In keeping with Massumi, affection is transmitted as a contagion, tangential and associative; an offshoot that temporarily inhabits subjects only to later abandon them for new spaces. The non-narrative character of these affects and the repercussions of their entrance into artistic practices are factors which are theorized by Ngai, who associates them with the thickness of verbal, sonorous, and visual languages and with a tendency towards noise, seriality, and repetition. In the following section I will explore some of the implications of pulsional and affective difference in Galician performance poetry. As we will see, the difference between the pulsional and the affective is related to the distinction between accentual and timbral poetics.

Accentual and Timbral Poetics
Before entering into the difference between timbral and accentual in poetry performance, I will linger briefly over the concept of voice, which to a large extent enables us make this distinction, and the difficulty of fixing this term historically and theoretically. As pointed out earlier, it is surprising that voice has not been more carefully explored as the source of theoretical research and as the technical resource for poetic action. "Poetic voice" and "lyric subject" are used as interchangeable terms or synonyms without the recognition that the voice does not necessarily need to be remittable to the sphere of the "I." Contemporary theater, at least since Beckett, abounds in bodiless voices of multiple enunciation, a fact that should encourage deep reflection on the performative complexity of the onstage word, be it poetic or otherwise.

Several historical and literary factors explain this lack of attention. Up until the end of the eighteenth century, when the influence of prescriptive tradition began to wane, the privilege of rhetoric over poetry made the terms "poetry" and "figurative language" almost equivalent. Later, the romantic poets explored the locative dimension of lyric poetry, paving the way for a conception of the poem which was no longer solely compositional and rhetorical. Despite this, certain later interpretations of poetic romanticism fostered the identification between the poetic text and self-revelation, thereby ascribing the poem to the voice of the poet in question. The possibility of recognizing the multiplicity of the poem's voices was reduced due to this automatic remission of the poem to the sphere of the "I." In the twentieth century, after the poem's formalist and post-formalist relegation to that of a dialogical setting (Bakhtin, 1988) and the almost exclusive attention of the semiotic foci for structure at the expense of agency, literary pragmatism made the study of the voice depend upon a theorization of lyric enunciation. Recognizing that the poem is a complicated speech act, although undoubtedly a means to poetic analysis, should not constitute the only possible approach, because such a view often overlooks the fact that poetic voices may be composed to circulate through air, and not just on paper.

The undeniably corporal quality of the term – it is obvious that saying "voice" is not the same as saying "narrative instance" – leaves little room for abstraction. Thus, in an analysis of the effects generated by the voice in poetic action, critics often turn to terms such as "tension-distension," "stop," "attack," or "repose," which generally converge with technical terms taken from music theory. Possibilities are then opened up for establishing correlations between the properties of the physical voice (timbre or color, pitch, intensity, accent) and the qualities of the poetic voice. In this essay I will focus on two sonorous categories which are crucial to an analysis of "voice": "timbre" and "accent." These are well-defined and sometimes opposing descriptors of contemporary poetic practices. In the following pages, I will distinguish between timbre and accentual-based performative poetics, using examples from contemporary Galician poetic performances.

Timbral performance grants predominance to the expressive axis and is related to affect. Affect refers to an emotional quality which transcends the individual subject as well as the narrative trajectories of the poems. The timbre – also termed "color" in musical theory – is that which is most specific to each voice. Taking the term metaphorically and expanding it, timbral performances would then be stage practices that are characterized by a "style consciousness," frequently manifested in an author's poetics in which communicational immediateness is subordinated to other values, such as expressive singularity or the capacity to shatter the receivers' ideological, intellectual, moral, or axiological expectations.

The use of the term "timbral" in an analysis of Galician performance poetry seeks to map out a field of performance, opposed to an understanding of poetry as representation, as a horizon where the relationship between world and language is conceived and presented to the public as problematic and in which the fissures between world and language strengthen the production of aesthetically and ideologically subversive content. It is in this sense that timbral poetics, even those distanced from communicative propositions, are not usually indifferent to the possibilities of communitarian participation. Without engaging in *social poetics* in the most conventional sense of the word, many of the actions based on timbre are founded on the presupposition that the poetic *performance* can be, through the temporary suspension of the norms that govern social space, a site of emancipation or even utopia.

The concept of "utopian performance," as developed by Jill Dolan (2001, 2005), can be useful in describing the emotional and social connection that the viewer experiences during the performance. Dolan began her career as a researcher with a study titled *The Feminist Spectator as Critic* (1991). In similar fashion, the public who attended the feminist performances of Chus Pato, María Esteirán, and María Ruído in Galicia were involved in the construction of a utopian space of transgression and the questioning of gender rules and conventions. This public experienced the critic's standpoint in at least a double sense: 1) insofar as they managed to reconstitute (in a remarkable feat of hermeneutics) the complex web of meaning set in motion by the participants – the result of an efficient interlacing of verbal and visual codes; and 2) insofar as they made it evident in their decoding praxis that the unveiling and deconstruction of social norms was a task of a political nature.

For this reason, in spite of the effectiveness of her model, Dolan can be criticized for excessively restricting the scope of the term "political." In one of her works, her resistance – even anxiety – in conceding certain political functions to performance is quite perceptible in her concentration on its emotional character:

> Perhaps instead of measuring the utopian performative's "success" against some real notion of effectiveness, we need to let it live where it does its work best – at the theater or in moments of consciously constructed performance wherever they take place. The utopian performative, by its very nature, can't translate into a program for social action, because it's more effective as a feeling. Perhaps that feeling of hope, or that feeling of desire, embodied by that suddenly hollow space in the pit of my stomach that drops me into an erotics of connection and commonality – perhaps such intensity of feeling is politics enough for utopian performatives. (Utopia 19–20)

It is not clear as to why the "hollow space in the pit of my stomach" must necessarily remain dissociated from what we understand as politics. Could it not, for example, refer to steps prior to the awakening of a conscious action? Perhaps a review of some timbral-based Galician poetic performances might assist us in more subtly pinpointing the complexity of the connections between the emotional and the political. The performance *A Sereíña* (1993) illustrates the affective dimension of contemporary poetic performance. Verses by Chus Pato counterpoint María Ruído wrapping a rope around herself from her feet up to her waist. This in turn was videotaped by María Esteirán. Once projected on stage, Esteirán's video constitutes a visual splitting of the action carried out by Ruído, a recurrent practice in postmodern art, but one which here acquires specific nuances derived from the possible connections between escopophilia and violence. Without ceasing to be rope, the stage and film object that serves as protagonist in the performance also becomes a mermaid's tail and the actress's body changes into a monster, a hybrid creature like those populating the pages of Chus Pato's poetry collection *m-Talá* (2001). Fairytales, feminine submission, social violence, and (self-) mutilation pass before the spectators' eyes, and succeed – to recall Dolan's article – in turning them into both critics and feminists. *A Sereíña* (1993) shows onstage that generic assignation is a project with subjective costs. The performance generates reception contexts that are at the same time both intellectual and emotional. In doing so, the performance preluded the inscription of gender issues in the Galician contemporary poetic setting, one of the most recognizable characteristics of this "poetry of the nineties."

The cultural imprint of fairytales as one element of the conformation of generic labeling would also become the material for the performances of Yolanda Castaño.[12] As a performer, she has participated in happenings that have received considerable attention from the media. Many of these were explicit elongations of what might be the central theme of her poetry: the moral ambivalence of beauty, stemming from a problematization of the feminine body which does not escape the temptations, at times intentional, of objectification and erotic fetishism. We must read her attempt to simulate suicide in the Pambre Castle in this way. It is a visual performance which unmistakably ties in with the reflections on the connection between aesthetics and violence which make up her last book of poetry, *Profundidade de campo* 'Depth of Field' (2007), from which I quote the first stanza of the poem "Highway to Heaven":

> Na autoestrada quedan marcas de curvas imposibles,
> liñas vacilantes que acaban directas contra a mediana.
>
> Cómo quedaría a miña beleza de espiga
> tronzada e sangrante contra o cristal do parabrisas,
> e cál sería o estado exacto dos meus peitos
> que xa non caerían
> nunca máis?[13]

When reciting her poetry, Yolanda Castaño knows how to take advantage of the identification between utterance and enunciation, consciously working the intonation and modulation curvature in each phrase in order to match her purposes. Her way of reciting refers explicitly to the verbal contexts of seduction sometimes thematized in her own poems. We can imagine the impact of this eroticized voice as it makes reference to the contemplation of the poet's own cadaver, seen as the final work of art.

Castaño's interventions in the poetic field draw their strength from physical presence and repetition. Performative in the most literal meaning of the term, these actions associated with the diction of verses are recognized as secular rituals of love and death by the public, who might accept or reject them. In this respect, the landmark study by Karen Mills-Courts, *Poetry as Epitaph*, takes on a meaning far too literal. It is not that poetry is thought of as a dead voice, but that during the reading the voice and the images that this voice summons evoke a visual illusion: the listener contemplates the cadaver of the poet.

Applied to the study of performance, queer theory offers an explanation as to why such visceral reactions should occur in response to some of Castaño's poetic interventions, which are often received suspiciously by the most traditional sector of feminist criticism. As opposed to what occurs in *A Sereíña*, Castaño's discourse does not respond to strategies of emancipation. The mythical resonances of her shows – based on legends, cartoons, or fairy tales – do not carry a normative or transcendental meaning which allows one to distinguish between good and bad, perversion and innocence, or ugliness and beauty. Rather, they are games of disguise where the performative and even arbitrary feminine character flourishes together with the generic-sexual roles.

The question is to what extent Castaño, undoubtedly the artist of the nineties most connected to new media, is able to activate the space of utopian communication referred to by Dolan with her timbral performances. Her successful activation of these spaces is bound up with an inward-turning where the timbral dimension, despite not being completely beyond questioning social norms, maintains a strong connection with self-expression. The perhaps deliberate ambiguity of purpose impedes an application to political projects, at least when these projects are seen in the larger context of community.

The concept of "utopian performatives" is most fitting for an analysis of the joint happenings of Ana Romaní and Antón Lopo. In the aforementioned *Lob*s* (1998), the authors attempted to reveal the conventional, even arbitrary character of generic-sexual designation. They also attempted to generate a space in which gender indetermination was effectively lived as such by the actors and spectators. Hearkening back to some of the considerations on the body put forth in the first section of this essay, in *Lob*s* we find generically marked enunciative verses. However, these were frequently the direct opposite of what was expected, in line with heteronormative conceptions, in order to write a new history of sexuality in the present through the bodies of Lopo and Romaní. The uniqueness of their verbal and gestural poetics, ascribable to the area of performance which we have been calling *timbral*, is in keeping with the opening of a utopian horizon that enables spectators' access to new possibilities in the social order. It is in this sense that such timbral poetics can also become politics of sound.

We will now turn to the category of *accent*, taken here in a technical-poetic sense (though not far from the sociological and dialectological connotations that are normally used in linguistic studies). Accentual performance, characteristic of the work of authors like Anxo Angueira (Manselle, 1961), Celso Fernández Sanmartín (Lalín, 1969), and Leo Campos (Matamá, 1973), mobilizes the performative value of dialects and sociolects, thereby establishing an intentional connection between voice and place, and conceding a pulsional rather than affective tone to subjectivity.

In *affect studies*, pulsion is defined as an oriented and linear movement. Therefore, poetic performance based on accent clearly favors communicability. Often, in an attempt to guarantee communicability, the performers organize their performances around narrations. Celso Fernández Sanmartín, for example, constructs his poetic happenings – minimalist in terms of set – by assuming the role of "storyteller." This role is also very present in his poetic writings and uniquely comes to life in books such as *Sen título* 'Untitled' (1995) and *Fucsia, talladas, estampados, boca* 'Fucsia, carvings, prints, mouth' (2001). Here, it seems fitting to contrast the stage work of Fernández Sanmartín with Walter Benjamin's analysis of the storyteller as a mediator of cultural contents. When stories are in danger of being lost, as in modern industrial societies, the storyteller's role – in accordance with the dialectic between patrimony and technique – enters into a crisis. Insofar as his shows generally rest upon a performative updating of traditional stories, the question must be asked to what extent the performances of Fernández Sanmartín tacitly question the destruction of a world and a way of life in favor of values associated with modernization. In this sense, we would no longer be dealing with Dolan's "utopian performatives," but rather with "local performatives" founded upon a critical reflection on the cultural homogenization imposed by a globalized present.

The conceptual opposition of "local performatives" to "utopian performatives" emphasizes the fact that accentual performances usually place the voice in a specific *locus*. Consequently, its level of cultural translatability is less than that of timbral performances. Similarly, happiness conditions[14] in accentual performances usually depend not so much (or not always) on the audience's capacity to imagine alternative spaces as on their ability to effectively put themselves into the physical and ideological coordinates envisioned by the performers. The use of accent in Galician poetic performance usually connects performative practices with politics of a communitarian nature. Depending on the understanding of *communitas*, accentual poetics can be founded on the sense of belonging to a linguistic-cultural whole or, in a less nationalistic sense, to collective identities based on parameters such as age (youth cultures), opposition to hegemonic cultural forms (countercultural movements, generally urban), or geographic origin (rural or rural-urban cultures).[15]

Projecting the category of accent, taken in its most literal sense, onto an analysis of some of the aforementioned poets and performers can be quite revealing. Anxo Angueira, Celso Fernández Sanmartín, and Leo F. Campos privilege dialectical markers in their poetic discourse. In the case of Campos, these markers are charged with a clearly ironic value. The performances of Campos, who defines himself as a punk singer-songwriter, are literary unintelligible without a basic understanding of the sociolinguistic situation in Galicia. His performances owe much to his use of the *gheada* and *seseo*, remnants of spoken Galician which, up until very recently, were stigmatized and are still relegated to non-formal oral contexts.[16] Galicia itself becomes both the object of, and stage for, his scathing parodies. The humorous treatment of diglossia or the use of *castrapo* (the mixture of Spanish and Galician) for satirical purposes make up two of the most fundamental aspects of his performances. These can be linked to a long tradition of Galician poetic performance, which, from Antón Reixa to the Colectivo Ronseltz (active from the 1980s through the 1990s), has found in Campos one of its self-proclaimed heirs.

If the success of the performances of Leo F. Campos rests on his capacity to encourage humoristic reflection on the linguistic conflict in Galicia, the accentual thrust in Fernández Sanmartín and Anxo Angueira is related to communicative values such as confidentiality. In this sense, the rhetorical function of the accentual performance rests on the existence of a public which socially desires spaces that produce authenticity, with all the problems inherent to this notion. As we have already seen in the case of Fernández Sanmartín, authenticity largely resides in the possibility of setting up, via fictional means, a circuit of social communication spliced with informative rather than experiential modes. Trust, in the context of a poetic performance that is a macro-act of complex speech, is created by pragmatic rather than essentialist means.

However, the meaning attributable to what is made socially operational by Galician poetic performance must be questioned. To what extent, for example, do accentual approaches still satisfy some particular social impact of the poet's word? In some cases, this impact is connected to the transmission of knowledge relevant to the community – a factor which might explain the narrative direction of Celso Fernández Sanmartín as well as the critical use of humor in Leo F. Campos. In others, it is associated with the latency of an oracular dimension of the poetry, which some poets are able to periodically update. Uxío Novoneyra (Parada de Moreda, 1930-Santiago de Compostela, 1999) fulfilled this latter role in his public appearances, and it is no coincidence that, if indeed parody is a sort of homage, the Colectivo Ronseltz has referred ironically to this role in its poetic shows of the 1990s. Surely the bard figure also founds the way in which Anxo Angueira recites Rosalía de Castro, focusing on the accentual dimension of a poet who can be read from other enunciative positions.[17] And though Leo F. Campos and Anxo Angueira are quite distanced from each other in both age and style, it is revealing that the two designed a poetic show together based on *Fóra do sagrado* 'Outside of the sacred' (2007), in which Angueira's verses, in accentual diction, were distorted by Campos's guitar. The confluence of these two performers would seem to indicate that the generational dynamics in the evolution of written poetry (which set apart projects by Campos and Angueira) might not coincide with the evolution of the performative scene. In Pierre Bourdieu's terms (1992), an accentually based poetry performance favors the "exportation of capital." The older poet incorporates the punk aesthetic of the junior poet and the junior poet the value of popular authenticity tied, in the Galeguista's social imaginary, to the accentual aspects exhibited in Angueira.

The relationship between timbral and accentual poetics is of a dialectical rather than differential character and they should not be understood in an ontological sense as being characteristic of the "essence" of certain performances, but as tools which can distinguish between different modes of reception for poetic performance in Galicia. Considering poetic performance as an emerging cultural manifestation does not mean presenting it as a hodge podge of characteristics or attributes, the way literary genres were thought of not too long ago. On the contrary, this emerging genre of performance poetry can be understood as a practice that can easily be reabsorbed according to diverse, and even opposing, poetic and political criteria. The timbral and the accentual can coexist in the same author and even in the same performance. Poets frequently explore these possibilities, starting off with an accentual practice and then turning towards the timbral, or vice versa. Since the early stages of her career María Lado has used accents as a relevant dimension of her stage performances. Especially in her public readings of poems, her own as well as that of other authors, *gheada* and *seseo* imbue her discourse with locative significance.[18] The presence of dialectal traces of maritime Galicia in Lado's discourse might indicate not so much a nationalistic fascination with origins as a spontaneity and anti-rhetoricism characteristic of what is referred to as the "poetry of the nineties" and its zealous endeavors to correct the poetic *oficialismo* or formality of some earlier trends.[19] However, her most recent work with electronic music or her video poems, in which she appears either alone or accompanied by Lucía Aldao, can be described as timbral.

It is even possible for the accentual and the timbral to converge during the same performance. This is the case in the most recent performance by Anxo Angueira and Leo F. Campos, based on the book *Fóra do sagrado*. The convergence of the timbral and the accentual can also be observed in the collective happening which was the outcome of the postgraduate seminar "Poesía e prácticas performativas" 'Poetry and Performative Practices,' led once again by Campos, this time joined by Xiana Arias (A Fonsagrada, 1983).[20] Arias and Campos had already shared the stage in a recital project with background guitar for the presentation of *Ortigas* 'Nettles.'[21] Arias, who works as cultural journalist at CRTVG (Compañía de Radio Televisión de Galicia), marked her first poetic and musical forays with readings of poems over sonorous backgrounds created out of fragments of songs by the Velvet Underground. But it was in the happening conceived for the previously mentioned seminar that she most clearly reveals herself as a performer by preparing an ambitious performance, both in terms of its theoretical underpinnings and the difficulty of execution. Wearing a wig and red lipstick, the author speaks a monologue in which she interweaves verses from *Ortigas* with verses from her forthcoming publication *Acusación* and other unpublished poems.

While speaking, Arias works with a series of objects (a doll, a ball, a rope), which she extracts from a trunk. Her monotonous diction, sleepy voice, and the repetition of actions regulated by automatism (jumping rope, bouncing a ball), accentuated by the continuous bass of Leo F. Campos, produce an intense contrast with the incisive and direct meaning of her verses, which cover the gamut of the accentual-communicative.

The performance constituted a revisiting of childhood scenes and an exposure of the perverse nature of many of its rituals. The poet's choice of costume – highly effective in its stage presence, in spite of its minimalism – recalls the theory of Joan Riviere, a psychoanalyst from the 1930s and an important figure for queer theory, who thought of feminism as mask and performative repetition. From the point of view of the interaction between timbral and accentual poetics, performances like those by Xiana Arias and Leo F. Campos suggest that the political in poetic performance is most effective in the meeting, through voices and bodies, of the affective and the pulsional.

The Location of Voice in the Galician Poetry Performance
Throughout this essay I have attempted to explore some possible lines of inquiry into the Galician poetic performance over the past fifteen years. The analysis of the function of the body, emotions, and the voice in these performances has sought to single out the Galician poetic setting in distinction to that produced in other cultures. At the same time, this study has attempted to produce analytical categories which might be applicable to other contexts. I have endeavored to show that just as one of the effects of trauma is the loss of voice, performative representation can serve as an element of identitary social feedback in historically minoritized literary discourses. In this context, a historical and cultural conception of emotional expression would open up new perspectives on the ways in which pulsional and affective contents generate effects of a political nature.

In advocating an analytical focus based on the stage use of emotions, I hope to challenge the dissociation, implicitly or explicitly maintained by the critics, between the supposedly subjective territory of affectivity and the supposedly objective territory of social intervention. As different as the aesthetic means used in these different types of performances may be, their participation in the ideological nuances surrounding modernity and postmodernity convert them into conscious or unconscious instruments of political action.

The distinction between timbral and accentual poetics, largely correlative to the opposition "utopian performatives" and "local performatives," has led to a different way of approaching performance practices in Galicia. I have attempted to suggest that, in general, timbral poetics operate better both with contemporary aesthetic codes and with new global political practices current since the 1970s, particularly those connected to gender and transgender movements. It is more difficult to assign contents and forms to accentual performances, which tend to draw from the singularity of the Galician national character and seek to represent this character in a sometimes essentialist manner. Once again, the Galician stage hosts tensions between the local and the global, even though it must be insisted that this tension can lead to valuable results from the point of view of the performances' aesthetic impact and social effectiveness. This is what occurs in the happenings authored by Chus Pato, María Esteirán, and María Lado, who incorporate codes that are simultaneously connected to local identities (Galicia as a unique historical subject) and universal identities (woman as subject of the contemporary feminist project).[22]

In spite of the richness and versatility of Galician stage poetry, the circuit of performance poetry and written poetry finds itself in tight interdependence. The fact that some of the aforementioned happenings took place within the framework of book presentations allows this to be clearly seen. Thus, in closing I would like to introduce some reflections on the social implications of readings, as it is this practice that confers a special centrality onto the voice and body of the poets. It might be said that communities such as the Galician continue to share something akin to a bardic consideration for their poets and that these communities continue to be most semiotically affected by public recitals. Since the 1990s Galician poetry readings have tended to renew themselves as an oral genre, closely approaching performance poetry.

The "poetry of the nineties" was one of the implicit arguments of this chapter: it is the unwritten plot that allows one to understand, for the most part, what happened with poetry that, like performance, was not destined for written circulation. Many of the authors mentioned here recognize a duality between their actions as poets and their actions as performers. This duality can even open up a profound distance from the written texts, although they must still be kept in mind. Nonetheless, I would venture to say that the logo-centrism of Galician poetic performance (from which few poetic endeavors escape, one of these being Antón Lopo's previously mentioned "Co ceo ás costas") is no coincidence. The word, be it written or spoken, timbral or accentual, continues to have an important role in communitarian representation. At the same time, the location of voice continues to be pertinent as a defining mark of Galician poetic performance.

A second dimension of my analysis has been the political effectiveness of different performance styles. The fact that performances based on what I have been calling "timbre" choose to disregard linguistic markers which would assign them either dialectic or social connotations does not mean that their political functioning is less effective than that of performances based on accent. In fact, a timbral performance might hide an accentual one and vice versa. The question, therefore, is to expand the field of what is considered political without restricting it solely to the realm of nationalism, while considering the undeniable impact of claims based on markers such as sexual genre or transgender. Timbre and accent allow us to start drawing the outlines of a possible politics of sound applicable to the most recent activity in the world of Galician poetry.

Notes

1. See Méndez Ferrín.

2. For a discussion of the concept of generation in Galician literature from a critical standpoint, see Nogueira; for a more theoretical stance, see Arturo Casas ("A cuestión"; "De Pondal").

3. See Lyotard.

4. In the wake of recent psychoanalytical approaches, authors such as Jane Gallop (Daughter's Seduction; Thinking), Sigrid Weigel, Judith Butler, and Joan Copjec ("Sex"; Imagine) have set out possible guidelines for the contemporary analysis of various intersubjective practices that take bodily presence as the protagonist.

5. Antón Lopo (Monforte de Lemos, 1965) is the author of books of poems such as Sucios e desexados 'Dirty and desired' (1988), O libro dos amados 'The lover's book' (1996), and Pronomes 'Pronouns' (1998), as well as of novels such as Ganga 'Bargain' (2001).

6. This aim is present in the trajectory of the author at least since A palabra e a cidade: intervención no espazo 'The Word and the City: An Intervention in Public Space' (2004), a performance presented in the Foundation Vicente Risco de Allariz (Ourense), October 30, 2004, in the 21st edition of GALEUSCA, a meeting of writers in the Galician, Catalan, and Basque languages.

7. Statements by Antón Lopo to the newspaper El Correo Gallego (16/06/2006). "Antón Lopo e Iván Prado callejearon 'Co ceo ás costas' por Compostela." www.elcorreogallego.es/index.php?idMenu=3&idNoticia=55763.

8. "The body constitutes a deposit of metaphors. In its economy with the world – [with] its limits, fragility, and destruction – the body serves to dramatize, and to some extent write, the social text."

9. Important performances of Ana Romaní (Noia, 1962) include her collaboration with Antón Lopo in the show Lob*s (1998), a stage-code rewriting of the poetry collections Arden (by Romaní) and Pronomes (by Lopo), and the shows Estalactitas 'Stalactite' (2002), featuring Anxos Romeo and Lupe Gómez, and Catro Poetas Suicidas. Intervención Poética Contra a Levidade 'Four suicide poets: Poetic intervention against lightness' (2002).

10. Derrida converted the sentence "I love you" into the material for two seminars, one of them delivered in 1992 at the École des Hautes Études de Paris, the other – an improvised version of the first – delivered at the University of California, Irvine.

11. For the difference between pulsional and affective in the area of affect studies, see Sedgwick; Massumi; Ngai; and Terada.

12. Yolanda Castaño (Santiago de Compostela, 1977) first became know as a poet in the mid-1990s with books such as Elevar as pálpebras 'Raising the Eyelids' (1995), Delicia 'Delight' (1998), and Vivimos no ciclo das Erofanías 'We Live in the Erofania Cycle' (1998). Since the beginning of her career she has experimented with media such as video, television, and photography. For her television program Mercuria she has conceived of and produced video poems by authors such as Xabier Cordal, Celso Fernández Sanmartín, Anxo Angueira, and Estevo Creus.

13. "On the highway the marks of impossible curves remain,/Hesitant lines that end head on against the guard rail.//What would my gleaned beauty look like/split and bleeding against the windshield,/and what would be the exact state of my breasts/that would now/ never again sag."

14. See Austin.

15. Bravú, a musical movement of the 1990s that attempted to reconcile rural and urban cultures in pop and Galician rock fits into some of the parameters of characterization which we have denominated here as accentual.

16. Both gheada and seseo are phonetic alterations of the phonemes /θ/ and /g/. The

gheada is created by pronouncing the phoneme /g/ obstructive velar as [ɦ] (aspirated, voiceless). *Seseo*, which can be implosive or explosive, according to its position in the phonic chain, is created by pronouncing the phoneme /θ/ like /s/.

17. At the start of this chapter I made reference to the centrality of the foundational figure of Rosalía de Castro (Santiago de Compostela, 1837-Padrón, 1885) in Galician poetic discourse. Author of books of poetry such as *Cantares gallegos* 'Galician Songs' (1863), *Follas Novas* 'New Leaves' (1880), and *En las orillas del Sar* 'On the Banks of the Sar' (1884), Castro was also an actress, journalist, and narrator.

18. María Lado (Cee, 1979) is a performer and author of books of poems such as *A primeira visión* 'The first vision' (1997), *casa atlántica, casa cabaret* 'atlantic house, cabaret house' (2002), *berlín* 'Berlin' (2005), and *novembro* 'November' (2007).

19. The high volume of Lupe Gómez's voice in her reading from books like *Pornografía* 'Pornography' (1995) can be interpreted in the same way: her shouting radically and transparently opposes the standard of correctness and grandiloquence that was the custom among the hegemonic poets of the preceding decade.

20. The seminar took place at the Faculty of Philologies of the University of Santiago de Compostela during the Master Mundus Crossways in European Humanities Program (2008/2009).

21. The video is accessible at www.youtube.com/watch?v=ak2YKklpEXg.

22. Ruído's most recent projects – including the film essay *Plan Rosebud*, award winner in the New York Independent Film Festival (2008) – delve deeper into this identitary crossroads, introducing themes of identitarian hybridization resulting from Galician emigration throughout Europe and America.

Bibliography

Austin, John L. *How to do Things with Words*. Oxford: Oxford University Press, 1962.

Butler, Judith. *Undoing Genre*. London: Routledge, 1994.

———. *Precarious Life: The Powers of Mourning and Violence*. London: Verso, 2004.

Casas, Arturo. "A cuestión xeracional e o canon no marco dunha nova periodoloxía comparada." *Iucundi acti labores. Estudios en homenaje a Dulce Estefanía Álvarez*. Ed. Teresa Amado Rodríguez. Santiago de Compostela: Universidade de Santiago de Compostela, 2004. 230–38.

———. "De Pondal a Novoneyra: o proceso xeracional en tanto foco poetolóxico." *A semente da nación soñada. Homenaxe a X.L. Méndez Ferrín*. Ed. Francisco Fernández Rei. Santiago de Compostela, Vigo: Sotelo Blanco, Edicións Xerais de Galicia, 2008: 133–38.

Castaño, Yolanda. *Profundidade de campo*. A Coruña: Espiral Maior, 2008.

Copjec, Joan. *Imagine There's No Woman: Ethics and Sublimation*. Boston: MIT Press, 2004.

———. "Sex and the Euthanasia of reason." *Supposing the Subject*. London: Verso, 1994. 16–44.

Dolan, Jill. "Performance, Utopia, and the 'Utopian Performative'." *Theatre Journal* 53.3 (2001): 455–79.

———. *The Feminist Spectator as Critic*. Michigan: University of Michigan Press, 1991.

———. *Utopia in Performance. Finding Hope at the Theater*. Ann Arbor: University of Michigan Press, 2005.

Gallop, Jane. *The Daughter's Seduction: Feminism and Psychoanalysis*. London, Ithaca: Macmillan Press, Cornell University Press, 1982.

———. *Thinking Through the Body*. New York: Columbia University Press, 1988.

Jáuregui, Carlos A. "Introducción. Del canibalismo al consumo: textura y deslindes." *Canibalia. Canibalismo, calibanismo, antropofagia cultural y consumo en América Latina*. Madrid, Frankfurt: Iberoamericana, Vervuert, 2008. 13–46.

Jirku, Brigitte E., Cecilia López Roig, and Herta Schulze Schwarz. "Introducción: Ein Weites Feld." *Cuadernos de Filología* XXX (El cuerpo en la lengua y literatura alemanas: Ein Weites Feld) (1998): 5–11.

Konstan, David. *The Emotions of the Ancient Greeks: Studies in Aristotle and Classical Literature*. Toronto, Buffalo, London: University of Toronto Press, 2006.

Lyotard, Jean-François. *La Condition Postmoderne: Rapport sur le Savoir*. Paris: Editions de Minuit, 1979.

Lopo, Antón. "Antón Lopo e Iván Prado callejearon 'Co ceo ás costas' por Compostela." elcorreogallego.es. Web. 6 October 2009.

Massumi, Brian. *Parables of the Virtual: Movement, Affect, Sensation*. Durham: Duke University Press, 2002.

Méndez Ferrín, Xosé Luís. *De Pondal a Novoneyra: poesía galega posterior á guerra civil*. Vigo: Edicións Xerais de Galicia, 1994.

Mills-Courts, Karen. *Poetry as Epitaph: Representation and Poetic Language*. Baton Rouge: Louisiana State University Press, 1990.

Ngai, Sianne. *Ugly Feelings*. Harvard: Harvard University Press, 2005.

Nogueira, María Xesús. "A poesía galega actual. Algunhas notas, necesariamente provisorias, para un estado da cuestión." *Madrygal. Revista de estudios gallegos* 6 (2003): 85–97.

Reddy, William M. *The Navigation of Feeling: A Framework for the History of Emotions*. Cambridge: Cambridge University Press, 2001.

Romaní, Ana. *Love me tender. 24 pezas mínimas para unha caixa de música*. Santiago de Compostela: El Correo Gallego, Concello de Santiago, 2005.

Rosenwein, Barbara H. "Worrying about Emotions in History." *The American History Review* 107.3 (2002): 821–45.

Sedgwick, Eve Kosofski. *Touching Feeling: Affect, Pedagogy, Performativity*. Durham: Duke University Press, 2002.

Terada, Rei. *Feeling in Theory. Emotion after the "Death of the Subject"*. Cambridge, Mass.: Harvard University Press, 2007.

Weigel, Sigrid. *Body and Image Space: Re-reading Walter Benjamin*. London: Routledge, 1996.

Zizek, Slavoj. *The Parallax View*. Cambridge: The MIT Press, 2006.

Producing World and Remnant: Dialogue with Chus Pato

Arturo Casas

the outside of the poem: its height, eye colour, the sex to which it belongs; when
it eats, sleeps, walks
it is different than when we say: thought, i, consciousness?

does the poem have an inside/outside?

do all these words (intellect, mind, reason…) belong to the inside?

is it private, the language the poet uses when configuring the inside of the poem?

is there an outside?

   is it private?

      language is a labyrinth of pathways
      a traffic

(Pato, *Charenton* 50)[1]

"I have never found a concept that was grasped in a word." The phrase is Jacques Derrida's (83). I take it as my starting point because I see his words as rich with possibilities for discussing Chus Pato's poetics.[2] In terms of what her poetics say as well as when they are read in the negative. One can imagine that Derrida and the poet would concur that discourse (understood as the result of an act and of enunciative conditions), that the text (understood as interwoven from remnants and non-monological registers), that *writing* itself, as process, network, hybridization, advance, indeterminacy of its own subject, as *horde*, already contains all concepts, and along with them, the world.

This is no trivial matter, for our very understanding of what poetry is today depends on it, even if this understanding cannot be stated in specifics and is not something that can be demarcated, here or anywhere. It cannot be reduced to the *word* and its ordering. Yet, from Hölderlin on, poetry traditionally retains a foundational capacity, perilous in the face of history: it maintains both world and life in immanency. In the shift that stretches from Mallarmé to other avant-gardes, this tradition still holds and is key to a volcanics of poetry: the surging bed of lava – destruction/production – that captivated the surrealist movement and that Chus Pato revisited as mytheme in her *Hordas de escritura* (2008).

From mineral to animal, from architecture to fluvial beds, space, earth; space contemplated with a soil scientist's eye and with tools to register transformations, changes, at times over long periods. The poetry of Chus Pato is one of mutation, from a present that observes history and, out of it, projects our collective future, in mutual understanding and recognition.

Gender, nation, language, body, culture; and erosion, humus, metamorphosis, death. But no concept can be grasped in a word. Not even in *life*, *humanity*, *poetry*, or *end*. Pato's writing, from *Urania* (1991) to *Secesión* (2009), presents a different cartography, other limits, another habitus, other possibilities for understanding and speaking, other ways of communicating and reading. There are few poets with whom it is impossible not to dialogue. Some of us insist that Chus Pato is one of these.

Chus, to what extent do you consider the poetry you write to be affected by knowing that at certain points in time, you yourself will embody it with a presence, with your voice, your body, or your presence in front of an audience?

I can say right away and truthfully: there is no relationship, because again and again the act of writing determines itself. It begins and ends in itself and has no affinity with anything but itself. Having said this, the nuances involved, also true, are complex.

Over and over, for nearly twenty years now, I've read my texts in public and in private. I read in private when I prepare a public reading. I rehearse, to put it simply. When I do, a voice emerges from the writing itself, along with bodily movements that take shape non-violently and in harmony with the text; whether seated or standing, I move, and my voice is generally quite slow, and I breathe and listen to my breathing, I write the poem anew as I utter it and in returning myself to the moment/s of writing, I experience a kind of pleasure. I am alone with my writing and I know how I must dub the text with my voice and body.

Something quite different occurs when I read in public. For years, reading in public used to fill me with dread, and all I wanted was to get it over with as soon as possible and get out. I felt a kind of shame that is hard to explain; it had to do with the fact that I didn't feel authorized to read to (impose on) an audience what I had written. I distrusted not the texts but myself – and worse yet – the very audience. I thought that surely they were there for reasons that had nothing to do with what I wrote – for political reasons, for example. This has to do, clearly, with the fact that mine is a literature of resistance, a fact that blurs the line between defense of language/nation and the poem's sovereignty (my first public reading was at an anti-NATO protest). Let's just say that I always suspected that the public was there for reasons that were not literary. Of course there's also my shyness, but this isn't relevant. As you can see, I was really in a bad state when I had to read.

This has changed in recent years as I have begun to feel surer of myself and surer that the audience is actually interested in what I have written. In recent years, when I've been able to read in public, my experience is closer to that of reading in private, transferring my voice and body to the site of writing. It's not an interpretation, which doesn't interest me at all. It is a going forth. . . a being able to go forth. All in all, I'm still far from being able to move, breathe, and produce sounds as I do in private. I still have that feeling of shame, though I am getting better in this respect.

In keeping with what you're saying, what does the *supplement* of the audience's co-presence, outside private space, consist of? Is this really a supplement/implement or does it depend in some sense on circumstance and on the variability of any specific spatial framework? I'd also like to ask you to expand a bit more on what you've described as this movement of re-finding or re-experiencing the act of writing in the act of reading/performance.

I perceive the audience as both presence and responsibility. What I would like is to bring them into what I call the site of writing. There are many ways to describe how I understand this site. Today I'd say that it is a state in which the distance between word and thing is at its greatest, but precisely because of this maximum distance, and in it, it is easy or possible to frame word and thing, to bring them close, which simply means to perceive what is freed or detached in language. In other words, there is an open fracture in the language of instrumental reason, in this language of consensus which is the language of idolatry: in the fracture, idols burst. Here lies the beauty that is the human capacity to create language: this capacity is so amazing that it hurts and overflows in its own monstrosity. It is also a black sun, a blind spot that must be traversed. Writing poetry, from my perspective, is a journey of arrival, sojourn, and departure from that site: the poet remains there for as long as she can stand it (writing is also an exercise of bodily resistance, of bodily exposure to the fracture).

Anyway, when I read in public, I want to bring those who listen to me into that site, and to do this, I have to go there myself. It's not always easy for me because, among other things, it is an exposure in front of others, an unlimited exposure. It is really an act of love, like making love in public. My responsibility is to ensure that the journey is possible. I begin with the idea that they are there to hear what I write and in gratitude for this, I show them the site where I write, bring them to this place where language is a sense that exceeds the senses. Of course, I don't achieve this, but it's what I'm trying to do.

Does this movement toward a sort of stripping of performance from enunciation have any political thrust?

Let's take one step at a time. I'm not against poetic performances. What I am against are didactic poetic performances. Let me explain: as I indicated earlier, I understand poetry to be a sense that exceeds the linguistic aspects of a language. Thus, when it comes to transmitting poetry to others, there is no room for "let the audience come, and I'll do something or other," or "I must make it possible for them to understand." "They" are not stupid and there's no need to explain anything to them, because they arrive already knowing (the didactic approach makes me angry). In short, behind some performances is a desire to hunt down and capture the poem. This I can't stand. It is this sort of "didactics" and capture that I object to.

Poetic "normality" does not exist: poetry is a state of linguistic exception and the audience is those people who demand and accept this state of exception. Any claim to "poetic normality" is something that has nothing to do with poetry. This, of course, is a political position. It amounts to a "take your grubby hands off the poem"; the poem doesn't belong to you, it's public.

Personally, what I would most like is to be able to learn all sorts of techniques so I can do it better, and I wouldn't rule out cooperating with other artists to succeed in making this transmission I desire possible. It is impossible for me to rely on, though, because I belong to a generation that never even imagined that one could make a living as an artist, let alone as a poet. Younger people today do have the freedom to imagine this. We didn't, but I don't rule out being able to do it someday.

Apart from the physical site, which varies and has decisive impact on a poetry reading or performance, there is also an abstract site of encounter that exists when we speak of the co-presence of poet and audience. In this respect, Carolee Schneemann has mentioned the existence of a *projective space*, in some ways already dramatized prior to being materialized, which stems from the body, the voice, and the expressions of the person who enunciates and recites the poem. How do you view the relation between performativity (including, if you'd like, this performative didactic) and dramaticity? This line of thought interests me in particular because your poetry, even before *m-Talá*, dramatizes subjectivity, so much so that in some ways it can be thought to call it into question. Having said this, I don't really think this is the case, but rather that what is questioned is precisely the foundation that gives rise to a certain notion of lyric, or of lyric in every sense of the word.

I understand articulated language as a technology; in other words, I conceive it to be an invention of human bodies. There is no doubt from where I stand that there is a correspondence between writing and human voice that involves not only an animal voice, but also a voice of language(s), traversed by this technology we call articulated language. I definitively accept, with all its possible deviations, that there is a correspondence between animal voice, linguistic voice, and writing, between writing and the body. In this sense I understand or could understand this abstract site of encounter to which Schneemann refers, though I don't know if she meant it this way.

With regard to the second question: lyric and subjectivity. . . What I write is not written or directed against the lyric, but out of what I see as a confusing of lyric and poetry, of lyric and poem, or, in other words, the reduction of the poem to the lyric poem.

In answering your second question earlier, I offered a definition of poetry as a sense that exceeds linguistic sense, and I would now add that the poem is that construction which pushes against or attempts to exceed the limits of the language of consensus; limits are borders or enclosures that can be understood not as devices that enclose, but rather as a zone that is porous, like a mountain pass. A poem would be that writing which tries to capture what lies outside a language's enclosure. It involves two movements: thinking languages as shut inside a border (instrumental language) and then imagining an outside and asking, what's out there? My favorite answer is "we don't know," although, for example, "outside there is a mountain, outside is my body and the chair I'm sitting in, and the computer I'm writing on; I'm outside and inside at the same time."

Thus the poem cannot be reduced to what is conventionally referred to as lyric; to do so would be equivalent to saying that everything that isn't a portrait isn't painting. And this all has to do with subjectivity, with the way the poet understands subjectivity from his or her angle. For me it is quite evident that whoever writes has subjectivity, that he or she is a *subject,* to put it clearly, and that it is an "I" which writes. This is very different from thinking that this "I" actually is the centered "I" assumed by lyric. On the other hand, I think any "I," any subjectivity, is not only a stage (a dramaturgy) but an interminable assemblage of stages (of dramaturgies), as much dramatic as comic as tragic, and that articulated language is constitutive of all of them.

To me, the projective space you mention in your question can be understood as a consensus that takes place prior to the reading: the one who reads in public and those who listen are all there and knew beforehand that they would be, ready to be inundated by a written text (by a sense, by a transgression of the enclosure of the language of consensus) heard via a voice that is simultaneously the voice of a mammal and a voice articulated in a language, and ready to be inundated by the five senses, above all I think by hearing, sight, intelligence, and touch; in other words, to be stirred by a voice that reads a written text and that transports them, transporting itself as well, toward what is set loose, freed, in the linguistic capacity of human beings (in the cave).

This voice that reads the written text becomes one with the body of whoever listens to it and with its own body.

The writing and reading of poems in public is a technology for entering and stirring the body, one's own and those of others.

I don't know if what you're saying has anything to do with the appeal to the receivable in Barthes, which he relates to texts he calls readerly or writerly. It strikes me as interesting that your epigraph to *Secesión,* **your most recent book, was the very passage from Barthes that articulates this (Barthes 118).**

Secesión marks the end of a process that can be unveiled as such. There is a cut; this cut initiates the process that leads to secession. This cut in which I write is called Thebes. Thebes is the name that designates my native land, both literary and political. The process consisted in cutting into the bloodstream and diverting it towards a place where it can more easily breathe. This bloodstream is both a biological and linguistic blood.

I read Barthes when I first came upon him, around the age of twenty. The one who was reading him then was Antigone, Antigone who is always too busy and doesn't pay much attention. Years passed. Now the one who reads is Ismene: Ismene has all the time in the world. It was a pleasure to reread Barthes, not only for what I learned, but also because I understood so much more – my neurons began to dance with delight.

The one who writes, and not only *Secesión,* is Ismene, and her writing doesn't renounce its native lands, but is not willing either to be a third corpse. She passes, and reverently, through the crypt where the bodies of the mother and sister are still lulled by the metallic breeze that blows from Oedipus's blind eyes, but she does not stay there. This writing is intent on freely entering into a relationship with the blood, and not the blood of the eternal: it desires the new, life, and words for this novelty. The new is not whatever is in style; the new is what begins, what begins incessantly: the origin.

Ismene read Barthes when the process of the cut was nearly at an end. I found the quote and knew that this was what I craved, a text that is received "like a fire, a drug, an enigmatic disorganization."

What I want to ask now might seem redundant in relation to what you've just explained. The question doesn't refer so much to what authorship is, as to how the entity of authorship functions. To what it means to be an author, a woman author, today. In particular, I would like to hear your thoughts on two aspects that I think define all writing. One is intertextuality and the other is performativity. It's strange that, if we troll through the conceptual history of these notions, we bump up against ideas of tradition and intentionality, respectively. But, obviously, other positions exist, unthinkable in an operative sense prior to Kristeva, to pinpoint a name and point in time.

In my case, the author is an invention of writing. I want to write phrases here like: the author, she's I, the author is the others and is thus I, the author is the character who goes by this name in my writing, the author is the assemblage of characters-author-she who display themselves in the poem and is that element (feminine, in this case) which belongs and doesn't belong to the assemblage and which limits the series. The author is a refined despot, the author is a businesswoman who hires women narrator-poets so they can write what she tells them to, and the author is I myself as writer, the author is the reader and is the readers who circulate as characters in the books I publish. . . the game is infinite. Also: the author is a legal entity who, using the name with which I sign, vouches for the originality of what I publish, certifies that there is no plagiarism, that nothing is rigged; the author is an economic entity who receives my royalties in her bank account. The author, male or female, is a cataclysm that emerges in the history of Literature and from there moves into readers and in some cases into an entire society (we've all said at some point "this is Dantesque" or "we/they're like Romeo and Juliet" or "these shadows and streams are Rosalian" or even "this gunpowder, this magnolia, this lineage is Xosé Luís Méndez Ferrín and I demand freedom for my people"). An author, male or female, is a password that admits us to another dimension that restores our auditory, sensory, and cognitive wavelengths. An author is a poetic performativity that shoulders the writing of the poets who came before her, and all her own writing, along with a future time, that not yet written, that which had never been written, which others had never written, that which had written itself in a time that still does not exist and in an immemorial past of which there is no memory. The author is the subject that is the mask for that inconsistency, that mote that is Chus Pato, the name with which I sign what I publish.

Agamben, in one of his books, I don't remember the title now,[3] informs us – and I take up Agamben here extensively from my notes – that in Latin *auctor* meant the representative of an underage youth or anyone whose acts had no legal validity, and the *auctor* conferred upon this person the necessary complement of validity. So an author, derived from *auctor*, is that person who fills the place of another who cannot be present.

Agamben continued to assert that, among old meanings of the term, was that of "vendor" in the sale of property, that of one "who advises or persuades," and, finally, that of a witness. In all of these cases the intervention of the "author" always implies a duality in which insufficiency or incapacity are complemented by the author's act, so as to give them value. Thus, says Agamben, we have the sense of "founder of a race or a city," which poets granted to the term *auctor*, and the general "to bring into existence," which Benveniste identifies as the original meaning of *augere*. Agamben goes on to say that the classical world knew nothing of *ex nihilo* creation, for any act of creation involves something further, unformed material, incomplete being, that must be perfected and nurtured. Every poet is always a co-creator, every author a co-author. This is how the *auctor*'s act completes those of the incapacitated; he or she gives life to that which cannot live unaided. We can also say the opposite: that it is the imperfect act or incapacity that the author appears to correct that makes the acts or words of the *auctor-witness* meaningful. An act by an author who pretends to live solely on her own behalf, is meaningless.

What I want to emphasize here, via Agamben, is the dual structure of the term *author*, as difference and complementarity, and how, as Agamben says, it indicates both an impossibility and a possibility of writing, or, in my case, of a non-poet and a poet. The authorial subject is excised, because its only consistency is that of this disjunction and, yet, it cannot be reduced to it. To Agamben, this is what "being subject to a de-subjectivization" means. To me, this non-assignable character of the author is nothing more than the price of this excision, of the indissoluble intimacy between non-poet and poet, between an impotence and a power of writing.

The authority of the author – I continue to quote Agamben from my notes – consists in that she or he can write only in the name of being unable to write. The author does not, of course, guarantee the truth of statements stored in the archive, but instead the very impossibility of their being archived, their exteriority with respect to the archive. For this reason, because a poem can only be written where there is an impossibility of writing it, an author exists only when a de-subjectivization takes place. The non-poet (Liberdade Aguirre in *Charenton*, for example) is the one who is most fully the author, and for this reason it's not possible to separate the author from the non-author.

We could say that being an author, a poet, means placing oneself in relation to the language of those who have lost it, installing oneself in a living language as if it were dead or in a dead language as if it were living, at any rate, outside the archive as well as the corpus of what has already been said. Thus we can't be surprised by Hölderlin's thesis[4] according to which "that which remains is founded by poets," which shouldn't be understood in the trivial sense that the work of poets endures and lasts over time. It means that the poetic word is that which adopts the role of remnant, and can, in this way, bear witness. Poets (and authors) establish writing as that which remains, which survives the possibility, or the impossibility, of writing.

Non-enunciable, and impossible for the archive, poetry is the language in which an author succeeds in testifying to her inability to write.

She – the author – is/when the mother tongue which will never be mine passes through me and writes the poem.

The ideas you bring up – remnant, testimony, and the dialogue-dichotomy between what can and cannot be written/enunciated – leads me to my next question, a change of direction that brings us to writing as object of contemplation. What is your access to poetry as something to read? On what does your process depend? And what happens when you read poetry?

I read poetry from a position of relaxation, sitting on a sofa so I don't get interrupted by a sore neck. It's very different from sitting down to prepare classes. Which is to say: there's no desk, no papers, no pens, no computer. For me, reading poetry is an activity that requires total concentration; it's a bolt of lightning. The main problem is when I can't continue; I always want to read the whole book without stopping and I fail, of course, because a book of poems can't be embraced in one go, even if I'm stubborn and try to do so. Of course, I'm drained when I finish, but I keep going till I'm totally exhausted. I know no greater pleasure than reading poetry, and in reality what I do is write the poem as I read it. Reading has an advantage over doing one's own writing as the poem is already there; yet this writing that I read still takes me time; I go back over it again and again, and it is always characterized by that lightning bolt I just told you about.

Reading poetry simply depends on whether I have a new book of poems and on whether or not I like the book, for to be precise: not all books of poems are poetry. Yes, it depends on this, on having a new book; later they are shelved in my study, and they quite often reappear from there, some more than others. I'd say they reappear in shifts, and some reappear quite often.

When I read poetry I read poetry; I don't do anything else. Sometimes I read it with my eyes closed and in a complete temporal suspension, which is to say, I don't need the book in front of me.

And when you re-read your own poetry?

I can almost reply that once a book of mine is published, I never pick it up again. The only exception is if I'm preparing a public reading, a process I've already described to you, and then sometimes, very rarely, I read other poems in addition to the ones I've prepared. More than once I've paused with delight over what's written and I like the feeling of not fully recognizing myself in what's there. I know, of course, that it was me who wrote the poems, but they are as much mine as anybody's; in other words, I'm anyone, any reader, of course.

Regarding rereadings of one's own work and of that of others appropriated in the act of reception: what do you think today of your collaborations most directly rooted in the concept of performance? I refer not only to your work with María Ruído and Ignacio Vilariño but also, of course, to your participation in the celebratory, protestatory and emancipatory collective interventions of the cultural group *Redes Escarlata*.[5]

I have to say first that none of these performances were my idea, and that I've always felt like a guest and view my interventions as privileges accorded me by Ignacio Vilariño and María Ruído, both visual artists and not poets, so I participated in acts that sprang from visual ideas rather than texts.

Ignacio Vilariño was in his final year of Fine Arts in Pontevedra and asked me to participate in what would be the final project for one of his courses. The performance took place in the interior courtyard of the Faculty, a building that was formerly an army barracks. Thus, it was a big space, outdoors, circumscribed by the four interior walls of the building – glass and steel walls painted in enigmatic blue tones. There, Ignacio had placed chairs for the audience – his classmates – in the form of a Latin cross, so that each spectator lent their body to the raising, if you will, of this cross, while remaining isolated from the others. I was in the center (like the altar in a cathedral, laid out like a Latin cross, clearly Catholic). I was seated and my place was marked with an equilateral triangle – a symbol of the divine. I read texts from *Heloísa*, the most recent book I had published. During the reading I felt an enormous push. It was the force of the earth that mysteriously rose up and, overcoming gravity, found contact with the skies (it was a cloudy day with some sun, but mostly cloudy). What Ignacio Vilariño had created was a sort of ship or vehicle, part spatial and part biblical, Sputnik mixed with the rapture of Elijah; there's no doubt that he succeeded in convoking the four elements and having them modify our material being. It was an unforgettable experience, though I still say nothing religious can be deduced from it.

When I met María Ruído, I'd spent years away from studying or living with the visual arts. María was a huge catalyst for me, and a link to a world I'd abandoned and was about to recover (it was the beginning of the 1990s). For her, as for Ignacio, poetry had a place of great importance and she wanted it to be present in her work. Our first action was held in the NASA performance space, that "spaceship of artistic services." Those were its early days, and NASA was more a project than anything else. For those who have never been in Santiago de Compostela, the NASA is an enormous space which was previously an automobile repair facility. At the entrance was the pit for working on cars, and it was there that María decided to hold the performance. I remember Xesús Ron and Miguel de Lira, now acclaimed and well-known actors, sweating like dogs because this hole had been filled with dirt and they had to shovel it out. Finally the pit was empty: it was rectangular, deep, and narrow. The show was entitled *Mateino porque era meu* 'I Killed Him Because He Was Mine.' The poster was magnificent: María had altered Caravaggio's painting *David and Goliath*, substituting her face for David's. The effect was impressive. The theme, of course, was a denunciation of violence against women (I must point out that, at that time, no one in Galicia dealt with these issues. María was a real trailblazer, in this and in many other ways). My poems were broadcast in that pit, completely transformed by María via a recording which played in a loop. It was a success, especially for the children in the neighborhood – which was still quite working class – who didn't want to get out of the pit, despite their parents' pleas. Nor did some teenage couples, who undoubtedly felt quite comfortable in that sort of womb with a voice.

In the meantime, María went off to study with Esther Ferrer. Upon her return we started *Pato Esteirán Ruído,* a production cooperative composed of the three of us, with María being the linchpin to the whole initiative. We mounted the performance

A Sereíña 'The Little Mermaid', today owned by the *Centro Galego de Arte Contemporánea* (Galician Centre for Contemporary Art), in the Galán theater; it was a great success and dealt with how romantic love mutilates women. María faced the audience, with a thick rope coiled at her side, a chair, and, on a coffee table, a television set. As María started to undress herself, the television projected a Japanese version of *The Little Mermaid*, and Esteirán recorded a live video film which was projected on a huge screen on the back wall. Once naked, María began to coil the rope around herself from her ankles up to her chest. When the performance ended, she was still trapped and unable to leave. While I read texts that I wrote for the performance, María toppled herself onto the floor; two people entered and carried her to the back wall, where she wrote in French: *Je t'aime*. We even had a party in the NASA, with music sampling, and recorded it all on film; we danced till sunrise. It was entitled *Ethic of Care*, in homage to Foucault's last writings.

And what can you tell us about the *Redes Escarlata*?

It's something completely different. The *Redes* was born in a context in which some people felt it opportune to create a kind of new cultural front that would unite culture and political intervention – Republican and independentist politics. The antiglobalisation movement was at the fore and the Internet was taken up as a weapon. So the *Redes* were born, and within them was a group of poets that has never stopped growing. These poets organize the readings that the *Redes* sponsors. A few highlights:

- All the poetic actions have, from beginning to end, had a marked political hue.
- The readings are intended to agitate and propagandize.
- This intention had nothing to do with the texts themselves; poems were not read for their political message but because the poet chose to read them, and in many cases the poems had no explicit political message.
- We wanted to occupy as many different public spaces as possible.
- Anyone can belong to the group; it is not necessary to have texts published, not even one poem.
- The group is intergenerational.
- There is no hierarchy that allocates a bigger role to well-known authors, who read for the same length of time as those who have not published or who are shockingly young.
- Meetings are convoked via the Internet, a novelty at the time the *Redes* started.
- Any member of the group can organize a reading.
- To belong to the group, one must be a member of the *Redes*.
- We have organized poetry readings with more than twenty poets.

I remember some particularly relevant interventions, which I'll describe here.

Torga Bookstore and the Rúa dos Zapateiros (Street of the Cobblers) in Ourense
In keeping with its name, the street is medieval, cobbled, and not very long; at more or less its midpoint is the Torga Bookstore, which specializes in Galician and Portuguese books. Visual artist Xoán de Dios and his brother Josechu made huge paper paintings of the facades of the buildings of the street where the Teatro Principal, one of the city's emblems, is. These paintings were hung with great effort from the houses on the Street of the Cobblers, so that they vanished behind their pictorial doubles. The bookstore was emptied and doubled in the same way as the street, the floor covered with books, more than a thousand volumes scattered about. In the center, a helicoidal column made of books rose to the ceiling, ending at the navel of a large-scale reproduction of Velázquez's Christ. The public congregated in the street and poets read in their midst or inside the bookstore. The poets' voices were broadcast all along the street outside.

Participation in the Prestige Macroconcert
The *Redes* participated in the organization of this concert, held in protest after the tanker *Prestige*, loaded with almost 80,000 tons of oil, sank off the Galician coast in November 2002, a major ecological disaster. The poets of the Redes read their works before more than five thousand people congregated in the Sar pavilion in Santiago de Compostela.

Reading on the Island of Arousa to protest the black tide caused by the Prestige
For this action, we carried the enormous placards painted by Xoán de Dios in protests against the *Prestige*. Amidst these, and in front of the estuary, we read poems. In the open air, naturally.

Action in the streets of Santiago de Compostela on St. Valentine's Day
We convened in the Praza de Abastos, and from there the poets strolled on their own past various places in the city, approaching people and whispering poems to them. People's reactions were varied, as one might suppose. At a given point, the poets all met up again in order to bring traffic to a halt; they sat down in chairs set in a row along a pedestrian crossing and recited love poems, to the surprise of drivers and pedestrians alike. No one called the police.

Poetry reading in the abandoned village of Santalla a Vella, Lóuzara, district of Samos (Lugo)
Once we had the idea of occupying public spaces, we thought up this intervention to bring attention to the process of depopulation in rural Galicia. We met in Lóuzara and, from there, drove down to the abandoned village of Santalla in several cars. It was a spring day. Once in the village, each of us selected a house, a woodshed, a ruin, a staircase, etc. from which to read a poem. So we did that. Each reading was

recorded and documented. Later, a film was made from this material, though it was never shown in public. It still exists.

Another productive collaboration was the one with Antón Lopo
I worked with Antón Lopo in his performance piece *Dentro* 'Within.' I'd like to note that this was the sole intervention that blossomed from and was carried out in poetry, if only to show that poetry and the writing of poems aren't always the same thing and that poetry goes far beyond most poems that are considered poetry; and that, in Antón's view, poems are only, and simply, literature.

At some point Lopo attended a workshop run by Marina Abramović, *Cleaning the House*, in the area near the Ulla River. On one of his walks, he spotted a marsh in Portocarreiro that totally enchanted him. In 2003, Antón decided to look after the marsh, to take care of it. He began to invite a series of friends to go on morning walks with him there. He decided to take us to one particular place, a place once part of a traditional farming operation that was now abandoned, or would have been, without Antón's dedication (and undoubtedly would be abandoned once more when Antón decided to leave).

You might say that Antón Lopo decided to put us in touch with a physical, moral, and mental ruin that for a brief moment had been restored to its past state, though with different ends in mind. So I walked all morning in the marsh with Lopo. At a given point, I lay down on my back in the grass and spoke to Antón, a text later published in the book that documented the performance.[6] My words had to do with my feeling of belonging to the planet, visualizing my spine held in the curve of the Earth, which is a geometric pleasure, an ellipse that extends from birth to death and that defines me: I felt myself embryo and daughter of the Earth, growing in Earth's placenta, and that death had already occurred in the womb. Antón photographed those moments, and he photographed the hollow that remained when I stood up: this hollow was a navel, a place of enchantment, which I neither know how to interpret, nor do I want to. We spent the rest of the day swimming in the river, talking of fear, of our difficulties in controlling anxiety, and of the river, and we swam. At some point I reminded Antón of his poem about the river, one of the most beautiful poems I know. Antón photographed me in the river. These photographs were later exhibited in the gallery at the Casa da Parra as part of the exhibition. *Dentro* was later published as a book.

Poetic intervention in public spaces has been a hallmark of Galician poetry in the last twenty years. This period coincides roughly with that in which you surged into public view very actively as a poet. At some point in the mid 1990s, you published four books, pretty much one after the other: *Heloísa*, *Fascinio*, *A ponte das poldras*, and *Nínive*. The emergence of new ways of presenting poetry marked, at that time, a sort of consensus to reformulate the idea of the poetic speaking subject and constituted, as well, a huge change in the reception of poetry. It was a complex time because, in

that restructuring of forces, women's poetry emerged with incredible energy, and there was also an unprecedented renewal of the live or circulating repertoire. A new canonicity emerged as well, in the technical sense of the selection of new frameworks or characteristics that merited consideration as models that would replace prior ones. Your influence as writer and referent in that sociocultural and political space was considerable at that conjuncture, and you yourself served as architect, master builder, shift supervisor, and construction worker in these changes. You've spoken of this on other occasions. How do you see it now, from today's perspective? How do you analyze these two processes: the exit (perhaps temporary) of poetry reduced-to-a-book, and the public events associated with your name, which have had such major repercussions over the past fifteen years?

It seems to me that in Galicia, and I suppose it's no exception, whenever there's a micro or macro historical change, and clearly the passage from Francoist dictatorship to the current constitutional monarchy was one, there is a movement that operates a bit like this: "here we are, we've arrived at the summit, at the golden age of Literature." It is an affirmation that acts to immobilize reality, to settle power struggles, all without thinking too deeply, and it's amazing because right away reality starts proving the dictum wrong. That said, proving it wrong takes time and a lot of energy. If you ask me, this is what happened in the fifteen years you mentioned: reality has disproven the idea that we have again reached a new summit and can gaze out and feel pleased with ourselves. Reality, rather, showed that in poetry only the unexpected is poetry, only that which doesn't repeat what's already finished and which opens the world anew, has energy and endures.

Then, just like that, without anyone asking, the poets of the nineties appeared on the scene, a whole generation which, like any generation, was very different from prior ones; the poets were also very different from each other. And inevitably, lots who appeared were women who wrote poetry and who did it in very different ways (they can't be reduced to the common denominator of biology, that which is called *feminine*). And these poets saw themselves forced to create space for themselves, because they found almost all doors closed to them; no one called them, no one involved them. So they grew and grew, and completely altered, just as you've noted, not only the way poetry could be written but also the contract with readers. And they worked so hard and had so much faith in the poem that they brought it into all the bars, to all the public squares, and to all the museums. I mean to say that they worked without stopping, created their own publishing imprints and did all the amazing things they did and continue to do. One of these, very important to me, is that each writes in their own way. I was lucky to start publishing late; in other words, I didn't start publishing at the same time as those of my biological generation. I did it at the same time as these young poets, and even if I would qualify my relationship with them as one of belonging rather than inclusion, I still participated in and was part of this whole explosion. Already by the end of the 1990s new formulas were appearing, and each year new poets show up, new alternative publishers, new ways of writing and relating to poets and to readers and the public, who show up at all sorts of events derived from poetic doings, in which, on many occasions, the body speaks the word and indicates the sites or places.

In general, in my opinion, the poem utters the names of truth, names born from bodies, from our surprise that this is what we are, beings capable of language(s) that blossom in real places and utter word(s) (yours, mine, ours, theirs: stones, bricks, plastics, flowers, butterflies, olive trees/of the south, of the north, of the east, of cyclone, cloudburst, city, field, everywhere, yours, mine, ours, theirs). The poem, today, is almost always written down, but can live only in the voice of the one who invented it or who interprets it; or it cannot be written down and – always, in my view – poetry, the muse, is a wavelength that exceeds the poem, that takes in much more than the poem. The muse goes and lives in wind, waters, computers, archives, in what is not yet born, in the dead; it's no one's, it doesn't just belong to the poem, it belongs to anyone: it doesn't belong to the one who writes it either, or to the one who reads it. Poetry and the poem are a kind of grace, an offering, a gift that is ours but that we can't sell or give away, which is to say that it is never ours even though it is for us. Poetry and the poem are free, they acknowledge no owner, and thus poetry doesn't belong (even as it does belong) to Literature, nor to the book. I like to think that when our species shuts its eyes and inside the eye the animations of dreams burst open, that there . . . everyone, all of us, the entire species is a poem and is used by the Muse.

Now, to get back to the thread of my argument, yes, in these years which bridge two centuries and begin a millennium on the calendar that we inherit from Christianity, poetry in Galicia did change, but at no time did it lose one of its initial characteristics: that it is a grand poem of struggle and resistance that, though it receives no support whatever from its government (as is normal in every literature, and this condemns it to an obvious precariousness and invisibility), is free as it has no master.

Also, and on this note I'll stop, criticism has evolved too, certain sectors of criticism. Others continue where they were: loyal to a way of thinking (not only the canon) that they think still applies though it is constantly invalidated by reality. Political conceptions of the poem evolved, some anyhow; others remained faithful to the idea that poetry has to serve a master, and in all this time, theory – some theorists – were there, attentive, supportive, putting wind in the sails, giving support from their intelligence; and some publishers, some newspaper supplements, helping to configure a landscape of impressive power, given we're a small country almost no one knows.

One last reflection relating to what you've just said. You teach History and in the 1980s did active research and investigation[7] in this field. I consider your poetry to be

a poetry of investigation as well, and I want to zero in on one element in particular, which is partly related to this. I always recall the phrase of a historiographer who said that the word "history" (as *narratio rerum gestarum*, and also as discipline, as historiography) is really a neologism arising from the development of philosophy of history via Vico, Voltaire, and other eighteenth-century thinkers. Before this, *history* existed as voice, clearly, but toward the time of the French Revolution its meaning changed profoundly, in particular with the introduction of the note of causality. I believe that we are now witnessing a similar change in relation to History and also in relation to *histories* and stories that circulate and that recount our story. And I believe that here there is, or could be, the basis for introducing a new schemata of the epistemic space occupied by theoretical work and critical intervention. What do you think we can expect, on the epistemic level, from the changes that are ushering in this new world "of knowledge and information," in particular in relation to knowledges and practices traditionally classified as "humanist"? And to what degree do you think this has an effect on the sociocultural space of the literary and, specifically, on that of poetry?

In the same way that I say that "the author is an invention of writing," I can affirm that "contemporary History is a refined construction." Now is not the time to demonstrate such a claim, but yes, this is what I think. History is freedom guiding the people, guiding peoples, and History is Walter Benjamin writing about the angel and thunder of History, of Progress, of unlimited faith in reason and of the destruction of this faith, of this confidence. Thus, beginning with Benjamin (from the time of the *Lager*) things stopped being contemporary and History shattered into a thousand pieces, no longer the story and promise of Eden on Earth. This word "Earth" is the only word that marks the difference between freedom guiding people(s) and History as a Judeo-Greek, i.e. Christian, story of salvation. The diverse chronicles, the grand gestures of which your author speaks, are something else again. But no God, no story, is with us today, just a faith. And I can't say more about that faith, that word that I just wrote down.

Two notes here: nothing of religion and everything of faith, the ability to move mountains. No story, thus, and only one action: to move mountains. I'd like to add that in the auditorium of the Faculty of Geography and History in Santiago de Compostela – a quasi-Napoleonic building in which I studied – there is still a ceiling fresco of the nine muses. History lives, too, and we live, under the protection of this name, Clio, with her scroll always open and her trunk of books, under the name that is Memory's child. This fresco has the power to calm my nerves, grant me a certain tranquillity. With respect to the poem, one last thought: no beautiful words, but sobriety, which is to say, prose.

Galicia, October 2009
Translated by Soidade Aguirre

Notes

1. Original Galician text: "*o exterior do poema: a súa estatura, a cor dos seus ollos, o sexo ao que pertence; cándo/come, durme, camiña/é diferente a cando dicimos: pensamento, eu, conciencia?//existe un interior/exterior do poema?//todas estas palabras (intelecto, mente, razón...) pertencen ao interior?//é privada a lingua que o poeta utiliza cando configura o interior do poema?//existe un exterior?//é privado?//a linguaxe é un labirinto de camiños/ un tráfico*" (Pato, *Charenton* 54). Arturo Casas and Chus Pato wish to express their sincere thanks to Soidade Aguirre for her translation of the interview.

2. Chus Pato (Ourense, Galicia, 1955) is professor of History and Geography and author of eight books of poems: *Urania* (1991), *Heloísa* (1994), *Fascinio* (1995), *Nínive* (1996), *A ponte das poldras* (1996), *m-Talá* (2000), *Charenton* (2003), and *Hordas de escritura* (2008). In 2009 she published *Secesión*, a volume of prose texts that explore worlds, inhabited or visited, along with texts that probe – among other things – writing, identity, and language. Iris Cochón edited and translated a volume of her selected poems in Spanish, *Un Ganges de palabras* (2003) and Xosé Manuel Trigo translated *Heloísa* into Spanish (1998). Three books of Pato's have appeared in English, in translations by Erín Moure: *from m-Talá* (2003), *Charenton* (2007), and *m-Talá* (2009). Her *Hordes of Writing* will appear from the same presses in 2011. Pato's poetry has also been translated into other languages, among them Portuguese, Serbian, and Polish.

3. Translator's note: *Remnants of Auschwitz: The Witness and the Archive*. Pato quotes and paraphrases from Agamben's discussion of the author and witness on pages 148–51.

4. Translator's note: from the last line of Hölderlin's poem "Andenken" or "Remembrance": "Was bleibet aber, stiften die Dichter" ('But what remains, is founded by the poets').

5. Translator's note: "Scarlet networks," more or less, though that term normalizes the Galician one. "Scarlets Network" perhaps.

6. The text published in the book that accompanied Antón Lopo's exhibition *Dentro* at the Casa da Parra in Santiago de Compostela in 2006, was the following "Would that I could lie down,/fit/my spine to the planet's curve/ until it forms/an ellipse that beckons me to nothing//and its geometric pleasure./It is the most perfect form I know for returning/to absolute companionship:/embryo and placenta.//Because death first starts/in the womb/of the mother" ("*O que faría sería tombarme,/encaixar/o meu espiñazo na curvatura do planeta/até formar/unha elipse que me conducise á nada//e ao seu pracer xeométrico.//É a forma máis perfecta que coñezo de volver/á compaña absoluta:/ o embrión e a placenta.//Porque a morte sucede antes,/no ventre,/na nai.*") Lopo's project in Portocarreriro was four years in preparation. A total of sixteen people participated, more or less under the same conditions as Chus Pato. Most of these experiences, along with texts and photographs, appear in the 2006 volume, which bears the following epigraph: "Arrive at the edge of the abyss/and do it:/leap/to the other side" ("*Chegar ao bordo do abismo/e facelo: /saltar//ao outro lado.*")

7. Translator's note: The word for "research," in Galician as in other Iberian languages, is "investigation," a word that better reflects what the interviewer is talking about. Therefore, I doubled the translation here to include both words.

Bibliography

Agamben, Giorgio. *Remnants of Auschwitz: The Witness and the Archive*. Trans. Daniel Heller-Rozen. New York: Zone Books, 1999.

Barthes, Roland. *Roland Barthes by Roland Barthes*. Trans. Richard Howard. Berkeley: University of California Press, 1994.

Derrida, Jacques. "As If It Were Possible, 'Within Such Limits'." *Paper Machine*. Stanford, CA: Stanford University Press, 2005.

Pato, Chus. *A ponte das poldras*. Santiago de Compostela: Noitarenga, 1996 (2nd ed., Vigo: Galaxia, 2006).

———. *Charenton*. Vigo: Edicións Xerais, 2004.

———. *Charenton*. Trans. Erín Moure. Exeter and Otawa: Shearsman Books & BuschekBooks, 2007.

———. *Fascinio*. Muros: Toxosoutos, 1995 (2nd ed., Vigo: Galaxia, 2010).

———. *Heloísa*. A Coruña: Espiral Maior, 1994.

———. *Heloísa*. Trans. Xosé Manuel Trigo. Madrid: La Palma, 1998.

———. *Hordas de escritura*. Vigo: Xerais, 2008.

———. *Nínive*. Vigo: Xerais, 1996

———. *m-Talá*. Vigo: Xerais, 2000.

———. *from m-Talá*. Trans. Erín Moure. Vancouver: Nomados, 2003.

———. *m-Talá*. Trans. Erín Moure. Exeter and Ottawa: Shearsman Books & BuschekBooks, 2009.

———. *Secesión*. Vigo: Galaxia, 2009.

———. *Un Ganges de palabras*. Trans. Iris Cochón. Málaga: Puerta del Mar, 2003.

———. *Urania*. Vigo: Calpurnia, 1991.

Poetry and Autofiction in the Performative "Field of Action": Angélica Liddell's Theater of Passion

Anxo Abuín González

Intermedia: Performance as Expanded Field

As its Latin etymology suggests (coming from the verb *spectare,* "to look") the term *spectacle* generally refers to all that is viewed or contemplated. In a more restricted meaning, a spectacle would be a manifestation of any of the arts involving *acting, execution,* or *performance.* This includes theater, opera, radio, film, and television (referring, in particular, to those events which occur on the set); improvisation or musical and poetic directing, dance, circus, mime, cabaret or variety shows; sports and other collective rituals. This category of stage art is characterized by the collective basis of its production and representation (theater companies, orchestras, dance troupes, sports teams, etc.) – though often differences are perceived with regard to leadership or direction. Also particular to stage art is its possible variance with regard to the order of the preexisting work on which it is based (a dramatic text or score). In contrast to the "duration of persistence" and static nature of physical objects, performance implies the idea of development or of "process" in time: spectacles are always subject to shifting identities. Spectacles are singular because of their ephemeral nature and because of the co-presence – from a socio-communicative standpoint – of emissor and receptor (the spectators). Existing along with all this are obstacles to achieving falsification; the absence and ontological impossibility of iteration, since any attempt at rigorous and identical repetition of any of its fragments would be useless[1]; the game, and its refusal, also rank as the spectacle's main conventions, cementing an authentic and implicit fictional contract between producers and receivers; and finally, pluri-coded and multimedia language is always a constitutive property of any spectacle.

It goes without saying that all these manifestations are susceptible to combination, and thus to alteration. In the 1960s art undergoes all sorts of criss-crossing where genres mixed with other genres and media with other media. Dick Higgins, "polyartist" and member of Fluxus, consecrated the concept known as *Intermedia* in 1966, which, while recognizing antecedents such as Giordano Bruno, Samuel Taylor Coleridge, Marcel Duchamp, or his own mentor John Cage, attempted to delimit the new art of the age: "Much of the best work being produced today seems to fall between media" (n. pag.). This "betweenness" wasted no time in being applied to the idea of theatricality with the arrival of the happening as the art of radical juxtaposition. Thus, the happening developed as an *intermedium*, an uncharted land that lies between collage, music, and theater. It is not governed by rules; each work determines its own medium and form according to its needs. The concept itself is better understood by what it is not than by what it is.

The world has become heterogeneous, multiple, and plural. Art goes beyond artistic and aesthetic categories, splintering into a great variety of practices, ideas, and concepts, among these the happening as *expanded field* – as the poly-aesthetic fusion of visual art, literature, and music.[2] Performance is understood as a manifestation characterized by interartistic dialogism and the confluence of media, especially the plastic, visual, and musical. And yet it is the nature of the artistic product that is affected in its conditions of *uniqueness, autonomy, delimitation, permanence, intentionality, coherence,* and *cohesion.*

According to the celebrated definition given by Michael Kirby in 1965, "a performance using a variety of materials (films, dance, readings, music, etc.) in a compartmentalized structure, and making use of essentially non-matrixed performance, is a Happening" (qtd. in Sandford 34). The happening is organized in this way because its structure eschews coherence and thus, permits the intervention of indetermination and chance; and also, because the happening mobilizes various genres and media, which sometimes converge and at other times oppose each other. Contemporary performance, which in a certain sense is heir to the avant-garde tradition of the happening, was unable to adjust to being parceled or compartmentalized. Performance resists being defined as a subsidiary happening or something second-rate, a form of imitation (or interpretation) of a previous model. Let us take *Learning Piece* (1970) by Vito Acconci as an illustration. It has been described by the author in the following terms:

> Playing, on tape, the first two phrases of a song (Leadbelly's "Black Betty"). Repeating the two phrases and singing along with them, until I have learned them and gotten the feel of the original performance. Playing the next two phrases; repeating four phrases until I have learned them. Continuing by adding, each time, two more phrases until the entire song is learned. (qtd. in Meyer 6)

The piece is configured as something unfinished, as a learning process undertaken by the artist, which is transformed beneath the gaze of the spectator. In the terminology of Roland Barthes, we find ourselves before a "texte scriptible" ("writerly text"), defined as "a perpetual present, upon which no consequent word can be set, for 'le texte scriptible' is us in the process of writing . . . the game . . . which shuffles amidst the plurality of entries, the overture of networks, the infinity of languages" (11). The text unfolds like a "galaxy of meanings" without beginning or end, submitted to reception and reversibility. To interpret it is to recognize its plurality, to accept its dispersion, somewhat like the "labyrinth-image" described by Román Gubern (1966) as opposed to the "scene-image," which reads the visible order and the alteration of the natural as full of unforeseen events and surprises.

The authority of the text has been somewhat erased, just like the concept of the original. This is accompanied by a radical opposition to the conventional uses of language that undoubtedly has its roots in the transdisciplinary experiments undertaken by Futurism and Dadaism in the 1920s, later followed by the neo-avant-garde. Vito Acconci, champion of interdisciplinarity and aesthetic promiscuity, has labored notably in the sphere of poetry, as have almost all of the authors whose trajectory we will observe in this essay. Recognizing the uselessness of formal and generic frontiers, he concentrated his efforts in a performative and multimedial experiment of an intensely reflexive and self-conscious dimension:

> Art for my generation was a kind of non-field. It didn't seem to have any inherent characteristics of its own. Art was a field into which you could import from other fields, so I felt free to come to it from the closed field of poetry, in which the parameters were set. Besides, I was interested in what all the arts had in common – the author mediating between the object and the viewer. (qtd. in Poggi 255)

Among the distinctive manifestations of performance art, one stands out in its conception as a multimedia modality in which diverse, non-heterogeneous elements intervene. Henry Sayre saw in performance the rupture of the text due to the incorporation of "exterior" forces (reality, physical space, the spectator, other technological mediums) with the goal of creating an intrusive dynamic which would impede any fixation of sense. For Acconci, the poem's page soon became a cell which confined the process of the "I" exercising control in its movement towards the margins (5). It also limited any urgency to become closer to a communitarian "you." Sayre remembers that Acconci considered poetic writing as a "field of action" (a phrase borrowed from William Carlos Williams) which soon proved irrelevant: "I was using the page as a field for movement, there was no reason to limit that movement, there was no reason not to use a larger field (rather than move my hand over a page, I might as well be moving my body outside)" (qtd. in Sayre 94).

His body therefore became his own writing space. It is important to point out that the performative comprised an *outside/inside* dialectic which was quite enriching from a generic, media, and referential point of view. The notion of *field* became enormously important in Acconci's shift back to the visual, which the critics date precisely to 1968. He undertook projects such as *Soap and Eyes* (1970), *Hand and Mouth* (1970), *Run off* (1970) and *Trademarks* (1970), which constitute a metatextual delving into the relationship between subject and object, observed and observer – an approximation to a phenomenology of sight associated with a material corporality, "spermatic," and "fecal" (Auslander 78), which hints at the omnipresent idea of pain or death. From this point onward, the work of Acconci can be thought of in terms of poetization, expansion, and interaction. Ostensibly, his poems were already metalinguistic, while at the same time tending to map the uses of language: less "filling in space" in a movement towards the margins than "revealing a meaning." Thus, poetry materialized, passing through the limits of the written word and entering into other adjoining disciplines close to this process of creation – film, video, body art, and architecture.

Performativity and Poetization

Acconci's experimentation is representative of the itinerary undertaken by many playwrights during the second half of the twentieth century. In the experiences nearest to the performative, the objectivity traditionally attributed to the theater genre disappears and the text finally gives way to an unpredictable poetic universe. The performative space opens up equally, intensely, to the lyrical and autobiographical, or the autofictional, as we will see. Ruth Maleczech, member of the experimental New York Company Mabou Mines, underlines the inconvenience of the classic understanding of theater and includes an autofictional dimension in the performance area:

> It wasn't interesting to play parts in other people's plays anymore. Also, it probably wasn't interesting for directors to do new interpretations of often-done plays either. Something else had to happen . . . It's not just due to performance art, but to [writer/ director Jerzy] Grotowski's idea that it was no longer necessary for the actor to realize the author's intention when he wrote the part. Once that became clear, then a piece becomes the story of the lives of the performers. So the context is changing and within that changing context, you see the life of the performer. We're not really working with any material except ourselves. (qtd. in Howell 11)

Artists such as Meredith Monk, Joan Jonas, and Robert Wilson also could not think in terms of only one discipline. Rather, they responded to multidimensional creative impulses which mixed the visual, spatial, aural, and verbal (shortened, fragmented, invented, and electronically distorted words). Collaborations by performers and poets were common, as in the project American Beat Poetry (1981), in which Laurie Anderson, together with William H. Burroughs and John Giorno (author, in his own right, of the project Giorno Poetry Systems), worked together to put on a series of recitals in U.S. nightclubs. Before this, Anderson had participated in similar experiments with John Cage and Merce Cunningham.

This field interference solidifies in de-territorialized landscapes in which one medium struggles against another. The spectator, protagonist of all the operations, feels like a nomad and is at the mercy of continuous displacements: this configuration of the audience is submitted to frequent metalinguistic turns in poetic texts, such as Anderson's *United States* (1983):

> You're driving alone at night.
> And it's dark
> and it's raining.
> And you took a turn back there
> and you're not sure now that it was the right turn
> but you just keep going in this direction.
> Eventually, it starts to get light and you look out,
> you have absolutely no idea where you are. (qtd. in Sayre 145)

In Anderson's work, the appearance of new technologies and the choice of a multimedia format point towards the "language of the future" made up of subversive noises and disturbing urban sounds. She sees theater as a means to discover mechanisms of authority and power and as a form that activates itself against social structures and the "role models" that condition the place of women in society. Her shows combine a sort of attenuated rock concert with a poetic lecture, amplified by a potent sonorous and visual imaginary. Her writing recalls Gertrude Stein and David Antin in its open poetry and unbridled orality.[3] It forgoes punctuation and adheres to unique registers that relay a disconcerting and uncomfortable feeling when listened to.[4] The first four parts of *United States* constitute a montage-collage of instrumental compositions, narrative monologues, poems, dramatized anecdotes, minimalist dances, light paintings, Chinese shadows, visual effects, and film or slide projections. Again, the figure of the nomad surfaces in Anderson's words: "My whole intention was not to map out meanings but to make a field situation. I'm interested in facts, images, and theories which resonate against each other, not in offering solutions" (qtd. in Howell 12).

To a certain extent, Anderson connects with the "feminist autobiographical solo performance" of Holly Hughes and Deb Margolin and the "monopolylogues" used by Lily Tomlin and Anna Deavere Smith.[5] In these cases social criticism takes it upon itself to create desires and hope for the community, a confidence in the possibility of something better in the world constituting what Jill Dolan has called *utopian performative*:

> Utopian performative describes small but profound moments in which performance calls the attention of the audience in a way that lifts everyone slightly above the present, into a hopeful feeling of what the world might be like if every moment of our lives were as emotionally voluminous, generous, aesthetically striking, and intersubjectively intense. (5)

Performance becomes a vow, "not because it can only promise possible change but because it catches its participants – often by surprise – in a contract with possibility: with imagining what might be, could be, should be" (Pollock 2). Despite this, the utopian frequently finds itself in conflict with what Zygmunt Bauman terms *postmodern wisdom*, based on a disbelief in the idea of truth as an absolute, or in reason and progress: "What the postmodern mind is aware of is that there are problems in human and social life with no good solutions, twisted trajectories that cannot be straightened up, ambivalences that are more than linguistic blunders yelling to be corrected, doubts which cannot be legislated out of existence, moral agonies which no reason-dictated recipes can soothe, let alone cure" (*Postmodern* 245). The postmodern mind does not therefore aspire to find universal formulas and recognizes that values of ambiguity, risk, danger, and hatred will always be present in our lives. At any rate, theater revamps a different present in which the clash of human identities questions the social rules and norms on behalf of the spectator, the true critical subject of an improbable epiphany coming out of the naïve belief in reality's change. In this way, "the neutral interpreter," "disinterested" in relation to the object to be judged, is done away with, replaced instead by one who is politically active and involved in exercising responsibility against injustice, poverty, and war (Greham 5).

Much of the aforesaid fits stage practices customarily referred to as "devising theater." At least two elements are quite evident in this "collaborative" theater: it perceives the text as a very general, at times non-existent guide and places a maximum importance on the functioning of rehearsal and improvisation techniques. As a result, representation is thought of as setting in motion an open process which oscillates continually between life and art. It is a process of constant transformation in which the audience is the only and final guarantee of an attempt to approach meaning. Thus it is customary to find "a layered, fragmented and non-linear text, one specifically courting various perspectives and viewpoints" (Heddon and Milling 192). Along these lines, Nick Kaye comments:

> The postmodern in art and performance . . . occurs as a making visible of contingencies or instabilities, as a fostering of differences and disagreements, as transgressions of that upon which the promise of the work itself depends and so a disruption of the move toward containment and stability. (23)

This is the case in some of the most notable antecedents of "devising performance" (the San Francisco Mime Troupe, the Open Theater, the Living Theatre, the Performance Group – not to mention what is known as *happening* or the historical avant-garde) and in experiences along the lines of Sheffield Forced Entertainment's company. Tim Etchells, leader of the group, suggests conceiving stage space as a place where opposing sensibilities collide. His notion is rooted in the idea of play:

> Play as a state in which meaning is flux, in which possibility thrives, in which versions multiply, in which the confines of what is real are blurred, buckled, broken. Play as an endless transformation, transformation without end and never stillness. Would that be pure play? (53)

Performance art is characterized by being playful, liminal, and liberating; it can infiltrate a text, "dispossessing it" and displacing authorial power toward the margins. The structure of performance includes a moderate serendipity which cannot be comprehended by rational systems of thought: instead of being configured, like most texts, around a plot, it is constructed in terms of networks that can appear disorderly, but that contain unique forms of internal order. Performance deconstructs authorial power and its illusion of Presence, substituting it with an energetic source of deferred and hypothetical power, as Jean-François Lyotard would say, and creating renewed levels of meaningful complexity.[6] The modern North American drama and its new language has not been able to move away from this attitude towards performative, as José Antonio Sánchez has pointed out in *Dramaturgias de la imagen* (1999). He names the elements common to both theater and performance: the indifferentiation of actor-character and the appreciation of the physical presence of the actor; the identification of stage time with presentation time rather than with that of the representation; the blurring of the limits between fiction and reality; the aesthetic value of objects, with emphasis on isolated detail (if they are connected to the rest of the spectacle); associative structuring and composition; the superposition of different languages; and transdisciplinarity in the creation of multimedia spectacles.

In works by The Wooster Group (Elizabeth LeCompte) or in the autodramas of Spalding Gray, the contradictory nature of text and world is placed on center stage, so to speak. The drama and the performance dynamically interact; both cultures remain, but not without substantial changes in their respective configurations. The Wooster Group appropriates materials of any kind in its spectacles in order to create a hybrid and intermedial collage where limits disappear and the text becomes unstable and absolutely provisional. Thus, the spectator is encouraged to "make the kind of choices usually considered the province of the writer and/or the performer," and the piece requires the public "to realize the multitude of possibilities on which it opens" (Savran 55). Themes are also typically postmodern: identity in the context of globalization, the insufficiency of language, the world's unreality (simulacrum), death in its most violent manifestations (converted into spectacle), the isolating of the human being in a new consumer society, etc. Theater therefore moves onto the terrain of political activism or, if you wish, counterculture (the rebellion against established values). It also places the spectator next to the playwright, in the position of witness: "The art-work that turns us into witnesses leaves us, above all, unable to stop thinking, talking and reporting what we've seen" (Etchells 18). Autobiographical performance can be associated with the idea of *a watchful eye/I of the world* (Heddon 163) present in contemporary reality by a testimonial necessity, but also resultant of a somewhat interventionist impulse.

Postdramatic Autofiction

On the modern stage, a place of emancipation from any central or textual authority, "the text 'performs,' the performance 'textualizes'" (Pavis 301). This type of theater rumbles through the frontiers that separate representation and reality, imagination and authenticity, subject and object. The stage construction of personal identities causes the spectator to question what is true or false – the uncertainty as to which events are lived experiences and which are narrative or poetic inventions. Autobiographical performance plays around with the idea of *non-acting* and of life directly exposed to the spectator. Thus, it hopes to establish a more direct communicative link with the audience, which Tim Etchell refers to as "in-the-same-roomness" (18). Representation is converted into a space for memory, testimonies, and denunciation, a space-in-between for shared reflection on the nature of being human. At times, autobiographical presentation may even show an exaggerated version of oneself, as Laurie Anderson emphasizes when speaking about her "talking styles" as a type of mask: "For instance, I've used about eight talking styles today, starting with a phone call about a death in the family and talking with my mother, then screaming at the lawyer in my most efficient, business-like style" (qtd. in Howell 14). Her spectacle *Happiness* (2002), her most autobiographical piece to date, describes her response to the events of September 11. It also shares her identity experiments in an Amish community and as an employee at McDonald's (Govan, Nicholson and Normington 67–68). In some respects, it is this "eruption of the real" that ensures a whole and mixed spectacle: "In this way a new hybrid generation arose, often with biographical content, at the intersection of body art, stage poetry, and cabaret, which carried the idea of working exclusively with the reality of the actor (author/artist) in real time, renouncing fiction and seeking a direct dialogue with the spectator" (Sánchez 128). It is a game of identities dealing with human existence in which the "I" comes together in successive tropes like a system of meaning: "the *announced self* of both autobiography and the mask of persona, the monolithic self versus the polyvalent construction of conflicting selves, the self that is conscious of history and explicits it behind each line of a work" (Silliman 369).

In these and other cases which assimilate themselves into models of "Platform storytelling," we find ourselves in the territory of autofiction, insofar as these practices construct a "mega-identity" before the spectator's eyes (Wilson 70). In the celebrated approach by Serge Doubrovsky in his novel *Fils* (1977), autofiction is characterized as a sort of psychoanalytical personal exploration.[7] Doubrovsky's idea was later used to designate a type of narration in the first person – fictional in nature (marked by paratextual traces) – where the empirical author appears homodiegetically bearing his or her own name. Autofiction lucidly exposes the "experience" lived by the real author, maintaining the appearance of the autobiographical yet openly playing on the edges between fiction and reality. It is a narrative pact that is frequently expressed as follows: "I, real author, am going to tell a story, protagonized by me, which never took place." Philippe Gasparini (2004) prefers to apply the formula "Est-il je?" In other words, "Is it the author or a fictional person who is telling us their life?" Autofiction therefore entails a mixture of narrative codes which are considered incompatible and constitutes a textual exercise that showcases either a "false sincerity" – to cite Rousseau's famous comment regarding Montaigne's *Essais* – or a sickly *egotism*, if we accept the Anglicism with which Stendhal attacked Chateaubriand's "abominable" taste in speaking of himself. Autofiction implies the appearance of a *mise en abyme* in which the enunciative situation is converted into an object of mimesis, in a sort of reflexive or mirroring split which, to a greater or lesser extent, breaks the discourse's linearity. Now is not the time to go into the metanarrative implications of these practices or how they point to literary expression as an artificial mechanism or fictional construction.

Theatrical autofiction, at least initially, can be situated in the sphere of the mixed epic-lyric, due to the presence of an authorial *alter ego* that would break away from the interpersonal realism of current *bourgeois drama*, as it is called by Peter Szondi in *Theory of the Modern Drama*, i.e., preoccupied with ideas of the world's totality, illusion, and reproduction. Perhaps it is worth wondering, as Christian Biet and Cristophe Triau have done, whether dramatic theater, seen in the Aristotelian manner as an "absolute drama," has only been a myth – akin to a theoretical aspiration (242). This would be even the case with Diderot (see the clear narrativity in the experiment by Lysimond and Dorval in *Entretiens sur le Fils naturel* 'Conversations on the Natural Son,' 1757). The stage spectacle is submitted to continuous leaks, or escapes, which playwrights of the last century succeeded in converting into fundamental themes for their craft. At any rate, theatrical autofiction tends to narrativize the stage and to subordinate theatrical action and interpersonal dialogue, favoring instead the monologized and lyrical reflections of a central "I." Therefore, it might be fitting to speak of a *discursive dramaturgy*, based on the imbalance between history and discourse, or of *mixed mediums*, which opt for the meshing of epic with lyric elements. This phenomenon is worth observing from a figurative perspective, posing a degree of similarity between the character-narrator and the author in-the-flesh by means of narrative operators as diverse as age, profession, and sociocultural sphere.

From a point of view concerned exclusively with set design, it seems necessary to apply the term *autofiction* to the theater of Memory and Death by Tadeusz Kantor.

Georges Banu (1990) describes the ceremonial style of the Polish creator as "personal" and autobiographical theater, where individual memory is placed on stage for the spectator. Kantor was extremely marked by Dadaism and the *happening*, as well as by influences from painting and sculpture. His figure of the man in the corner, at the same time creator, actor, and spectator, evokes certain aspects of Asian theater, especially the structure of Nô. There, the *waki* causes the dead heroes to rise again, although in Kantor's work it is perhaps more fitting to speak in terms of marionettes, phantoms of the past, and cemeteries of the dead. In *The Dead Class* (1977) or *Wielopole, Wielopole* (1980) we find airtight universes possessing their own laws. Kantor jettisons his "I" in order to place it on the other side of the mirror, like a *meneur de jeu* in an imaginary space, showing the infinite becoming of the possible variations of life in action *in fieri* – between chaotic effervescence and the most calming tranquility, between noise and silence. The actors know that his active presence enables him, furthermore, to interfere in their interpretation by changing the order of the scenes, adjusting the volume of the music, or changing the placement of objects. Kantor explains the procedure as a metatheatrical rupture of expectations:

> I am a private person, I am the author. But what brings me happiness is this role of a provocateur, i.e., the director should be hidden, he is not needed on stage. But I stand there . . . because this illegality fascinates me . . . because I destroy illusion, since I appear on stage as if to say: I do not like that. (qtd. in Klossowicz 112)

The non-linearity of the memories comes from the repetition and superimposition of distinct and autonomous spaces and times. These spaces and time contract or dilate according to the will of the "autofictionneur."

It is impossible to speak of *autofiction* without referring to the "solitary word" placed onstage by theatrical monologue. The character who holds a monologue can match his or her identity with the author's, or choose to disperse it in an explosion of the multiple and contradictory. Both cases translate to coming out of the darkness to exhibit and project an intimate "I" out towards the exterior, in a solitary and often problematic enunciation. The narrative power of the monologue has been especially utilized by postmodern aesthetics, with its tendency towards the dislocation and fragmentation of theatrical time in all its manifestations. The physical limitations of the stage are transcended and virtual spaces are created, dramatizing the thinking of characters who suffer. These characters, like those found in works by Samuel Beckett and Harold Pinter, tell stories, thus reliving their memories and revealing themselves in the process.

In the territory which Hans-Thies Lehmann (1999) refers to as *postdramatic theater* (in which we would include the work of Kantor, at least for its precursory importance) autofiction gains considerable relevance, as Richard Schechner pointed out years ago. Postdramatic theater is, according to Lehmann, offered to the spectator as a pure stage event – a pure presentation or presence ("presentification") that seeks to erase the idea of reproduction and repetition of the real. Postdramatic theater focuses on the juxtaposition of the lyrical, epic, and dramatic, and looks for the heterogeneity of formal languages (even the abolition of "aesthetics" itself has its adherents). Postdramatic theater goes a step further than epic theater, which was abandoned as a possible solution in the 1980s and 90s. This in turn opened up a post-Brechtian stage on which the narrative description of a world through mimesis (a unifying and totalizing representational principle) is abandoned in favor of a questioning of perception, of "floating attention" (not structured on a semiotic order), parataxis (not hierarchy), and plethora (chaotic accumulation). Theater comes into play here more as a shared than a transmitted experience. In addition, it is more a process than a result, more a manifestation than a meaning, and more an energetic impulse than information.[8]

Autofictional examples in the postdramatic realm are very evident, from Marina Abramović and Allan Kaprow to Spalding Gray, who represents a hyperactive "I" on the divan in dialogue with its own corporeality. This can be seen clearly in his shows with the Wooster group (in *Trilogy*, for example, based on the autobiographical texts which surround events such as his mother's suicide) or in *Gray's Anatomy* (1993). In this context, the denomination *autoperformance* (coexisting in the English-speaking world with solo performance, self-performance, or artist's performance) is worth noting. The term *autoperformance*, to which *The Drama Review* dedicated an interesting special issue in 1979, can be taken to mean a "presentation" conceived of and represented by the same person. As the dominant tendency on the postmodern stage, the term is used by Robert Wilson, who sometimes includes himself as the creator of the pieces he represents. It is also used by Richard Foreman, who normally appears as the visible "controller" of his shows. However, its true dimension is reached precisely when there are autobiographical implications or when the relationship between the *performer* and the life material used on stage is taken as a theme.

Theater of Passion: Angélica Liddell

It is not difficult to find an example from the Spanish scene. In the introduction to *Leda*, her first published piece from 1995, Angélica Liddell defines her dramaturgy as "theater of passion," where the body, materialized as visual territory, is represented. The word only receives its justification because it guarantees the privilege of the lyrical-poetic verse: "Later I opted for the stage word so that the poem could be contemplated" (*Leda* 89). This is an interesting consideration that confirms the ambivalent nature of Liddell's work, which is invariably completed by other referents, such as music and painting, and which has as its goal the most direct and "brutal" creation of emotion on stage. The principle of repetition acts, furthermore, as a means of subverting the order of language, the causality of discourse, the chain's linearity, and the teleological succession of facts, provoking the instability of both enunciation and the character enunciating. In *Leda* Liddell utilizes reality, or empirical living, as a point of departure for getting at the essence, the purity, the "deep interior of things" through strategies of abstraction and deformation. Instead of imitating visible things, the real experiences are interpreted in order to extract beauty and feeling from them, according to a diagram which implies renouncing objectivity in favor of the idea of poetization. Irreality is offered to the senses in theater (through sound, rhythm, movement…), aiming for the creation of the maximum disturbance for the spectator: "In effect, the work of art must transform the individual. It acts upon his vital organs, either destroying them or generating others, or metamorphosizing them. At any rate the transformation calls for a total restructuring of the system, which will modify the view of the subject's world" (Liddell, *Leda* 93).

In *Leda,* the disturbance comes from the impact of images that sometimes affect the corporal capacities of the spectator, as in the case of the monologue of the Incubatriz in scene IV, or in a reflection on the power of language that will not necessarily remain constant throughout its path: "What does the word father mean if it is repeated one hundred times? (without concealing pronunciation difficulties as the repetition advances.) Father. Father. Father . . . " (129). This story of brothels and dead swans puts the credibility of the artist at stake:

> Why do you write verses if you can't behave like your verses? Have you tried it? Well, don't bother because you will only succeed in making a grotesque face. Dumb, petty, and mediocre imbeciles! I don't accuse you of dirtying, because that is man's irremediable condition. You're can't resist dulling purity. What a failure. How disgusting. (136)[9]

El tríptico de la aflicción – consisting of *El Matrimonio Palavrakis* (2001), *Once Upon a Time in West Asphixia* (2002), and *Hysterica Passio* (2003) – is, like *Leda*, a "story of terror of Gothic inspiration" (Cornago 315) that presents stories of perversion, suffering, and death, of monsters and of personal and family guilt, with the aim of the spectator reaching a "cathartic shock": "Theater is a moment of suffering, a shared pain. The relationship with the spectator is one of sensuality insofar as it is a challenge to sensibility, a challenge with regards to human suffering or human allegories" (Liddell, qtd. in Cornago 319). In *Lesiones incompatibles con la vida* (2003), a performance that functions as an epilogue to *Tríptico*, the stress is placed on the importance of the body, sacrificial or ceremonial, as an autofictional tool of social subversion in the theater.

> My body is my protest
> My body renounces fertility
> My body is my protest against society, against injustice, against lynching, against war.

My body is criticism and compromise with the human pain.
I want my body as sterile as my suffering.
My body is my protest.[10]

The body is the place of pain and cruelty, of physical transformation, or, in extreme cases, of suicide and death. Without a doubt, it is theater of life, such as the one imagined by Antonin Artaud. However, here we also find ourselves before a "theater of attractions," as Sergei Eisenstein described it. This is an aggressive theater that submits the spectator to a series of emotional disturbances via the representation of actions onstage – in complete exaggeration of the spectacle. These actions are freely chosen at the same time that they disturb the resources being represented onstage. Referring to Mikhail Bakhtin, it could be said that the theater has become *carnavalized*, insofar as it transgresses hierarchies and confuses the sacred with the profane, the sublime with the ridiculous. In emphasizing or extolling the joys of bodily existence (especially food and sex), these works close in on the liberating idea of subversion pitted against official authority and established monological values.

In *concrete* theater (Lehmann 153) the immediacy of the human body is insisted upon, as in the case of Jan Fabre, whose work demands an intensified perceptibility in the face of elusive meaning or meaning which perpetually begs resolution. Postdramatic theater invents a new body that defies the limits of the real world. Bodies are reduced or expanded, are disguised or exposed, always with the anxious need to stand up against rules and patterns. The actor's body is discovered as both "itinerary" and "living," as both sensation and personal memory.

Pedro Manuel Villora (2009) situates the point of inflexion in the dramaturgy of Angélica Liddell around 2003, when, after finishing the "trilogía de la aflicción" 'trilogy of affliction,' she abandoned theatrical models coming close to ritual and entered into the territory of social themes with the "trilogía de actos de resistencia contra la muerte" 'trilogy of acts of resistance against death.' In 2009, Liddell connects these two stages with the poetic genre when she decides to publish two texts from this period in the poetry collection "Fuente del Abanico" 'Fan fountain.' These texts are *Frankenstein*, which premiered in 1998 in the Sala Cuarta Pared (though it was originally a puppet show), and *La Historia es domadora del sufrimiento: 2006* 'History is suffering's tamer: 2006' – a piece we will return to later. To these works we can add *Los deseos en Amherst* 'Desires in Amherst,' a book of poems written in 2002 and published in 2007 in the collection *Poemas desechables* 'Disposable Poems.' For the moment, it is enough to point out the deliberate generic indefinition of her texts, which, as has been mentioned, move through the poetic and scenic without worrying about strictly fitting into either one. In *Frankenstein*, for example, we find the same obsession with poeticizing reality by deforming it – in this case, through the confrontation between reason and a compulsive, monstrous, and mythical sexuality – as found in *Leda*. The brief poems of *Los deseos en Amherst* mingle the same longing for purity with the confirmation of the body as a deposit for pain and death.

In Liddell we find the explicit poetic will closing in on the word with an "open lyric vocation" (Cornago 62), which is at the same time sustained in her work through the voice and sonority (pleas, prayers, entreaties, etc.), and in the performative dimension of the word-body. In the trilogy of "actos de resistencia contra la muerte" – *Y los peces salieron a combatir contra los hombres, Y como no se pudrió… Blancanieves*, and *El año de Ricardo* – published in 2007 (although the works premiered in 2003, 2005, and 2005, respectively), Liddell insists on considering theater as a space for suffering. This space must necessarily include the spectator, fictionalized in the form of Señor Puta, to whom part of the monologues is directed. Here, reality is more perceptible as a referent: basically, the war and barbarism that lead to the extermination of the human being – whether soldier or immigrant. In *Y los peces salieron a combatir contra los hombres* 'And the fish rushed out to do battle with the men.' fleeing black people on rafts are devoured by fish while well-accommodated tourists contemplate them from their sun loungers on the beach. In *Y como no se pudrió… Blancanieves* 'How Snow White…didn't rot' has children dying each day because of warfare, while people impassively observe their image on the news. And *El año de Ricardo* 'The year of Richard,' a free version of *Richard III*, shows how evil is among us, forms a part of our nature, like an absolutely banal presence that is politically and economically desecrating. The dead Africans accumulate, but we should not worry because as the whore character, dressed in a Spanish flag skirt, says: "los negros están fuera del lenguaje" 'blacks are outside of language' (*Y los peces* 16, 24). The whore is represented here by Angélica, as Snow White, enslaved and converted into a child soldier. And Ricardo, a sick and degenerate person, exacerbates the wickedness of the Shakespearian antihero, legitimated in the first person and now almost ironically converted into a writer dedicated to culture, routine, and the exploitation of war:

> I know now that many have died because of me.
> But I didn't hate those people
> I didn't know them at all.
> I did it for their own good.
> I'm not a murderer.
> It was simply a question of ideas.
> In war no one is to blame,
> All sides are equal. (*Y los peces* 109–10)[11]

We stand before a true *cultural sniping* against the dominant culture founded on the autobiographical game: the personal is political, the masquerade reveals the contingency of social relations.[12] Meditation on the association between the human beings and their desire for self-destruction continues in *Belgrado. Canta lengua el cuerpo glorioso* 'Belgrade: Sing the glorious body, tongue' from 2008, in which the theme of the war (in Yugoslavia) takes on a more traditional form in the protagonism of two journalists, Agnes and Baltasar. They confront a permanently degraded reality and once again discover the evil underlying a sickly society throughout time.[13]

In this second phase of Liddell's career, the poetic impulse is accompanied by a principle of individualization, rooted in the "fierce reaffirmation of the individual, which flows out into the disappearance of the character in favor of the voice of the author, without character and without plotting, in light of the plot of the war, the author presents himself without a plot" (Liddell, *Un minuto* 69). The author's protagonism is an act of resistance in the face of man's disappearance and the failure of humanism that underlines the necessity of the intimate and private in an "author's naked discourse," or "the great confessional *strip-tease*" (71). The ethical intensifies in its reference to man's misery, suffering, and autodestruction, which "does not cease in any of its forms" (68).

In *Boxeo para células y planetas* 'Boxing for cells and planets' from 2006 we see the application of certain notions coming from the postdramatic which are at the same time quite close to performance: the need for a fragmented perception of reality (the narrative monologues are cut by different disconcerting actions), a tendency towards distortion and discursive instability (from the word to either screams or silence), parataxis, intermedial density (with special attention to visual media, which appear in the transparencies of certain *collages*, in the family movie, and in video recordings of the public), de-sacralization, corporality (consider the bites that the artist inflicts on her own arm prior to showing it to the audience), interaction with the spectator, who must come to her aid with medicines during the spectacle. In the figure of Pascal Kahn ("Pascal is the protagonist of our story"), the narrator becomes a witness to what others do or suffer, in an appeal that reaches a planetary dimension thanks to Pascal's hobby of creating collages from newspaper fragments:

> In spite of his attachment to himself, Pascal Kahn continued to investigate his double condition of flesh and bones man and humanity man, attempting to discover his identity through collective horror. He once again turned to taking mortal leaps between immeasurable distances. He reviewed war's physiology again and again, using newspaper clippings. Sometimes Pascal identified with the catastrophes. In these moments the individual and the collective connected with each other.[14]

Making the most of the advantages of his semi-fictional nature (the pact with oneself, for example, but also the freedom to incorporate any topic into the biographical story), the narrator-witness of *Boxeo* sees himself capable of rebelling against the values and practices of the dominant culture, making what is denied or marginalized visible. The autofictional is converted into an act of resistance, of intervention (not without an aspect of revelation and reinvention) in the world, a utopian act to a certain extent, which causes what could or should be, but is not, to be imagined. Thus, the age of the witness is inaugurated with the creation of a space for that which is personal (an autotopography), a selective and expanded map, accounting not only for the central aspects, but for peripheral or missing elements as well. This is also the case in *Perro muerto en tintorería: los fuertes* 'Dead dog at the dry cleaner's: the strong' from 2007, a piece which reflects on the failure of Enlightenment thought and on a Europe (and a stage) lacking a conscience. The character of El Perro, played by Liddell herself, speaks out against the public, in the same way she had against the artist's narcissism or against the creator's paralysis:

> Only by offending those who hire me
> and those who pay to see me
> do I free myself from the feeling of servitude.
> Offending makes me feel less a slave,
> Less stupid than the public and the master.
>
> ...
>
> The true spectacle
> is always in the stalls.
> I expand my stage
> To the world where the entire society acts
> Theatrum mundi.
> Theatrum mundi.
> The stalls
> Are a reproduction of the universal
> paltriness.
> In this way the spectator
> Becomes the Fucking actor of his Fucking actor. (52)[15]

The contemporary stage has restored the body of the actor as a physical and social territory, a space for doubt and subversion: this is my body, this is my history, I have brought it here for you, and we do not need more representations. Radical theater undresses the body and submits to an extenuating action, apparently lacking sense. In *Perro muerto* there are fights, spitting, caressing, eating, masturbating, and raping: "eating, drinking, sleeping, and fornicating, aside from this, everything is vanity" (Liddell, *Belgrado* 55). It is one more manifestation of *liquid* art (Bauman 2007) – constantly changing, without conclusion, an unstoppable sequence of beginnings awaiting the final destruction of the subject. Theater is what comprehends the total decomposition of social forms, of suffering and fear, of hatred and humiliation, of "human waste" robbed of any useful function. And yet, behind the work of Liddell there is an ethical responsibility that encourages a relationship with the Other. This meeting points to a feeling of responsibility that Emmanuel Lévinas allegorizes in the idea of caress (64, 71–2, 78) and that Zygmunt Bauman (being for the other) defines as something infinite and never satisfied from which any social possibility is constructed.

The art of theater is an art of time that posits time in relation to death (personal, cultural, and planetary destruction) in a process of never-ending metamorphosis. Reality strongly intrudes in Liddell's monologues by way of a true story (the meeting and subsequent relationship with Pascal) told from a dark perspective, thanks to a central "I" who imposes a very special view of the world, one critical and reflexive, and at times obsessive. Lehmann points out that often the actor in postdramatic theater plays no "role" whatsoever, but merely offers up his figure for the spectator's contemplation (217). This is indeed the case in this self-showing, with the additional dimension that Liddell is the playwright and director of the show. *Mi relación con la comida* 'My relationship with food' from 2005 was already a monologue in which 'details of disgusting daily life' abound, to be used like a weapon against a "well-intentioned" narrative. The text is presented directly and aggressively as a personal experience, as an authentic and immediate thought that is ultimately aimed at the spectator, who is seated on the bench of the accused.

> The spectators should participate in the human failure, they should be frightened of themselves, of the consequences of their gluttony, of the human possibilities of horror, they should simultaneously juggle the individual search for happiness with a consciousness of humanity's failure. (57–8)[16]

In a tiny text first published on the Internet and later as a book, *La Historia es domadora del sufrimiento: 2006* (2009), which is thematically connected with *Boxeo*, Liddell lays out all these questions in a sort of *captatio benevolentiae*:

> I ask that you be benevolent with me.
> Perhaps you think that speaking about oneself is arrogance.
> But the self-portrait is simply the product of the anguish coming from the absence of a theme.
> I resolve the lack of plot with "I."
> Don't accuse me of narcissism. (52)[17]

Once again the theme is genocide as a condition intrinsic to human nature, seen in this case from a comparative and universal perspective. No art is worthy if it pertains only to one individual case. Beckett's creatures, such as Vladimir, expresses this well when he comments to Estragon, his vagabond companion, "But at this place, at this moment of time, all mankind is us, whether we like it or not. Let us make the most of it, before it is too late! (155).[18] In Liddell's case, the stage presence of the "I" is accompanied by a metanarrative speech, accentuated perhaps because her shows often give the impression of being created at the same moment they are enacted, with the urgency of one who knows that theater can still be a medium of resistance against power and death. Beyond the idea of an exercise in solipsism or showing an individual cycle, Liddell speaks about everyone in this "life narration" – about today's world, dealing with the most immediate present without hesitation or restraint, focusing on the starts and stops of a society in permanent crisis. Hers is a theater of the real that flees from ludic and cheap exhibitionism in order to take part in resistance with eyes wide open before a multiple, heterogeneous, and politically unsatisfying reality.

Notes

1. This is especially true for film and television. Spectacles reach the public in the form of recordings (a video or DVD, for example), which to a certain degree supposes the transformation of its particular state from singularity to multiplicity or plurality – a phenomenon that might qualify as a case of "transcendence" or as a secondary mode of artistic existence.

2. See Rosalind Krauss's "Sculpture in the Expanded Field" and Olivier Lussac's *Happening and Fluxus*.

3. See the oral and performative nature of his "talk-pieces" *Tuning* (1984) or *What It Means to Be Avant-Garde* (1993).

4. See Goldberg's *Laurie Anderson*.

5. Karen Finley, Fiona Templeton, Holly Hughes, and Leonora Champagne are other relevant names – and the list goes on. For several anthologies of feminist *performance* texts, see Champagne (1990), Russel (1997), and Bonney (1999).

6. In commenting on the theater of Artaud and Brecht, Lyotard, in *Des dispositifs pulsionnels*, defines the energetic based on the intention to produce the highest intensity, in excess or in defect, due to the flow of passions and the force of presence, or due to the absence of a power hierarchy.

7. For the origin of the autofiction concept, see Gasparini (12ff.). He explains that in reality the first to use the term was Jerzy Kosinsky in reference to his novel *The Painted Bird* (1965), precisely with the intention of negating the simple autobiographism of a story which tells the life of a Jewish boy in wartime Europe. In recent years, research on the concept has expanded exponentially and is constantly being updated, as can be observed in recent special issues of *Magazine Littéraire* (2007) and *Poétique* (2007).

8. The idea of *energetic theater* comes from Jean-François Lyotard's approach to Brecht and Artaud. Energetic theater – a flow of pulsions based on the force of presence – arises in the attempt to "produce the highest intensity (in excess or by defect) of what is there, without intention" (97).

9. "¿Por qué escribís versos si no podéis comportaros como vuestros versos? ¿Lo habéis intentado? Pues no os molestéis porque sólo conseguiréis una mueca grotesca. ¡Torpes, mezquinos, mediocres, imbéciles! No os acuso de ensuciar porque es condición irremediable de los hombres. Sois incapaces de dejar de entorpecer la pureza. Qué fracaso. Qué asco."

10. "Mi cuerpo es mi protesta./Mi cuerpo renuncia a la fertilidad./Mi cuerpo es mi protesta contra la sociedad, contra la injusticia, contra el linchamiento, contra la guerra./Mi cuerpo es la crítica y el compromiso con el dolor humano./Quiero que mi cuerpo sea estéril como mi sufrimiento./Mi cuerpo es mi protesta."

11. "Ya sé que por mi culpa han muerto muchos./Pero yo no odiaba a esa gente./No los conocía de nada./Lo hice por su bien./No soy un asesino./Era simplemente una cuestión de ideas./En la guerra nadie tiene la culpa,/todos los bandos son iguales."

12. The term "cultural sniping" is taken from Spence's eponymous book.

13. See, for example, the dialogue between Baltasar and Dragan in scene IV (Liddell, *Y los peces* 43–52).

14. "A pesar del apego a sí mismo, Pascal Kahn seguía investigando su doble condición de hombre carne-hueso y hombre-humanidad intentando descubrir su identidad mediante el horror colectivo. Volvía a emprender saltos mortales entre distancias inmensurables. Pasaba una y otra vez de la fisiología a la guerra utilizando recortes de periódico. Algunas veces Pascal se identificaba con la catástrofe. En ese momento lo individual y lo colectivo se asociaban."

15. "Solamente ofendiendo a los que me contratan/y a los que pagan por verme,/me libro de

la sensación de servidumbre./Ofender me hace sentir menos esclavo,/menos necio que el público y el amo./. . ./El verdadero espectáculo/ está siempre en el patio de butacas./Amplío mi escenario/al mundo donde actúa la sociedad entera./Theatrum mundi./Theatrum mundi./ Cada patio de butacas/es una reproducción de la mezquindad/universal./De ese modo el espectador/se convierte en Puto actor de su Puto actor (2007a: 52)."

16. "El espectador debe participar del fracaso de lo humano, debe asustarse de sí mismo, de las consecuencias de su glotonería, de las posibilidades humanas del horror, debe manejar al mismo tiempo la búsqueda individual de la felicidad con la conciencia del fracaso de la humanidad."

17. "Os ruego que seáis benévolos conmigo./ Tal vez penséis que hablar de uno mismo es arrogancia./Pero el autorretrato es simplemente el producto de la angustia/por la ausencia de un tema./Resuelvo con el yo la carencia de argumento./No me acuséis de narcisismo."

18. See Liddell's commentary in "Un minuto dura tres campos de exterminio: la desaparición del espacio y del tiempo" (70–2).

Bibliography

Acconci, Vito. "Notes on my Photographs, 1969–1970." *Photographic Works 1969–1970*. New York: Brooke Alexander, 1988. 5–6.

Aston, Elaine, and Geraldine Harris, eds. *Feminist Futures? Theatre, Performance, Theory*. New York: Palgrave MacMillan, 2007.

Auslander, Philip. *From Acting to Performance: Essays in Modernism and Postmodernism*. London: Routledge, 1997.

Barthes, Roland. *S/Z*. Paris: Seuil, 1970.

Banu, Georges. "Le Narrateur et le *Waki*." *Kantor, l'artiste à la fin du XXe siècle*. París: Actes Sud, 1990. 74–77.

Bauman, Zygmunt. *Postmodern Ethics*. London: Blackwell, 1993.

———. *Tiempos líquidos. Vivir en una época de incertidumbre*. Barcelona: Tusquets, 2007.

Beckett, Samuel. *Waiting for Godot*. London: Faber and Faber. 2006.

Biet, Cristian, and Cristophe Biau. *Qu'est-ce que le théâtre?* Paris: Gallimard, 2006.

Bonney, Jo, ed. *Extreme Exposure. An Anthology of Solo Performance Texts from the Twentieth Century*. New York: Theater Communication Group, 1999.

Champagne, Leonora, ed. *Out from Under: Texts by Women Performance Artists*. New York: Theater Communication Group, 1990.

Cornago, Óscar. *Políticas de la palabra: Esteve Grasset, Carlos Marquerie, Sara Molina, Angélica Liddell*. Madrid: Fundamentos, 2001.

Demastes, William W. *Staging Consciousness: Theater and the Materialization of Mind*. Ann Arbor: The University of Michigan Press, 2001.

Dolan, Jill. *Utopia in Performance: Finding Hope at the Theater*. Ann Arbor: The University of Michigan Press, 2005.

Etchells, Tim. *Certain Fragments: Contemporary Performance and Forced Entertainment*. London: Routledge, 1999.

Gasparini, Philippe. *Est-il je? Roman autobiographique et autofiction*. Paris: Seuil, 2004.

Goldberg, RoseLee. *Laurie Anderson*. New York: Harry N. Abrams, 2000.

Govan, Emma, Helen Nicholson, and Katie Normington. *Making a Performance: Devising*

Histories and Contemporary Practices. London: Routledge, 2007.

Greham, Helena. Performance, Ethics and Spectatorship in a Global Age. London: Palgrave MacMillan, 2009.

Gubern, Román. Del bisonte a la realidad virtual. La escena y el laberinto. Barcelona: Anagrama, 1996.

Heddon, Deirdre. Autobiography and Performance. London: Palgrave MacMillan, 2008.

Heddon, Deirdre, and Jane Milling. Devising Performance. A Critical History. London: Palgrave MacMillan, 2006.

Higgins, Dick. "Synesthesia and Intersenses: Intermedia." UbuWeb. Web. 18 September 2009.
Howell, John. "Acting/Non-acting. Interviews with Scott Burton, Ruth Maleczech, Michael Smith, Elizabeth Lecompte, and Laurie Anderson." Performance Art 2 (1979): 7–18.

Kaye, Nick. Postmodernism and Theatre. London: MacMillan Press, 1994.

Klossowicz, Jan. "Tadeusz Kantor's Journey." The Drama Review 30.3 (1986): 98–113.

Krauss, Rosalind. "La escultura en el campo expandido." La originalidad de la Vanguardia y otros mitos modernos. Madrid: Alianza, 2007. 289–303.

Lehmann, Hans-Thies. Le Théâtre postdramatique. Paris: Actes-Sud, 1999.

Lévinas, Emmanuel. Le Temps et l'autre. Paris: P.U.F., 1991.

Liddell, Angélica [a. Liddell Zoo]. Belgrado. Canta lengua el misterio del cuerpo glorioso. Bilbao: Artezblai, 2008.

———. Boxeo para células y planetas. Archivo virtual de artes escénicas. 2006. Web. 20 September 2009. <http://artesescenicas.uclm.es/archivos_subidos/textos/242/angelicaliddell_boxeocelulas.pdf>.

———. El Tríptico de la Aflicción. Acotaciones, 12 (2004): 67–170.

———. Frankenstein. La Historia es domadora del sufrimiento: 2006. Sigüenza: EugenioCanoEditor, 2009.

———. "La historia es domadora del sufrimiento (I)." Diagonal. 2006a. Web. 20 September 2009. <http://diagonalperiodico.net/article3253.html>.

———. Leda. Madrid: CNNTE, 1995.

———. Los deseos en Amherst. Valencia: Poemas desechables, 2007b.

———. Mi relación con la comida. Madrid: SGAE, 2005.

———. Perro muerto en tintorería: los fuertes. Madrid: Centro Dramático Nacional, 2007a.

———. "Un minuto dura tres campos de exterminio: la desaparición del espacio y del tiempo." Dramaturgias femeninas en la segunda mitad del siglo XX. Espacio y tiempo. Ed. José Romera. Madrid: Visor, 2005a, 67–75.

———. Y los peces salieron a combatir contra los hombres. Y como se pudrió... Blancanieves. El año de Ricardo. Bilbao: Artezblai, 2007.

Lussac, Olivier. Happening and Fluxus. Polyexpressivité et pratique concrète des arts. Paris: L'Harmattan, 2004.

Lyotard, Jean-François. Des dispositifs pulsionnels. Paris: UGE, 1973.

Magazine littéraire 11 (2007).

Meyer, Ursula. Conceptual Art. New York: Dutton, 1972.

Pavis, Patrice. La Mise en scène contemporaine. Origines, tendances, perspectives. Paris: Armand Colin, 2007.

Poétique 149 (2007).

Poggi, Christine. "Following Acconci/Targeting Vision." *Performing the Body/Performing the Text.* Ed. Amelia Jones and Andrew Stephenson. London: Routledge, 1999. 255–72.

Pollock, Della, ed. *Remembering: Oral History Performance.* New York: Palgrave MacMillan, 2005.

Russell, Mark. *Out of Character: Rants, Raves, and Monologues from Today's Top Performance Artists.* London: Bantam Books, 1997.

Sánchez, José A. *Dramaturgias de la imagen.* Cuenca: Universidad Castilla-La Mancha, 1999.

—. *Prácticas de lo real en la escena contemporánea.* Madrid: Visor, 2007.

Sandford, Mariellen R., ed. *Happenings and Other Acts.* London: Routledge, 1995.

Savran, David. *Breaking the Rules: The Wooster Group.* New York: Theatre Communications Group, 1988.

Sayre, Henry M. *The Object of Performance: The American Avant-Garde since 1970.* Chicago: University of Chicago Press, 1992.

Silliman, Ron. "Who Speaks: Ventriloquism and the Self in the Poetry Reading." *Close Listening: Poetry and the Performed Word.* Ed. Charles Bernstein. New York: Oxford U.P, 1998. 360–78.

Spence, Jo. *Cultural Sniping: The Art of Transgression.* London: Routledge, 1995.

Szondi, Peter. *Theory of the Modern Drama: a Critical Edition.* Minneapolis: The University of Minnesota Press, 1987.

The Drama Review 23.1 (1979).

Víllora, Pedro Manuel. "Ayer y hoy de Angélica Liddell." *Frankenstein y La historia es la domadora del sufrimiento. 2006.* Angélica Liddell. Sigüenza: EugenioCanoEditor, 2009. 7–11.

Wilson, Michael. *Storytelling and Theatre: Contemporary Storytellers and their Art.* New York: Palgrave MacMillan, 2006.

Roberto Echavarren's *Atlantic Casino* and *Oír no es ver*: The "Neobarocker" Body in Performance

Irina Garbatzky

This essay explores the intersections among performance, installation art, film, and poetry in Roberto Echavarren's (Uruguay, 1944) film *Atlantic Casino*, inspired by Echavarren's poem of the same title, and in his installation *Oír no es ver*, based on his poem "Pacific Palisades." The topics to be developed include: 1. Writing in exile, in a foreign land and language, and thus developing an extraterritorial poetic voice; 2. Echavarren's use of glam rock as the discourse of the underground scene, which entails his appropriation of elements of the renewed North American avant-garde movement while avoiding any elitist critical artistic position and adapting elements of popular culture to shape new social subjectivities; 3. The creation of a non-central subjectivity and a concept of the body based on a performance merging rock and neo-baroque.

Neobaroque was a Latin American poetry movement started by José Lezama Lima in the mid-twentieth century. In the 1970s, Severo Sarduy identified this movement as a new trend. It was characterized by poetry with a proliferation of significants and an apotheosis of artifice (Sarduy 1385). Features of neobaroque poetry include parody, intertextuality, and eroticism, along with exaggeration and semantic over-elaboration, which ultimately conceal unequivocal meaning. The movement resisted linear, realistic writing, resorting to free association, condensed images, and non-verbal languages (such as visual arts, theater, and music). This type of writing also used a long, narrative verse that exceeded the limits of metaphor. The relevance of neobaroque was not only stylistic: it boosted a line of Latin American thought that identified cultural hybridization with baroque. Osvaldo Lamborghini, Arturo Carrera, Néstor Perlongher (Argentina), Roberto Echavarren, and Marosa Di Giorgio y Eduardo Milán (Uruguay) are some of its representatives. Neobaroque was a key element of Echavarren's work, especially when he published *La planicie mojada* 'The wet plain' in 1981. As noted by Eduardo Milán: "Roberto Echavarren's writing caught the eye of the critics when he published *La planicie mojada* . . . he used a verbal device, at the core of which was meaning . . . referenced aslant, casually implied, in an attempt of intertwining it into a canvas of meanings" (13). In 1990 Echavarren published a compilation of neobaroque poetry entitled *Transplantinos*. In the foreword, Echavarren describes the movement as utterly innovative, yet distant from homogenizing avant-garde notions. Echavarren did not think of neobaroque as an avant-garde communion, but rather as an impure community: as the circulation of individuals and the creation of a plural space that contained "otherness."

Atlantic Casino: Poetry Performance in Film

Between the late sixties and the early nineties, after leaving Montevideo, Roberto Echavarren established himself first in New York and then in London. Exile was his answer to the search for a way of life that was simply not possible in Uruguay back then. By moving away, he mimicked an escape-like motion, a concept that Amir Hamed (1996) created to describe twentieth-century Uruguayan poetry. For Echavarren, this physical relocation was reinforced by the dominant authoritarian constructs of the body at the time.

About Echavarren, Hamed asserts: "Due to the coordinates of the dominant discourse, the body could only be summoned into the rationalization of political fight; faced with an ideological attack, the body draws in, falls back, and any efforts to reappropriate it and eroticize it need to simultaneously revert the poet's relationship with language. Trusting your own body means revising your poetic language entirely" (87). Even though he left Uruguay before the military coup in 1973, Echavarren's trip can be analyzed as part of the "microscopic, molecular exiles" that were not recognized as exile. Néstor Perlongher introduced this concept when referring to the search for subjectivity in the context of dogmatic discourse in Río de la Plata ("El espacio" 274). In an interview in 1985, Perlongher explains there were "sexual exiles" at the time of dictatorship: "being gay in Argentina was unbearable. You were caught the minute you were out in the street. It was not even about having sex, it was because of the way you walked, your long hair, your looks. . . . It was exile indeed, on a microscopic, molecular scale, where people would just decide to leave, alone or in small groups, not realizing their status as exiles" (273–74).[1] Echavarren points out: "I believe I lived in those countries because of the stylistic display associated with new lifestyles related to rock music" ("Explicacíon" 239).[2] He is referring to the turning point that rock represented in terms of creating alternative conditions for conceiving of the body. From Elvis's hips to long-haired heavy metal icons, rockers' image building practices defied the ruling gender model and constituted a milestone in the timeline of androgyny.

Echavarren can be located in the intersection between London and New York in the seventies, when glam rock peaked as the most marginal counter-cultural trend. Clearly opposed to earth-toned hippyism, the "glam fans" made the establishment uneasy with their excessive make-up and artificial look. In spite of their feminine hairdos and tight pants, these musicians – whose story is portrayed in the film *Velvet Goldmine* (Todd Haynes, 1998), which unites Oscar Wilde with David Bowie, Iggy Pop, and Lou Reed – failed to imitate both men and transvestites.[3] The notion of art was inseparable from the body's ability to express itself. Much like dandies, rockers wanted to break down the barrier between the stage and everyday life and thus make art part of life. The development of their unsettling style also questioned the norms of appearance and gestures as dictated by fashion.

The poem *Atlantic Casino* was written in English and later translated into Spanish by Echavarren himself. These relocations or shifts are signed by an idea of extraterritoriality that transpires into genre: in 1989, Echavarren shot a medium-length film also entitled *Atlantic Casino*, in which glam rockers recite the poem. At this point, the question of shifting or translation becomes central to his poetry, not only in the sense of geographic relocation and linguistic translation, but also in the shift between expressive genres. Throughout the following years, questions regarding the poetic language *in* film, theater, essay, artistic performance, or rock would inform Echavarren's work.

Ana Porrúa points out that written poetry is transformed into oral poetry through the recitation itself and within listening traditions, often exceeding the signs and marks of written poetry. Reading out loud may or may not follow the tone suggested by the poem, and could even transform the historical horizon in which it was written.[4] This means that the person who recites a poem, chooses the sound family in which they want to stand. This moment of vocal recreation, with a certain degree of openness, also implies a certain closing of meaning as it condenses, in the voice of the person who is reciting, all the escape lines a poem may contain, especially in the case of the modern constellated poem.[5]

To find a tone that would reproduce but also distort the poem, while avoiding the use of a unique personal voice, must have been the hardest challenge for Echavarren. This explains why *Atlantic Casino* has a plural voice: several rockers repeat the poem by heart and appropriate it by changing the sequence of verses. The decentering of the authorial voice is highlighted by the fact that Echavarren himself is virtually invisible in the film; he only appears in a single, isolated scene. He is paralleled to the rest of the rockers in terms of his appearance, but he sets himself apart by being the only one who is sitting behind a desk, sheltered by sheets of paper and his computer. This is the one time when the written poem is represented as such and pop and neobaroque strategies are used simultaneously: Echavarren reading his own poem *in* the film, *which is* the poem itself, is a tautology, almost a *mise en abyme*. Then again, the person who is reciting is not meant to be identified as Echavarren; he is the icon of a poet reciting a poem. We can go even further and say that he is not actually a poet, but the poet's parodied double, the critic. He reads the following verses:

> A delirium of interpretation kills pop.
> We call it rasping.
> It destroys pop by cocooning it.
> Un delirio de interpretación mata el pop.
> Lo llamamos rallador.
> Destruye el pop al encapucharlo.[6]
> ("Atlantic Casino," 259)

In the film, parody is reinforced by the odd combination of Echavarren's glam look and his foreign, Latino accent. Echavarren explains that, writing in a language other than his mother tongue, he had no desire or need to use the language of "dictionaries"; instead, he wanted to dig deep in the flow of musical slangs. In his own words, "conversations about these topics and music magazines became my lexical sources" ("Debates" 298). He later realized how much the oral traits of the poem would compromise the act of reading it, because they would turn it into a recitation with strained pronunciation: "When I read them out loud I realized . . . I was not the best interpreter for those verses" ("Explicación" 239–40).

The decision to break down the poem by including multiple voices also results in an invitation to the viewer. In the sequence of scenes, there is a series of rupture movements and close ups that either places the audience inside the film diegesis or outside it. At the beginning of one of the first sequences, the conversation between the rockers excludes the viewer from the diegesis; rockers are dancing in the shadows and walking in and out of the building. Shortly after, however, rockers address the viewer directly, looking at the camera that pans the scene or takes still, close-up shots. The viewer becomes an interlocutor, exterior to the scene, but still someone the rockers can look at and who can recognize them in turn.

A last type of character-audience relationship serves our analysis even better, as it involves a dynamic closeness. Steve Fraser, the starring musician in the movie, is putting on his make-up and jewelry, and talking to himself in front of the mirror. The camera is set up so that the viewer can only see the rocker's image reflected in the mirror; thus, even though he is talking to himself, he appears to be staring at the viewer. This triangular setting locates the viewer inside the room, as if the fourth wall had disappeared and he could wander around. The viewer is participating in an almost imperceptible way. Based on the film's spatial opening towards the audience and its experimental use of poetic language in different styles of expression, *Atlantic Casino* can be analyzed within the realm of performance,[7] the "live art" that juxtaposes multiple disciplines in the context of the artistic search for the dematerialization of works of art, action art, and conceptualism.

Echavarren's work with performance modes is connected to the re-thinking of avant-garde cultures in 1960s counterculture. In *Mapping the Postmodern*, Andreas Huyssen highlights the elements of postmodernism that express protest against and criticism of the establishment. Post-modernism (defined as a relational phenomenon in terms of modernism) questioned high modernism's rejection of popular culture. Huyssen locates this moment of rejection in the rise of counterculture during the 1960s. 1960s postmodernism tried to revitalize the heritage of the European avant-garde (Dada, Surrealism and Duchamp), criticized the "institution art" adopted by American modernism, and tried to reach out to popular culture in a way that high modernism could no longer do.[8]

During the seventies and eighties, the outlook changed and the utopia exhausted its potential. Nevertheless, the heritage of counterculture, together with an eclectic and largely affirmative culture, led to the emergence of the protest movements of minority cultures, which Huyssen considers truly innovative and hopeful for the future: "The postmodern harbored the promise of a 'post-white', 'post-male', 'post-humanist', 'post-Puritan' world" (274). This contextual reference – which is in fact part of a deeper debate about the return of the avant-garde[9] – partially explains why Echavarren uses rock as the element that bridges poetry and film, instead of other frequent motives of avant-garde films, such as *Orpheus* by Jean Cocteau or *Salomé* by Werner Schroeter, two directors who greatly influenced Echavarren's work.

Ignacio Prado's work on *Atlantic Casino* (2000) includes a brief overview of the history of experimental video and opposes avant-garde to underground filmmaking. Prado places Echavarren in the second group and states that American avant-garde and rock were not really intertwined. His categorization is meaningful, especially for film:

> the avant-garde academic elite has always considered popular music as a medium for the masses, which was not to be included in their soundtracks. It was the underground film that partially opened to popular music, to share its rhythm and rebellious message. . . There are very few examples of collaboration between important rock musicians and avant-garde artists in the United States. Not even the team of Andy Warhol and Velvet Underground can be considered a good example. (284)

This adds to the conceptualization of tension put forward by Huyssen: tension exists between the pop vernacular and art, and the American avant-garde is suspended between the two. According to Prado, Echavarren chooses underground as a style for his art because it defies the establishment; however, there might have been more than one reason for Echavarren's choice of rock music. In the first place, as stated above, glam represents for Echavarren a space of transgression, allowing a body that is "outside of gender" in terms of sex and identity. In the film, rockers are nomads and outsiders. The cast of the film – with the exception of Fraser and Scott Gray – is not composed of renowned musicians or actors; the rockers "portray themselves," enacting their daily performance with their make-up, clothes, and gestures. These dark, vague bodies are the foundation for the search for "lustful erratic" subjectivities (Echavarren, *Medusario* 14).[10] His rockers are mutants because their forms are "without reason" – their "abjection," in the words of Judith Butler, has such an intense unsettling power that, based on their exclusion, the rockers point to "what can be read" and are the condition to build the masculine-feminine binary opposition.[11]

Styles of subcultures build the foundations for a heavily layered body. The rockers' bodies in the movie represent the density of a neobaroque body – a body with overlapping signs, images, and objects; a body that prioritizes surface over anatomy. In other words: the body of a *neobarocker*.

> A gogo dancer in a silver minidress,
> a twerp, lime-green crimplene budgerigar teeter
> . . . .
> A peeled corpse alive under the strobe
> . . . .
> A hoard of the dead milling around in the neon
> . . . .
> We're rats! We're rats! We're scum!
> We're pigs! We're vile! We're debaucheries!
> We're sluts! Even our managers are pigs!
> Sooner shot than forgotten.
> Un bailarín a gogó en un minivestido plateado,
> un tipejo balanceándose, papagayo estrujado verde lima
> . . . .
> Un cadáver despellejado revive bajo el reflector
> . . . .
> Un cúmulo de muertos chillones y amanerados se arremolina alrededor del neón
> . . . .
> ¡Somos ratas! ¡Somos ratas! ¡Somos mugre!
> ¡Somos cerdos! ¡Somos chusma! ¡Somos degenerados!
> ¡Somos perras! ¡Hasta nuestros managers son cerdos!
> Antes fusilados que olvidados.
> ("Atlantic Casino," 243–47)

This fragment features an accumulation of anatomies (androgyne, human being, corpse). This accumulation pushes baroque motifs (corpses, make-up, mirrors) towards rock, in order to break down the traditional model of the body and help free it from the constraints of its identity.

There is a clear call for disorganized, aggressive bodies. The rocker faces the camera directly with a violence that expands in multiple directions. In one of the scenes, a group of rockers attacks a single rocker and eats him alive. This cannibalistic ritual is reminiscent of communities' foundational ritual violence and becomes central to underline the irony. As Fraser repeats in a close-up, "Would you like someone to gauge out your eyes?" '¿Quieres que alguien te ajuste los ojos?' Adjusting our vision, focusing on what is blurred and distorted, could be deemed derisory in such a community farrago. But it should probably be read differently: someone has to adjust our eyes, to force us to look closely at what has been distorted. Faced with modern culture's foundational masked violence and its destructive attitude towards delicate forms, rockers resort to group violence. Band members leave the stage; they mingle with the jumping, dancing audience. The film highlights the fact that all rock events aim at erasing barriers and attempt to create/produce a ritual scene of collective sharing.

Even if Echavarren appears to agree with Huyssen on the fact that rock and pop as postmodern movements can create modes of resistance to the system, it is worth noting that Echavarren, being a Uruguayan based in the United States, appropriates these countercultural models from a critical point of view. It seems that the excitement of his writing on the subject of alternative styles leaves room for a certain level of criticism, even humor:

> Northerners are trend-setters.
> As they lack a mild climate
> they themselves must become the jungle they lack
>
> Los nórdicos indican nuevas tendencias.
> Como carecen de un clima templado
> Ellos mismos deben volverse la jungla que les falta
> ("Atlantic Casino," 252–53)

The following testimonial will serve the purpose of describing the way the author gathers these "new trends" in performance, poetic films, installation poetry, and even rock underground culture. In an interview about *Atlantic Casino*, Echavarren revealed that he could not think of the traditional poetry reading when trying to picture the recitation of the poem in English. It was then that he decided to use a different medium:

> Once they [the poems Atlantic Casino and Pacific Palisades] were written, I realized that if I went to a poetry reading and recited them with my foreign accent, the poems would not be understood at all. The audience of poetry is nothing like that of a rock concert, let alone the glam style of rock music. The contrast would have been too great. Me reading a poem to a group of very respectable people, with my foreign accent, would not create any effect, it would just be out of place, it would not work. ("Debate" 298)

Echavarren admits and embraces the moment of alienation in which he is "out of place," removed from any territory. He transforms this situation into a method for poetic creation, based in linguistic and geographical displacement, in aesthetical and sexual transgendered-ness, in syntagmatic: *neobarocker* proliferation. This migration was also central to neobaroque poetry, which navigated between baroque-modernist repetition and the hallucinogenic-experimental experiences of the avant-garde.

Oír no es ver: A Poetic Installation

Two texts by representatives of the *neobarroco* were crucial to the redefinition of the notion of 'avant-garde': Néstor Perlongher's "Foreword" to *Caribe Transplantino* and Echavarren's "foreword" to *Medusario*.[12] They both carefully distanced themselves from avant-garde purism and rejected its dogmatic nature. Perlongher writes:

> Neobaroque seems to be a result – one could figure – of the intersection between the flux of baroque . . . , and the outburst of surrealism. We should eventually trace back . . . the spreading of surrealism in its Latin-American version, how these wild lands helped radicalize the derealization of official styles – realism and its derivations, such as "social poetry" . . . Neobaroque poetries, as Roberto Echavarren points out, somehow borrow aspects from the avant-garde, especially its search for experimentation, but cannot be considered quite avant-garde. They lack the avant-garde's sense of conscious homogenization of styles and suppression of syntax. (25–26)

Perlongher also connected surrealism's "heritage of derealization" to the lack of "a homogeneous literary floor" (27) and the nomadism of neobaroque writers: "Sarduy was in Paris, Roberto Echavarren and José Kozer in New York, Eduardo Milán in Mexico" (29). In conflict with "the aspirations of a profound realism," new poetry would end up "paddling in muddy river waters" (30). This muddy "paddling" entailed that the inscription of language on the materiality of the body was a defining element of the connection between life and art.[13] The representatives of the neobaroque sought to open up a space that permitted locating the body in everyday ethics and singularity.

Therefore, it comes as no surprise that Echavarren created a work in which rock's notion of the body intersected with that of the baroque: the installation *Oír no es ver*. As he puts it:

> In Mexico (in the former convent of Santa Teresa) I created, together with an artist (Saúl Villa), an installation that intended to show, in a visual language, the equivalence between rock and "baroque". The "baroque" environment of the building contaminated the interpretation. (Vianna Baptista 313)

The fusion between rock and neobaroque was put forward as a style that produced a model of the Body constructed without any ties to convention, in which the so-called superfluous became essential.[14] The exhibition juxtaposed Villa's objects, a series of mannequins in rocker outfits, with other elements: an ax cleaving an animal-print sports shoe, a picture of Jim Morrison covered in gel. This series contrasted a set of hangers, leather, studs and lamé with mannequins and swords.

In *Oír no es ver*, the elements of Echavarren's poem were distributed in space, maintaining the image of the modern constellated poem and playing with fragmentary articulations. The installation was presented in the form of long strips of paper with fragments of the poem, combined with Villa's objects. It was set up in two rooms; in one of them, the film *Atlantic Casino* was screened. During the exhibition, both artists also presented the book *Oír no es ver/To hear is not to see*, which provided a summary of their collaborative work.

The exhibition was located not on Breton's dissection table but in the convent of Santa Teresa la Antigua, a building that had once been home to Sor Juana Inés de la Cruz. The choice of location for the exhibition is significant, as it brings together multiple elements. The convent of Santa Teresa la Antigua was reopened as a cultural center for contemporary art and re-named X-Teresa Arte Alternativo in 1993. Created by a group of contemporary artists, the project started with public funding.[15] In 1994, the center was refurbished by architect Luis Vicente Flores, who kept the original architecture but placed laminated corridors and stairs made of iron and glass on top of them. The architectural style and the artistic projects the center hosted – especially the ones related to performance and sound art – were similar to those of other cultural centers in the 1990s: spaces that pertain to the end-of-art discourse, as it was originally conceived in the fifteenth century. In *After the End of Art* (1999), Arthur Danto points out a change in the role of the museum for contemporary art. He argues that the museum is no longer an institution that displays aesthetic works, but becomes a place that attempts to reach an audience that is claiming "museums of their own":

> When art changes, the museum may fall away as the fundamental aesthetic institution, and extramuseal exhibitions . . . , in which art and life are far more closely intertwined than the conventions of the museum allows, may become the norm. (213)

The main feature of such projects was their commitment to the realization of experimental projects on the institutional, ideological and architectural level. This was an institutionalization and entering of avant-garde practices into the legitimated and legitimating spaces of high culture – an entering that, in terms of Peter Bürger's *Theory of Avant-garde* (1974), takes place as part of a contradiction, as it signals the submission of the renewing trends in art to the capitalistic production model. We can see, then, how each of the variables that can be used to describe *Oír no es ver* – the opposing pairs of rupture art/autonomous art, auric tradition/street art, and in general terms the tradition/postmodernity pair – were agglutinated in the installation, turning it into an indivisible, ambivalent, androgynous work.

From the architectural point of view, such a condensation of rock and baroque was also achieved in the integration of the Latin American baroque tradition and the refigurations of the 1970s avant-garde, such as the bodies and images of glam. The X Teresa itself, as a historical building and art center, pivoted between the urban space and the museum and in doing so inscribed the exhibition in a certain duplicity: a penetration of the public sphere and an affiliation with the most exquisite scholarly heritage of Latin America.[16]

In this regard, we could say that the installation-performance *Oír no es ver* also proposed a space for an interdisciplinary and transitional crossing from Academia – as a silent, hierarchical, educated option – to relational aesthetics. Nicolas Bourriaud argues that the dynamic notion of art in the 1990s conceived the *oeuvre* as a process and especially as a space of circulation. The installation was the result of a post-production model, achieved through montage and the use of the entire history of Occidental art. In this sense, the instances of performance and exhibition are privileged, as they both intend to reunite the audience in a shared experience.

The utopian notion of community developed in Echavarren's poetry can be traced back to the avant-gardes. This is apparent in "Veo a través de ti" 'I see through you,' a poem included in *Oír no es ver*. It functions as "deferred action" in Hal Foster's sense. According to Foster, the signification of avant-garde events is analogous to Freud's definition of "trauma": one event is only registered through another event that recodes it. Thus, by way of a delicate alternation of anticipation and reconstruction, neo-avant-gardes acquire a status equivalent to that of historical avant-gardes. Moreover, they also become an essential part of the earlier projects by validating their interpretation and depth in the historical present.

Just like avant-garde movements, Echavarren aims for community. However, the community he envisions does not subscribe to a manifesto that crushes any form of divergence; quite the opposite is the case. In the poem, the grammatical mobility achieved by shifting the enunciation subjects characterizes Echavarren's invocation of a potential community. By shifting the subject focus, Echavarren moves from the first observed object (a dancer), to a *you*, followed by an *us*, and lastly an *I*, which finally turns into music (62). This is a long poem that shifts the subjects of enunciation. From the third to the second person: "mírate bien/¿por qué me miras?" (26) 'take a good look at you/why are you looking at me?,' then "Escalamos un muro", "Éramos íntimos", "no dijimos nada" (30-33) 'We climbed a wall, We were intimate, we said nothing' and then, "El amor verá a través de mí" (48) 'Love will see through me.' In the last verse of the poem, the first person turns into sound: "Me volví una condensación, un sonido único ininterrumpido por el silencio/y sin embargo, inmerso en él" (62) 'I became a condensation, a single sound uninterrupted by silence/and still, immersed in it.'

Echavarren appropriates some baroque strategies for achieving artificiality and multiplication – the blurring of the subject of lyrical enunciation, multiple variations between "I" and "you," barely seeing, vision filtered through mirrors, fragmentary vision, focus on self-exposed individuals – in order to reinforce the notion of a broader identity. Tamara Kamenszain calls the result "Echavarren's transvestite view":

> All yous . . . are turned on their backs. We could say they are not that invisible, they rather pretend they are, . . . they present the backside of their identity. And it is when they are turned on their backs when we can actually get to know them. If saying "facing" is associated with adjacency, and thus means "from the outside" – an object facing a subject in exteriority . . . – saying "from behind" can be associated with . . . "from within." ("Veo travesty" 118)

The motion described above, this entering into the other and listening to what the other has to say, can be useful to understand the type of subjectivity performed in the poem. Because if, as Kamenszain says, "poetry is pushing language into the zone of the other" ("Sólo"), this appropriation when enunciated in a first person plural calls for a community that is not homogeneous but rather inclusive of the otherness expressed through stylistic differences (in Spanish, the third person plural "nos-otros" includes the words "us" and "others").

The Rocker as a Model of the Performer

Echavarren's model of the performer is not the artist or the poet, but the rocker. He chooses music because it immediately performs different lifestyles. For him, rock becomes a rite of passage: "Rock is the meeting point for a bodily experience, for sexual politics, body politics, drug experimentation, a historical body, a bodily enclave, a dressing style, a hair style, an androgynous look, in clear opposition to the male and female icons of the 50s, still in fashion" (Rivero 322).

In *Veo a través de ti* the main character, a dancer, slips obscurely through the poem. In *Pacific Palisades* the body becomes a character and takes on an explicit role. Originally written in English, the entire poem is a somewhat ironic description of the rocker body. Towards the end of the poem, using italics, Echavarren theatricalizes the body by giving it a voice:

> *We've been around for a long time dressing up*
> *like we were musicians and hanging out at the bars*
> *and people assumed we were posers.*
> . . .
> *We are long hair, loud riffs,*
> *Cool clothes and lots of attitude.*
> *You know what happens when you take*
> *five guys with long hair? You put too much make-up on them*
> *and they wind up looking like chicks.*

> If these guys look better than your girlfriend,
> that's gonna piss you off.
> We are not trying to be chicks, or even act like them.
> We are just guys who enjoy wearing make-up
> and platinum boots held together by duct tape
> (Oír no es ver 101)

The use of italics allows the lyrical subject to reinforce the largely fictitious nature of any subjectivity experience. Echavarren states: "Rather than acknowledging a first person, lyrical or existential, I want to introduce an experience" (Vianna Baptista 316).

Rockers adopt a fictitious subjectivity that characterizes each performer (or: all performers), who either invents a character or stylizes his life which is then displayed on stage. The rocker character is therefore the ideal model of the performer:

> I thought Jim Morrison was the most appropriate rock performer character of the sixties, as he summarizes the motifs, experiences and conflicts that inaugurate our times. He represents the emergence of a new appearance for men and women in rock style, changes in their relationship, facing drugs, acknowledging the validity of experiences of minorities: women, black, Indians, homosexuals. It's not about confirming races or identities, but confirming qualities of experience or existences. (316)

The author identifies the birth of rock as a transgressive and overwhelming performance that took place between 1957 and 1964. The emergence of happenings, art performance, and Living Theater was part of the same movement. The strong link between art and rock performance is important here:

> We should take into account that people like Alice Cooper, Frank Zappa, The Doors and many other bands put on a show on stage. This theatrical gesture – be it magical, erotic or circus-like fireworks in its most banal versions is not just a representation. It is a mode that has realized the existence of a podium; the mode is not reduced to the stage, as it extends to the entire room. Band members come offstage and mingle with the audience or vice versa. They tend to break the line between stage and audience, . . . The rock show is not "bounded": because it is not strictly a show, but a continuous becoming in any vital space. (Arte Andrógino 40–41)

Just like happenings, rock "breaks away from the convention of the stage" (42). As in Artaudian theater, rock does not aim at the experience equivalent of a concert or a theater play, but at "a different experience that breaks away from the conventions of representation" (42). In all these situations, the audience is not treated with consideration but thrown into a shared group experience. Thus, for Echavarren, performance means a privileged moment that de-essentializes the establishment.

Oír no es ver as a performance/installation was not just about a rock-baroque pastiche. It was the result of a passage: Latin American baroque becoming rock. The installation marked the moment of transition in which Echavarren consciously resorted to neobaroque body strategies to devise an ephemeral figure of desire through tattoos, clothes, and accessories. This *neobarocker* model pushed written poetry into new realms, allowing Echavarren to create and use a device for experiencing subjectivity-in-performance, that is to say, an ever changing subject associated to an experience considered exterior to ordinary life.

Conclusion

Echavarren's positioning as poet and performer puts forward the extraterritorial situation of genre. This explains his shifting between languages and expressive styles, and adds new meaning to the use of neobaroque as a type of poetry that moves towards the disruption of form and towards escape. *Atlantic Casino* and *Pacific Palisades* represent a search for new subjectivities within poetic performance in Rio de la Plata.

The acceptance of performance as an artistic genre can be closely linked to a series of emerging postmodern movements, especially to the emergence of minorities and subcultures, and their claim for social legitimation. These movements draw on the re-emergence of avant-garde movements that had been taking place since the late 1960s and that advocated a different, countercultural way of artistic production, circulation, reception, and recording. Avoiding any dogmatic positioning, Echavarren – poet, critic, and performer – presents himself as a nomad. Through nomadism and by bringing together the adventures of neobaroque and rock in a unique ethos, he seeks to create a community that allows singular lifestyles and a non-hegemonic body.

Notes

1. According to Hamed, the "oddness" of Uruguayan writers lies in their inability to identify with their territory, which was uncertain, standing in forming a unique continuity with heteroclitic languages such as tango and *gauchesca*, and even French-Uruguayan poetry; a territory that was historically disputed by Brazilians and Argentines until 1830. This homeland uncertainty forced them to look for home in no place other than language itself. Hamed elaborates on Eduardo Milán's hypothesis that Uruguayan writers either seek exile in another country or within themselves, in their seclusion: "To its writers, Montevideo seems to work, not as a container, but as a barrier, as a margin or line that exiles them. And this sense of exile starts in the language in which writers recognize themselves . . . The escape is thus closely related to language, and this is just when Montevideo represents as a barrier for exclusion rather than a home" (17).

2. All quotes from interviews with Echavarren are taken from Adrián Cangi's *Performance. Género y transgénero*.

3. "Rockers are creative but not in a secondary order, merely camp or kitsch, as the two great icons of homosexuality; they are creative in an 'authentic' way: allowing for the singular, the particular – there is no such thing as identical mutants" (Echavarren, *Arte* 79).

4. Porrúa argues that Juan Gelman's recitation of "Yo persigo una forma" and "Era un aire suave" takes the work of Rubén Darío as a model. In both readings, Gelman creates a "narrative scene" that smoothes out the multiple accents.

5. Stephane Mallarmé (1897) condensed the idea of the modern poem, born together with free verse and poetry prose, in "Un coup de dés" (a throw of dice), based on the discontinuity of a poem through its visual dispersal on the page, just like sheet music, a text to be played in order to reproduce an idea.

6. These verses belong to *Atlantic Casino*; both versions are Echavarren's. The rest of the poems are cited in their original language: *Pacific Palisades* in English and *Veo a través de ti* in Spanish (with my translations).

7. In the words of Patrice Pavis performance art "brings together visual arts, theatre, dance, music, video, poetry and film, with no preconceived ideas. It takes place, not in theatres, but in museums or art galleries. . . . The accent is on the ephemeral and unfinished nature of the production rather than a complete work of art. Rather than the actor playing a role, the performer is in turn a narrator, a painter and a dancer and, because of the emphasis on the physical presence, a stage autobiographer who has a direct relationship with the objects and situation of enunciation" (333).

8. "In the form of happenings, pop vernacular, psychedelic art, acid rock, alternative and street theater, the postmodernism of the 1960s was groping to recapture the adversary ethos which had nourished modern art in the earlier stages, but which it seemed no longer able to sustain. Of course, the 'success' of the pop avant-garde, which itself had sprung full-blown from advertising in the first place, immediately made it profitable and thus sucked it into a more highly developed culture industry than the earlier European avant-garde ever had to contend with. But despite such cooption through commodification, the pop avant-garde retained a certain cutting edge in proximity to the 1960s culture of confrontation" (Huyssen 332–33).

9. Some of the most relevant texts on the avant-garde/neo-avant-garde debate, in addition to Huyssen's, are Bürger's *Teoría de la Vanguardia* (1987) and Foster's *El retorno de lo real* (2001). Ana Longoni struggles with the relevance of Bürger's approach to the Latin American avant-gardes in "La teoría de la vanguardia como corset."

10. In the foreword to *Medusario. Muestra de poesía latinoamericana*, Echavarren mentions how the interest in this interpretation of baroque is based (among other things) in the fact that "Our time is a turn of the screw concerning the complementary ideals of the nineteenth

century: illusory subjectivism and authoritarian utopianism. Information is the result of a conflict of powers. Individuals are divided not only by income or by class origins. They are also divided by their behavior and appearance. The regime of truth becomes fluid . . . . Any ideology is considered a fiction . . . . The interest in contemporary baroque in the present situation has to do with allowing for the singular, the particular, the lustful erratic" (14).

11. According to Judith Butler's *Cuerpos que importan* (2002), all bodies, in order to be constituted in culture, "perform" gender as they repeat behaviors, movements, gestures, and ways that are a repertoire of citations. Each body cites elements of this repertoire, always partially, renewing the heterosexual norm. But in this repetition, what matters is creativity. Butler mentions how "queer studies" reappropriated a derogatory term and transformed its meaning. Echavarren's rockers also "cite" a repertoire of gestures not as a way of mimicking the norm, but as a way to cite the unique way of constituting their subjectivities.

12. *Caribe transplantino* is the title of the neobaroque poetry anthology compiled by Perlongher in Brazil. Its foreword was later published in Echavarren, Kozer and Sefamí's *Medusario. Muestra de poesía latinoamericana*. The quotations are from this last edition.

13. It also meant lowering the Spanish Golden Century baroque, which had been resumed by Lezama Lima and linked to the classical cultural tradition of the Western world. Rio de la Plata's neobaroque put this heritage through the "mud" of politics and marginality. With Sarduy (1974) as a starting point, this new baroque was critical of the system: "The baroque space is that of superabundance and waste" (1250). In the 1980s, Perlongher's notion of "neobarroso" defined the scope of this modulation – in his particular case through Trotskyism and homosexual activism in a protest movement called Frente de la Liberación Homosexual.

14. In his writing, Sarduy explores how transvestism, tattoos, and jewelry – in other words, "what is written on the body" as simultaneously variable and immanent features – define the individual. "Just like Brecht's *Galileo*'s Pope starts taking hold of his authority and sense of truth as he gets dressed, the ritual of transvestism returns Mito to himself, to recovering his self-image . . . The superfluous becomes essential, what is added to the body become its sign" (Sarduy 1144).

15. As of 1998, it was renamed "X-Teresa Arte Actual." The history of the building can be found in the archive of the center's website. "In 1992, the civil association Ex Teresa Arte Alternativo, chaired by Eloy Tarcisio with the participation of Marcos Kurticz, Helen Escobedo, Felipe Ehrenberg, Maris Bustamante, and Vicente Rojo Gama, presented a project to Mexico's National Council for Culture and Arts, requiring that the building be released to be used in connection to non-objectual conceptual art. The requirement was fulfilled in 1993." See http://www.bellasartes.gob.mx/INBA/FmgShowFileByName?who=principal.MUSEOS_Y_%3Cbr%3EGALERIAS.Recintos.Ex_Teresa_Arte_Actual.Edificio.&fileName=extaa.pdf.

16. Both lines could be used to describe the artists' individual work: Echavarren's searches within neobaroque and Villa's work on urban intervention and mass communication. Villa himself belongs to a generation of Mexican visual artists that broke free from pre-1968 art and produced art in the 1980s. Villa's affiliation with the Mexican artistic scene in the 80s was taken from Debroise's catalog of the exhibition *La era de la discrepancia*. One of its articles explains the corpus selection and the line drawn in the late 1960s: "The student movement and the massacre of the 2nd October in Tlatelolco meant a change in the dynamics of art. The cultural crisis that surrounded the student movement was the turning point for the creation of artistic groups, the only way of surviving in those times of intolerance, repression or plain indifference, a thought that prevailed until the mid 80s" (Debroise 21). The 80s, on the other hand, were "the moment of public display of a variety of discourses on identity, spanning gay and feminine aesthetics, as well as the post-colonial claim for an American cultural constellation. The 80s we are interested in, are the ones that defy the notions of normal and redefine "political", separating it from the

notions of proletarian, partisan, unionized left movements, which was still present in the minds of groups in the late 70s" (22). In this selection, Villa's work is included, especially in the period ranging from the late 80s to the early 90s, as part of the "artists without trajectory" "certain new 'rebels' that called for Zapatism from their worldwide reach via the internet . . . or an acceptance of X generation aesthetics and assimilated gore, a pansexuality marked by all kinds of divergence (Saúl Villa, Rodrigo Aldana) and the deletion of limits between high culture and the rest . . ." (368). Additionally, Villa worked on visual campaigns about advertising in the public space together with Lorena Wolffer (see Barbosa Sánchez).

Bibliography

Barbosa Sánchez, Alma Patricia. "La perspectiva artística de la publicidad." *Pensar la publicidad* 1.1 (2007), 199–218.

Bourriaud, Nicolas. *Estética relacional*. Buenos Aires: Adriana Hidalgo, 2006.

Bürger, Peter. *Teoría de la Vanguardia*. Barcelona: Península, 1987.

Butler, Judith. *Cuerpos que importan. Sobre los límites materiales y discursivos del sexo*. Buenos Aires: Paidós, 2002.

Cangi, Adrián, ed. *Performance. Género y transgénero*. Buenos Aires: Eudeba, 2000.

Danto, Arthur C. *Después del fin del arte. El arte contemporáneo y el linde de la historia*. Paidós: Buenos Aires, 1999.

Debroise, Oliver. *La era de la discrepancia. Arte y cultura visual en México 1968–1997*. México: Dirección General de Publicaciones y Fomento General de la UNAM, 2007.

Echavarren, Roberto. *Arte andrógino. Estilo versus moda en un siglo corto*. Buenos Aires: Colihue, 1998.

———. "*Atlantic Casino*." Cangi 242–59.

———. "Debate sobre *Atlantic Casino*." Cangi 295–307.

———. "Explicación falsa de mis versos." Cangi 239–40.

Echavarren, Roberto, dir. *Atlantic Casino*. 16 mm, 40 minutes, color. New York, 1998.

Echavarren, Roberto, José Kozer, and Jacobo Sefamí. *Medusario. Muestra de poesía latinoamericana*, México: Fondo de Cultura Económica, 1996.

Echavarren, Roberto, and Saúl Villa. *Oír no es ver/ To hear is not to see*. México: X-Teresa, 1994.

Foster, Hal. *El retorno de lo real. La vanguardia a finales del siglo*. Madrid: Akal, 2001.

Hamed, Amir. *Orientales. Uruguay a través de su poesía. Siglo XX*. Montevideo: Grafitti, 1996.

Huyssen, Andreas. *Después de la gran división. Modernismo, cultura de masas, posmodernismo*. Buenos Aires: Adriana Hidalgo, 2002.

Kamenszain, Tamara. "Sólo hay poesía de amor. Interview with Silvio Mattoni." *La voz del interior*, July 2003.

———. "Veo travesti." Cangi 117–21.

Longoni, Ana. "La teoría de la vanguardia como corset." *Pensamiento de los confines* 18 (2006): 61–68.

Milán, Eduardo. "Roberto Echavarren: posiciones." *Aura amara*. Roberto Echavarren. México: Cuadernos de la Orquesta 9, 1988.

Pavis, Patrice. *Diccionario de teatro. Dramaturgia, estética, semiología*. Buenos Aires: Paidós, 2008.

Perlongher, Néstor. *Caribe transplantino. Poesía neobarroca cubana y rioplatense.* San Pablo: Iluminuras, 1991.

———. "El espacio de la orgía." Interview with Néstor Perlongher by Osvaldo Baigorria in *Papeles insumisos.* Buenos Aires: Santiago Arcos, 2004.

———. "Foreword." *Medusario: Muestra de poesía latinoamericana.* Ed. Roberto Echavarren, José Kozer, and Jacobo Sefamí. México: Fondo de Cultura Económica, 1996.

Porrúa, Ana "La puesta en voz en la poesía." *Punto de vista* 86 (November 2006).

Prado, Ignacio. "Música de rock, poesía y cine experimental." Cangi 281–90.

Rivero, Federico. "Una Guerra de estilos (Desde abajo hacia arriba)." Cangi 319–26.

Sarduy, Severo. *Obras completas* Vol. II. Madrid: Fondo de Cultura Económica, 1999.

Velvet Goldmine. Dir. Todd Haynes. Channel 4 Films, 1998.

Vianna Baptista, Josely. "Poesía reciente en el hemisferio (Pieles en la superficie iridiscente)." Cangi 311–17.

My Life and Performances

Roberto Echavarren

I started doing performances with the Uruguayan poet Marosa di Giorgio in the eighties. I remember one at the theater of the Alliance Française of Montevideo, with music by the Uruguayan composer Renée Pietrafesa, and a group of drummers playing candombe. Marosa and I read from each other's work, but at times we held a dialogue based on the poems. We projected slides of the Uruguayan coast I had taken as a teenager. We moved a lot, going up and down the stage, and through the alleys, and mixing with the public as we recited. This event was called "Pecarí labiado: una ópera popular," and it was truly popular, since a lot of people came, thinking perhaps that we would present a Maoist show. Another event with Marosa was called "Sur." Marino Rivero played bandoneón, and he played the tango with the same title, which Marosa liked a lot. Another performance ("Copos de oro") took place at the Goethe Institute; we were accompanied by a flutist. Another took place at the Ministry of Culture, with Marosa and Eduardo Espina. And still another, at the restaurant Lobizón, among the smell of fried potatoes. These shows happened during my holidays from New York University, which I spent in Montevideo. In those years, Marosa also did a few presentations of her own.

I spent three years in London and seventeen in New York. In London I participated in events organized by the Gay Liberation Front in the early seventies. They were for the most part big balls at the town halls, plus some street demonstrations. The balls were very creative, with costumes elaborated for the occasion, and various types of sketches. Perhaps one could also call performances the sometimes violent attacks on us by straight thugs at the entrance of the town halls.

Having lived in English speaking environments for some time, I wanted to generate versions of my poems in this language. A couple of translators offered their services, but I was not happy with the results. On the other hand, it seemed to me redundant and painful to translate the poems myself. I turned to another idea: to write directly in English, but in a certain way. As a foreigner, my speech was flat and simple. It occurred to me that it was not worthwhile to add my sober entreaties to the rich expression of native speakers. I therefore became – like Conrad, like Nabokov – a dutiful collector of idiomatic terms and expressions, to a degree that a native speaker would hardly become. My focus was precise. I was not interested in using words taken from a dictionary, or to employ every conceivable idiom. The reason I was in London, and later in New York, was to witness and, if possible, to take part in the stylistic developments linked with rock music. Conversations on this subject, and the music magazines, lent me lexical material. While American publications were keen on their pictures rather than the texts, the British reviews of records and gigs were full of witty manifestations. Despite the fact that I lived in the U.S.A., I was nourished by British printed material. I gathered those bits and pieces in order to elaborate my poetic narratives. They came together as a prophecy of the present, the traces of a new sensibility. The result was a series of longer poems. On reading them aloud in public, I realized that the audiences did not connect with them; they did not understand the stylistic attitudes alluded to by the poetry. With my foreign accent I was not the best interpreter of those verses. I thought that my most satisfactory piece was a longer poem called "Atlantic Casino." I decided to make a film with the same title, in which the image would be in accordance with the words. The actors in the film were rock musicians in full glam; those were the stylistic directives of the time (1988). The image interacted with the words. The accent of the musicians sounded streetwise, whereas the verses had a Shakespearean extravagance, not because the language was Shakespeare's, but because it shared that "Italian" exaggeration Borges saw in the Bard, which is but the concentrated wit of England. Later on I had occasion to concentrate on his language, as I translated *Troilus and Cressida* for a publisher in Buenos Aires.

After "Atlantic Casino," I wrote "Pacific Palisades." It is an even longer poem, and also a more baroque one. This time, instead of making a film, it occurred to me to use the piece for a plastic installation. I was helped by the Mexican painter Saúl Villa, and – with the support of a grant from the Fondo de las Artes of Mexico – the show was presented at the Convent of Santa Teresa, converted into an art gallery close to the Zócalo of the Mexican capital (1994). We published a book in connection with the show, *Oír no es ver/To Hear is not to See*, which includes photos of some of the objects of the installation plus the full text of "Pacific Palisades."

From the year 2000 onwards I lived in the Río de la Plata (Uruguay/Argentina), and became part of a group of poets and painters called Pira, around the Estación Alógena, a center for readings, performances, and courses in Buenos Aires. With Pira we organized several performances in different spaces: at the MALBA museum, at the Centro Borges, at the Centro de España in Montevideo, and so on, through the years, until the present. These performances, although structured around a loose script, have been largely improvisational. Besides the poetic texts, they turned increasingly into a musical jamming of electric and acoustic instruments, including dance and devices such as the "Dream Machine" (a turning cylinder illuminated from the inside, which, on rotating, brings a state of hypnotic trance on the viewers). The intent of these performances was, and is, to induce the audience's participation, either by playing musical instruments left at their disposal, or by entering the dance, so as to fuse the bystanders into a physical state of excitement and receptivity to the energies released by the event itself.

In a performance which took place at the theater of the MALBA museum in Buenos Aires in 2003, three poets intervened (Gabriela Bejerman, Nakh Ab Ra, and I) and also three boys disguised as "androgynes" with made up faces and tulle skirts. The "androgynes" interrupted our readings, participated in them by reciting or repeating some verses, ran on stage taking us hostage, and went into the public for different kinds of actions. We did another performance at the same museum in 2008. The participants were Gabriela Bejerman, Romina Freschi, Nakh Ab Ra, and I. This time we went through the whole building. We started in the lobby, reciting our texts under a wide red cloth. Afterwards we went up and down the mechanical stairs, with the public following suit. They followed us through two big rooms, where we traced our steps with playing cards, taking different positions, saying poems in turn as each one got to specific points in space. We ended our tour at the museum terrace, where we painted our faces and bodies, preparing a final celebration in which the public took part.

In a recent performance at the Estación Alógena, the public entered the room blindfolded. They were led by the participants and sat on the floor around the "dream machine." A group of improvisers produced a musical curtain that helped them relax. We later uncovered their eyes and the "dream machine" perfected the integration of the visitors. Glasses with salvia divinorum were passed around. In a short time the public started to dance to anything we played, no matter whether it was dance music or not. The musical atmosphere brought an incredible sense of liberation and free play. The guitars were processed with distortion, flanger, delay, and intervened physically with Chinese sticks placed through the strings to generate an unpredictable sound. The instruments became musical in a new way, without guarantees, transformed in a new venue for sounding out and exploring, a buzzing timbre generating virtual and ephemeral "chords." This "performance music" becomes critical in a way. It is not organized; it is not subject to tonic scales, harmonic sequences, or measured rhythms. It is not the expression of subjective feelings. It consists of synthetic micro-sounds at the service of an intensity that may be melodic at times, but as a whole becomes a very open musical landscape. Nevertheless, themes and leitmotivs emerged from that chiaroscuro field. There were not measured rhythms, but chaotic ones; not a homogenous plane, but a passage through heterogeneous levels. There were voices that took the microphone in order to sing, recite, babble, or shout. The ritornello was the performance as a whole, as a modular unity never equal to itself. There was a second sea of sound: the acoustic unplugged instruments. When the electrical instruments were muffled from the console table, one could hear the clinking of metal, glass, leather, wood, flutes, tambourines, and maracas. We were then aware of all the levels of maritime sustenance we were promoting. A good part of the public was also improvising. Each one chose an instrument. I took the microphone and started to recite some sort of psalmody. After which a slow musical crescendo started, involving some kind of rite. People went after it and progressed on its horseback, as it were, in order to appropriate and digest it. This psalmody culminated in a sort of general chant.

I have the impression that in any successful improvisation of space-rock-candombe a will for the unconscious expresses itself. Sometimes it takes off like a disastrous comet, and at other times with a gust of triumph, and new individuations come out of the unformed soup. It can be exhausting, and one feels rather like fusing into the whole instead of coming out with individuality. These are vital experiences, in order to become more attentive, or connected, in a loose way, to what changes inside and outside.

These performances are related to other intellectual pursuits of the Estación Alógena, such as two recent publications: a) *Nosotros, los brujos. Apuntes de arte, poesía y brujería*, edited by Juan Salzano (Buenos Aires, Santiago Arcos, 2008), to which I contributed with "Discusión del eros en *Paradiso* de José Lezama Lima"; b) *Deleuze y la brujería*, by Matt Lee and Mark Fisher, translated, edited and introduced by Juan Salzano (Buenos Aires, Las Cuarenta, 2009). From persecutions, the outcome of the codified interests of organized religions and the mechanisms of church control, to the accusations of superstition connected to the disenchantment of nature initiated by modern science, in particular in its rationalistic and instrumental version, sorcery, and everything related to its intermedial impulse (alchemy, magic, shamanism, and so on), has suffered various simplifications. If there was a philosopher akin to sorcery, it was Gilles Deleuze, since he subscribed to a vision of nature different from mechanicism, causalism, or the more traditional organicist finalism. Matt Lee and Mark Fisher have been the first to value and explore this aspect of Deleuze's work, and also Nakh Ab Ra, a poet and writer, founder of the Estación Alógena, who has explored the less codified sources of esoterism.

III. Locations of Performance

"Set in Stone": Lemn Sissay's and SuAndi's Landmark Poetics

Deirdre Osborne

The spoken word is always an event, a movement in time, completely lacking in the thing-like repose of the written or printed word.

(Ong 74)

On September 4th, 2008, amid a sea of pinstripe-suited white (predominantly male) City workers, Lemn Sissay, one of Britain's foremost poets, proclaimed his poem "The Gilt of Cain," set in Michael Visocchi's sculpture, at its unveiling by Emeritus Archbishop Desmond Tutu – one of the few black people present. As part of his poetic *oeuvre* Sissay has shouted his work from rooftops, had it set in the counterweight of London's Royal Festival Hall lift, projected onto building facades, engraved upon walls, and inlaid into pavements. The unveiling and proclaiming of "The Gilt of Cain" confirms the capabilities of poetry as a heightened form of "word-in-space" (Ong 120), where Sissay's contemporaneous (yet ultimately ephemeral) delivery and its setting in stone for perpetuity activated multiple performances of his poem, making it a simultaneously oral, aural, visual, typographic, and grapholectic enterprise.

"Proclaim" is used intentionally here (rather than perform, speak, or read), as Sissay, like many of his black British contemporaries, has long been housed critically within the category of performance poet or spoken-word artist (which he rejects) rather than poet – as though his writing should be qualified or formally marked out in some way from the greater field.[1] The performance medium is undeniably important for the majority of contemporary black British poets as distinct from what critics might refer to as page poetry. In asserting cultural indigenousness and citizenship, poetry termed spoken-word or performance poetry is a means whereby many poets (writing from various involuntary marginalities) have found their most strident poetic voice, a resistant orality to predominant socio-cultural norms.² Moreover, it is productive to consider the resonance between poetry as publicly uttered medium and the implications of Harryette Mullen's coinage "resistant orality," by which she characterizes specifically the creative voices of African American women's slave-narrative writing. For black poets in Britain similarly speak back to, speak out against, and rewrite (poetic) traditions, as "neo-millennial black British avant-garde poets," who, R. Victoria Arana argues, "do not at all see themselves as migrants, exiles, or nomads, but as British citizens with certain inalienable rights in their birthlands, the various (now 'devolving') but still United 'States' (rather than Kingdom) of a Britain no longer Great" (Arana 2002:49–50). Wright (2000), Dawes (2005), and Tutu (2007) have explored the complex ramifications of the live performance associations for the work of black poets in Britain, revealing various emancipatory, celebratory, reductive, and restrictive receptions in contexts spanning audiences and critics. Labeling can produce a fight or flight reflex, as Kwame Dawes notes: "a desire to run away from the label, or embrace it with defiance and as a kind of statement of race and aesthetics" (282). In parodic reference to himself in an objectifying third-person pronoun, Sissay challenges the condescension of the performance straitjacket:

> If Lemn Sissay's live audience is moved by his work—and he loves reading live—this does not equate with his readings being a "performance." He believes the description (in its everyday usage) implies an act. And an act implies an untruth. Indeed it is often used as a disingenuous accolade, particularly in Britain. To truly see the misapplication of the term simply look at its supposed opposite (or supposed opponent)—"Page Poetry". Lemn Sissay believes this too to be a bizarre banal non-descript term and can find neither page nor performance poetry in the Princeton Encyclopedia of Poetry and Poetics. (Morning Breaks 70)³

As Dawes rightly argues, "The poem is the thing. Its value can be tested on the page and in performance . . . A poet ought to be able to choose her own 'performance space'" (284).

In drawing upon Michel de Certeau's poetic valuing of the everyday life that thrives amid the gaps of larger power structures, this explores the performativity activated by what I term landmark poetics. The linguistic modalities illustrated in de Certeau's "Pedestrian speech acts" invite application to poems on monuments and landmarks due to the "distinction between the *forms used* in a system and the *ways of using* this system (i.e., *rules*), that is, between two 'different worlds,' since 'the same things' are considered from two opposite formal viewpoints" (97, 98). I will discuss not only Sissay's example but also the work of his contemporary, SuAndi, whose poems are inscribed in Manchester's first black public monument at Dulcie School (now demolished) and in the promenade of poetry plaques, "Words on Discs," that line Salford's centenary walkway to the Lowry Arts Centre, Manchester.⁴ SuAndi's corpus further features the experiences of people not habitually celebrated in poetry: black and mixed-heritage women, disabled people, low-paid workers, and young people. Her project is not one of idealization, sentimentalizing or heroizing of struggle, but one of intimate poetic markings of lives lived, disregarded, and invisibilized in mainstream social and cultural representations.[5] Moreover, many of her finest poems are inscribed in the margins of programs, magazines, and other publications, not as doodling (which arises from daydreaming or distractedness) but as a focused marginalia, a mental multi-tasking amid various simultaneous stimuli that produces a distinctive and autonomous work, responsive to the original medium but not necessarily forming a thematic connection to it.

Landmark Poetics
The carving of poetry into sculpture and other landmarks can cleanse a space of prior negative associations and nurtures the experience of shared memory (via a poem) that is exposed and accessible to all passers-by. It also opens up a literal and literary interface between the concrete and the abstract, an ensemble of relations which can juxtapose past and present, local and international contexts, to function as a memorial and commemoration. Unlike poetry spoken or performed aloud, the reception of landmark poetics is unmediated orally or aurally (the poet is not physically present during its infinite delivery); its actualizing is dependent upon the paradox of public introspection – in the mind's eye and internal voice – of the reader and spectator. It functions as a public record and public art.

SuAndi's Salford Walkway poems and Sissay's "The Gilt of Cain" are responsive to black history locally and globally as they assert black people's crucial presence in the legacies of slavery and commerce which have shaped contemporary British society. As children growing up in 1960s and 70s Britain (when racism was politically, culturally, ideologically, and institutionally entrenched), SuAndi and Sissay carved out identities, in their professional lives and poetry and drama, that named and defied the discrimination they faced in order to foreground self-authenticating representations of black and mixed race people's experiences.[6] Their landmark poems offer a universality of appeal and responsiveness that opens up common ground between margin and center in cultural production. This multiple medium thus undoes the double bind that Julien and Mercer identified in relation to black film: "black subjects who speak in the public sphere: if only *one* voice is given the 'right to speak,' that voice will be heard, by the majority culture, as 'speaking for' the *many* who are excluded or marginalized from access to the means of representation" (198). The work of both poets revives but also revises the past complexities of "the culturally constructed nature of ethnic identities" of Julien and Mercer's "De Margin and De Centre" to create the margin as a public presence, central to and at the center of the work.[7]

Sissay and SuAndi's landmark poetics counter the historically overlooked contributions of black people to British culture, making a spatial, ideological, and creative intervention that converts past disregard into present-day commemoration, a repository for the future. As a combination of artistic expression and social retrieval that also offers an implicit social critique, the landmark poems which create the landmark poetics represent the innovative ways in which black experience is restored to British cultural heritage. While this is an imperfect project – as Walter J. Ong points out, "we can never forget enough of our familiar present to reconstitute in our minds any past in its full integrity" (15) – it assumes a recalibrating function, as there have been inarguably more triggers and traces preserved for remembering white-majority British society than for its black citizens. The interface between poem and public monument underscores the importance of recognizing this distinctive aspect of contemporary poetry and its positioning within contemporary British culture. As Sue Hubbard has noted, poetry as public art "needs to have a visual and conceptual dynamic, a spatial rhythm to echo its poetic musicality. It needs to grow out of and engage with the space in which it is to be situated rather than be imposed on it."[8]

Intrinsic to landmark poetics is that it is on general view and yet lies in wait, in a state of preserved ever-readiness; offering an illusion of fixity, stability, and inertness, but not inertia. This performance potential is manifold temporally and contextually. Like de Certeau's pedestrian enunciation, the landmark poem is "caught in the ambiguity of an actualization, transformed into a term dependent upon many different conventions, situated as the act of a present (or of a time), and modified by the transformations caused by successive contexts" (117). If the individual encounters the (already made) poem as a passer-by or in visiting it by design, de Certeau's "triple 'enunciative' function" of the pedestrian speech act gains another aspect as the walker then becomes a reader, speaker, or viewer of the poem in relation to the spatial signification they uniquely activate in relation to it. Their picking out of "certain fragments of the statement in order to actualize them in secret" is governed by an ensemble of ambulatory possibilities which is dependent upon "the crossing, drifting away, or improvisation of walking privilege," the negotiating of interdictory elements and the transforming or abandoning of spatial elements in the poetic encounter.[9] The interrogation of the three-dimensionality of a landmark poem diversifies potential perspectives by which to consider poetry's form and function, space, place, position, access, and design – materially and symbolically. It also generates a public place for introspection in the performability it invites in the reader and spectator, who read it to themselves or aloud, or touch it, or view it without reading the words. The ordering of Sissay's and SuAndi's landmark poems is open to individual construction to a certain degree, for, as the words are grouped on various columns in Sissay's work or discs in SuAndi's, the reader is not presented with a sequentially complete body of a poem but must engage with the separate parts to fashion this whole. Taking up de Certeau's habitability, this configuration, "opens up clearings; it 'allows' a certain play within a system of defined places. It 'authorizes' the production of an area of free play" (106).

A Graphic Tale

The performability and performativity of Sissay's poem "The Gilt of Cain" creates a tension between contexts: the flat surface or the printed page and the three dimensions of the live delivery of a sculptural piece.[10] Sissay's ironic standpoint towards the relationship between spoken-word and poetry as read is demonstrated in the poem's obvious polysemy and homophonic and multi-accentual qualities, initially activated by the speaking of "gilt"/guilt, which becomes reduced to a singular meaning of "gilt" upon reading. Even though many oral, aural, and visual attributes of spoken-word (gesture, facial expression, pacing, tone, volume, and other cadences) are lost upon the poem's typographical capture (in Visocchi's sculpture, the wall plaque, and the 2008 anthology *Listener*), Sissay still manages to defy the reductive association that black poet inevitably equals performance poet, as problematized earlier. In other work by Sissay, the performance on the page of poems such as "Advice for the Living," where words form the shape of a coffin and "**** THIS", and the word-scatter of "Gambian Holiday Maker" (all from *Listener*) joins the ekphrastic "Slipping" and bold type of "Erratic Equipoise" from *Morning Breaks in the Elevator* (1999) to challenge any reader or speaker of these poems to actually be able to articulate them aloud. The point made by these poems' typographical constructions (and their whole point) is lost if you cannot see them, as speaking the poem cannot convey their typographical effects.

Sissay's previous landmark poems have tapped into the heritage of visual poetic word placement that ranges from classical Greek influences to George Herbert's "The Altar" to the mid-twentieth-century Concrete poets. With "The Gilt of Cain" Sissay ratifies the poem as conduit for social remembrance. However, the commissioning process reveals that the synthesis between visual impact and literary value of the public art sculpture indicates as much about the relationship of black poets to mainstream British culture as it does about the redefining of black people's roles within British history and commerce.

Sissay rejected the initial plinth design "that represented Parliament, the Abolitionists and the Church, and the sugar cane represented the people, the Slaves . . . [where] my poem was set to go on top of the plinth." As he argued, this conveyed the sense of enslaved people waiting for the English to liberate them, making such liberators celebrated over the liberty achieved. As he pointed out to the Scottish sculptor Visocchi, "on top of the plinth, it won't be seen by anybody, so how are you going to incorporate it?" (personal interview, 2008). Furthermore, he found himself in a familiar position black artists have experienced in encounters with white-dominated institutions (especially around the issue of reparation for slavery) concerning accountability, denial, and guilt. His insistence that the words of the poem be carved into the sugar cane columns was viewed by the sculptor as tantamount to defacing the purity of the sculpture's surfaces, making it in some ways an act of graffiti. The implication of a black poet's words as interlopers or acts of defacement in relation to a sculpture commemorating the beginning of the end of slavery shows how guilt shaped the project as much as gilt. This resonates with the dynamics of the canonical exclusion many black artists in Britain experience, artists for whom, as Sissay's poem notes, "history is no inherent acquisition." Sissay observed,

> Guilt is such a self-serving emotion if it's not acted on. I wanted to say you're working with a black man here who by virtue of who he is, will have more knowledge about this issue, has made certain suggestions which you have not even taken on – and this is the kind of thing that can happen to black people in all kinds of scenarios. (personal interview, 2008)

Although he was able to nominate which sections of the poem were to be inscribed upon the columns representing sugar cane, there were fewer than originally intended and so the full four octaves did not end up on it. Various single lines are inscribed and the complete version is recorded upon a wall plaque facing the sculpture. Sissay's insistence at the inscription of lines meant that the poem was not marginalized in the overall sculpture and produced a social and aesthetic equivalence. Yet, the converse is also detectable, as the rhyming scheme of the octaves (aabbcccc ddeeffff gghhiijj kkllmmoo) is disrupted by its fracturing upon the columns (as it is not when published in successive stanzas), which emphasizes the way the poem looks (as constituent of the surface composition of a sculpture) over the poetic effects its author has engineered. The arrangement of the poem on the columns thus affects possible interpretations of it. Similarly, SuAndi's twenty-two stanzas placed separately on plaques on the walkway to the Lowry Centre (to be discussed next) also invite interpretations based upon where the reader/spectator happens to walk and whatever point of the poem they encounter first, giving them an intensely localized authority rather than de Certeau's "local" one. (106).

As guilt/gilt is key, so are Cain/cane, and Sissay drew upon two primary grapholectic sources of religion and commerce, the bible and Bloomberg's glossary, as foundational texts for his research.[11] As Ong has noted "Writing gives a grapholect a power far exceeding that of any purely oral dialect" with the vast resource of "a recorded vocabulary of at least a million and a half words, of which not only the present meanings but also hundreds of thousands of past meanings are known" (8) and it was this resourcefulness that Sissay employed to create his poem:

> I think the things that came out of the poem most of all were the religious references and the City language . . . you know the story of Cain and Abel where Cain says "Am I my brother's keeper?" it was a gift from the endless well of creativity. Bloomberg's glossary, it was great that glossary. It just introduced you to so many

new words and a whole new language. I knew that if I researched properly, then the poem would find its own way. I let the poem sort of gallop away and sort of just rode it. (personal interview, 2008)

Sissay anticipated numerous audiences for his work, not only those attending his live delivery of it but also the people in future who will intentionally seek it out or come across it: "I'm aware that the Caribbean community will visit it and Americans will come and visit it as well. But if I'm really honest with you I think at the forefront of my mind was the City worker walking past it and stopping for one minute and catching one line" (personal interview, 2008).

At the unveiling and performance of the poem, the space and place activated an interaction between the simultaneity of past and present, creating a measuring stick for evaluating not only the legacy of the slave trade but also the position of spoken-word poetry in contemporary cultural expression. The history of the trade of centuries ago (human bodies dehumanized into commodity) is evident. In the southern approach to Fen Court, the charged polysemy of the ominous pub sign, "The City Flogger," dually evokes the flogging of people by lash or as goods being sold. The podium which features in the sculpture calls to mind an elevation charged with associations; one that has performed multiple services as a site from which homilies or impassioned abolitionist arguments were delivered or on which slaves were auctioned. In its proclamation, Sissay's poem took on the qualities of a jeremiad that enhanced these reverberations from history as performances of epic proportions. At its unveiling, Sissay was elevated above the pinstriped-suited, white crowd with a microphone and chose to read his poem, a reading rather than a recitation. He later noted how he used his knowledge of the audience and space to shape this:

> If they'd have all been black actually it would have been a different reading because I would have been much more animated, they would have got it much more. I just found solace in the poem and not in the audience. I was aware that the audience could have felt uncomfortable because self-criticism is not something that the City does. (personal interview, 2008).

From windows that surrounded the Court, office workers presented a sea of white faces looking down on Sissay's poetry reading, adding a further dimension to the spatial dynamics. As these people would not have heard Sissay's delivery and were too far away to view the wall plaque, their motivations for looking can only be surmised. The observing of the scene below is reminiscent of de Certeau's looking down upon Manhattan from the former World Trade Center, where he noted the differentiations between an official, ordered, daily life which exists alongside that which is connected to drifting and dreaming. Furthermore, for those on the ground, the panopticon effect of the surrounding high-rise office buildings is unavoidable, as Fen Court is an enclosed courtyard with narrow access points north and south. The elevation renders the onlooker as voyeur, observing from afar as though from the summit of the city, not only architecturally but also conceptually as *the City* and all it stands for. The disconnectedness mirrors the lack of direct visibility of the slave trade on home shores, which had screened the British psyche from its consequences as the ships that entered its ports had already exchanged their human cargo for commodities such as sugar, coffee, tea, and cotton before docking in Britain. This resonates with de Certeau's philosophizing of a city's contradictory properties: "But in reality, it repeatedly produces effects contrary to those at which it aims: the profit system generates a loss which, in the multiple forms of wretchedness and poverty outside the system and of waste inside it, constantly turns production into expenditure" (96). It should be remembered that it was when slavery was no longer financially rewarding and economically efficient that its abolition was hastened.[12]

In Sissay's anthology *Listener*, the poem's commercial terms are italicized (as they are not on the wall plaque), self-consciously evincing the poetical shaping of his research and also orchestrating how his poem should be read in terms of stress and rhythm, reliant upon sibilance and near *rime riche* effects: "And great traders *acting in concert*, arms rise/as the *actuals* frought on the sea of *franchise*/thrown overboard into the *exchange* to drown/in distressed *brokers*' disconsolate frown." Juxtaposition of the horror of slaves hurled forcibly from ships in the middle of the ocean with the fervor of the trading activity (identifiable in "the *actuals*," a macabre almost paronomastic pun that reminds us of the actual live human beings – so crucial yet so dispensable) alerts the reader/listener to the real cost of the enterprise, one where livelihood is given more worth than a live person. The brokers will be disappointed, "distressed," "disconsolate" at most; the slaves, having been first wrenched from liberty, denied free will, then murdered, are dead. In contrasting the two fates in this crescendo of commercial performance, Sissay rebalances the historical ledger and thus undoes any claims of the trading floor and the City to valorization, when they are so steeped in the trade in human beings.

In monumentalizing the forgotten and anonymous black people who were the enslaved currency of the City's past transactions, Sissay's utterance of his poem sang out as an assertive presence, a vocal counterpoint to the legacies left by the powerful institutions of religion and commerce in serving the shameful trans-Atlantic slave trade. The evangelism of the trade becomes hammered out in the rhythmic use of abstract nouns and alliteration in the second quatrain of stanza two, promising an epiphany through the collapse of the temple of greed:

> In *accounting liquidity* is a mounting morbidity
> But raising the arms with such rigid rapidity…
> Oh the reaping the raping rapacious *fluidity*,
> The violence, the vicious and vexed *volatility*.

However, Sissay defers this satisfaction of collapse as the City survives and, titan-like, "The roaring trade floor rises above crashing waves: / The traders buy ships, beneath the slaves." The ambiguity of the latter line suggests the actual nameless, enslaved people lining the cargo holds of slave ships and recapitulates the image of those thrown overboard whose bodies are beneath the waves. It is in this third octave that a change in the uniformity of Sissay's rhyming scheme occurs, as the last quatrain is divided into rhyming couplets, heralding the approach of abolition and the future. The image of the "machete" and the onomatopoeic "Crick crack *cut back* the Sugar Rush" alludes to the contemporary shackles of addiction and violence with which many young black men in urban Britain have been associated in socio-cultural representation.[13] Subtly, Sissay allows the interplay of the modern and historical usages a moment before his poem begins its path to its presumed commissioned endpoint, the lauding of William Wilberforce.[14]

However, Sissay's delivery style at the unveiling adroitly conveyed the paradox of the City funding such a commemoration. The poem's stress pattern, coupled with his accent, in uttering the final lines encapsulated this perfectly. "I answer by nature by spirit by rightful laws/My name, my brother, Wilberforce." The successive "by" through to the enjambment, builds up an emphasis which is then halted by the comma after "name." At this point, (unconsciously, as he confirmed in an interview) Sissay's pronunciation enabled a nuanced reversal of the expected solidarity and shared valorizing of the abolitionist Wilberforce. Sissay's stress of *my* was followed by the pronounced ambiguity, "Will be force," undercutting the printed name Wilberforce and giving the poem an entirely different aural ending. As Sissay observed, "the City benefits from slavery and the City celebrates the end of slavery – it's like there's something missing there isn't there? It's basically black people" (personal interview, 2008).

Both spoken and inscribed, the poem visually and aurally challenges public sculpture's traditional role in glorifying and commemorating military acts or conquests, to replace this with subject-matter that has been ignored historically, in processes of national archiving and remembrance. It is restorative as an act of speaking back at history's exclusions and as an act of speaking out, as Sissay, a black British poet, places his art in the contemporary cultural canon, which has traditionally sidelined or excluded the work of black poets.

A Graphic Trail
SuAndi's "Words on Discs," which line the walkway to the Lowry Arts Centre in Salford (see Figure 1), also clearly pave a route from the past through to the present – as the poetic voice of one plaque reminds an imagined or anticipated dismissive reader, "Don't snub your nose/at history,/the future lives on the past/of folks like we." In this celebration of the port's epic history, there is no mention of slavery but a focus

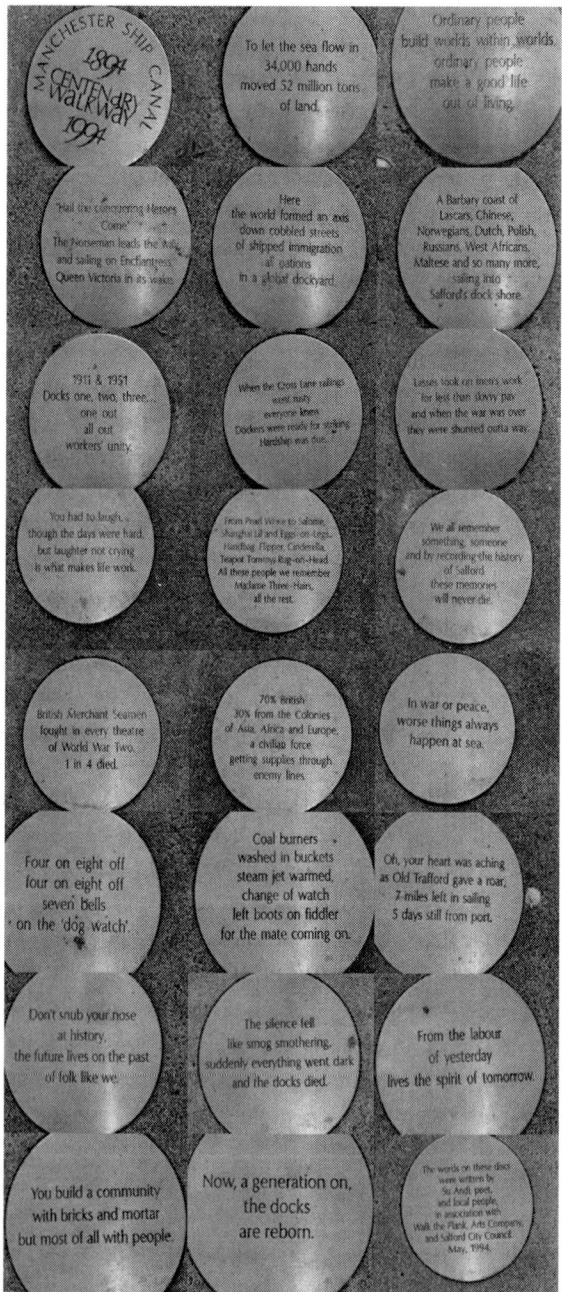

Figure 1: Poems on Discs written by SuAndi and members of the community, Manchester Ship Canal Centenary Walkway. Photograph by SuAndi.

on the working classes, "Ordinary people" who comprised the docklands demographic over the centuries, producing an energetic internationalism well before the concept of globalization, "all nations/in a global dockyard."

The architectronics of epic poem of twenty-two stanzas, which have been fashioned onto plaques or word discs, creates portals for reader and spectator which might be seen to embody the formalist concept of the *sjuzet* in that they shape the raw material retrieved in an arrangement (the stand-alone segments, the stanzas) but do not represent a true sequence of events, as these might have occurred sequentially or temporally. The positioning of the discs along a walkway might suggest a direction for this engagement and yet, this is confounded by the lack of directions. Evoking de Certeau's theorizing of the pedestrian's poetics, it is possible to walk forwards, backwards, backtrack, miss discs out (knowingly or unknowingly), and to cross from one side of the walkway to the other. The poem hands over its textuality and deliberate segmentation to the reader's own haphazard choreography, conscious or unconscious, and the version of the whole poem they will create. The reader/walker is thus not confined to any particular linear narrative direction. Each disc can be autonomous and is self-sufficient in its evocations, images and information – albeit only a fragment of a series. This testifies to the partial perspectives that have been handed down as history, while at the same time offering discrete pockets of knowledge. As SuAndi has written, "You build a community/with bricks and mortar/but most of all with people."

On the page of the Salford City Council pamphlet, the poem's only published (as distinct from public) version, this fluidity of potential modes of reading the poem bridges two seemingly antagonistic methods: synthesis (a combining of elements brought together) and analysis (breaking something down into its constituent parts).[15] The poem can be read vertically or horizontally or even diagonally. The reader's compositional opportunity mirrors the choreography of the walkway. Thus, SuAndi's stand-alone stanzas function (both as discs and in printed form) to celebrate and retrieve the Salford dockyard *her*stories and *hi*stories in order to forge *our*stories where the reader/recipient, through making their own connections, participates in the (re)birth that happens with each encounter.

Beyond the Margins

Sissay's style of uttering his poetry is one that constantly undoes expectations of how audiences and poets relate to each other. In speaking his work live, he strategically spills over the edges of his poem vocally, in a style which supports Gräbner's argument that Sissay is an example of a poet "showing doing" and hence quite consciously performing as a poet ("Is Performance Poetry Dead?" 81). Ong argues that "corrections in oral performance tend to be counterproductive, to render the speaker unconvincing. So you keep them to a minimum or avoid them altogether"

(103). However, Sissay's DJing of his poetry, interrupting the expected continuity to point out meta-textual aspects as though he defies being pinned down (or recorded), appears to undo the notion of any poem uttered ever being a finished entity. This meta-textuality of delivery (which did not occur at the unveiling of "The Gilt of Cain") can be considered in tandem with SuAndi's commentaries upon the origin of particular poems and her distinctive peppering of such polemical writing with extracts from them, as well as her acts of marginalia wherein what is foregrounded in the oral and aural genesis of the poem can be that which is peripheral to its starting point.

Edgar Allan Poe wrote, "in the marginalia, too, we talk only to ourselves; we talk therefore freshly – boldly – originally – with abandonnement – without conceit" (1844), characterizing the space where marginalia can be written as liberated from the constraints of the text proper, around which it skirts. Of her poem "She Telling Secrets," SuAndi notes how she wrote it "around the edges of the conference programme" ("She" 47), while "She Will Smile" (printed in this volume) was penned around the border of a magazine, now thrown away. The inscribing of the borders of printed material unrelated to poetry with a poem evokes the tentative exercising of creativity (no blank sheets of paper to hand) and the fitting in of one's creativity around an established majority discourse – a familiar position historically for women writers and black or mixed-heritage women writers in particular. But as both poems demonstrate, the sentiments expressed, the form, poetic strategies, and voices that SuAndi creates, centralize the peripheral in her realizations.

"She Will Smile" represents a wistful poetic voice that reflects upon telltale signs of aging and the minutiae of personal bodily changes: "She runs hands a little coarse from always doing" (signposting the busyness that characterizes her life), "Over a girth she never noticed spreading/And raise her breasts back into a cleavage/Now long gone." Her self-contemplation seems to catch her unaware until now. Written in the margins of a women's magazine, a genre which traditionally exudes unattainable ideals of womanliness to exploit material acquisition and female readers' anxieties about their body image, SuAndi's poetic riposte reminds the poem's reader of the majority of real women who hover around the margins of this projection of an ideal, ageless, flawless womanhood. The speaker's perfectionism and limitations are conveyed in an extended retrospection, alerting us to her internalized self-reprimand and perpetual feelings of falling short of what is expected: "And by her own judgment/ Fails to measure up to standard . . . And chastise all her errors with tears." The poem becomes a tribute to the speaker's motherhood as the most perfect achievement in the face of all of her previous critical self-judgments. Yet, it is a joint venture between parents: "A miniature perfection of her/And the man who loved her enough/ To place his child within her protection/And name her mother." The tempering of the "perfection," however, is achieved through the disquieting effect of "enough," circumventing any nostalgic sentimentalizing of conception and maternity. The ordinariness is just as noteworthy. The man's placing of the child (suggesting care, purpose, and responsibility) and naming of her as mother reshapes the woman-centered biological aspect by which women's opportunities in history have been curtailed and restores a semi-sacredness without mawkish rhapsody, emerging as it does from "dirty clothes" and the speaker's regrets over perceived shortcomings.

A continuity accessed by the poetic voice's visceral senses – "Often she inhales it/Holding dirty clothes to her cheek" and "how her heart would whimper/Each time she lost sight/Of this so precious gift" – confirm that SuAndi's poetic voice is not sorry for herself nor does she elicit sympathy from the reader. The poem marks out merely a moment in one woman's life of emotional memory, a pensive and unfinished reverie captured through aposiopetic thoughts: "Yes indeed – some days/She wished she'd never." The enjambment of the poem's form, without even a final full stop, fulfils what Stephanie Trigg has offered in relation to a white Australian poet, Gwen Harwood, "at the same time invoking memory, and the irresistible power of poetry to move beyond itself . . . to suggest the possibility of a life outside language" (5). SuAndi presents models of independent-thinking women who are faceless and anonymous in public consciousness and pays tribute to women's fortitude in motherhood in much the same way as her poetic predecessor, Harwood. However, while Harwood's mothers can be left bereft of their own identity after child rearing – "To the wind she says, 'They have eaten me alive'" ("In the Park"), or, in "Suburban Sonnet" where "She practices a fugue, though it can matter/to no one now if she plays well or not" – SuAndi's glimpses eschew resignation to a fate of social and self-worthlessness in favor of self-acceptance.

SuAndi's marginalia poems play with the illusion of privileged access to her personas' private voices but in emphasizing the specificity of one consciousness, although empathic identification can occur, she creates poetic voices that undo Julien and Mercer's concern that "if only *one* voice is given the 'right to speak,' that voice will be heard, by the majority culture, as 'speaking for' the *many* who are excluded or marginalized from access to the means of representation" (198). The poem "She Telling Secrets" explores, warts and all, the oscillation between self-acceptance for black women, privately shared understandings of socially adaptive codes, and the role of the public voice in potentially aiding and abetting in the perpetuation of negative stereotypes of black women. Inspired by a conference paper she heard on the work of Britain's leading black playwright, debbie tucker green, the poem creates a scrutiny of how black women are publicly portrayed.[16] SuAndi's technique of writing commentary which explains its genesis, functioning as complimentary to the poetic voice, creates an ambiguity of either being deeply critical of the paper's speaker or of what she spoke about, (debbie tucker green's work), thus confusing the reader as to who the addressee might be. The poetic voice admonishes the addressee as anchored in a stigmatizing negativity about black women's image-making that is devoid of historically informed references and it interpolates positive alternatives: "Don't' tell about ghetto style breeding," "Don't' tell about sweet looking men . . . /With not one word of interest in any sistah," but "Tell about the church", "'Rice and Peas' keeping warm," "Tell about white gloves," "And elegant men in trilby." She positions her addressee as educated, "See she uniformed to school/Cheeky to college," but lacking the knowledge of life's protocols, an internalized self-surveillance and self-regulation requisite for survival in the surrounding hostile society, "So why she never learn/No speak our business in public/White people be listening/And best we tell them nothing." However, SuAndi herself states that while the poem's urging to hold one's tongue, was her poetic response to the actual conference paper, her emotional response prior to this (which caused it to be written) was actually, "my giggling, toes curling, delighted response to hearing words that even I, some days, dare not speak out loud . . . Hearing with clarity things said that, some days, others have used to question *my* sanity" ("She" 49). Encapsulated within this is a shifting standpoint that at once acknowledges continuity, inheritance, and alteration. It acknowledges the necessary gate-keeping of the previous generation (the micro survival strategy in the macro environment), and the needful public assertion of a present-day, British-born sensibility which her polemic articulates as "Heavens! If we keep it all to ourselves how will our experiences and 'their' experiences really interrelate . . . because no matter what we remember, we can never go back. Yesterday *is* done" (49). The poem thus serves as a responsive confessional both accusatory and conciliatory. A tripartite inter-text results, created between a black woman academic's conference paper about a black woman playwright and SuAndi's fashioned poem, which candidly examines the unmentionable in the conference paper: the no-go areas assumed for black writers in mainstream culture and black people's replication, too, of stigmatizing tropes of black experience in the public arena.

Critical Ground

Both SuAndi and Sissay adopt styles of delivery and subject matter that speak back at oppression or undo any notion that they do readings of their work. Sissay has been described as having "the motormouth energy of a spoken-word star" (Le Gendre 2000: 47). Marmion observes that in the monodrama *Something Dark* (2008), he "performs his life story like an improvised jazz routine. Quite often you've got no idea what he's on about, yet you're always being swept along by his riffing" (Marmion 303). Lauri Ramey has commented that "SuAndi is known for presenting an on-stage persona that is direct and sassy, wisecracking and poignant, political and opinionated, often controversial, and encompassing both history and topicality" (Ramey 292). SuAndi herself also makes this comparison: "My poetry is as impetuous as my personality" (qtd. in Kalu 137).

Their poetry begins as a work of interiority and introspection. SuAndi explains: "I compose and write all my performance pieces in my head, complete. Anything that begins on the page remains on the page" (email exchange, 2008), while Sissay begins solely by writing his work down – it is not improvised or devised during his live utterance, despite his meta-textual observations about the process. In live readings neither poet spontaneously alters what they have created in advance on the page; they simply activate the extroversion of the repertoire of delivery techniques demanded by a live context of articulation. The compositional and editing process is very much a grapholectic exercise.[17] As their work frequently slips between and re-works literary genres and performance traditions, this raises questions about the need for critical languages which can meet the demands of the forms and experiential aesthetics they forge. Gräbner identifies how the performance of poetry requires this very apparatus of engagement:

> The performance of poetry is a challenge to the methodologies we have used so far to read poetry. It demonstrates that our realities and the ways to understand them and engage with them have changed. . . . Academic theory needs to respond to the challenges posed by the performance of poetry by developing the methodologies that are necessary to frame performed poetry within the bigger picture of social, cultural and political developments. ("Performance Poetry and Theory")

Although the difference between the act of performance and reading is unresolved here, Gräbner does call for the evolution of a more inter-referential analytic process to catch up with the generic innovations. Similarly, Tutu has highlighted the formal and generic synergies that spoken-word elicits, which fall beyond the "scales predetermined for other poetic genres," where it is impossible to divorce "the aesthetic of this developing genre from its social context" (157, 159). Self-termed Black British writers like Sissay and SuAndi have not unilaterally experienced the advantages derived from patronage or longevity in Britain's cultural processing of their writing comparable to those enjoyed by their white contemporaries.[18] For many black British writers, the constraints of representationalism have often impeded experimentation in subject matter and form, and also tempered the flourishing of critical models that tackle the artistic merits of the work.[19] Expectations of what black British writers *should* produce are often at odds with what they *want* to produce.[20] Dawes has voiced his uneasiness about the terminology associated with the cultural and critical processing of black British poets: "It has become an unfortunate assumption that Black poets in Britain are 'performance poets' first, – writers who are fixed in the world of performance . . . like all reductionist labels, it demeans the work that is being done by these writers and encourages laziness in those who respond to the work" (283).

As a counter-stance to this inhibitory dynamic, constructive critical engagement should firstly recognize indigenous black British writers as *bona fide* constituents of contemporary British culture – more so than their generational predecessors were allowed to be – and secondly consider how the work is created and constructed: its aesthetic qualities, the artistic aspirations that motivate its genesis, and for whom or for what reason it is fashioned.[21] As a prism through which to view the uniquely British manifestations of African oral aesthetics, Wright notes how performance poetry "provides an ideal conduit to engage with Black performativity owing to its orality, its capacity to equivocate between the aesthetic and social functions of performance and its popularity within Black communities . . . language as spoken and ritual as performed" (272). Communality is fundamental to the art form. Ong has testified to the unity between speaker and audience achieved by the spoken word: "Because in its physical constitution as sound, the spoken word proceeds from the human interior and manifests human beings to one another as conscious interiors, as persons, the spoken word forms human beings into close-knit groups" (73). As applied to the genres of spoken-word or performance poetry, a contract of public contact is created that runs counter to the historically exclusive brethren (of introspective, white, Oxbridge-centered poetic traditions) who read from their works.

As socio-cultural norms can disregard, devalue, and oppress certain groups of people based upon race and sex-gender categories, similarly too, prevailing aesthetic traditions can denote which writers' work merits inclusion or exclusion within the British literary canon and its associated networks of endorsement and legacy formation. SuAndi and Lemn Sissay create work as indigenous Britons which inherits and references African diasporic *and* European poetic and performative traditions to traverse a number of cultural and generic boundaries. Through permeating the tradition of the commemorative monument and monumentalizing habitually peripheral cultural perspectives via inscription in sculpture and other landmarks, SuAndi and Sissay's landmark poetics produces an intriguing and unique representational aesthetic where the experientially unfamiliar (in relation to mainstream culture) functions as a challenge and catalyst for revising cultural expectations about how we view, re-view, read, and experience contemporary poetry. In considering how SuAndi and Sissay's landmark poetics relate to their oral delivery through live performance and typographical life, on the page or as inscribed upon other surfaces, the "new dimensions to our realities" to which Gräbner refers in "Performance Poetry and Theory" may be explored and the parameters designating socio-cultural perpetuity for some and not others tried and tested.

Notes

1. As I have argued elsewhere, Sissay's work frequently "reinforces the powerful, self-fashioning capabilities of the art of poetry as counterstance and counterbalance; to prevailing social norms that devalue and oppress certain groups of people based upon race and sex-gender categories; *and*, to prevailing aesthetic traditions which denote inclusion or exclusion within the British literary compass and its markers of artistic merit" ("Our Mothers" 230, emphasis added).

2. Spoken-word sharpens the divergences between poetry as written to be read on the page – as an act of introspection – and poetry written with an ideal endpoint of being relayed as an extroverted utterance to an audience. So while spoken-word poetry is not reading aloud but is an interactive engagement with an audience, this does not *necessarily* equate with activating a repertoire of performance strategies by which drama is articulated, although much cross-fertilization obviously occurs stylistically, generically, and formally. In a theater context, critic Michael Billington habitually laments that (black British woman dramatist) debbie tucker green's plays are poems not drama, describing *stoning mary*, in a review, as "more like an acted poem than a play" (28) and discerning in *random* "a pungent poetic voice and an eye for detail. But fine writing is not the same as drama" (284). By contrast, D. Keith Peacock finds inter-referentiality unproblematic when applied to (white men) Beckett and Pinter, "Like Beckett, Pinter's whole career in the theatre . . . has been characterized by a poet's search for economy and clarity of expression in words, movement and visual imagery" (161).

3. However, he does not deny his enjoyment of delivering his poems to a live audience: "When I'm performing in front of an audience, I love it. I like people and I like the audience and I want to do a good job" (Barker).

4. Salford Wharf Centenary Walkway, Salford City Council, Salford Quays Project Office. For Sissay's poems as landmarks see www.lemnsissay.com. For SuAndi, see www.victorianbaths.org.uk/documents/Women's Walk and www.actsofachievement.org.uk/blackhistorytrail.

5. Examples of these poems include "Darren," "The Barmaid," and "Just Slow" from *Nearly Forty*, "20–22 Hours From Blackburn," "Passing," and "Sex, Love, Rape" in *Style in Performance*, and "Those Who Have Not Considered Living" in *There Will Be No Tears*.

6. While their work is published in numerous poetry collections, SuAndi and Lemn Sissay have also written and performed auto/biographical monodramas. *The Story of M* (2002) and *Something Dark* (2004; 2008), "intimately dramatize their odysseys to self-knowledge, through retrieving and paying homage to their respective mothers' struggles – in raising or rejecting them – in a surrounding, hostile, white-dominated English society, of the sixties and seventies" ("Our Mothers" 2010: 231).

7. Literary activism has been inextricable from both poets' professional lives. See the entries for Sissay by Deirdre Osborne and SuAndi by Lauri Ramey in Arana.

8. See www.poetrysociety.org.uk/content/archives/publicart/hubbard/opening.

9. De Certeau identifies these as follows: "The act of walking is to the urban system what the speech act is to language or to the statement uttered. At the most rudimentary level, it has a triple 'enunciative' function: it is the process of *appropriation* of the topographical system on the part of the pedestrian (just as the speaker appropriates and takes on language); it is a spatial acting-out of the place (just as the speech act is an acoustic acting-out of language); and it implies *relations* among differentiated positions . . . It thus seems possible to give a preliminary definition of walking as a space of enunciation" (97–8).

10. The poem in the sculpture in Fen Court, City of London, was the result of lobbying by the Afro-Caribbean community and black peer Baroness Lola Young for a sculpture that would commemorate the abolition of the Slave Trade

Act. It was developed in partnership with British Heritage, Futurecity Arts, and the Church of St. Mary Woolnoth. The original church stood on the site until 1811 and slave-trader turned preacher and abolitionist Reverend John Newton (who penned the hymn "Amazing Grace") was rector of the parish from 1780 to 1807.

11. This is an alphabetically ordered glossary of financial terms, a resource of over 8,000 entries and 18,000 links compiled by Campbell R. Harvey (2000). See www.bloomberg.com/invest/glossary/bfglosa.htm.

12. As C.L. Innes notes, the historian C.L.R. James "marshals evidence to demonstrate that Wilberforce was merely a tool of mercantile interests in Britain, and that it is the loss of the American colonies and rivalry with the French and their prosperity derived from the colony of San Domingo that changes British attitudes between 1783 and 1807" (208).

13. Since Gus John's influential study *Race and the Inner City* (1970), sociologists and cultural theorists have identified the State's equating of blackness with problems such as criminality, deprivation, and disaffectedness. See Hall, Critcher, Jefferson, Clarke and Roberts's *Policing the Crisis: Mugging, the State, and Law and Order* and Solomos's *Race and Racism in Britain* amongst many works which explore this.

14. Peter Fryer observes: "The demand for the abolition of slavery and the emancipation of the slaves was central to the British working-class movement that emerged in the 1790s, which black people helped to organize and lead" (9). Although there were noted white abolitionists such as Thomas Clarkson and Granville Sharp, Fryer identifies that the person most associated legislatively with the Act of 1807, William Wiberforce, "climbed on the band-wagon at the last minute when he realized it would win him votes" (9). Slavery was finally abolished throughout the British Empire in 1833.

15. Obviously, the localized longevity of the poem set in stone creates a different legacy to a printed version in a book and confines audience access (and thus potential interpretations of the work) to those able to physically visit Salford.

16. See Goddard (2007) and Osborne (2007) for critical work on debbie tucker green.

17. Even in their monodramas this process continued. SuAndi describes how "I wrote *M* following a mediocre production that closed with homage to white women who had endured racism following their inter-racial marriages. Lois Keidan felt it was the strongest section and encouraged me to write more, as fact is always more interesting. Forty minutes into my return journey to Manchester I'd done as advised with tears running down my face. It took very little more writing to complete" (*Story* 1).

Sissay recollects that in rehearsals of *Something Dark*, "I sat with a director, who said to me, 'forget everything you've ever known concerning performance poetry, this isn't it' . . . . So I had to act like an actor. I'm blocked, every section of the play is a five-minute block, a ten-minute block or whatever, and every section is thought about, the vocal, the sound, the body, you know . . . whenever I wanted to change the lines as an actor in rehearsals, the director would say well no, 'the writer wrote it that way and that's the way you do it.' It was wonderful" (Osborne, "Lemn Sissay's Life Source" 323).

18. In 1986 SuAndi became the Freelance Director of Britain's largest and longest-running Black cultural organization, the Black Arts Alliance, working in communities, creating networks amongst black artists and writers, professional and otherwise, noting, "we will not die out because we actively recruit the next generation and the next generation who will in turn recruit the next generation" (SuAndi, *Acts* 94). While this exemplifies a longstanding intervention into fears regarding longevity that accompany many black British artists' work, in 2009, the Arts Council of England terminated the BAA's core funding after twenty-three years.

19. Yasmin Alibhai-Brown has criticized the closed-shop coterie of white critics who "don't get it when it comes to black and Asian artists and writers" and accuses them of distorting

critical inaccuracies which falsely inflate the imagined merits of black and Asian literature: "Aroused by encounters with the unfamiliar and unknown . . . they end up giving us inflated valuations, instead of considered, intelligent and scrupulously dispassionate verdicts, which we have a right to expect." Victoria Arana notes the tendency for "discussions of contemporary 'black' British writing" to emphasize "the social and demographic features of the writing," rather than considering "its quality as writing, its artistic features and objectives, or its aesthetics" (viii).

20. Courttia Newland was unable to find a publisher for a science fiction novel after the successes of his novels and short stories which focused upon the experiences of working-class urban, primarily black youth (personal interview 2006). Kwame Dawes identifies "the need to try and change the world that has made things so difficult for the Black British poet to freely create powerful art" (298).

21. The back cover of *Tender Fingers in a Clenched Fist* (1988) quotes the twenty-year-old Sissay on being identified as British. "I am British," he says there, "of course I'm British. But being British and black are two different things and my birth certificate pays no account of who I am. I want to be accepted here as British but the system here doesn't accept the Britishness of Blacks." This volume, on the whole, demonstrates how Sissay's earliest pathways into the cultural landscape produced radical, denunciatory, (re)activist work in subject matter and poetic techniques.

Bibliography

Alibhai-Brown, Yasmin. "Black art can be bad, just as art by whites." *The Independent*, 5 February 2005.

Arana, R. Victoria. "Black American Bodies in the Neo-Millennial Avant-Garde Black British Poetry." *Literature and Psychology* 48.4 (2002): 47–80.

Barker, Lewis. Unpublished personal interview with Lemn Sissay. 2004. Courtesy of Kadija Sesay.

Billington, Michael. Review of *random*. *Theatre Record*. 10–23 March 2008, 284.

———. Review of *stoning mary*. *The Guardian*, 21 March 2006, 28.

Certeau, Michel de. *The Practice of Everyday Life*. 1984. Trans. Steven Randall. Berkeley, Los Angeles and London: University of California Press, 1988.

Dawes, Kwame. "Black British Poetry: Some Considerations." *Write Black Write British: From Post Colonial to Black British Literature*. Ed. Kadija Sesay. London: Hansib Publications Ltd., 2005. 282–99.

Fryer, Peter. *Aspects of British Black History*. London: Index Books, 1993.

Goddard, Lynette. *Staging Black Feminisms: Identity, Politics, Performance*. Hampshire, GB and New York: Palgrave Macmillan, 2007.

Gräbner, Cornelia. "Is Performance Poetry Dead?" *Poetry Review* 97.2 (Summer 2007): 78–82.

———. "Performance Poetry and Theory." www.57productions.com. Web. September 2006.

———. "The Poetics of Performance Poetry." *World Literature Today* (online edition) 82.1 (January–February 2008): n. pag.

Hall, Stuart, Chas Chritcher, Tony Jefferson, John N. Clarke, and Brian Roberts. *Policing the Crisis: Mugging, the State, and Law and Order*. Basingstoke: Macmillan, 1978.

Harwood, Gwen. "In the Park." *Poems*. Sydney: Angus and Robertson, 1963.

———. "Suburban Sonnet." *Poems/Volume Two*. Sydney: Angus and Robertson, 1968.

Hubbard, Sue. "Opening Spaces: Poetry as Public Art." www.poetrysociety.org.uk/content/archives/publicart/hubbard/opening. Web. September 1999.

Innes, C.L. *A History of Black and Asian Writing in Britain*. 2002. Cambridge: Cambridge University Press, 2008.

Julien, Isaac, and Kobena Mercer. "De Margin and De Center." *Black British Cultural Studies: A Reader*. Ed. A. Baker Houston Jnr., Manthia Diawara, and Ruth H. Lindeborg. Chicago and London: University of Chicago Press, 1996. 194–209.

Kalu, Pete, ed. *Peace Poems*. Manchester: Crocus, 2002.

Le Gendre, Kevin. "A snake called Hope." *The Independent* 21 May 2000: 47.

Marmion, Patrick. Review of *Something Dark*. Theatre Record 5 (2004): 303.

Peacock, D. Keith. *Harold Pinter and the New British Theater*. Westport CT: Greenwood Press, 1997.

Ong, Walter J. *Orality and Literacy*. 1982. London and New York: Routledge, 2002.

Osborne, Deirdre. Email exchange with SuAndi. July 2008.

———. "Lemn Sissay's Life's Source: An Interview and Commentary." *Hidden Gems*. Ed. Deirdre Osborne London: Oberon Books, 2008. 318–26.

———. "Lemn Sissay." *Dictionary of Literary Biography: Twenty-First-Century "Black" British Writers*. Ed. R. Victoria Arana. Sumter, South Carolina: Bruccoli, Clark, and Layman; & Detroit, Michigan: Gale Research Company, 2009. 261–72.

———. "Not 'in-yer-face' but what lies beneath: experiential and aesthetic inroads in the drama of debbie tucker green and Dona Daley." *Dictionary of Literary Biography: Twenty-First-Century "Black" British Writers*. Ed. R. Victoria Arana. Sumter, South Carolina: Bruccoli, Clark, and Layman; & Detroit, Michigan: Gale Research Company, 2009. 222–42.

———. "'Our Mothers, Ourselves': Staging (I)dentity politics in SuAndi's *The Story of M* and Lemn Sissay's *Something Dark*." *Contemporary Poetry in Crisis*. Ed. Charlie Armstrong, Sean Crosson, and Anne Karhio. Basingstoke: Palgrave Macmillan, 2010. 230–47.

———. Personal interview with Lemn Sissay. July 2008.

Poe, Edgar Allan. "Democratic Review." November 1844. books.eserver.org/fiction/poe/marginalia.html/document_view. Web. 15 October 2009.

Ramey, Lauri. "SuAndi." *Dictionary of Literary Biography: Twenty-First-Century "Black" British Writers*. Ed. R. Victoria Arana. Sumter, South Carolina: Bruccoli, Clark, and Layman; & Detroit, Michigan: Gale Research Company, 2009: 291–8.

Sissay, Lemn. *Listener*. Edinburgh: Canongate, 2008.

———. *Morning Breaks in the Elevator*. Edinburgh: Payback Press, 1999.

———. *Rebel Without Applause*. Newcastle upon Tyne: Bloodaxe Books, 1992.

———. *Something Dark*. Osborne, "Lemn Sissay's Life Source," 327–347.

———. *Tender Fingers in a Clenched Fist*. London: Bogle-L'Ouverture, 1988.

Solomos, John. *Race and Racism in Britain*. 1989. London: Palgrave Macmillan 2003.

SuAndi. *Acts of Achievement Colloquium 2001*. Ed. SuAndi. Manchester: artBlacklive, 2002.

———."Cultural Memory and Today's Black British Poets and Live Artists." *Dictionary of Literary Biography: Twenty-First-Century "Black" British Writers*. Ed. R. Victoria Arana. Sumter, South Carolina: Bruccoli, Clark, and Layman; & Detroit, Michigan: Gale Research Company, 2009. 31–49.

———. *Nearly Forty.* Liverpool, UK: Spike Books, 1992.

———. "She Telling Secrets." *Dictionary of Literary Biography: Twenty-First-Century "Black" British Writers.* Ed. R. Victoria Arana. Sumter, South Carolina: Bruccoli, Clark, and Layman; & Detroit, Michigan: Gale Research Company, 2009. 47–9.

———. *Style in Performance.* 1990. Manchester: Pink Heater Press, 1991.

———. "The Story of M." *4 For More.* Ed. SuAndi. Manchester: Black Arts Alliance, 2002. 1–18.

———. *There Will Be No Tears.* Manchester: The Pankhurst Press, 1995.

Trigg, Stephanie. *Gwen Harwood.* Melbourne: Oxford University Press, 1994.

Tutu, Samera Owusu. "The Resounding Underground: Performance Poetry in the UK Today." *Dictionary of Literary Biography: Twenty-First-Century "Black" British Writers.* Ed. R. Victoria Arana. Sumter, South Carolina: Bruccoli, Clark, and Layman; & Detroit, Michigan: Gale Research Company, 2009. 157–69.

Wright, Beth-Sarah. "Dub Poet Lekka Mi: An Exploration of Performance Poetry, Power and Identity Politics in Black Britain." *Black British Culture and Society: A Text Reader.* Ed. Kwame Owusu. London and New York: Routledge, 2000. 271–88.

Eartha Kitt Once Told Me

SuAndi

Eartha Kitt[1] once told me that if I wanted to hang out with Eartha then where were we going. However, if I wanted to hang with Eartha Kitt I would need to come to one of her shows because I could only find Miss Kitt on stage. I understood at once what she was telling me, and it wasn't simply that she didn't let fans into her private time, but that the stage self and the personal self were, and had to be, two separate identities. Otherwise, the performer might start sitting down to breakfast. Eartha needn't have worried. I had been schooled in reality by a tough and warm band of performers on the outer regions of the entertainment circuit in local pubs and in comedy and small-small scale art venues.

"Ladies and you blokes listen up, tonight for your entertainment we have here on stage!" Jo Brand, Henry Normal, Nick Toczek, Lemn Sissay, and SuAndi. And so it went on, as our little group of performers were mixed and matched in local gigs. We were not a company, as the line-up would often change. Sometimes Steve Coogan was on the bill. Other nights it would be Kevin Fegan, Clare Mooney, and the late Linda Smith, and my identity would often change from a Manchester poet to Caribbean, the former being true, the latter not.[2]

Lemn was already established as the Ethiopian poet. Whereas me, I was still "up and coming," often ending up on the program immediately following Jo's satirical wit with its sexy overtones – no wonder one group of lads in Leeds complained that I wasn't funny. I wasn't. But Jo gave them a mouthful and they were disgruntled but remained reasonably quiet.

It wasn't that I was heckled because of a lack of popularity. Actually, to be honest, a couple of times Henry Normal and I sat not with the audience but with the staff who had forgotten to advertise our gig. No, not heckled . . . but I did stumble a few times, to be picked up and dusted off by my co-performers. Their guidance and advice was boosted by a particular knowledge-sharing that could only go on between Lemn and I as the only (most of the time) two Black performers on the bill.

As each of the group went on with their careers, some diversifying, all of them gaining higher profiles as they established their successful careers, I started to listen to my own voice and slowly began to understand that what made a performance poet special was the ability to speak in a voice that they, the poet, believes in.

This is particularly important to me as so many of my writings are soliloquies. Something else I learnt from being with this particular amazing array of multi-talented artists was that we were all finding our own voices and sharing these stories, framed by our life images.

> We move with memories
> Voices we remember
> In places we no longer recognize
> Like tides they wash over us
> So that if we stand perfectly still
> Possibly, we can hear the sea[3]

I believe that, as people of African descent, we can always hear the sea. That sound is part of our history. The sea, the huge transporter that carried us further and further away from our families, our people, our land, our true homes.

> Did you know that the sea voices a hunger?
> That cries constantly at the bows of small boats
> And the hulks of cruise liners
> Like a thirsty dog lapping its empty bowl ("At Sea")

However, I am jumping my own timeline. I think I am right in saying that whenever I have been interviewed I am always asked this one question, "Who has inspired you?" It is a difficult one to answer, particularly if the interview is just before a performance with another writer, for one has to be careful not to cause offence.

In my own timeline of writing, my first inspiration was my mother, for it was on her life that I completed my first full piece of writing. Putting her life, her biography together as a family history led to my ICA (Institute of Contemporary Art) commission of what became "The Story of M." Although this production was to happen many years later in my career, my mother remains my first voice of inspiration. Her Irish genes were so embedded in oral history that my story telling is an art inherited. However, no-one was really interested in women like her, ordinary working class women.

> I am an ordinary woman
> Nothing special
> Ordinary. Nothing. Nothing. Ordinary.
> There is nothing to show

> Nothing to tell
> Ordinary. Nothing. Ordinary. ("Ordinary Woman")

Here was the connection, even though the barriers of the race line were still wide and high, there was a connection between the English working – "under" – class woman and Black women trying to find not their voices, but a means to communicate.

I was a co-founding member of BlackScribe, a Black women's writing collective.[4] The years I spent with BlackScribe, and in particular the three other co-founders Tina Tamsho, Carline Montoute, and Elaine Okoro, were fundamental to my development as a writer. There were other inspirations, none more so than Lemn Sissay, but here I want to concentrate on women. Because we women have been forced by a global patriarchal society to be seen and not heard. Our tongues have swollen in our mouths, we have almost choked on our words, gagged on our stories, and swallowed so many life experiences that our collective ability to stand up and move forward is truly amazing. We are the sisters and sistahs who have been writing on the edge and have lifted the words from the page into the spoken word arena.

It will be difficult for me not to dedicate this chapter as homage to other writers. However, if I did so I would be doing them a disservice, for I have no knowledge as to how they conceive their work. I can only truly speak for myself and, as a poet, that is the best starting point for the creative flow.

My first poems came from the two different points of who I am. On the one hand, there was confidence in me the woman, feline, female; I was slimmer and younger. I didn't have a man and didn't care because I knew I could have one if I so chose. Even a few extra pounds could not undermine me.

> I long to be thin but I'm fat
> A sexy kitten but I'm fat
> A long willowy wisp of feminism
> But I am a fat that's a fact I am fat.
> But honey before you take leave of me
> Step up close let me wrap you in the whole of me
> When you discover the length and the breadth of me
> You'll be glad that I'm fat that's a fact (SuAndi, "I Long" 59)

The other extreme was political but the voice was muffled. I was writing about Africa, a country I didn't know as a living space. I was writing a history of hurt and pain, a history of slavery and abuse. I still write on these topics but I have grown more comfortable within myself, so, though Africa is the root base of my soul, England is my home. My voices are closer, closer to my own experiences where the chock of slavery is now the smothering blanket of racism. But I refuse to be suffocated and when I raise my voice, I am in a choir of others.

It is their voices that inspire me. They are the sisters, the white women who have downed tools and lifted up pens in order to write their way through life. There are my Sistahs, the Black women with whom I share a commonality of experience that shape us into duets, quartets, choirs of hundreds of voices, and always when necessary we give each other space to be the soloist. Is this carrying a metaphor too far? I think not. For the performance of poetry is simply lyrics where the music plays in the mind.

Let me return to Eartha Kitt. Eartha was appearing in pantomime[5] at the Palace Theatre Manchester when Granada Television rang to suggest she review my CD *Soliloquy*, a collection of poetry. Although I said yes, I was worried. What did I have in common with this international star? We came from different places, were from different generations: we were different in every way aside from the fact we were both of African heritage. How stupid of me. From the moment we met, Eartha did nothing but talk about my work. She wanted to record one or two things, turning thereby my poetry into lyrics. There was that commonality of understanding of experiences. The fact that Eartha was Black meant that certain pieces had a certain resonance for her. Over the years I have found that my work speaks to many women from different cultural backgrounds.

> When reading SuAndi's poetry, I found so many that I related to, even though this artist is living a completely different experience than me. This is the value of inclusiveness that Afrocentric art strives towards, . . . I am a white, female student in Middle America who has found a connection to a Black British (Liverpool) woman and artist of Nigerian descent. If that ain't Afrocentric inclusivity, then I don't know what is![6]

Afrocentric inclusivity; now there's some terminology for you.

When I wrote "Cultural Memory and Today's Black British Poets to Live Artists," I thought the chapter would be rejected for its lack of academic depth. My theory is simple and not new (I expect).

> How clever this cultural memory is, for it allows for the possibility of remembering and forgetting, so that there is a fusion representation of the present with the past. And in some cases, for some writers who indeed have no first-generation inkling of their ancestral home. Then the form of their art practice, the style of their work, particularly in stage format, will reveal itself without their necessarily calling on it. It will simply be there, a part of them just like their genetic make-up. Their cultural memory will simply one day wake up and begin to revive, regenerate and inspire them. So like myself, that youthful silly female obsession with size and weight is replaced, not by a politicalised chanting voice of dissent for all things English and British, but with a deeper understanding of self-positioning on a global stage where so many are still waiting at the back door. Not the stage door! The back door! Down the dark alleyway, still waiting to get in. (SuAndi, "Cultural Memory" 40)

What poetry allows the writer to do is to share who we are. The poems that I was forced to read in school told me nothing about where I was or where I came from in society, they told me nothing about me. I never heard a living poet until I had started on the long road of writing myself. In the late eighties at Cornerhouse Manchester, there was a festival of poetry – I don't remember the name. I sat and listened to poet after poet, and what I was to discover, to my never-ending delight, was that when the Black poets performed it was truly a performance.

I was already writing. I had just a couple of performances under my girdle (not that I wore one then – or even now, for the record – but I can't say belt in this chapter of female writing, well can I?) I am not trying to say that all the white poets merely "read" their work, but when a true performance poet took to the stage, you could feel the attention of the audience, sense their desire to be taken on a journey that would evoke any of the emotions from sorrow to laughter, passion to understanding. Once again, I thanked the gods that I had developed a performance style before I ever saw or heard of Dr Maya Angelou, to whom, in the beginning of my career, I was often compared. I have always disliked it when people feel it necessary to liken the work of one poet to another. "Oh you are just like . . ." There are clones about, I have seen Lemn's style on a number of occasions and none of them have been male writers. However, at the end of the day, the voice is the voice of authenticity in the work. It is the work that cannot truly be duplicated and as I have already said, I have heard some bad attempts to do so.

I am chaos. I am not a dedicated set-amount-of-hours-each-day, writer. My locations are where life places me. My inspirations are often the overheard. Sometimes they are visually inspired.

On my first trip to New York, I visited a photographic installation by Carrie Mae Weems, "And 22 Million Very Tired and Very Angry People," at the New Museum of Contemporary Art.[7] The catalogue was a three or four-fold sheet. I found a pencil and began to write along the edges of the paper and in the margins. I lost this writing for a couple of years and when I finally located it I developed it into *This is All I've Got to Say* (1993), my first ICA commission as the performance poet moves to the Live Art stage.

I used to say that for me there were very clear demarcations in my writing. If I write direct to paper then the poem would live in print, it might occasionally be read within a performance but it would never be a performance piece in itself. I realize now that this is not entirely true. Some work has to be jotted down immediately because my brain is anxious to move on to other matters. This means that poems can begin their life on the edges of newspapers, serviettes, theater programs and very, very often, conference papers. At other times I let my brain set up its own notepad so that in the middle of a conversation, for example, the edge of my brain is taking notes. Sometimes it is capable of getting the first full draft together in my head whilst I am shopping, having dinner or whatever social interaction. I am told that when I do this, my head tilts slightly to one side. It is I believe, the only give-away. It is perhaps also a signifier of madness.

Conferences are great places of inspiration for me. It is often writing born out of boredom. If I am not responding to some comment made by a speaker, usually one that makes me angry, then I am focusing on the delegates until someone in particular fuels my concentration.

This is one example, from when I watched a women hassled by the necessity of having to bring her new baby with her, trying to mix the professional self with motherhood. Embarrassed every time her baby makes an audible sound and then smiling with such serenity as it lies content in her arms.

SHE WILL SMILE

She will smile
Retell stories
Laugh a little
Shake her head
And occasionally sigh
Confession being good for the soul
She'll admit with gay abandonment
Yes indeed – some days
She wished she'd never

Holding her breath
She runs hands a little coarse from always doing
Over a girth, she never noticed spreading
And raises her breasts back into a cleavage
Now long gone

Perfume cheap
Or ridiculously expensive
Could never wash away the scent
That lingers
And the truth be known
Often she inhales it
Holding dirty clothes to her cheek
And breathing

She aims for perfect
And by her own judgement
Fails to measure up to standard
So no small wonder
She disappoints herself
And chastises all her errors with tears

> Why did no one warn her
> She'd never be able
> To do, see, everything
> Be, here, there, everywhere
>
> And of how her heart would whimper
> Each time she lost sight
> Of this so precious gift
> Bestowed by nature
> A miniature perfection of her
> And the man who loved her enough
> To place his child within her protection
> And name her mother (SuAndi, "Mother")

It is pretty hard living your life with voices in your head. Ntozake Shange's[8] "life on the edge," has been well documented. I have never seen Ntozake's *For Colored Girls Who Have Considered Suicide/When the Rainbow Is Enuf* (1975), but I have read it in what she describes as a choreopoem, and 99.9% of it makes total sense to me. That is not true of all her work, simply because of the Latino influences in her writing, but when we have performed together, audiences remarked on how similar our very different performances are – which is pretty remarkable considering that there exist two very different languages between England and the United States of America.

I believe what Ntozake terms a choroepoem is very different to performance poetry as a genre in itself.[9] Ntozake wrote *For Colored Girls* to be performed, whereas performance poets are not actors. I like to consider my own performances as small scenes in a one act presentation, with each scene being taken on by a specific persona. I pledged to myself that I would never bore my audience with an explanation of the poem, so I have developed a style of linking each scene and slipping into "character" so that the audience is (I hope) surprised when they realize that SuAndi has left and the stage is now occupied by "someone else." Surely these are the 'masks" that Dunbar refers to:

> *We wear the mask that grins and lies,*
> *It hides our cheeks and shades our eyes,—*
> *This debt we pay to human guile;*
> *With torn and bleeding hearts we smile,*
> *And mouth with myriad subtleties.* (Dunbar 1896)

Jackie Kay[10] once told me how she was riding in a train in Scotland not long after 9/11, when a group of lads asked her where she was from. No matter what she told them they had insisted that she was a Muslim, therefore (in their eyes) a terrorist.

Jackie told me how her fear slowly began to rise until eventually they got bored of her and left the train.

This forced identity switch on this Scottish-born Black woman is a simple example of how we move across identities that always place us outside of the mainstream: not that any one of us wishes to be a collaborator with those who would oppress those we see as part of our extended family. I don't know if a poem has yet resulted from Jackie's experience, but I am pretty confident that one will eventually be written.

In many ways our writings as women – as Black women in particular – follow the beliefs of *The Theatre of the Oppressed*. As Barbara Santos explains, this method, created by Augusto Boal and based on the Aesthetic of the Oppressed, focuses on the combat against the aesthetic invasion to our brains, to the domain of ideas and perceptions and authoritarian imposition of pre-established conceptions of what is beauty, certainty or desirable. It fights against the strategies perpetrated by the oppressive system that uses aesthetic ways – sound, image, and word – to influence and convince the oppressed they are incapable of creating, participating, and, specially, deciding by themselves."

> *I am not defeated by rejection*
> *It serves to heighten my determination*
> *Of this one thing, I am sure* (SuAndi, *Mary Seacole*)

I wrote that!

They are part of Mary's closing words in the opera *Seacole*. When I was first approached to write the libretto, I had no idea what the word meant, and I had difficulty looking it up because I couldn't spell it. Nevertheless, one pledge I have managed to keep since I became a writer is never to say no at the first post. To express an interest, get more detail, and then decide if I am capable of seeing the project through.

Rejection is almost the life commodity of a writer and most definitely of women.

However, just as with any consumer, we have the option to buy in or opt out. I prefer the latter. To measure oneself on the negative of any one other is simply self-destructive. As women, we must be strong enough to re-evaluate. As writers we must be prepared to edit, rewrite, share with someone we trust, edit it again, and consider – is it worthy of our skills? And in a strange way, as Performance Poets, we must always consider whether it is exactly what we want our (the) audience to hear, because in a strange way people hold us (you) much more to what you said over anything written down. It is almost as though the fact that they heard it (or indeed a friend heard it) has much more validity over anything in print. There is danger in the spoken word, for it takes you from writing on the edge to center stage.

Notes

1. Eartha Kitt: African American cabaret Artist, singer and actress 1927–2008. http://www.earthakitt.com.

2. Jo Brand: English Comedian and Novelist. http://www.vivienneclore.co.uk.

Henry Normal: comedian, television producer, poet, and writer. He is Managing Director of Baby Cow Productions Ltd., which he set up with Steve Coogan. See http://www.babycow.co.uk.

Lemn Sissay: poet, playwright. http://www.lemnsissay.com/lemn/index.ht.

Kevin Fegan: poet, playwright. http://www.kevinfegan.co.uk.

Nick Toczek: comedian, television producer, poet, and writer.

Claire Mooney: singer. http://www.clairemooney.co.uk.

Linda Smith (1958–2006): stand-up comic and comedy writer.

3. Extract taken from a narrative produced for Chantal Oakes video installation, Preston, Lancashire, 2008.

4. For a complete bibliography of BLACKSCRIBE, see www.lancs.ac.uk/fass/projects/movingmanchester/docs/Moving%20Manchester%20Complete%20Bibliography.doc.

5. Pantomime (informally, panto) is a musical-comedy theatrical production traditionally found in Great Britain.

6. Personal e-mail from Ianie Henry, Senior Program Assistant of the Department of Theater Arts, University of Louisville.

7. www.newmuseum.org.

8. Ntzoake Shange: African American poet, playwright, author, and educator. www.bridgesweb.com/blacktheatre/shange.html.

9. Shange defines choreopoetry as poetic drama that moves, sings, and speaks to the immediate feelings, soul, and spirit of our inner most being.

10. Jackie Kay: poet, novelist, and playwright born in Edinburgh, Scotland in 1961 to a Scottish mother and a Nigerian father. www.contemporarywriters.com/authors/?p=auth54.

Bibliography

Boal, Augusto. *Theatre of the Oppressed*. 1975. London: Pluto, 2008.

———. *Aesthetics of the Oppressed*. New York: Routledge, 2006.

Dunbar, Paul Laurence. *We Wear the Mask. Lyrics of Lowly Life*. London: Dodd, Mead, and Company, 1896.

Shange, Ntozake. *For Colored Girls Who Have Considered Suicide/When the Rainbow Is Enuf*. New York: Scribner, 1975.

SuAndi. "At Sea." 2006. Unpublished.

———. "Cultural Memory and Today's Black British Poets and Live Artists." *"Black" British Aesthetics Today*. Ed. R. Victoria Arana. Newcastle: Cambridge Scholars Publishing, 2007. 31–49.

———. "I Long to be Thin." *BlackScribe*. Manchester: GMVC, 1990.

———. *Mary Seacole*. Opera libretto, 2000. http://www.gyenyame.org.uk.

———. "Mother." 2009. Unpublished.

———. "Ordinary Woman." *Style in Performance* 9 (2002): 59.

———. "Soliloquy." Originally published as "Playing for Life." *Style in Performance* 9 (2002): 5.

———. *This is All I've Got to Say*. London: Live Art, 1993.

Heterotopical Routes through Barcelona: The Reshaping of Public Space in the "Galactic" Poetry of Jaume Sisa

Mercè Picornell Belenguer

The marginality of poetic production distributed in non-institutionalized circuits and media is reinforced in cultural contexts that are in a process of reconstruction following years of repression and censorship.[1] This is what happened in Catalan culture in the 1970s, against a backdrop of national identity policies based on an ideal of unity in the face of bad luck and loyalty to the type of tradition that tends to demotivate dissident discourse and the experimental creations produced within it, either by ignoring them or integrating them as marginal creations which only allow the centrality of more canonical production to be confirmed. Towards the end of the Franco period, Catalan poetry became an amalgam of different tendencies in which, among others, the residual claim for the type of symbolist lyricism that was canonical before the Spanish Civil War lived side by side with committed readings of historical realism, and also with experimental creations diffused through underground publications and on public stages linking the musical production and plastic arts of the time. From this interartistic point of ligature, poetry came out of the books and began to occupy the public space, circulating in a new network of cultural diffusion (alternative art galleries, music festivals, public poetry readings, etc.) but also as a reinvention of the imagery associated with the space and identity to which it subscribes.

This essay aims to study how this reinvention takes place in the representations of Barcelona by Jaume Sisa, a poet and singer who first appeared at the end of the 1960s in connection within "Grup de Folk."[2] We will see that, despite their naive appearance, Sisa's poems and songs denounce the possibility of representing the city in essentialist terms. They put forward a new poetics and politics of recognition based upon the acceptance of the variety of backgrounds that coexist in the contemporary urban space, as opposed to the "place of memory" imagined by those struggling to reconstruct the Catalan identity as a recuperation of an idyllic heritage. In other words, in Sisa's works, the culture of the democratic city is founded on contradiction and simulacrum, and is therefore, as we will see, more related to camp aesthetics than to the search for authenticity that we find in most contemporary Catalan literary production. During the 1970s, Sisa's work would evolve towards the creation of his own poetic world, staged in some of the new cultural spaces – such as the now mythical Zeleste venue or the first Catalan rock festival, Canet Rock (1975) – as well as others that have not become part of the traditional topography of historic sites in the Catalan capital, such as La Paloma, an industrial premises converted into a dance hall in 1903 that remained one of the reference points of Barcelona night life until a few years ago. These venues and events constituted a fringe of creative freedom in the Spain of the late Franco period, places where young creators had a sense of occupying the public space as well as voicing their concerns, without having to depend on the constraints of the type of publishing company that existed in Catalonia at the time, which was marked by an ideology of defending Catalan culture that determined the selection of products for publication and shaped their reception. Thus, spaces that had been traditionally considered simple leisure venues were charged with a lyrical content that would not dissipate until the end of the seventies, when, with the arrival of democracy, conventional artistic circuits began to take on new experimental projects that enjoyed greater audience projection but were often less intent on making a statement.

To reflect on the reformulation of the proposals for experimental poetry in the seventies, this text looks at the re-shaping of the imagery of Barcelona in the poetry of Jaume Sisa, works that were published on paper but sung and staged in numerous shows in which psychedelic lyrics combine with kitsch stage sets recreating decadent cabaret performances, circus imagery, and old-fashioned musical galas.[3] Specifically, in this analysis, I will take as the object of study *Lletres Galàctiques* (1984), a book that, according to the author, includes two types of composition: "Lletres *musicals*" 'musical lyrics' (or songs) and "Lletres *de paper*" 'paper lyrics,' which are often poems or poetic proses of different lengths that are linked thematically with the different music albums of the composer. I will also illustrate my analysis by referring to the album *Barcelona Postal*, an *assemblage* of songs, hustle and bustle, and photographs that offers a curious re-reading of the touristic and symbolic imagery of the city. We will see how Sisa's performed and written poetry is submitted as an intervention in the symbolic space of the city, as a reformulation of its representations produced from the celebration of the heterogeneity of cultural backgrounds that exists within it. That heterogeneity contrasts with the models for recovering the "symbols of Catalan identity" that determined the policies for cultural reconstruction from the more *nationalist* sectors during the late Franco period and the Transition to democracy. These policies were concerned with the task of recovering cultural prestige and reducing the interference that had been caused by the Francoist imposition of the Spanish language as the only vehicle for learning and culture.

The Heterogeneous Memory of a *Liminal* City

The city that Sisa recreates in his work both is and is not Barcelona. In other words, it is the myth of the modern, rebellious city created in the seventies, a myth which would be modified in the eighties to give way to the urban materialization that has become known as the "Barcelona model" and, from the nineties onward, to a broad critical review that would culminate in public debate on the sense and "results" of the Universal Forum of Cultures 2004.[4] In the story of what Joan Ramon Resina has called in the title of his recent book "the rise and decline of an urban image," the Barcelona of the Transition period embodied the crisis of the time. Barcelona in the seventies was a city opposed to order: a city of urban chaos but also one of political mobilization, which, with Franco's death and the end of the unitary utopia of anti-Francoism, began to diversify its struggles. This imaginary city of the post-Franco period was also a community situated within a conflict of interests involving a collision between different ways of understanding urban identity. Resina writes:

> Peopled by liminal beings, post-Franco Barcelona lacked a sense of origin. With Franco or against Franco, many would not suffer Barcelona to remember itself. No longer Catalan and not yet completely Spanish, Barcelona was suspended in a bottomless present made of pure potentiality. Being no place in particular, it could be thought as the threshold to all places. (8)

The Barcelona of the Transition was a city in the process of being defined, a *liminal* city which some would not allow to recover "its own" memory. However, I would like to add that once the single discourse of Francoism had been overcome, the "memory" of the democratic city could not be anything but an area of conflict in which different ideas about which cultural heritage needed to be reinscribed coexisted. How can we place the first works by Sisa in this *liminal* place? I postulate that his urban representations are situated in an intentionally ambiguous manner in this conflict of identities, taking advantage of the drive of the conflict itself to transgress the univocal conceptions of public space and national memory to which they subscribe. The singer-songwriter appropriates the liminal space for himself; he makes it one of the different potentialities that characterize the city in Transition, emerging from the darkest years of the Franco dictatorship to prepare for a democracy that has yet to be reinvented. That is why the cultural references in Sisa's work are intentionally incoherent, the result of a recycling of cultural backgrounds which contain all kinds of characters. So it is no coincidence that his best known song "Qualsevol nit pot sortir el sol" 'The sun may come out any night' – which was banned by the censors at the Canet Rock festival (1975) but has now almost become the hymn of a generation – conjures up a magic festival of characters from a wide range of children's imagery, from Obelix to Frankenstein's monster and from the Catholic comic hero of the Franco era, Roberto Alcázar, to the Catalan pre-war cultural symbol of the Patufet.

Both the combination of heritages and the juxtaposition of images used as the single cohesive link in his poems and songs mean that Sisa's urban universe is not sketched as a hybrid scene that is, in the words of Néstor Garcia Canclini, the result of a mixture of diverse cultural backgrounds (14), such as those that converge in modern cities (22). In Sisa's work, superimposition never seeks to mix, but is rather a game of contrasts, the curious collision caused by the everyday meeting of these multiple heritages; it attempts to show the heterogeneity rather than to postulate synthesis. To analyze his urban representations as more than a paradigm that celebrates hybridism, we need a model featuring diversity, such as that constructed by Antonio Cornejo Polar when talking about what he calls "heterogeneous" literatures; those literatures characterized by the inclusion of a duplicity of sociocultural signs without necessarily attempting to make a coherent sum of them. The discourse of the migrant, for example, according to Cornejo, "duplicates the territory of the subject and offers it or condemns it to speak from more than one place" (841). In fact, the various heteronyms in which, as we shall see, Jaume Sisa's styles and backgrounds end up distributing themselves, may be the result of an ironic attempt to resolve the "offer" or creative "condemnation" referred to by the Peruvian critic.

This place of multiple enunciation enables Sisa to characterize himself in an interview published in 1976, simultaneously as a "local singer, a simple boy from the Poble Sec neighborhood of Barcelona, who humbly and lovingly sings his songs" (Durall 14) and – introducing a qualification that he would use resourcefully to designate his work – as a *galactic* singer-songwriter, situating himself between the microhistory of the neighbors from his traditional Barcelona neighborhood and the unfathomable mystery of the movements of the cosmos. This intentional ambiguity can also be found in the mix of styles and genres of his songs. When asked, in the same interview, "How would you describe what you play? Songs, *sardana*, country, pop, rock, jazz?," he replied unabashedly, "I am one of the precursors of the 'new Catalan style' or 'nou style català'" (Durall 14). Imposture is constant in the work of Sisa: evidently one cannot be the precursor of a style that has not yet emerged. This ambiguous placement is a determinant of the reception of Sisa's work during the seventies, both in counter-cultural environments, obsessed with identifying the subversive aspects of his songs, and in the most nationalist Catalan magazines of the time, which interpreted the presence in Sisa's songs of references considered to be *Spanish* and *subcultural*, and therefore not fitting in with the coherent design of his project for the national reconstruction of Catalan culture, as the result of a simple "nostalgic evocation."

This play on the ambiguity of identities and the apparent incoherence that Sisa wove into his initial works can be seen in the representations of Barcelona in his texts. The imagery of Sisa's city is one of chaos and his descriptions contain abundant references to lengthy and unconnected enumerations. It is the city that contains, as in the song "Carrer" from the *Orgia* album (1971), "an Alpha Romeo and thirty cardboard grannies/ a buddhist monk/an Englishman and a teacher/two young ladies with thick lipstick/ [and] a grand old general, paralyzed from head to toe" (1984: 22).[5] Sisa recreates this enumerative description in the different works of poetic prose in *Lletres galàctiques*, which are dedicated to the city itself. In the "Sinfonia Atòmica" 'Atomic symphony,' for example, description becomes a simple chain of images and dispersed qualifiers:

> Melody Symphony Atomic urban citizen Subterranean Casco Antiguo Las Cloacas dos aceras architects upside-down ripped-apart topsy-turvy suburban Waiter Atomic Bar Rincón J. Birbe company shopping plastic trumpets and hacksaws flutes unfinished symphony atomic explosively asphaltic in front of the Ateneu spitting twenty years photography at the sawmill cacophony canteens S.E.U. marimba supersonic symphony clean of crowds. (Lletres 30)[6]

In the poetic prose of the opening of "Lletres *de paper*" on the *Barcelona Postal* album, the city also becomes, more than a stage, a living landscape saturated with different cultural identities, where a variety of objects coexist: "the covert play houses, the American aircraft carriers, the drunken tourists from Andalusia, the breakwaters, the midnight walks, the cake shops . . . the rats, the vanguard exhibitions, the back of City Hall, the cheap meals, the rag paper monuments . . . " (*Lletres* 173-5).[7] This multilingual and non-synthetic representation of the city would be enhanced by a poetics based on fragmentation, the "spasmodic style" of research that Sisa himself talked about (*Lletres* 13) when describing his *galactic* poetry as the result of a "heterodox or combinatory representation of different systems" (*El Viajante*). This is an aesthetic proposal that would not be out of place in the context of the detours from realism identified by the critics in the literature of the young Catalan writers of the seventies, marked by a dichotomy between investigations into formal experimentation and the simple innovation of content. In this context, Sisa's *galactic* poetry is close to the trials of the experimentalists and we could also place it, for example, next to the call for incoherence as a creative strategy by the Ignasi Ubac writer's collective – a group that published a whole series of programmed articles in the newspaper supplements of the time, influenced by the works of Barthes, Kristeva and Derrida, which were just arriving in Spain – or in relation to the writing of poems and prose that imitates the effect of automatic writing by authors such as Biel Mesquida and Quim Monzó. In the 1970s, Sisa did not qualify his work as avant-garde – and neither did his experimental writer contemporaries – but described his aesthetic option as the result of what he called a "de-intellectualized conceptualism." He therefore places himself in the context of the type of seventies creator who approached the parameters of conceptual art that dominated the experimental art world of the time from the point of view of literature. In fact, as Margalida Pons (2007) has commented, in a brief polemic in 1977 about the meaning of experimental literature on the pages of the *Tele/eXprés* daily, Jaume Melendres called for the term "conceptual literature" in place of other labels such as "alternative," "avant-garde," or "experimental literature" and defined literary conceptualism on the basis of the characteristics it shared with other artistic production along the same lines, which included the use of extra-artistic materials, an iconoclastic nature, and the elevation of everyday objects to the category of art.

Identity as Simulacrum: The Reuse of *Camp* Aesthetics
The most easily identifiable conceptual footprint in Sisa's work on the city can be found in both the staging of his songs as unrepeatable acts of performance art and in the combination of poetry with everyday urban images such as "found objects" – in other words, objects that are decontextualized as a result of their placement in a deliberately chaotic discursive context where they take on new meanings, where daily life mixes with the mystical and the vindication of Catalan culture does not contradict the recovery of popular Spanish post-war culture. From this mix of objects and cultural backgrounds, references and styles, it is impossible to shape a stable identity: from the Catalan recovery of the "signs of national identity" we move on to a representation of identity that is like a collage, made of *objets trouvés* found in the city streets. Thus the mixture represented is one made, according to the review of the album *Qualsevol nit pot sortir el sol* by music critic Jordi Garcia-Soler in *Serra d'Or*, "using procedures related to kitsch, seeking new and original expressive forms, slapdash and even 'bad taste' in appearance, almost the result of the author overcoming his sentimental education by clearly shocking methods that benefit from depth" (62). Sisa's aesthetic perhaps approaches kitsch in the sense that it takes advantage of the unconnected backgrounds to build representations that are nothing more than collages or simulacrums, which is why it is difficult for the work to attain the kind of depth that the critic views as positive. The aberrant mix of backgrounds and aesthetics in Sisa's work comes from an awareness of the image of identity that it promotes and of the contradiction to which it subscribes. It comes close to an avant-garde approach to kitsch, generating a new modern sensibility: camp.

Camp is the result of a reuse of negative prestige in the aesthetic manipulation of the aberrant, which, as Matei Calinescu writes, "under the guise of ironic connoisseurship, can freely indulge in the pleasures offered by the most awful kitsch" (230). In any case, the pleasing reuse of camp sensibility in Sisa's work would involve a low-conflict form of irony, which has more to do with a play on complicity with the receiver in terms of the recognition of a partially shared heritage than with the re-creation of ugliness or the wound of sarcasm. Sisa's texts use innocence, as Susan Sontag's camp does, simultaneously supporting and corrupting it. This can be seen in songs such as "El fill del mestre" 'The teacher's son,' where the innocent child that features in it begins by simply "making dolls" and ends up "setting fire to the house";

or in "Jugant a bolles" 'Game of marbles,' where childish lyrics seem ridiculous in relation to the tune that accompanies them, which is in the purist form of the Catalan "nova cançó," a group of Catalan singers committed to the nationalist cause and the defense of democracy, influenced by the music of George Brassens or Jacques Brel.

The album *Barcelona Postal*, made together with the painter and sculptor Antoni Miralda, is a good example of this aesthetic reuse of camp. Working with Miralda gave Sisa's urban world the form of a curious experiment, which, although distributed as a commercial album, was inspired by the ideas of conceptual art. The whole album takes the form of a kind of *assemblage*, the artistic technique that consists of bringing together heterogeneous materials of everyday use. In *Barcelona Postal*, however, the artistic support is as visual as it is sound-based. In this recording there are songs about the city in different languages and genres (*rumba*, swing, ballad, *pasodoble*, etc.); voices recorded in the street presented as a cacophony of the hustle and bustle of the city that connects us with interphone systems, market stallholders, and tourist comments about the food in Barcelona; and even recited fragments of the poem "Barcelona ja no és bona, o mi paseo solitario en primavera" by Jaime Gil de Biedma. The album is also illustrated by postcards of the city created by Miralda, which parody the monumental perspective that is offered by conventional picture postcards of the Catalan capital. There is a photo of the caravelle "Santa Maria" – a replica of the ship commanded by Christopher Columbus on display in the Port of Barcelona – but set in a filthy port; an image of Sisa and Miralda looking at the face of the Columbus statue in the old port, covered in pigeon excrement; a photo of Sisa surrounded by the type of people who do not usually appear on postcards; a photo of a large chocolate cake with a reproduction of the Barcelona monuments on it[8]; and a photo of a dish of little shields bearing the city's coat-of-arms (*escuts*) served in a broth and jokingly titled *Escutdella*, a word that refers to one of the most typical dishes in Catalan gastronomy (*escudella*), but which could also be pronounced "*escuts d'ella*," or, referring to the city, "*her* shields." In the last two photographs, the symbol of identity is converted into a gastronomic object with a clear cultural reference for the Catalan people and with only two possible destinations: either being eaten or going off. The album also links to the aesthetic of conceptual art in the use it makes of the postcard itself as an art object. Although it cannot be said that *Barcelona Postal* is an object of Mail Art – more than that it is a consumer object and, as such, lacks the principles of being free and of alternative distribution that is characteristic of that conceptual tendency – it is true that it comes close in terms of subverting the functions of the traditional postcard. In that sense, the "postcard" genre is linked to the particular poetics of space and identity that we see in Sisa's work. Barcelona, says the only song written by him on the album, is a tourist city and a domestic city. In the end, it is like a postcard. A postcard is a reduced, economic representation of symbolic heritage, almost a miniature memory place (*lieu de mémoire*, in Pierre Nora's words), whose task is to show memory from a distance. The postcard therefore disseminates an apparently representative image of the cultural identity of the place – whether that be, to give some examples that one might find in a Barcelona souvenir shop, a view of the Sagrada Familia, a folkloric scene of people dancing the *sardana*, or . . . a Mexican hat – but it also implies the absence of any roots in the place for the person who signs it and feels the need to remember it. Under the representation of the postcard, the symbolic sites of Sisa's city become places both in the present and in *memory*; they are *practiced* places that evade both the heritage-like character of memory places and the apparent emptiness of non-places.[9]

Poetry, writes Sisa in the prologue to the songs and poems on the *Orgia* album, satisfies our need for mirrors. But it is a kind of mirror that, in his work, mixes and deforms the urban objects that it represents. This complex kaleidoscope of city identities cannot be reflected by the molds used by what he calls "yesterday's poets," who were often inspired by the idyllic, rural landscapes of inland Catalonia. He illustrates this impossibility in the poem "Reflex de l'eco" 'Reflection of an echo':

> If in the midst of an existential target
> You woke me one day at the calmest hour
> With a suit stained with adrenalin
> Aroused by the worldly echo
> Of the buzz of urban roads
> I do not know if, in the end, I would believe it
> Or if I would need a scene of nature
> To see the extent
> Of such an untranslatable, silent and personal act. (Sisa, *Lletres* 227)[10]

The poet therefore awakens at the heart of an existential crisis in an urban setting that does not allow him to clearly recognize his own state, and that clarity, he writes ironically, may be revealed more assuredly in a "natural" scene. That is why, in the following verse, he rewrites the lines in inverted commas and places them in a non-urban context, enabling him to express himself in "another register, more in keeping with the archetype": "I will wake on the riverbank, with no problem/And little by little the river will carry me/The weeds carried by the soul/Freed to abysmal depths" (*Lletres* 227).[11] The irony gathers strength if we read the lines in the context in which, as Lluís Bartomeu Meseguer observes while reflecting on the words of the "nova cançó," the singer-songwriters of the time had constructed an imagery linked with nature in a Romantic-type search for origins and identity determined by the ties between ground-homeland-country (*terra-patria-país*). All the more ironic, then, when one sees that in the review of Sisa's album *Qualsevol nit pot sortir el sol*, by musical commentator Jordi Garcia-Soler in 1975, it shares a column with other new recordings such as "Fent camí" by the *Esquirols*, specialists in mountain songs, where the link between hiking and the existential and/or national search (very deeply rooted in the Catalan tradition) is shown in songs about defending identity, authenticity, and spirituality that would become hits of the time in scouting circles and in some Catalan Catholic parishes.

Sisa's urban environment, however, does not even admit what he calls the "archetypal" register in poetry that attempted to reflect the beauty of natural scenes, nor the apparent "authenticity" of mountain songs. Those who walk through the modern city cannot do so by following the hiker's cairns; they have to improvise their route in an interspersed and chaotic setting. The modern city, writes Manuel Delgado, "cannot be reduced to a single discursive unit, because of the endless versatility of the events that take place there, its layered structure, the constant mix of between continuity and oscillation that it displays" (17). Sisa's representations show that incoherence or illegibility of the city through poetics based on an apparently arbitrary chain of well-known objects. This is the sense in which Sisa sketches a *topical* space – where common places seeking the emotional identity of the receiver abound – but one that is also *hetero*topical, in the sense that Michel Foucault gives the term in his introduction to *Les mots et les choses* (xix): a place that admits impossible connections of objects between which no meeting point can be identified, no point at which it could be possible to find stable links.[12] Barcelona is, according to Sisa in his "Simfonia atòmica" 'Atomic Symphony,' a city that is "upside-down ripped-apart topsy-turvy" and the urban chaos cannot find any order through maps. The only thing that can give it a coherent sense is the inhabitant who turns the places in the city into spaces that are walked through and charged with sense. "Thus, the street geometrically defined by urban planning," writes Michel de Certeau, "is transformed into space by walkers" (117).

The Changing Point of View of the Walker
Looking at Sisa's texts, one can see that the author's urban topography does not respond to the map coordinates but is articulated around a single axis and marks an opposition to the two options available to the citizens trying to make sense of it: "leave home and start walking or remain seated on the chair" (*Lletres* 77). This inside/outside opposition in Sisa's texts refers as much to the dichotomy between the home and the street as it does to the superimposition of the real world and the imaginary state that is reached by opening up ones awareness to what Aldous Huxley called "the doors of perception." Sisa's houses are neither hippy communes nor the designer buildings of the utopian architects of the time. On the contrary, they are modest low-class flats: damp spaces that smell of light wells and are only "brought to life by small children" (*Lletres* 65). But in Sisa's texts, the home can also be a place to find oneself. That is what he writes in the words *of paper* "The Philippine stitch doesn't slip": "The doorbell rings/I open up/and I arrive home/go in a go into the wardrobe/And I see myself" (*Lletres* 36).[13] These kinds of effects are constant in Sisa's texts. The house, he writes in "1er guió" '1st script' is a place where one can

go in only to "come out again in costume" (*Lletres* 35) onto a street that is, in fact, a stage set where anything could happen. Julià Guillamon (31) notes, however, that if there is one relevant space in the houses that appear in Sisa's poems, it is the balcony – the threshold between inside and out where the poet can just stand and watch or express himself to the outside world by shouting – "Breu exposició" (*Lletres* 32) – crying – "Primera comunió" (64) – or . . . pissing – "El fill del mestre" (52). His balconies look down onto a street represented as a maze of asphalt but also as an inhabited place. The image we get is that of the wanderer who walks the street with nothing more than the walk itself as an objective. It is the image that would be obtained through one of the practices advocated by the situationists: *dérive*. According to Guy Debord, *dérive* is what happens when you let your steps be guided by both an unconscious will to talk and by the urban environment itself.

Sisa's Barcelona streets are those of a city inhabited by prototypes – the shopkeeper, the nun, the prostitute, the notary, the waiter, and the cloth trader on the left-hand side of the Eixample – but also the unreal characters placed beside them. Among the latter is the friendly official neighborhood "Star counter" to whom Sisa dedicates one song and three pieces of poetic prose, a kind of *galactic* security guard, successor to the Three Kings of the Orient, who counts stars at night and during the day lives hidden under the stairs of a house. In the representation of characters such as this one, Sisa's unreal world becomes part of the daily life of the city; it is the result of a kind of magic realism in which the magic has lost its capacity to transform us; it is the illusionism of a childish or innocent magic trick that can only make us half smile or throw our perception of reality off balance for a moment. In many of his most unreal texts, it is the known and identified place that opens the door to this magic world. This is the case in some of Sisa's best-known songs, such as "El trist i desconsolat enterrament de la meva esposa" 'The sad and distressing burial of my wife,' where the Cathedral square in Barcelona becomes a place where the concierges, night watchmen, soldiers, and police officers dance the *sardana*, the polka, and the waltz in a funeral that has become a sad carnival in which the celebrations cannot hide death. Also, in the song "La Catedral" 'The Cathedral,' the gothic windows of the building become "doors to another life."

This other life or consciousness allows us to fly, as another song says, through "Blue orbits," and is the subject of numerous poems and pieces of prose that form part of a new type of literature, what one might call a *"trip* lit" that first appeared in Catalan literature in the works of Jaume Sisa and Pau Riba. Sisa's psychedelic descriptions seem to be linked to the exploration of consciousness, which Allen Ginsberg indicated as being the main goal of a creative experience induced by drugs.[14] They are also the result of an aesthetic contagion of imagery and writing by authors who had become models of modernity for alternative young people, such as Ginsberg himself, Jack Kerouac, and William Burroughs. Sisa's psychedelic stories are journeys towards what Ginsberg called "unused brain zones." They do not construct alternative worlds but imaginary spaces that remind us constantly of their simulated state. "Dreams are life in a dreamed cabaret," he writes in "Galactic Cabaret," where if we make life the subject of the sentence, it could in fact be just a dream of the inhabitants of that imaginary cabaret.

Heteronyms: The Impossibility of Having a Single Identity
Dreams and mirrors appear often in Sisa's compositions. The mirrors – spaces, according to Foucault, that are both virtual and real, and therefore between utopia and heterotopia[15] – allow a multiplication of identity, a dispersion of the "I"s that Sisa has used throughout his career. In particular, from 1984, the multiple cultural backgrounds that condition his creations start to become specific autonomous identities to the point where Jaume Sisa became yet another character in his own work and he could refer to himself in the third person. Faced with taking on the multiple backgrounds that exists in his imagery, Sisa proposes a heteroclite dispersion of his identities, identities that become stereotyped characters behind which he presents himself to the public and to whom he assigns a background that is as individual as it is national. Among them we find Ventura Mestres, a lieutenant from Tarragona who is studying Sisa's own literary work; Armando Llamado, a singer who lives in Segovia, sings Latin American songs, and publishes volumes of poetry under the pseudonym Arcadio Reynes; Ricardo Solfa, a man of "decadent talent" who sings boleros; and *El Viajante*, a character who allows reflection on space travel through the parodic reformulation of a professional profile that Sisa very much admired, that of the commercial salesman who walks through the city with a suitcase full of samples of different types of objects.

This heteroclite dispersion of identities that allows the multiplication of heteronyms is not as innocent as it may seem, however, since it allows Sisa to adapt to different political and cultural contexts. It means that we cannot state outright that Jaume Sisa is a bilingual singer who has betrayed the coherence of other singer-songwriters who stayed "faithful to their language." If anyone complains, it is Ricardo Solfa who sings in Spanish. This multiplied identity thus becomes a set of masks in the political game of the Transition from the Franco era to democracy. In the poetic prose "Parlant idiomes" 'Speaking languages' Sisa ironizes to the point of absurdity the links between language and identity when he writes, "Although I'm not a polyglot, I don't know how to speak, if it's not in another language, with scarcely anyone. Hotel porters, towel manufacturers, the Aragonese, footballers and music hall musicians . . . Foreigners, on the other hand, seem impeccably far away to me, even though often they cannot be understood" (*Lletres* 71).[16] Identity is just one more card to play in Jaume Sisa's game of imposture in a context where the call for national rights has become an irremediable responsibility for anyone who produces literature and music in Catalan. Sisa, on the contrary, tried to relate to a partially invented tradition of Catalan surrealists who ironize the ancestral condition of their own myths. The song "Dumbo, dumbito," from the *Roda la música* album, for example, offers a modern-day fable that rewrites the story of Saint George, patron saint of Catalonia, in an urban setting:

> Glass swing doors
> The guardsman keeps watch
> Don't let the fair imp escape
> The betrothed of the blue prince
> Automatic tannoy announces:
>
> "The revolution is pure sensation"
> Saint George prepares the lance
> With the rose in his lips
> Barricades and bumper cars in the street. (Sisa, *Lletres* 198)[17]

In this confrontation between the blue prince and the surrealist Saint George – who is reminiscent of one of the volumes of poetry by avant-garde Catalan poet Joan Salvat-Papasseit in terms of "the rose in his lips"[18] – the fairy ends up appealing to her savior to turn the warriors into statues: in other words, to make myths into simple urban monuments.

The irony in recovering the "signs of identity" that Sisa must assume as a writer and singer in Catalan appears in poems like "La revolució" 'The revolution,' where he reflects on how fatigue should both "have" and defend an identity:

> The time has come to interpret the code and the beat
> Of a language unified by joining tail and head
> From the transnational balcony
> When we lost the origin of identity, oh, what a relief! (*Lletres* 215)[19]

The irony here is reinforced in an intertextual reference identified in the last line of one of the most cited lines from "Jo vinc d'un silenci" 'I come from silence' by Valencian singer-songwriter Raimon, champion of the "nova cançó" genre, in the bold affirmation of one of the phrases which was to become an emblem of multiple causes in the defense of the Catalan language and culture: "Qui perd els orígens, perd identitat," literally "When you lose your origins, you lose your identity." Sisa's origins are heterogeneous, however, and do not give way to a single identity. He constructed his place of poetic enunciation by distancing himself from the production of the anti-Franco singers, who had grouped together under the "nova cançó" tradition, both aesthetically and in their provocative declarations. In 1976, when asked in an interview "Do you think songs should represent a political statement?" he replied "Yes, I do, but I also think that I don't believe what I think" (15). And when the same interviewer deliberately asked him "Where do you think you are heading, musically? Towards heavier Catalan rock?" he answered "I am heading, as I said before, towards my own style with a philosophical-metaphysical base in the galactic tradition" (15). Being *galactic,* like Sisa, could also mean a way of being (or not being) Catalan.

From *Desencanto* to Recognition?

The album *Transcantautor: última notícia* would mark Sisa's provisional retirement in 1984, his moving to Madrid, and the beginning of his creation in the Spanish language. Maybe his old work did not fit in with the new times. Despite the way the *desencanto* had apparently led to a lack of confirmation of the expectations of freedom following the death of Franco,[20] some of the old Spanish underground artists were well-known or worked as presenters on the public TV network. Maybe this new scene made Sisa think of the wealth of possibilities that moving to the Spanish capital, and to the Spanish culture, would offer. The press conference announcing his disappearance from the Catalan cultural scene was justified by the need to "find the person behind the character" (Batista 33) of Jaume Sisa, who no longer had anything to say. It was the end of a project that was the result of an awareness that the world, so he said, "cannot be changed by songs." Even so, Sisa seemed happy with that ending and stated, "I think that my records will be appreciated in time" (Batista 9). He therefore left the door open for a comeback and it was unlikely that he would do so through the front door of recognition and integration. In a recent interview on the Catalan Vilaweb news portal, filmed inside a taxi driving through the Barcelona streets, Sisa rejected outright the *underground* label and reconfirmed his support for the political figure of Pasqual Maragall, the socialist Mayor of Barcelona whom he had abandoned in 1984.[21] And that is what happens when one defines oneself with an identity like *galactic,* voluntarily indefinite, incoherent, and elusive. In that sense, maybe Sisa was never as galactic as at the Mercè Festival in Barcelona in 2008, a festival where somebody well-known in the Barcelona cultural scene is selected to front the celebrations. Here, the singer-songwriter presented himself as another of the characters in his own songs.[22] He posited his critical discourse against the kitsch setting of the local police in parade dress and of officially invited left-wing intellectuals who were comfortably seated in the Hall of Honour of Barcelona City Hall. The latter is a political institution that seems to be interested in reimposing the exciting and modern urban image of the Transition onto the present city of wild urbanism and circulatory chaos. An image, therefore, that is aesthetically compatible with the *retro* style of the clothes sold in what appear to be second-hand shops and the uncomfortable vinyl-covered sofas of the *vintage* cafés that proliferate in the Catalan capital, but that over time has lost the subversive claim that its aura of modernity may have had in the seventies.

Notes

1. The research for this essay was conducted within the research project "Experimental Catalan Poetry from 1970 to 1990: Discourses, Representations, Reception, Diffusion, and Sociocultural Context" (Ministerio de Ciencia e Innovación, FFI 2009-07086 FILO). I gratefully acknowledge the help of Fiona Kelso (Servei de Llengües de la UAB) and Emma Saura in translating this text into English.

2. The "Grup de Folk" (1967–68) was the initiative of a group of young musicians who, mirroring North American protest songs by singers such as Bob Dylan and Pete Seeger, attempted to reinvent popular songs in Catalan, organizing some of the first large alternative music concerts in Catalonia, such as the Parc de la Ciutadella Folk Festival, which brought together nine thousand people in Barcelona in mythical 1968.

3. Images can be seen in the documentary "Passa, passa, Sisa" directed by Lurdes Cortés for *Gran Angular* on the Spanish national TV station in Catalonia. See www.granangular.cat.

4. For an analysis of this evolution in the critical perception of the city, see the work of Josep M. Montaner and Zaida Muxí, Brad Epps, Conrad Kent and Donald McNeil in "Special Section: Barcelona and the Projection of Catalonia" from the *Arizona Journal of Hispanic Cultural Studies* (2002). The Forum of Cultures was planned as a meeting point to reflect theoretically on cultural diversity, promoted by Barcelona City Council. The results of the forum were basically the urbanization of an area peripheral to the city and a considerable sum of debts. In all, it generated broad debate about the cultural and urban planning policies of the municipal institutions.

5. "[U]n alfa romeo i trenta velles de cartró/un monjo budista/un anglès i un professor/dues senyoretes amb els llavis molt pintats/[i] un gran general paralitzat de cap a peus" (*Lletres* 22).

6. "Sintonia Simfonia Atòmica urbana ciutadana Subterrània Casco Antiguo Las Cloacas dos aceras arquitectes desgavellada desgarrada descapçada suburbana Camarero Atómico Tomás Bar Rincón J. Birbe companyia compra trompetes de plàstic i xerracs pitos inacabada sintonia atòmica explosivament asfàltic davant i l'Ateneu escupint vint anys fotografia a la fusteria cacofonia menjadors SEU [Sindicato Español Universitario] marimba supersònica simfonia neta de multituds" (Sisa, *Lletres* 30).

7. "[L]es cases de joc clandestines, els porta-avions americans, els turistes ebris d'Andalusia, els trencaones, les caminades nocturnes, les pastisseries . . . Les rates, les exposicions d'avantguarda, els voltants de l'Ajuntament, las comidas económicas, els monuments de paper d'estrassa . . . " (*Lletres* 173–5).

8. These are the monuments made into *mones*, the chocolate cakes eaten during Easter in Catalonia.

9. I take the term "practiced place" in the sense of Michel de Certeau (117; 130), when he distinguishes between the concept of place (the order that organizes relationships of coexistence) and space (determined by the movements produced within it). This distinction is not made by Augé in *Non-lieux*, where the opposition occurs more between the place as the space filled with identities and the non-place as that which does not permit the cultural backgrounds that the symbolic places foster to integrate.

10. "Si al bell mig de la diana existencial/Em despertés algun dia a l'hora calma/Amb el trajo maculat d'adrenalina/Desvetllat per l'eco mundanal/De la remor d'urbanes vies/No sé pas si, tot sencer, jo m'ho creuria/O em caldria garantia d'escenari natural/Per reconèixer la mida/D'un fet tan intraduïble, silenciós i personal" (Sisa, *Lletres* 227).

11. "Despertaré vora la riba, sense nosa/I poc a poc el riu se m'endurà/Les males herbes que l'ànima disposa/Siguin lliurades a fondàries abismals" (*Lletres* 227).

12. Foucault, in *The Order of Things*, introduces the concept of heterotopia by reflecting on the taxonomy referred to by Jorge Luis Borges in the story "El idioma analítico de John Wilkins," where the established categories do not accord with our perception of the world and there is no possible space where they can become clear. This causes concern about the possibility of alternative spaces that could constitute a utopia. In a different sense, the concept of heterotopia would be the central subject at a conference given by Foucault in 1964 at the Centre d'Études Architecturales. At that conference he sketches the complex and vague theory of "other spaces," which, contrary to other utopias, are physically real but at the same time isolated from conventional locations. According to Foucault's examples, they include cemeteries, boats, museums, as well as locations involving a ritual displacement, such as honeymoons. For an analysis of the uses that the concept has since had in the field of geography and urban planning, see the comments by Michiel Dehaene and Lieven De Cauter in the introduction to *Heterotopia and the City* (2008).

13. "No s'escorre el punt filipí": "Truquen el timbre/Obro/i arribo a casa/entro i pujo a l'armari/I em veig" (*Lletres* 36).

14. For more about psychedelia in Catalonia, see Guillamon (29).

15. Foucault writes: "The mirror is, after all, a utopia, since it is a placeless place. In the mirror, I see myself there where I am not, in an unreal, virtual space that opens up behind the surface; I am over there, there where I am not, a sort of shadow that gives my own visibility to myself, that enables me to see myself there where I am absent: such is the utopia of the mirror. But it is also a heterotopia in so far as the mirror does exist in reality, where it exerts a sort of counteraction on the position that I occupy. From the standpoint of the mirror I discover my absence from the place where I am since I see myself over there" ("Of Other Spaces" 24).

16. "Encara que no sigui políglota, no sé parlar, si no és un altre idioma, amb quasi ningú. Porters d'hotel, fabricants de tovalloles, aragonesos, futbolistes i músics de varietés... Els estrangers, però, em semblen impecablement llunyans, encara que sovint no els entengui" (*Lletres* 71).

17. "Portes de vidre giratòries/El carabiner vigila/No s'escapés la fada rossa/Promesa del príncep blau/Altaveus automàtics informen:/ 'La revolució és pura sensació'/Sant Jordi prepara la llança/Duu la rosa als llavis/Barricades i auto-xocs al carrer" (*Lletres* 198).

18. Joan Salvat-Papasseit is the best-known Catalan avant-garde poet, and author of the book *El poema de la rosa als llavis* (1923).

19. "Arribat és el moment d'interpretar la clau i el compàs/D'un llenguatge unificat sintetitzant la cua i el cap/Des del balcó transnacional/ Quan perdem l'origen i la identitat, ai, ai, quin descans!" (*Lletres* 215).

20. Jo Labany and Helen Graham define *desencanto* as "the mood of political disenchantment/disappointment that prevailed in the later years of the transition period (1979–1982), anticipated by the film *El desencanto* (Chávarri, 1976)" (421).

21. The interview can be seen on the Vilaweb portal at www.vilaweb.cat. During his presidency of the Generalitat de Catalunya (2003–2006), Pasqual Maragall symbolized the left moderate alternative to the conservative nationalism of the government of Jordi Pujol (1980–2003). For more about Maragall's government of Barcelona, see Marín (2008). For a contextualization of Jordi Pujol's politics, see Lo Cascio (2008).

22. The recording of the official opening, an ironic and critical speech seasoned with a few songs, can also be seen on the Vilaweb portal: www.vilaweb.cat.

Bibliography

Augé, Marc. *Non-Lieux. Introduction à una anthropologie de la surmodernité*. Paris: Seuil, 1992.

Batista, Antoni. "Jaume Sisa es retira de la cançó (1)." *Avui* 22 June 1984: 33.

———. "Jaume Sisa es retira de la cançó (i 2)." *Avui* 23 June 1984: 9.

Calinescu, Matei. *Five Faces of Modernity*. Durham: Duke University Press, 1987.

Castellet, Josep M. "Mitologies de la nova generació." *Serra d'Or* 121 (1969): 45.

Certeau, Michel de. *The Invention of Everyday Life*. 1980. Berkeley and London: University of California Press, 1984.

Cornejo Polar, Antonio. "Una heterogeneidad no dialéctica: sujeto y discurso migrantes en el Perú moderno." *Revista Iberoamericana* 176–7 (1996): 837–44.

Dehaene, Michiel, and Lieven De Cauter. *Heterotopia and the City*. New York: Routledge, 2008.

Delgado, Manuel. *Sociedades movedizas*. Barcelona: Anagrama, 2007.

Durall, Jordi. "El món d'en Sisa." *Ajoblanco* 9 (1976): 14–15.

Foucault, Michel. *The Order of Things*. "Of Other Spaces." 1967. *Diacritics* 16.1 (1986): 22–7.

———. 1966. New York: Routledge, 2002.

García Canclini, Néstor. "Introducción a la nueva edición. Las culturas híbridas en tiempos globalizados." *Culturas híbridas*. México: Grijaldo, 2001.

Garcia-Soler, J. "I la cançó al vent." *Serra d'Or* 190 (1975): 62.

Guillamon, Julià. *La ciutat interrompuda*. Barcelona: La Magrana, 2001.

Epps, Brad. "Special Section: Barcelona and the Projection of Catalonia." *Arizona Journal of Hispanic Cultural Studies* 6 (2002): 193–288.

Labanyi, Jo, and Helen Graham. *Spanish Cultural Studies*. Oxford: Oxford University Press, 1995.

Lo Cascio, Paola. *Nacionalisme i autogovern*. Barcelona: Afers, 2008.

Marín, Martí. "Crisi, transició i democràcia (1973–2007)." *Història de l'Ajuntament de Barcelona*. Ed. Manel Risques. Barcelona: Enciclopèdia Catalana, 2008. 270–95

Melendres, Jaume. "Literatura conceptual." *Tele/eXprés* 10 August 1977: 15.

Meseguer, Lluís B. "Les metàfores de la nova cançó." *Actes del desé col·loqui internacional de llengua i literatura catalanes*. Barcelona: PAM, 1995. 351–79.

Picornell, Mercè (2008). "Deconstruint Franco: el carnaval identitari de la transició." *Poètiques de ruptura*. Ed. Maria Muntaner, Mercè Picornell, Margalida Pons, and Josep Antoni Reynés. Palma: Lleonard Muntaner, 2008. 77–110.

Pons, Agustí. "Carta privada a Jaume Sisa." *Lletra de canvi* 23 (1989): 42–43.

Pons, Margalida. "Formes i condicions de la narrativa experimental (1970-1985)." *Textualisme i subversió: formes i condicions de la narrativa experimental catalana*. Ed. Margalida Pons. Barcelona: Publicacions de l'Abadia de Montserrat, 2007. 7–79.

Resina, Josep Ramon. *Barcelona's Vocation of Modernity: Rise and Decline of an Urban Image*. Stanford: Stanford University Press, 2008.

Sisa, Jaume. *El Viajante Sisa Mestres llamado Solfa*. Madrid: El Europeo, 2000.

———. *Lletres galàctiques*. Barcelona: Llibres del Mall, 1984.

———. and Antoni Miralda. *Barcelona Postal. 1982*. Barcelona: K-Industria, 2007.

Sontag, Susan. *Against Interpretation*. New York: Dell, 1966.

Absent Cities: Text, Performance, and Heterotopia

Zoë Skoulding

The performance of poetry implies a location and a particular site of encounter with an audience, whether in real or virtual space. The relationship between this site and the space beyond it can be seen variously; the rarefied atmosphere of some poetry readings might occasionally suggest that there is little connection between the two, while others, for example those in which poetry asserts a strong regional identity, might be viewed as continuations of structures and norms that extend beyond the venue and into everyday life. In the following discussion of poetry that relates specifically to the city, I am concerned with approaches to poetry and performance in which such continuities are challenged, and with the ways in which performance can act as, in Foucault's terms, a critical "counter-site," outside of everyday spaces yet related to them. The performance of a written text unfixes the poem by bringing it into conjunction with lived spaces; the poem at the moment of performance enters into relationships with its surroundings, material and social. However, these relationships are all mediated by the poem; they are changed by a text that is both present, because it is embodied, and absent, because it is contingent, momentary, and never heard in the same way twice. In an attempt to address questions raised by my own practice, which I shall discuss later on in this piece, I will first explore the work of three writers, Fiona Templeton, Hazel Smith, and Geraldine Monk, all of whom have engaged with the idea of the city through performances that imply a range of relationships with city space.

The city, as understood by theorists such as Michel de Certeau (1984) and Henri Lefebvre (1991), is a nexus of social interactions within the spatial practices of everyday life. In this essay I will explore relationships between the structures of the city and the spatial practice of performed poetry, focusing on the notion of heterotopia, described by Michel Foucault as

> capable of juxtaposing in a single real place several spaces, several sites that are in themselves incompatible. Thus it is that the theater brings onto the rectangle of the stage, one after the other, a whole series of places that are foreign to one another; thus it is that the cinema is a very odd rectangular room, at the end of which, on a two-dimensional screen, one sees the projection of a three-dimensional space. (25)

The performance space itself is both inside and outside lived experience: the theater or cinema opens on to the street and members of the audience come in with its dust on their shoes, but the scenes evoked in it are separate from the life of the street, unfolding further layers of geographical and temporal complexity. The paradox is often normalized and forgotten in the escape into realistic screen or stage fiction, but poetry, because of its more insistent artifice, might offer other ways of exploring the tensions and possibilities of the performance as heterotopia. Foucault argues that such places, common to all cultures, are "something like counter-sites, a kind of effectively enacted utopia in which the real sites, all the other real sites that can be found within the culture, are simultaneously represented, contested, and inverted" (24). It is therefore a space in which different ideologies co-exist, and where homogeneity is resisted. In this essay I explore the relationship between real and represented sites, including the city, the site of performance, and the text.

There is a risk that heterotopias, by existing outside the dominant order, may tacitly reinforce it. Lefebvre was critical of Foucault's emphasis on the marginal, commenting:

> this tactic, which concentrates on the peripheries, simply ends up with a lot of pinprick operations which are separated from each other in time and space. It neglects the centers and centrality; it neglects the global. (Survival 116).

Lefebvre's view of heterotopias as "mutually repellent spaces" (*Production* 366) suggests a notion of interrelationship between spaces rather than regarding otherness as a characteristic of excluded spaces, a point suggested by Doreen Massey's question, "Surely all spaces/places are heterotopias?" (Golding 224). It is therefore helpful to distinguish three main aspects of the term as it will be used here. As well as being, primarily, a separate and inverted space of difference, as Foucault describes it, the heterotopia may, secondly, be seen as an orientation towards place that recognizes its otherness, a point emphasized by Fran Tonkiss, who points out that "it is possible to think about spatial otherness by starting out from spatial practice. This has less to do with the unusual order of certain peculiar spaces, than with the potential for more everyday spaces to be disordered through tactics of use" (135). A third angle, which relates to both of the others, is suggested by Foucault's first use of the term "heterotopia" in the preface to *The Order of Things*, which emphasizes its linguistic nature:

> This is why utopias permit fables and discourse: they run with the very grain of language and are part of fundamental dimension of the fabula; heterotopias . . . dessicate speech, stop words in their tracks, contest the very possibility of grammar at its source; they dissolve our myths and sterilize the lyricism of our sentences. (xix)

The heterotopia therefore illustrates "the boundaries of the imaginable, an area in which our thought encounters objects or patterns that it can neither locate nor order" (Dehaene and de Cauter 43). A performance of poetry can bring together both the linguistic and spatial aspects of the term: I focus here on texts that in various ways both employ and contest lyric expression, and on determining to what extent, and to what ends, their performance might create an "other place" or reveal the multiplicity already present in places.

The poet Laura Elrick, drawing on Lefebvre, has argued convincingly for a reappropriation of lived space, suggesting "a possible grounding of poetics in spatial practices that challenge the 'nature' of capitalist space, a practice that rejects the separation of our bodies from the spaces we inhabit."[1] Such a view of poetry and public space owes much to avant-garde movements of the twentieth century, notably the Situationist International, who in the 1950s called for a breakdown between the boundaries of art and life by focusing on situations that would transform the everyday public sphere rather than on the specialized areas of art and literature (Gray 15–8). Jules Boykoff and Kaia Sand have documented the contemporary legacy of this work in the U.S.A. in "guerrilla poetry" that occupies public spaces in "an interruptive and interventionary model of poetry rooted in artistic practices that insert poetic language into public space, thereby challenging its apparent neutrality and surfacing its political history" (16–7). In dismantling the border between political activism and public art (for example in graffiti), the authors usefully examine the political role of physical intervention in urban space, through performance or the material presence of text. However, a view of both body and city as mutually constructed, technologized, and increasingly in dialogue with virtual spaces suggests that the challenge to neutrality might be extended to aspects of performance that are less obviously embodied. I will discuss works that occupy a range of positions within a spectrum that runs from the physical to the virtual, although all of them are concerned with the politics of public spaces.

Relational Space in Fiona Templeton's *YOU – the City*
I will consider first a performance that takes up the challenge to insert poetry disruptively into public space. If it is not, strictly speaking, poetry, it is by Scottish poet Fiona Templeton (living in New York) and is based on a dramatic text in which poetic artifice and a questioning of the structures of language are strongly foregrounded. Her play

YOU – the City was performed in Manhattan (1988), London (1989), and The Hague (1990) for an audience of one at a time, as each member of the audience or "client" arrived by appointment and engaged in a series of encounters with a group of actors. Rather than into "acts," the play is divided into "interacts," in which the client is addressed throughout the poetic monologues as "you." The text is published as a book with alternatives for the actors' improvisations and a selection of audience responses from the production of the play in New York, so the text is incorporated into the site-specific circumstances of its performance; what holds it together is a set of relationships that echo the chance interactions of the environment beyond it. As Redell Olsen points out, "Templeton's work involves the creation of a network of communication that takes place alongside those that already exist in the city." Within that network,

> the "you" of the live subject becomes the one constant of the performance at the same time as it is the structure that is most radically challenged. What remains constant is not the audience's passivity but their ability to influence the course of the production, so they are kept in a state of perpetual "liveness" rather than being subsumed into a fourth wall.[2]

The pronoun "You" is repeated to the point that it becomes unstable, revealed as a linguistic construction that depends on the nature of the dramatic encounter for context and meaning:

> You may turn to another but never away from me. And the mystery of my other you makes me mine, you meaning I don't understand, not you meaning I do. I need not be you. You don't seem myself. You must be you. So I will be like all of you, because you open and do not divide. (Templeton 49)

As Templeton observes, "The word *you* changed from being egoistic to being social" (135). Rather than taking place in the closed box of a theater, the performance space is created relationally, actors and clients linked by reciprocal eye contact as described in the actor's spoken text:

> Your eyes will look right through. Do you really think you would have taken such a risk if you yourself were to be implicated? How can a shadow be waiting for you to come closer? You wish you could turn and read some guidance in my face, some sign telling you how to answer.
>
> . . . .
>
> But you'll still not avoid meeting my eyes. (107)

The notes on the performance include an actor's comments on one client, a poet himself, who refused to return the actor's gaze; having expected "pure poetry," he "only wanted to hear the words" (107). However, the structure of the performance makes it difficult for the audience to remain passive: actor and audience alike are involved in the production of dynamic and relational social space, in contrast to the Cartesian, container-like space of the theater. As Templeton explains, the play critiques the boundaries of illusion:

> Since YOU deals with relationship, it also evokes privacy. But not the privacy of reaction of the individual in one of a thousand theatre seats, protected in anonymity and in numbers, in a distance which reduces the human spectacle to a television-sized illusion switched off by trips to the "real" bar, in the one-sided darkness of the voyeuristic position and the superiority of its demand . . . . (139)

Foucault states that heterotopias "presuppose a system of opening and closing that both isolates them and makes them penetrable" ("Of Other Spaces" 26), suggesting that they are territories subject to regulatory control. In performance, the borders of such territories vary: the theater, for example, usually has clear boundaries between the bar and the auditorium, while in *YOU*, the borders of the illusory space are far more mobile: "In the middle of the street, in the middle of the real, at a few inches distance, what client and performer held in the air between them was the reality of artifice as a deal" (Templeton 140). The performance is enmeshed in the city and separated from it, both by the participants' knowledge of the artifice and the fact that the performers are speaking from a poetic text. The effect is "to create a space of illusion that exposes every real space . . . as still more illusory" (Foucault, "Of Other Spaces" 27). This is exactly the effect experienced by one of the audience members:

> I was in the middle of the city and all of a sudden that two-dimensional world which I know is three dimensional but is always two dimensional as I walk around, suddenly became three dimensional. I remember standing in that kid's playground and thinking, what a set. (Templeton 54)

The private, one-to-one encounter of the performance is importantly set within the wider context of the city itself. Privacy becomes not anonymity, but individual responsibility, modeling rather than simply describing a version of the city in which individuals can become actors, discovering political as well as dramatic agency across the porous boundary of the heterotopia. Templeton suggests that "Like an analogue of the mind in the world and vice versa, the city is an experience of simultaneous interiority and exteriority" (140). In this tension between public and private space may be seen "a strategy to reclaim spaces of otherness on the inside of an economized 'public' life" (Dehaene and de Cauter 4).

Hazel Smith's Hypertext and Non-place
The relational understanding of space and subjectivity that emerges in *YOU – the City* has a relevance, as Redell Olsen argues, to "contemporary metaphors of the city used

to conceptualize a virtual geography of cyberspace." Hazel Smith's hypertext piece "Wordstuffs: The City and the Body,"[3] produced in collaboration with musician Roger Dean, explores textual relationships between bodies and cities in what was then the new environment of online media. Smith's position as a British-born writer living in Australia throws an interesting light on the dislocations between body and place that arise in her work; like Templeton, she is an expatriate within a complex postcolonial context. Her work operates differently, though: if *YOU* asserts the physical presence of both actor and client, the hypertext may seem to be a performance at the other extreme, in which the aleatory possibilities of text and sound combinations are triggered by the viewer-reader-listener's touch; the author and performers are absent, and the text is an unfolding set of digital connections within virtual space. However, the viewer becomes co-author and co-performer in choosing a way through the text and the pace at which it is delivered.

Texts fall apart as they are negotiated, and different registers intersect. Alliterative and more obviously "poetic" lines such as "time warps in the weave of talk shows/ the cancer and craft of consumption" are cut across by fragments of academic discourse, which are themselves disintegrated. For example, the statement "a hyperscape – a heterogeneous, global, constantly changing site characterized by difference. The hyperscape occurs when the body and city are dismantled and reconstituted" appears whole in the text version of the piece, but online as:

> *ismantled*
> *heterogenous, global, constantly changing site characterise*
> *difference. The hyperscape occurs when the body and city ar*

Both body and city are understood as textual subjects: to dismantle language and mix discourses is to reframe relationships between the two, and it is in this sense that entering the hypertext can be understood as both performative, according to Judith Butler's use of the term (179), and performance, in the viewer's interactive physical engagement with keyboard and screen. However, in another section, the poem describes the points of rupture between the body and mediated representation of it, in this case through mapping:

> Maps do not inscribe human beings. But arms, legs, and heads tear through their grids and curves, and bodies arched and curled somersault over their straight, uncompromising sides.

This reframing takes place on the computer screen, within virtual connections that increasingly intersect with lived spaces. "Hyperscape" is a term on which Smith elaborates in her later critical work, and she uses it to link landscape and cityscape with textual and virtual spaces, seeing it as "distinguished by the co-presence of opposites"

(*Hyperscapes* 1). As such, it implies an expanded vision of the heterotopia in which its boundaries, instead of opening and closing, are simultaneously dissolved and multiplied. Rather than creating a definable and physical "counter-site" within the city, the virtual performance of poetry, as Smith presents it, becomes part of a fluid set of relations encountering multiple borders. Of the writers I am discussing here, Smith makes the most overt connection between performance, city space, and gender, drawing on Donna Haraway's notion of the cyborg to disrupt a view of body and city as unchanging or uncontested. As Elizabeth Grosz has pointed out, if the city is imagined in an isomorphic relationship to the body, that body is by implication masculine, so to rethink that relationship demands a view of body and city "not as megalithic total entities, but as assemblages or collections of parts, capable of crossing the thresholds between substances to form linkages, machines, provisional and often temporary sub- or micro-groupings" (*Space* 108). Smith describes her collaborative project as "a creative enactment of Grosz's theoretical ideas. The hypertexts interlink cities and bodies – both parts and wholes – in different times and places, from the medieval to the modern, from Kuwait to Australia, with an emphasis on marginalized, racially vilified, and futuristic bodies" (Smith, "Cursors"). In breaking down not only the ideas of city and body, but also the roles of author and reader/listener, the text re-orders boundaries within the performance as a means of interrogating those that structure the spaces beyond it.

Within and beyond the city, the subject inhabits an environment described by Smith as:

> the place that is everywhere and nowhere
> a no-place a non-made a no-man a knot place
> the place that is where in the not that is when
> (Dean, Smith and White n. pag.)

These lines resonate with Marc Augé's definition of the "non-place," the interstitial spaces of transit and connection between places that hold definable meanings for individuals; while he was referring to airports and supermarkets, cyberspace has also been discussed as a "non-place" by Bolter and Grusin. If "The City and the Body" explores the overlap of lived spaces and the spatial practice of non-places, then this, too, constitutes a form of heterotopia, as argued by Dehaene and de Cauter, who note that "Heterotopia embodies the tension between place and non-place that today reshapes the nature of public space" (5). The reader is, over a decade on from its creation, increasingly likely to encounter Smith and Dean's piece within the frame of other virtual interactions, flicking between it and email or other websites. As Dehaene and de Cauter point out, "Rather than interrupting normality, heterotopias now realize or simulate a common experience of place" (5).

One Place and Then Another: Movement and Performativity in Geraldine Monk's "Hidden Cities"

Given her declared interest in what she describes as "the emotional geography of place,"[4] one might expect the poetry of Geraldine Monk to be more firmly centered within the localities of the northern English cities in which most of her work has been written. In many ways it is, and she has written entertainingly about the impact of regional speech patterns on her approach to language. However, a relationship between place and movement pervades her work, as in a performance piece presented in 2000 as an alternative bus tour of Manchester entitled "Hidden Cities" (*Noctivagations* 63–70). The final section, "(Unlocated)," begins:

> So all this past is come to pass and a body aches/in one place and then another/ body aches in another/place and a face/cracks and creaks in time to/some emotion or another time/is faced and the space is vacated/and another is filled with/a past and a body that ached in/one place and then another body ached in another place and a face cracks and/creaks in time to emotion/or another time is faced and the space is vacated and another is/filled with a past is/come to pass and a body aches/in one place and then/another. (70)

This is a piece written for performance, yet visually, too, there are clues to its approach to space: the title is bracketed as if to suggest suspension, and the forward slashes, less pronounced than line breaks, create both pause and onward movement. In the pattern of repetition and difference that builds up in the poem there is a series of echoes or after-images, the distance between a phrase and its repetition complicating the question of here and now, or the deictic aspect that one might expect of a guided tour. The relationship between a body and the place it inhabits shifts continuously through repetitions and variations: place and body are mutually produced and performed through these repeated verbal gestures. The sound patterning, because it is a series of riffs not subordinated to linear thematic development, keeps all the sonic elements of the poem in play simultaneously, so that the word "past," for example, will not stay in the past but resurfaces in "come to pass." The poem relies on particular kinds of movement, just as the whole performance takes place within the context of a moving bus.

In the lead-up to this final poem, different locations around Manchester are explored in a sequence that moves between sensory apprehensions and an appreciation of a layered past that is in conversation with the present and future. Such temporal layering is reminiscent of Foucault's comment that "heterotopias are most often linked to slices in time – which is to say that they open onto what might be termed, for the sake of symmetry, heterochronies" ("Of Other Places" 26). Monk's poem is located within its performance context, within a given time, and the understanding of place presented here is one that is open to change, asserting the need to re-assess the inequalities of the past that persist into the present: "We start and shiver in this place of a once deep industrial valley . . . A past under our feet skewered with stations of unconsecrated crosses" (Monk, *Noctivagations* 64). The insistence on the layering of the past in Monk's work is, as Sean Bonney has pointed out, reminiscent of Walter Benjamin's "monad," a revolutionary point in history where "thinking suddenly stops in a configuration pregnant with tensions, it gives that configuration a shock" (Benjamin 254). Such moments erupt in Monk's work, the tensions of the past allowed to rupture the present, and Bonney fruitfully explores their political efficacy in what he describes as a heretical tradition that incorporates not only the witches and dissenters of the past but also the class struggle of the present. Pointing out that "poetry that is worth the name actually makes a reality, one that exists outside of the surveillance cameras and media metaphysics that make up the experience of living in a modern city," he applauds the necessity of Monk's work in creating a socially active response to her environment (Bonney 77).

Bonney's analysis presents two different "realities," that of poetry and that of surveillance cameras, as if they are separate spaces, yet the most compelling parts of his argument in fact concern the interpenetration of spaces as past and present are juxtaposed: poetry, history, and the current conditions of the contemporary city are negotiated simultaneously. The heterotopia, in Foucault's description of it in terms of a theater, encompasses shifting temporal relationships as scenes unfold and change. The poetry performance on the bus is separated from the everyday urban environment, yet as it moves it creates multiple relationships with the city it describes, as incompatible sites are connected through the journey; it also recalls Foucault's example of the boat as heterotopia. Through movement, the poem inverts and suspends the structures of the city while remaining engaged with them.

Like Smith's work, Monk's poetry critiques the notion of the city's parallel relationship to the human body. Elizabeth Grosz asks: "Can architecture be thought, no longer as a whole, a complex unity, but as a set of and site for becomings of all kinds?" (*Architecture* 70), imagining an environment of flux and change that is in a dynamic, co-constitutive relationship with the body and its physical presence. This resonates with Monk's poem "Cheetham Hill. Strangeways" (*Noctivagations* 66), which addresses the notion of a prison not as a space of enclosure but through an arc of movement that encompasses both its surroundings and the bodies within it, down to a microscopic level. An imagined eye or camera begins with a wide-angle view of the cityscape, closes its focus on the prison walls, crosses them, and then closes again on high magnification of the inmates' bodies or fragments of dead skin under the beds. We begin in the "Land of wholesalers/warehouses/hidden goods and useless goodies" before settling on the prison itself, as the language veers between differently gendered identifications: "Strangeways walls/deliciously curved. Even so it is a masculine building./A men-only building./Note the watchtower./Note inside: all turgid with pain stuff." However, rather than identifying the built environment as a whole with a human body that exists independently of it, the poem breaks down both, and in doing so exposes and critiques the gender norms that shape public space. The cells of the prison give way to the cells of the organisms within them, and just as in the poem "the oscillatory disequilibrium of cells originates from external causes," so the prison and the lives of those inside it are imagined as enmeshed in the oscillation of social and political circumstances in the city beyond it. It is in this sense that Monk's work, like Smith's, might be seen as performative, constituting new relationships in language, as well as in the different and more literal sense that this piece is written for a specific performance context (and my focus here has excluded discussion of Monk's highly dramatic reading style), as each encounter with place is a verbal gesture that produces both space and the subject's shifting identity within it.

Anti-Utopias: Words, Sound, and Collaboration
In this final section I will discuss my own practice in writing and sound-based performance, a collaborative project with Alan Holmes that has developed alongside my collection of poems *Remains of a Future City* (throughout the following I alternate between first person singular and plural, depending on whether I am discussing our joint practice or my own contribution to it). Some of the poems draw on a Situationist text, "Formula for a New City" by Ivan Chtcheglov (alias Gilles Ivain), who calls for a re-visioning of the city that will restore a mythic power to its different quarters (Gray 15–18). The text itself becomes an imaginative journey through such places as "The Noble and Tragic Quarter" and "The Square of the Appalling Mobile," and Chtcheglov argues that through drifting in the city, and through the re-awakening of individual desires, urban alienation may be overcome. Drawing on these sources to write poems creates ironies: Chtcheglov's vision concerns lived space, but poetry creates yet another abstraction, existing in the world of art rather than everyday life. Nevertheless, his manifesto is also a text and it maintains an ambiguous connection with the city of Paris that appears to have inspired it, echoing Paris's scale and variety while incorporating features from other cities, real and mythical, from Mexico to Vienna. While appearing to invite an innocent, immediate approach to the city, Chtcheglov's text in fact creates multiple connections with other places and other versions of utopia. In this sense, the text may suggest some qualities of a heterotopia, and it was this aspect that I began to explore both in writing my own poems and in a parallel process of developing a sound-based performance.

My method involved writing in response to specific localities, often close to where I live in north Wales, but also in various other European cities, then juxtaposing these texts with phrases from Chtcheglov's manifesto and other sources. The semantic link between *dérive* and derivation implies both a wandering between different places, like the diverted course of a river, and the connection between different texts. In the drawing together of notes from *dérives* with derived text, together with the exploration of the relationship between physical and textual wandering,[5] I have been interested in how juxtapositions of real locations can suggest an unreal space and a new set of possibilities. Often, I have walked with Alan Holmes, who makes recordings of particular sound environments, then digitally layers them to create sound collages in which the aural qualities of different places are mingled. Sometimes the effect is disorientating, drawing the listener's attention to the constructed and mediated nature of the sound, for example where the shrill cries of children at an outdoor event are cut out and placed alongside clanging doors in a reverberating underground space (Skoulding and Holmes, *You Will Live*). Elsewhere, he searches out correspondences between places, setting them in dialogue: the poem "Building Site" has been performed along with recordings of construction work in Vienna and Prague.[6] It ends:

> Look,
>   now you can see in the ruins how
>   buildings took hold and pushed up
>   through your bones, rubble, walls of earth,
>   this tangle of useless pipes. (Skoulding 10)

The poem bears the traces of a journey through texts by other writers, including Ludwig Wittgenstein's description of language as a city (8), but its concluding deixis also points to the everyday detail of building detritus. Using recorded sounds in performance has not been intended to bring the poem into the physical world, as "real life," but to exploit the tension between physical and linguistic spaces. Recorded sound of an environment appears to offer an embodied experience of a place, yet recording too is a selective, artificial process; we draw attention to these dislocations and to the new connections that may be made through performance. The recordings are altered in length, though they may be cut and juxtaposed with each other, or occasionally with musical elements. They are never otherwise treated, so the dimensions of distinct spaces can still be heard, for example in the level of reverberation on a piece of metal dropped in a cathedral, or the sound of traffic blending into the city. The poems, in terms of the physical texture of the voice, become part of the overall sound, yet they retain cohesion as poems, even when fragmented syntax underscores the discontinuities of sound, as in the following:

> the wall down the
> movement of internal
> displacement fractures
> the wall a sentence
> crumbling into air (Skoulding 22)

The framing of the text as poetry, and as artifice, makes it possible to echo the disjunctions that are also a feature of the field recordings. A more consistent approach to this area of music would be to use only random, overheard voices, sampling and manipulating them along with the other sounds. However, by working within a clash of chance and artifice, we aim to bring together two separate genres rather than creating a synthesis in which the elements become homogenized.

The heterotopia contains different elements simultaneously, and the performance is a palimpsest of everything that has gone into the process of writing and composing: first there is walking, reading, and recording, then the gathering and shaping of words and sounds, then the combination of these elements in front of an audience which will in turn create a further layer by bringing their own interpretations to bear on what they hear. In combining words with layered sound collages, we aim to keep interpretation open: the collaborative aspect means that there are always at least two perspectives, and therefore infinite ways of listening to the gap between them. However, words easily dominate, and the question of how to prevent them from doing so, how to preserve my own authorial absence from them in performance, is one that has influenced the development of this work in two areas in particular: firstly, the use of translation, and secondly, the use of looping and effects on the voice.

Translation has been part of the background to this work in that one stimulus to its development has been the opportunity to perform it at a number of events where translation has been provided. For these particular poems, concerned as they are with the shared spaces of the city, translation is valuable in introducing another voice, and for that reason, we aimed to present translation in performance in such a way that it would be on an equal standing with the English source text. Writing in English in the bilingual context of north Wales creates an awareness of the interplay between linguistic, social, and physical spaces, a need to understand how different languages and cultures co-exist within the same physical dimensions: the bilingual culture itself has been described as a heterotopia (Beneventi 120). Although we work in a small city with its own distinctive context, these are also the conditions of every Western global city, and they raise questions for English, specifically. If English as a global language threatens other languages, how can the spaces around English be enlarged? The translated text allows English to fall silent, to be absent, and to be heard in relation to other languages. In several performances the translation has been recorded in advance and is played on a small cassette player to accentuate the technological mediation inherent in the process; however, the soundscape provides a mesh within which both languages can be heard as rhythm and texture, embedded within other aural elements. English is recast within a pluricultural heterotopia in which it is no longer the sole or dominant element.

Our method of working deliberately embraces the reading aloud of texts that some of the audience will not understand, and which we often do not understand ourselves. In the performance, language and sound combine to become part of an exploration of how we hear places; sound sources, like a foreign language, may be difficult or impossible to decipher. The borders between languages have been productively explored by the Canadian poet Erin Moure, who suggests: "To enable a language (returning) is also to allow intrusions, and to enable intrusions or their possibility as *part* of the cultural order. . . . Sometimes only the 'overlap' makes borders of a zone visible" (75). Like much of her work, this points to a more radical intermingling of languages than is evident, as yet, in our own project, but to "enable intrusions" is a paradoxical term that embraces the disruptive edge of difference in the heterotopia, emphasizing a boundary while crossing it.

Working from the idea of the city, we aim to "enable intrusions" by re-ordering the physical zone in which the voice exists, as the discontinuity of languages is reflected in discontinuous use of live and recorded sound. Several of the poems refer to the materiality of the voice, for example, "You Will Live in Your Own Cathedral," which works through the possibilities of the voice as part of a built environment rather than as an expressive medium:

> The cathedral of words is buttressed
> against the pressure of lips falling open
> on air caught in a windpipe.
>
> The cathedral of winds whispers
> through airwaves, cables or repeated loops
> in the pitch glissando of speech. (Skoulding 9)

During the process of writing the poems I acquired a guitar effects unit and began to use it on my voice: layers of sung notes form a bed for the spoken words, and phrases can be looped and repeated to turn the words into textures. The gradual decay of sound, and the way in which the voice could also be distorted and destroyed, suited my interest in the city as a site of both construction and demolition. By looping my voice I can create the effect of many voices, and although all the voices are mine, I am absent from them all. As they are treated and degenerate, they lose their connection with my body and begin to evoke other environments – a gurgling drain, a machine, wind.[7]

The processes we use, along with many other aspects of the contemporary experience of technologized sound, were described by Francis Bacon in 1627:

> We have also sound-houses, where we practise and demonstrate all sounds, and their generation. . . . We have certain helps which set to the ear do further the hearing greatly. We have also divers strange and artificial echoes, reflecting the voice many times, and as it were tossing it: and some that give back the voice louder than it came, some shriller, and some deeper; yea, some rendering the

voice differing in the letters or articulate sound from that they receive. We have also means to convey sounds in trunks and pipes, in strange lines and distances.[8]

While this is a utopian vision of ultimate control over sound in time and space, it prefigures a postmodern reality in which everyday life is saturated with recorded sound and long-distance communication. Our collaborative work has been a response to the current inescapability of these conditions; we have explored the material and geographical disjunctions that work against the homogenizing effects of globalization, simultaneously exploiting and questioning the utopian possibilities imagined by Bacon and Chtcheglov. Setting live and recorded sounds against each other also becomes a means of interrogating the gaps between language and the physical environment of lived space.

Conclusion

Writing itself is one of the many technologies that dislocate the body from its surroundings, and if the heterotopia is seen as central to understanding patterns of difference within cities, the texts and performances I have described provide a means of recognizing the disjunctive and mediated qualities of lived space. That process of mediation may relate to various forms of dislocation: as an English-born writer living in Wales I am conscious of the histories of interaction between cultures that shape one's experience of public space; it is significant that two of the writers I have discussed are expatriates, while Monk's work often presents a view of the English north as a marginalized "other" space within the U.K. Gender, too, mediates, as is particularly evident in Hazel Smith's work, where the gendered body is understood as already textual, and therefore functions as a grammar that intersects with the production of space: the performativity of gender cannot be separated from the physical performances that constitute lived space. The body's boundaries, defined by language, become a crucial site of interface with the city, and the frictions I have described, along the boundary between the heterotopian site of performance and more extended spatial relationships, enable overlap and intrusions. While the physical performance of poetry brings it into lived spaces, its textual disembodiment and its apparent detachment from the practice of everyday life can create a parenthetical counter-site in which the city, as both lived and textual space, can be re-negotiated.

Notes

1. www.brooklynrail.org/2006/06/poetry/poetry-ecology-and-the-reappropriation-of-lived-space.

2. www.asu.edu/pipercwcenter/how2journal/archive/online_archive/vl_6_2001/current/iindex.html.

3. www.abc.net.au/arts/stuff-art/stuff-art99/stuff98/10.html.

4. www.westhousebooks.co.uk/gmonk.asp.

5. Lawrence Venuti draws out the connection between "*dérive*" and "derivation" (307).

6. These recordings were chosen specifically for a performance in Prague at Studio Rubin, 4 May 2007.

7. We have tended to make more use of vocal processing in live performances than in recordings (such as the CD that accompanies *You Will Live in Your Own Cathedral*) because, paradoxically, the treatment of voice has been a way of introducing more spontaneous and improvised elements into a live performance.

8. www.gutenberg.org/etext/2434.

Bibliography

Augé, Marc. *Non-places: Introduction to an Anthropology of Supermodernity*. Trans. John Howe. London & New York: Verso, 1995.

Bacon, Francis. *The New Atlantis*. http://www.gutenberg.org/etext/2434. Web. 25 May 2009.

Beneventi, Dominic. "Lost in the City: The Montreal Novels of Régine Robin and Robert Majzels." *Downtown Canada: Writing Canadian Cities*. Ed. Justin Edwards and Douglas Ivison. Toronto, University of Toronto Press, 2005. 104–21.

Benjamin, Walter. *Illuminations*. Trans. Harry Zorn. London: Pimlico, 1999.

Bolter, Jay David, and Richard Grusin. *Remediation: Understanding New Media*. Cambridge, MA: MIT Press, 1999.

Bonney, Sean. "What the Tourists Never See." *The Salt Companion to Geraldine Monk*. Ed. Scott Thurston. Cambridge: Salt, 141–121 2007. 62–78.

Boykoff, Jules, and Kaia Sand. *Landscapes of Dissent: Guerilla Poetry and Public Space*. Long Beach, California: Palm Press, 2008.

Butler, Judith. *Gender Trouble: Feminism and the Subversion of Identity*. London: Routledge, 1999.

Certeau, Michel de. *The Practice of Everyday Life*. Berkeley: California University Press, 1984.

Foucault, Michel. "Of Other Spaces." 1967. *Diacritics* 16.1 (1986): 22–27.

———. *The Order of Things*. London: Routledge, 2002.

Dean, Roger, Hazel Smith, and Greg White. *Wordstuffs: The City and the Body*. 1998. http://www.abc.net.au/arts/stuff-art/stuff-art99/stuff98/10.html. Web. 25 May 2009.

Dehaene, Michiel, and Lieven de Cauter, eds. *Heterotopia and the City: Public Space in a Postcivil Society*. London: Routledge, 2008.

Elrick, Laura. "Poetry, Ecology and the Appropriation of Lived Space." *The Brooklyn Rail* (June 2006): n. pag. Web. 25 May 2009.

Golding, Sue, ed. *The Eight Technologies of Otherness*. London: Routledge, 1998.

Gray, Christopher. *Leaving the 20th Century: The Incomplete Work of the Situationist International*. London: Rebel Press, 1998.

Grosz, Elizabeth. *Architecture from the Outside: Essays on Virtual and Real Space*. Cambridge, MA: MIT Press, 2001.

———. *Space, Time and Perversion: The Politics of Bodies*. St. Leonards: Allen and Unwin, 1995.

Haraway, Donna. *Simians, Cyborgs, and Women: The Re-invention of Nature*. New York: Routledge, 1991.

Lefebvre, Henri. *The Production of Space*. Trans. Donald Nicholson-Smith. Oxford: Blackwell, 1991.

———. *The Survival of Capitalism*. Trans. F. Bryant. London: Allison and Busby, 1976.

Monk, Geraldine. "A mini-biography." http://www.westhousebooks.co.uk/gmonk.asp. Web. 25 May 2009.

———. *Noctivagations*. Sheffield: West House Books, 2001.

Moure, Erin. *O Cidadán*. Toronto: Anansi, 2002.

Olsen, Redell. "Degrees of Liveness, Live and Electronic Subjects: Leslie Scalapino, Fiona Templeton and Carla Harryman." *How2* 1.6 (2001): n. pag. Web. 25 May 2009.

Skoulding, Zoë. *Remains of a Future City*. Bridgend: Seren Books, 2008.

Skoulding, Zoë, and Alan Holmes. *You Will Live in Your Own Cathedral*. Pamphlet/CD. Bridgend: Seren Books, 2009.

Smith, Hazel. "Cursors and Crystal Balls: Digital Technologies and the Futures of Writing." *TEXT* 8.2 (2004): n. pag. Web. 25 May 2009.

———. *Hyperscapes in the Poetry of Frank O'Hara: Difference, Homosexuality, Topography*. Liverpool: Liverpool University Press, 2000.

Templeton, Fiona. *You, the City*. New York: Roof Books, 1990.

Tonkiss, Fran. *Space, the City and Social Theory: Social Relations and Urban Forms*. Cambridge: Polity, 2005.

Venuti, Lawrence. *The Translator's Invisibility*. London: Routledge, 1995.

Wittgenstein, Ludwig. *Philosophical Investigations*. 1953. Trans. G. E. M. Abscombe. Oxford: Blackwell, 1968.

New *Loci* in Contemporary Catalan Art and Poetry: Perejaume's Performance of/on the Rural

Margalida Pons

The alloy between urbanity and the aesthetic avant-garde has been one of the most common binomials in the writing of the history of contemporary Catalan literary culture, as well as one of the most complex.[1] The problematic nature of this alloy comes not only from its *constructed* nature but also from the exclusions it entails, the most important of which is the implicit denial of non-urban space as a *locus* of research and disruption. This essay aims to first question the operativity of the city/progress and rural/tradition associations as applied to contemporary Catalan creation, and secondly to examine what the construction of the link between urbanity and modernity has excluded: forms of performative poetry that forge a new relationship with the non-urban space by re-using (or re-appropriating) its romantic aura to turn it into a scene of inquiry. The works of the poet and artist Perejaume, which unfold in the multiform realms of a new ruralism with avant-garde underpinnings, will be the testing ground for my reflections.

Early twentieth-century *Noucentisme* was viewed as an urban, citified current that strove for an updating of Catalan culture and society in contrast to the rural patriotism embodied by the late nineteenth-century authors of the *Renaixença* and *Modernisme*. In many writings on art and literature of recent decades, the city has been regarded as the *natural* place for the gestation and development of discourses of social protest and aesthetic experimentation. Thus, the underground poetry from the 1970s and the post-modern narrative from the 1980s, as well as the polypoetry that emerged in the 1990s,[2] have been viewed as intrinsically urban phenomena. In the 1970s, La Rambla and Plaça Reial, both in Barcelona's old quarter, were the backdrop of mobilizations against the Franco regime and its aftermath, as well as the site of ludic actions by the heroes of the countercultural movements, such as the multifaceted artist Ocaña and the underground illustrator and cartoonist Nazario. In the 1980s, Balmes Street, the main artery running through the bourgeois Eixample neighborhood, was the privileged setting of stories by Quim Monzó; the Bar Glaciar, right on Plaça Reial, witnessed the first polypoetic encounters held in the 1990s, in which authors like Carles Hac Mor, Josep Ramon Roig, Benet Rossell, and Xavier Sabater participated. On several occasions, Lis Costa has mentioned the "public poetry" that emerged in Barcelona two decades ago, a kind of poetry written to be performed live in front of an audience more than to be consumed in the traditional format of a publication on paper for private reading.[3] In his words to present the first Proposta Festival, the polypoet Eduard Escoffet claimed: "Barcelona has established a very particular relationship with poetry. Despite being a minority sector, the audience gathered by poetry readings is always numerous; and more remarkable yet is the fact that it leaves vast room for what could be called 'the risk practices' of poetry . . . Far from trying to create yet another focus of attention which would stump the previous ones, what we pretend with [this festival] is to complement Barcelona's poetry landscape."[4] The capital of Catalonia has thus become the prime venue for poetic performance – not just in Catalonia but in Spain as a whole.

The term "Barcelona model," which authors like Horacio Capel in the field of geo-criticism, Manuel Delgado in anthropology, and Joan Ramon Resina in cultural criticism have used to describe the metropolitan urbanism of the capital of Catalonia and the contradictions of the social system it generates, can be applied to literature as well to some extent. According to Delgado, the city has become a kind of top model, always perfectly coiffed, trained only to seduce, "monumentalized" for events like the 1992 Olympics or the Forum 2004, which painstakingly hides the marginalization and inequality in which certain population groups live – what Delgado calls, not without some misgivings, the "*real* Barcelona" (17). Similarly, the promotion – and institutionalization – of street culture and the performance that characterizes it, which was particularly strong in the era when the Socialist Party of Catalonia governed the city, has absorbed and *citified* such a wide range of propositions as the poetry of orality, *actions*, and video-poetry, presenting them as a unequivocal symptom (and compact sign) of modernity. These propositions, represented by events like the aforementioned Proposta Festival and the Barcelona Polypoetry Festival, have been permanently linked to an urban avant-garde. The specificity of the non-urban setting in which some of these expressions have emerged is thus relegated to the background. Furthermore, all of this took place at a time when the very country/city dichotomy ceased to function precisely because of the omnipresence of the urban. It has been noted that the fall of the Ancient Regime (which ended the legal differentiation between the urban and rural population), demographic growth, the Industrial Revolution, and the symbolic destruction of the city walls are the forerunners of an unquestionable fact: today the urban has spread so far and wide that we can only talk about "sprawling cities" with blurred boundaries (Nel·lo 17–9). In short, "if the rural/urban opposition is being overcome at this time, it is not so much due to a new concept of territory . . . as to the expansion of the urban to encompass the entire territory" (Corboz 26).

The Catalan literary establishment's obsession with urbanity as a desirable goal and as the exclusive hub from which culture radiates out may be explained by its eagerness to unearth a nationalism with romantic roots that identifies nation with territory (and that more specifically situates the essence of the homeland in a non-urban environment). The myth that contrasts the degradation of the *terra baixa* (made up of towns and cities) with the spiritual wealth of the solitary, rural *terra alta* has been around for a long time. In the nineteenth century, this *terra alta*, or high ground, was represented by the symbolic use of the Catalan mountain by the playwright Àngel Guimerà and the poet Jacint Verdaguer, but in the twentieth century it is also the site of a certain model of contemporary excursionist culture linked to conservative nationalistic politics (although it should be noted that there is another kind of excursionism, which we shall not discuss here, linked to progressive associationism). As Joan Nogué and Joan Vicente claim, "the mountain is and has been used by Catalan nationalism, especially by the more conservative, traditional strain of nationalism, to suggest national origins that are remote in time, not to say divine" (179–80). The warnings issued by journalist Agustí Calvet (or Gaziel) about Barcelona being a threat, set forth in a lecture in 1923, fall under the same myth: "Catalonia must suffer, by force, macrocephalia. This head [Barcelona] is too large for such a small body. The other members have to labor under the ravages that this excessive head wreaks in the entire organism. Beware, Catalans! Barcelona poses a real danger to Catalonia as a whole!" (Gaziel 27). However, today this myth has been replaced by another: that of the capital as the spokesperson for a hypothetical sociocultural totality. *Hypothetical* because it excludes part of Catalonia's geo-cultural area, from the counties of Valencia to the Balearic Islands, including the Empordà and midsized cities like Tarragona, Lleida, Sabadell, and Reus.

In experimental Catalan creations from recent decades, there is a use of the rural that is, in itself, a form of backlash. It is not difficult to find examples, including the intensive use of peasant language that characterizes the poetry of Mallorcan Damià Huguet; the revival of Empordà writer Carles Fages de Climent – described by Josep Pla as a brilliant localist – by Enric Casasses, one of the best-known contemporary poets of orality; the recurrence of the dialect from the city of Tortosa in the works by another oral poet, Josep Ramon Roig; experimental poet Patrick Gifreu's defense of Dalí's "ultra-localism"; and the *actions* by artist Alícia Casadesús and poet Víctor Sunyol in rural places like the county of Collsacabra. All of these expressions, which should be read parallel to the experiences of land art conducted by the conceptual artists, share a perception of the non-urban setting as a site for aesthetic inquiry.

Until now, this perception has not garnered much critical attention. One of the exceptions was the workshop "Thinking in the Province: New Ruralism in Post-Urban Modernity" (2009), coordinated by Joan Ramon Resina at Stanford University. In his introductory text, we can read that "the looming presence of the industrializing city reduces all cultural production conceived outside of the urbs to a new category: the non-urban," and he makes it clear that "[a]t the onset of the 21st century, an avant-garde of writers and literary critics focusing on regionalist discourse, provincial settings and other decidedly 'non-urban' realities has appeared and raised the question as to whether the rural remains a worthwhile research category."[5] After the hegemony of Urban Studies, the door seems to be open to an examination of the post-urban setting which enables us to explore new forms of creativity, yet also, let's not fool ourselves, to establish new realms of academic research. Regardless, the application of this new perspective of studying the forms of non-lyrical poetry enables us to re-examine its peripheral location within Catalan literature as a whole.

Best known as Perejaume, Catalan painter and poet Pere Jaume Borrell (born in 1957 in Sant Pol de Mar) explores a range of issues that include the interaction between nature and subjectivity and the combination of plastic, visual, and textual poetry. He has become notorious for his rethinking of landscape, shown in a large number of poetry collections, essays, paintings, installations, photographs, and exhibitions. Perejaume's graphic and written works construct a conceptual framework based on a poetic and political reading of place (in many cases, a non-urban place), which also becomes a venue of performance and of identity statements. His treatment of spatiality, which has common features, either coincidental or intentional, with the assumptions of Earth Art and with the theorizing of Bachelard, Blanchot, Henri Lefebvre, and Kenneth White, appears as an alternative to the critical "reglementary" languages of literary theory and art theory. In this conceptual framework, place operates as the raw material of the discourse, that is, as a language or code. In the next sections, I will discuss the basic ingredients of Perejaume's poetic system: collage, lexical invention, the territorialization of the subject, making poetic use of the concepts of size and miniaturization, redefining the signature and mimesis, and interpreting the landscape as a palimpsest saturated with looks.

Writing Landscape: Collage and Lexicon
The first underlying element of this new code is the notion of collage. In *Ludwig Jujol*, an essay hovering somewhere between artistic theory, poetic prose, and literary reflection, Perejaume compares two disparate characters: first, King Ludwig II of Bavaria, the builder of neo-mediaeval castles that were simultaneously the materialization and backdrop of his dreams; and second, Josep M. Jujol, the architect, draughtsman, and sculptor who worked with Gaudí and whose works reflect the landscape of the county of Tarragona. Both have a poetic and subversive relationship with

space. Perejaume joins them using the idea of collage, a procedure that he views not as simply a random union of dispersed objects and fragments but as an effort to nurture the maximum unity possible. Carles Guerra views this "random joining" as an inheritance from the Surrealists' policy of image production brimming with coincidental encounters, a policy that Perejaume extends to the realms of history, culture, and geography (124). By perverting the line of time with the scandalous pairing of the romantic monarch and the *Modernista* architect, the line of space is reinforced. What Ludwig and Jujol have in common is a miniaturist (*pessebrista*) approach to their physical environment: that is, the threefold desire to copy nature exactly, to represent it not inside a museum but – at scale – in nature itself, and to represent it using natural elements – that is, using nature itself as a code. On the other hand, "in view of the fragmentation of all discourses, in his works of art Perejaume seems to tell us that two objects placed side by side are still the only pure syntax capable of revealing some meaning to us" (Tarrida 24). Making the physical space the keystone of the poetics itself affords a prime vantage point for exploring these syntaxes, because space, unlike time, makes possible the simultaneity of the objects that inhabit it, their interaction *in praesentia*. The idea of collage has been applied more often to urban than to rural settings – I am thinking, for example, of concepts like *collage city*, coined by Colin Rowe and Fred Koetter in a 1978 essay to name the palimpsestic configuration and the clash of ideas that characterize the modern city. Applied to a natural environment, collage deconstructs the purported opposition between the immutability of the non-urban and the dynamism of the urban. King Ludwig imitated the wilderness in a palace garden and the architect Jujol imitated the Montserrat massif – one of the *lieux de mémoire* hyperconnotated in the history of the Catalan identity – on the façade of a rural sanctuary. This co-presence of geographically and morphologically disparate objects casts doubt on dichotomies like rural versus urban and natural versus artificial.

Another contribution from Perejaume's poetics is the creation of a new lexicon, which springs from an alternative view that aims to formulate a *natural language*. Traditionally, says the poet,

> Art history has ignored the mountain ranges, vegetation and widely varied water courses. At the turn of the century, everything was Paris, even the most obscure landscapes. We know that this is not true, that in 1900 Edvard Munch was working in Aasgaardstrand, Joaquim Mir in Cala Encantada, James Ensor in Ostend, Ferdinand Hodler at Lake Geneva, Claude Monet in Guiverny and Segantini in the Swiss Alps, but we stubbornly hang all these paintings on the walls in the capital of France. (Perejaume, Ludwig 63)[6]

These words are not just a warning about the "urbanization" of the historiography of art; they also entail a clarion call against restricting the explanatory causalities of reality to the metropolitan realm. Understanding the rural – or in this case the *natural* – as solely the place to which artists *flee*, spurred by boredom or by spleen, is equivalent to claiming its subsidiarity to the urbs. In response to these biases, Perejaume imagines a world in which the rural elements are not only in the foreground, but also generate ideas and language. Thus, his essays and poems feature lexical formations like *apessebrar*, *obreda*, *suroral*, and *verdagueres* (the latter an adjective based on the surname of the romantic poet Jacint Verdaguer). These neologisms seem to indicate that the mountain universe is sufficient for explaining the world without the need to resort to more abstract formulations. From the city as an explanatory microcosm we have shifted to the country and mountain as language. In *Oïsme*, Perejaume even goes so far as to uphold the natural character of this language: he talks about sound stones which store recorded sounds inside them, and he re-creates a scene in which three walkers bestow a name on a plain after closing their eyes and putting their hands flat on the ground to see what sounds they can hear (48-50). The section "Oïor" from the poetry collection *Obreda* develops a special meaning of the word *oir* (to hear), in the sense of listening to the earth's primeval sounds: "We hear, then, the landscapes of the voice: the sound figures that the voice makes when tracing the places where it goes" (233).[7] Toponyms and sonority are the basic ingredients of *natural writing*. Thus, there is talk of the *phonogenics* of places, of the toponymist who distinguishes the flavor of all names with his palate, of the phonation of a flame, of the euphony of places. Because of his tireless inquiry into the relationships between word and place, philologist Joan Coromines, the author of the monumental *Etymological and Complementary Dictionary of the Catalan Language*, is one of the artist's referents. In the exhibition "Amidament de Joan Coromines" (Measurement of Joan Coromines), which Perejaume himself curated, the artist compresses all the words from Coromines's work into a single sound file: he asks the members of the Madrigal Choir to utter all the entries in the etymological dictionary at the same time and records them. The result is an inchoate, elementary, total voice, a peculiar sound poem compressed to the point of exasperation, issued by a large number of subjects, which works as a palimpsest of unfathomable depth.

The Land as Subject: Scale and Signature

A new ingredient in this spatial poetry is the extension of the notion of subject to the land. In *Obreda*, we can read: "The world I see seems like a writer to me. The land is a confident, inexorable prosist" (142). And later on: "In the end, who holds the authorship?" (304) and "The forest is the author of a great obedience" (323).[8] In the *plaquette* entitled *Autors*, Perejaume interweaves subject and place from the very outset: "Montnegre, Mondrian, Mont-roig," one of the "poems" laconically says, making a heterogeneous collage with the name of the Dutch painter and two toponyms referring to villages and mountains in Catalonia. The self becomes spatialized but is not lost: it is placed on a par with the land to forge dialogues governed not by symbolism but by contact and displacement, on a horizontal plane that makes coexistence without domination possible.

This territorialization of the subject goes hand in hand with a recovery of the physical concept of scale for the poetic language – a crucial concept in the work of land artists like Denis Oppenheim as well. The book *Els cims pensamenters. De les reals i verdagueres elevacions* describes Verdaguer's conception of the Pyrenees as a temple of mountains. Perejaume compares Verdaguer – who has been avidly revived by Catalan performance poets like Enric Casasses, who has reissued forgotten texts, and Josep Ramon Roig, the author of the polyphonic piece *Verdaguer minimal amb acompanyament vocal* (Minimal Verdaguer with Vocal Accompaniment) – to John Ruskin, who viewed the Alps as the cathedral of the Earth. Underscoring these similarities means reactivating not just the old idea that nature copies art but also the awareness that other images live on, inscribed in the image of the mountain in an impossible chronology. *Els cims pensamenters* closes with a series of eight photographs that represent a pigment from the (artist's?) skin successively enlarged with a scanning electron microscope, until it becomes unrecognizable. Some of the images are reminiscent of peaks and mountain ranges. This kind of visual-corporal poetry harks back to the body works of the Boyle Family artistic collective, who in 1969 presented a series of photographs, enlarged with a microscope, of randomly chosen squares of Mark Boyle's skin.

The counterpoint to the microscope's enlargement is miniaturization. Perejaume pays a great deal of attention to miniaturization, specifically *pessebrisme*, miniature reproductions of the landscapes of Bethlehem, or nativity scenes, an artistic practice that was popular in Catalonia in the eighteenth and nineteenth centuries, and that today has been elevated to the rank of aesthetic category.[9] *Pessebrisme* entails making use of materials like cork, which, without forsaking their status as natural, come to represent other parts of nature: first, the "scale" reconstruction of a *perceived world* and secondly, the imitation of nature using homemade techniques and nature itself. In the words of Carles Guerra, "*pessebrisme*'s realism is twofold. First, because it aims to represent what is close by, and secondly because the materials used to represent the landscape are fragments from this very landscape" (179). And as Perejaume noted in an interview,

> The term "pessebrisme" had also been used with a pejorative nuance, in the sense that it meant something small, puny . . . To me seemed like a way that 19th century culture had developed (Italy and Bavaria also have a miniaturist traditions quite similar to that of Catalonia) that was great for illustrating what I wanted to explain about how one element of the land, at a different scale, ends up representing the land as a whole. Cork tree bark worked the same way the Zen garden worked in Oriental culture. (Sardà 109)

Pessebrisme miniatures are thus viewed as a form of "natural" metonymy: the entire land (Catalonia) can be represented by a minuscule element like cork, which is part of that land and furthermore dispenses with the need to undergo a process of symbolization. Therefore, the spatial poetry of *pessebrisme* has an identity-based dimension. This dimension, however, manages to elude the romantic-resistant discourse of "hallmarks of identity," which, in its spatial dimension, identifies Catalonia with a series of symbolic, sacred places, such as the Montserrat massif, the Sagrada Família, and even, more recently, Futbol Club Barcelona's stadium, Camp Nou. This discourse had been widely invoked by the representatives of Catalan resistance culture in the 1960s and 1970s that were determined to safeguard the referents of an identity that had been systematically attacked by the Franco regime. However, it had also been the butt of criticism from more experimental authors who had opted for a culture of inquiry more than a culture of conservation. The author Biel Mesquida, for example, talked about "the single, repetitive, boring and perhaps maddening slogan of Hallmarks of Identity" (23).

With his *pessebrista*, or miniature, actions, Perejaume replaces the traditional *lieux de mémoire* with his own "identity places." Thus, in the poem-object "Rambla 61," he represents a theater seat joined to a window-shaped screen, forming a transportable structure on wheels: the viewers may thus choose their own landscape. The artist even imagines the graphic figuration of this *"pessebristic* method of interpretation" (*Deixar* 114). It is a pencil drawing that portrays a human profile looking at a parcel of land. The eyes, the brain, and the parcel of land are joined in a triangle that indicates the twofold nature of the land: once perceived by the eyes, it has to be deciphered by the mind (and is therefore a secondary language), but at the same time it can speak directly to the intellect and therefore act as a primary code or language that bypasses the process of symbolization. *Pessebrisme* is also regarded as an avant-garde *modus operandi*. Joan Miró, Josep M. Jujol, Joan Brossa, J. V. Foix, and Antoni Tàpies are described as "heirloom avant-gardes" who have promoted the avant-garde in a naturalistic, rustic, specific place. We could add Dalí to this list of names.

Paired with the concept of scale is the idea of signature. Perejaume's signed territories, like his photographic poem "Mar signat" (Signed Sea) – a large-format photograph in which the name of the artist appears inscribed over the water – or the "correction" of the Folgueroles stream in Verdaguer's birthplace so that it traces the poet's signature, are elementary rubric forms. Some of these works call to mind other works, like *Rift* by land artist Michael Heizer, who inscribes the sandy desert surface with marks resembling geometric scars. Specifically, the correction of the stream poses the problem of authorship: just like land artists such as Walter de María, Nancy Holt, and Heizer himself, who use large technological means to render their works, including bulldozers, mines, helicopters, engineers, project leaders, etc. (Brun 128), Perejaume has to delegate part of the rendering of his works to technicians. Likewise, signing the land not only entails artificializing it, taking it as a canvas or appropriating it, but it also means treating it as a poem-object of elephantine proportions. Plus, it is a performative poem-object in that it has to be viewed in situ. The artist's book *Llegenda. Tres perejaumes. Monòleg d'un poeta i un pintor* (Legend. Three Perejaumes. Monologue of a Poet and a Painter), realized in conjunction with the poet Pere Gimferrer, reproduces Gimferrer's poem "Signe" (Sign) and then copies the same poem, this time signed by Perejaume, in what Vicenç Altaió regards as "a tautology on authorship and work" (25). With this appropriating, palimpsestic, and Borgesian over-writing, Perejaume turns the poem's original words into landscape: he territorializes them. At the same time, the signature calls to mind the obsession with rediscovering the link between discourse and author, and with preserving this link for the future (Burke 289).

Mimesis and Palimpsest

The legibility of nature leads us to the last point we shall examine here: mimesis and the process of constructing the landscape. In Perejaume's poetics, the verbal and objectual language – the word that designates the mountain and the piece of cork that represents the mountain range – work differently: if we take the piece of cork and put it in the foreground, it ceases to be a mountain range and becomes stubble, a border, a rock, and finally just cork. In contrast, if "I make a miniature scene of plaster, I can represent a faraway mountain range, and when drawing closer to put it behind a lifelike sea, with water you can touch, it remains a faraway mountain range. The language, then, is in fact a plaster miniature scene" (Perejaume, *Ludwig* 94).[10] Because of its symbolic or arbitrary nature, the verbal language shields the word-referent relationship. However, this shielding does not occur in the case of an iconic sign, like the cork used in the miniature scene, which makes multiple correspondences possible. That is precisely what *pessebrisme* brings as an instrument of speculation: it enables us to distinguish the mimesis that is operating through verbal signs from that other which uses "natural" signs. The former cements the meaning; the latter is polysemic, capable of an extreme reflection in the constant readiness for metamorphosis thanks to perspective and dimension.

If the "natural" sign makes it more likely for the object and what it represents to belong to the same sphere, then the boundary between the work of art and the world vanishes. The poem belongs to the setting, it melts into it. The poem "Bola nocturna" (Nocturnal Ball), published in the *Èczema* collection in 1980, is a good example of this. Subtitled "poema aerostàtic" (aerostatic poem), it took on the guise of a blue, pear-shaped paper balloon and was presented in a brown paper envelop. A sonnet was printed on the balloon. The poem was launched into the air several times, and each time it was lost in the nocturnal space. Closely related to the idea of weaving the poem into the setting, the idea of the frame, the boundary that separates the artistic from the non-artistic, is, as Carles Guerra has underscored (123), a constant topic of reflection. In Perejaume's graphic works, there are plenty of frames of all sizes, gilded or wooden, sometimes framing a painting, sometimes the peak of a mountain, and other times a void. However, these frames are always troublesome: they are useless, or they frame nothingness, or they enable you to see what lies outside them. Thirdly, the relationship between metaphor and referent has a twofold meaning: the metaphor contributes to the thing as much as the thing contributes to the metaphor. The first poem from *Obreda* describes this two-way movement: "discovery of images on the ground, underground/discovery of the ground in the images" (11).[11]

This "artificialization" of nature leads directly to the idea of landscape, which has interested a host of disciplines other than painting. Biology, philosophy, anthropology, and geography all underscore the non-evidence of landscape, its character of vantage point and especially its being an invention made from a certain distance. In his classic essay *The Country and the City*, Raymond Williams claims that only outsiders, those who do not live there, are capable of seeing a given landscape: "a working country is hardly ever a landscape. The very idea of landscape implies separation and observation" (120). And, in fact, "the farmer has never recognized himself in the image of the countryside as a happy Arcadia" (Corboz 26). To the farmer, who has to be concerned with changes in weather, soil quality, and the calendar for sowing, fertilizing, and pruning, the countryside does not exist as a landscape; it is solely a realm of active work. Alain Roger mentions Albrecht von Haller as the *inventor* of the Alps in his 1732 poem *Die Alpen* (97). Perejaume also cites Verdaguer as the inventor of the Catalan landscape, evoking the window in his study from which he caught glimpses of the Montserrat massif, musing: "No one is sure whether the massif was already there or whether Verdaguer was the one who put it there" (*Ludwig* 60).[12]

The critical literature on landscape has stressed its character of mental elaboration performed through cultural phenomena. Its link with hermeneutic activity has been pointed out: landscape does not exist without interpretation (Maderuelo 11, 17, 36). It has been said that the human eye is what turns a certain place into a landscape and manages to turn a parcel of the "natural" land into a sign of culture (Guillén 77–78). Landscape has been viewed as a tangible part of the territory, but also as a (picturesque) way of looking at it (Muir xiv–xv). This human glance never comes from nothingness. Our look, even if we think it is meagre, is saturated with latent, rooted models (from paintings, films, literature…) that shape our experience (Roger 20). The leaflet *El paisatge és rodó* (The Landscape is Round), published for the exhibition "Vuit artistes al cim pintrat" (Eight Artists at Cim Pintrat Mountain), includes the notion of the ponderous look imbued with culture: "The aesthetic contemplation of the landscape seems to refer less to the natural place itself than to our slanted perception of it, and even more to our concern with expressing it, retaining it and doing it at the hands of another observer. Without any doubt, it is a subject more similar to the image than to the location of the image" (Perejaume, *El paisatge*

9–10).[13] The act of perceiving each landscape thus occurs moment three times converge: the past (what the landscape evokes to us, the pre-existing images we relate it to), the present (the physicality, the immediately perceived visual and sound elements) and the future (the transformations in it that we imagine). Thus, in the prose piece "Paisatge de llum" (Landscape of Light) (*Obreda* 147), the artist imagines placing 5,000 candles in a wasteland that would cover five or six acres, and lighting them all at the same time. Similar to what occurs in the "poem projects" formulated by Joan Brossa, a poet with whom Perejaume has collaborated on numerous occasions, the real is combined with the potential, with the desire for metamorphosis, and, through the fact of "leaving it written," with survival.

Counter to the tradition that views it as static, in Perejaume the land-cum-landscape is changeable and even portable. In the action-poem "Postaler" (Postcard Rack), the artist carries a metallic display rack on his back like the ones used in shops to sell postcards. Once the display rack is placed in the chosen location, a series of small rectangular mirrors occupy the place meant for the postcards, so that when placed in different positions the postcard rack represents different settings, the only common thread among them being the rack itself. The "painting" (the images reflected in the postcard rack) is ephemeral, and the spatial element comes to the fore: not only because the reflected landscapes change but also because the circular structure of the postcard rack requires the potential viewer to walk all the way around it to perceive it in its entirety. The mobility of the subject-creator, who scales mountains, moves objects, takes walks, etc., is invested with artistic-ness. Curiously, the act of walking, from Baudelaire's *flâneur* to the transurban experiences of the group Stalker – and including the Dadaist "visits" and Situationist drifting – has been considered an eminently urban practice.[14] Thus, Michel de Certeau establishes a certain parallelism between the urban walk and the speech act: "The act of walking is to the urban system what the speech act is to language or to the statements uttered . . . It thus seems possible to give a preliminary definition of walking as a space of enunciation" (97–98). Perejaume transfers this "meaningful errancy" to the streetless realms of the non-urban.

In "Postaler," the poet exports Stendhal's maxim of creation as a mirror carried along a high road to the forest, and even goes one step further by making this mirror both multiple and rotating. "Since Verdaguer," he writes, "generations of *plein-air* outdoorsmen of words and places went around inventorying through invention, going around from one place to another. They seemed to know that mimesis *per se* is not possible, and they drew everything closer and distanced everything and incessantly chased it to and fro to turn things upside down" (Perejaume, *El pirineu* 84).[15] And in *El paisatge és rodó*, he insists that the landscape is "a flat thing that curves," "a still thing that revolves," "a flat thing stood upright" (9–10). The postcard, which works as a metaphor of the superimposition of images spurred by the different historical and ideological moments of perception, is a recurring theme in his work. A simple assembly dating from

1983 consists of a toy excavator collecting postcards with its shovel. In the artist's book *El bosc a casa* (The Forest at Home), wrought in conjunction with Joan Brossa, the images are old postcards that allow "new sentences to be written with old pictures" (Altaió 25). The postcard rack also allows faraway landscapes to be paired up, the simultaneity in the place of the postcard.[16] "With the postcards," Perejaume acknowledges, "I set out to geographize collage . . . . Geographize painting, geographize language, the work, the author. I am a geographizing machine. Even the people I love end up attaining a geographic presence around me. When any aspect ends up attaining this physicality of geographic relief, it offers the advantage of being accessible from all angles" (Sala 114). By transcending its physicality to become a place of knowledge, the natural space shifts, to use Fernando Aínsa's expression, from *topos* to *logos*.

Towards a *No-Logo* Approach to the Rural

Up to now, I have described a series of elements that define Perejaume's poetics. My aim with this survey was to reveal the preponderance of non-urban territory in his work as a code and as an instrument of artistic theorization. The last part of these reflections is related to the reception and placement of Perejaume's spatial actions within the Catalan poetic system. Many of his poem-actions are ephemeral and require the audience's *presence*. Others can only be captured by photographing the performance, so the real audience is absent. Would they exist if they were not seen? The disquietude of this question – the disquietude of the absence of an interlocutor – ties in with the inevitable question of the social dimension of his works. In the prologue to *Oïsme*, the poet Josep Palau i Fabre proposed a sociological-nationalist interpretation of Perejaume's work: "All of Perejaume's efforts seem to be targeted at reconquering the land in its entirety and in its virginity, in its primeval integrity. I cannot fail but to see in this gesture the attempt, achieved through extreme non-violence, to reconquer our land from the inside out, based on its threatened identity" (11). And he went on: "We are not merely witnessing a few admirable pages whose refinement might lead us to believe that they are art for art's sake. The sociological motives are lying there wide awake, itching to reveal our own drowsiness" (11). How has a culture that perceives novelty as something essentially urban grasped these sociological motives?

First of all, Perejaume's works are widely recognized. He is not a marginal artist but a creator with an increasingly important role in the emblematic spaces of institutional and artistic representation. The prominent venues of his actions and interventions include the Frankfurt Book Fair, the Miró Foundation, Barcelona's Liceu Opera House, and the campus of the Universitat Autònoma de Barcelona. However, the critics somehow seem to view him as an artist who is reviving a lost world more than a creator of alternatives. The reviews of *Obreda*, though full of praise, are very explicit in this sense: they qualify him as intuitive (Llavina 12), they talk about his "ancient world" (Rafart 29), and they claim that "in contrast to the richness of the woodland, the modern world appears paltry in the poems of *Obreda*" (Guillamon 7). Therefore, acceptance of the artist seems to hinge upon his inclusion within a neo-romantic paradigm of love of the land.

Joan Nogué claims that in Catalonia today there are two discourses on the landscape: first, the discourse of conservative nationalism that draws from archetypal landscape myths from the Renaissance but in practice ignores them and actually manages the land in a way that debases it, and second, the discourse of a heterogeneous civil society that staunchly defends this land. Perhaps this scheme could be expanded or further shaded, but it seems clear that the archetypal model of landscape has fallen into a crisis which has opened up a breach between the real and the imaginary landscape, and at the same time is facing the challenge of generating new landscapes with which society can identify: "the dilemma is posed to what extent we are going to be capable of generating new landscapes with which society can identify. Some new kind of landscape should be capable of being the object of social representation if we want to remedy the breach that exists today between the real landscape and the imagined and represented landscape" (Nogué 167). Perejaume's spatial poetry precisely falls into the cleft of this challenge. Today, in Catalonia, non-urban land seems to be an ambiguous signifier, or crumbling among the different discourses that are disputing it. Yet there are not only the two discourses that Nogué mentions – the one with a certain nationalistic bent and the other coming from a progressive, ecological civil society – rather, there is also a third discourse: the one that adopts the rural as the "brand" or "logo" of an urbanity it wants to paint as integrating and that, at international trade fairs, elevates the espadrille and *barretina* cap to the status of symbols of *today's* Catalan identity by antonomasia. Perejaume's commission to design the poster for the La Mercè festivities in Barcelona in 2004 might fall within this third discourse, although the artist's work somehow rebelled against decoratively including country folk in the urban discourse (which is one way of *convoking* country folk *without letting them speak*, of having them be present yet confined to the outskirts). The imageless poster took shape as a poematic form that contained this text: "Do we artists have to become peasants? Is a planted tourist a peasant? Can someone who has been a tourist become a peasant?" The questions aroused controversy and incomprehension in a variety of citizen forums.

In his quest for interstices that allow him to affirm his own theoretical autonomy beyond the romantic discourse and the trivializing discourse of the rural, Perejaume's work opens the non-urban space to the possibilities of a performance that becomes an active agent of cultural debate. It affirms *one* Catalan identity (based on one land, one tradition, and one inquiry), but it refrains from turning it into a uniform brand or an object likely to become a fetish, among other reasons, because it is constructed in a space that, by fleeing from the rules – even chaotic and collagist rules – of the urban, is difficult to map and therefore to control.

Notes

1. This article is part of the research project Experimental Catalan Poetry from 1970 to 1990: Discourses, Representations, Reception, Diffusion, and Sociocultural Context (Ministry of Science and Innovation: FFI 2009-07086 FILO). I gratefully acknowledge the help of Mary Black (Servei de Llengües de la Universitat Autònoma de Barcelona) in translating this text into English.

2. The term *polipoetry*, coined by Enzo Minarelli in his essay "Polipoesia, dalla lectura alla performance di poesia sonora" (1981), has gained wide acceptance in Barcelona since the end of the 1980s, and has become a relevant practice from the 1990s on. It designates a kind of poetry characterized by live performance, sonority, spatial significance, use of technology, and/or intermediality.

3. This has been mentioned in two heretofore unpublished contributions: the first is a lecture at Yuxtaposiciones, a poetry and polypoetry micro-festival organized by Experimentaclub in May 2008 in Madrid (www.experimentaclub.com/yuxt08.htm); the second is a paper presented at the Transformacions congress organized by the LiCETCT research group at the University of the Balearic Islands in July 2009 (www.uib.cat/catedra/camv/denc/transformacions/index.html).

4. See propost.org/proposta2000/proposta2000_introengl.htm.

5. See www.stanford.edu/dept/DLCL/cgi-bin/web/research/new_ruralism.

6. "La història de l'art ignora les serralades, les vegetacions i els variadíssims cursos d'aigua. Al tombant de segle, tot és París, fins i tot el més recòndit paisatgisme. Sabem que no és així, que, al 1900, Eduard Munch treballa a Aasgaardstrand, Joaquim Mir a la Cala Encantada, James Ensor a Ostende, Ferdinand Hodler al llac Leman, Claude Monet a Guiverny, Segantini als Alps suïssos, però ens entestem a penjar totes aquestes pintures als murs de la capital francesa." We have chosen to include the original Catalan versions of Perejaume's creative writing (essays and poems). All the other Catalan texts have been translated into English.

7. "Oïm, aleshores, els paisatges de la veu: les figures sonores que la veu fa de resseguir els llocs per on es desplaça."

8. "El món que veig em sembla un escriptor. El terreny és un prosista segur, inexorable"; "De qui és, al capdavall, l'autoria? . . . Talment l'escriptura d'algú la notem al cap i ens serpeja pels membres, o s'esdevé que una terra prengui, d'obrar-la, una carnositat autoral que reconeixem com a nostra"; "el bosc és autor d'una gran obediència."

9. This fad for miniaturization also appears, albeit with a very different meaning, in constructions such as Barcelona's Poble Espanyol (Spanish Village), a monumental complex built on the mountain of Montjuïc for the 1929 Universal Exposition. The complex reproduces emblematic samples of Spanish architecture. The use of Poble Espanyol as a vehicle of anti-Catalan discourse during the Franco regime spurred controversy. I owe this observation to Mercè Picornell.

10. "Si faig un pessebre de guix, puc representar una serralada llunyana i, en aproximar-la per posar-hi darrere un mar detallat, amb l'aigua a tocar, continua essent una serralada llunyana. El llenguatge, doncs, és, de fet, un pessebre de guix."

11. ". . . trobament d'imatges a terra, sota terra/trobament de terra a les imatges."

12. ". . . no sabem ben bé si la serralada ja era allà o ha estat Verdaguer qui la hi ha posada."

13. ". . . la contemplació estètica del paisatge sembla referir-se, més que no pas al mateix espai natural, a la percepció decantada que en tenim i, encara, a la preocupació per expressar-lo, per retenir-lo i fer-lo a mans d'un altre observador. Es tracta, sense cap mena de dubte, d'una temàtica més afí a la imatge que no pas a l'emplaçament de la imatge."

14. For an inventory and analysis of these practices, see Francesco Careri's essay *Walkscapes*. See also Delgado's *Ciudad líquida, ciudad interrumpida*.

15. ". . . generacions de plenairistes dels mots i dels llocs feien per manera d'inventariar inventant, tot anant d'un lloc a l'altre. Semblaven conèixer que la mimesi, com a tal, no és possible i ho aproximaven tot i ho allunyaven tot, i no paraven d'acuitar-se amunt i avall per canviar-ho de nom o de banda."

16. Speaking about Jaume Sisa and Antoni Miralda's album, *Barcelona postal*, Mercè Picornell defines the postcard as a representation halfway between the overload of *lieux de mémoire* and the triviality of non-places. See her essay in this volume.

Bibliography

Aínsa, Fernando. *Del topos al logos. Propuestas de geopoética*. Madrid, Frankfurt: Iberoamericana, Vervuert, 2006.

Altaió, Vicenç. "VisualKultur.cat." *VisualKultur.cat*. Ed. Vicenç Altaió, and Daniel Giralt-Miracle. Barcelona: KRTU and Institut Ramon Llull, 2007. 13–31.

Brun, Jean-Paul. "El land art, una nebulosa de prácticas sociales de creación entre gigantismo y fragilidad." *Estética plural de la naturaleza*. Ed. Pere Salabert, Herman Parret, and Dominique Château. Barcelona: Laertes, 2006. 125–36.

Burke, Seán. "The Ethics of Signature." *Authorship: From Plato to the Postmodern*. Edinburgh: Edinburgh University Press, 1995. 285–91.

Careri, Francesco. *Walkscapes. El andar como práctica estética. Walking as an Aesthetic Practice* [bilingual edition]. Trans. Maurici Pla, Steve Piccolo, and Paul Hammond. Barcelona: Gustavo Gili, 2002.

Certeau, Michel de. *The Practice of Everyday Life*. Berkeley & Los Angeles: University of California Press, 1988.

Corboz, André. "El territorio como palimpsesto." *Lo urbano en 20 autores contemporáneos*. Ed. Ángel Martín Ramos. Barcelona: Edicions de la Universitat Politècnica de Catalunya & Escola Tècnica Superior d'Arquitectura de Barcelona, 2004. 25–34.

Delgado, Manuel. *Ciudad líquida, ciudad interrumpida*. Medellín: Universidad de Antioquía, 1999.

———. *Elogi del vianant. Del "model Barcelona" a la Barcelona real*. Barcelona: Edicions de 1984, 2005.

Gaziel [Agustí Calvet]. "Les viles spirituals." 1923. *Faig Arts* 32 (1991): 25–34.

Guerra, Carles. "El pintor d'esquena." *Deixar de fer una exposició*. By Perejaume. Barcelona: Macba & Actar, 1999. 123–55.

Guillamon, Julià. "Perejaume en el jardín secreto." *La Vanguardia. Culturas* 13 August 2003: 6–7.

Guillén, Claudio. "Paisaje y literatura, o los fantasmas de la otredad." *Actas del X Congreso de la Asociación Internacional de Hispanistas*. Ed. Antonio Vilanova. Barcelona: PPU, 1992. 77–98.

Llavina, Jordi. "Perejaume: l'ombra del cor de la terra." *Avui Cultura* 13 November 2003: 12.

Maderuelo, Javier. *El paisaje: génesis de un concepto*. Madrid: Abada Editores, 2005.

Mesquida, Biel. "Barcelona quan sona." *La Bañera* 2 (1979): 23.

Muir, Richard. *Approaches to Landscape*. London: MacMillan, 1999.

Nel·lo, Oriol. *Ciutat de ciutats*. Barcelona: Empúries, 2001.

Nogué, Joan. "Nacionalismo, territorio y paisaje en Catalunya." *Paisaje, memoria histórica e identidad nacional*. Ed. Nicolás Ortega Cantero.

Madrid, Soria: UAM Ediciones & Fundación Duques de Soria, 2005. 147–69.

Nogué, Joan, and Joan Vicente. *Geopolítica, identidad y globalización*. Barcelona: Ariel, 2001.

Palau i Fabre, Josep. "Arièlica ment." *Oïsme: una escriptura natural a partir dels croquis pirinencs de Jacint Verdaguer*. By Perejaume. Barcelona: Proa, 1998. 9–11.

Perejaume. *Autors*. Barcelona: Cafè Central, 1991. *Ludwig Jujol.*

———. *Deixar de fer una exposició*. Barcelona: Macba i Actar, 1999.

———. *El paisatge és rodó*. Vic: H Associació per a les arts Contemporànies & Eumo Gràfic, 1995.

———. *El Pirineu de baix: Mont-roig, Miró, Mallorca*. Barcelona: Polígrafa, 1997.

———. *Oïsme: una escriptura natural a partir dels croquis pirinencs de Jacint Verdaguer*. Barcelona: Proa, 1998.

———. *Obreda*. Barcelona: Edicions 62, 2003.

———. *Què és el collage sinó acostar soledats? Lluís II de Baviera, Josep Maria Jujol*. Barcelona: La Magrana, 1989.

Rafart, Susanna. "Té quasi d'herba la paraula." *Caràcters* 25 (2003): 29–30.

Roger, Alain. *Breve tratado del paisaje*. Trans. Maysi Veuthey. Madrid: Biblioteca Nueva, 2007.

Rowe, Colin, and Fred Koetter. *Collage City*. Cambridge, MA: The MIT Press, 1978.

Sala, Toni. *Comelade, Casasses, Perejaume*. Barcelona: Edicions 62, 2006.

Tarrida, Joan. "El rei i l'arquitecte: la construcció d'un univers." *Lletra de Canvi* September 1989: 21–25.

Sardà, Zeneida. "Perejaume. Entintar els pics, escriure amb el Pirineu." *Retrats*. Barcelona: Publicacions de l'Abadia de Montserrat, 2007. 101–11.

Williams, Raymond. *The Country and the City*. New York: Oxford University Press, 1973.

The Contributors

Anxo Abuín González is Professor of Literary Theory and Comparative Literature at the University of Santiago de Compostela in Spain. He has published numerous articles on theater and performance studies as well as several monographs such as *El narrador en el teatro* (Universidad de Santiago de Compostela, 1997) and *Escenarios del caos. Entre la hipertextualidad y la performance en la era electrónica* (Tirant lo Blanc, 2006). He is also a coeditor of *A Comparative History of the Literatures in the Iberian Peninsula*, which appeared in 2010 with John Benjamins. He is currently directing an interdisciplinary project on electronic literature in Spain.

Arturo Casas teaches Literary Theory and coordinates the Centre for Research on Emergent Cultural Processes and Practices at the University of Santiago de Compostela. He is a member of the international network Poetics of Resistance and of scientific committees of journals published in Spain, Brazil, Estonia, China, the U.S.A. and the U.K. He is the author of numerous articles and book chapters as well as various books on his areas of specialization. Among others: *La teoría estética, teatral y literaria de Rafael Dieste* (1997), *La descripción literaria* (1999), *Elementos de Crítica literaria* (2004), and *Antoloxía poética*, a collection of poems by Uxío Novoneyra (2010). His current fields of analysis are the debate on literary history, modern and postmodern aesthetic thought, the contemporary essay, the Spanish Republican exile, and Galician poetry of the twentieth and twenty-first centuries from a comparative perspective. His latest work, *Resistance and Emancipation: Cultural and Poetic Practices*, coordinated with Ben Bollig, is forthcoming from Peter Lang.

Roberto Echavarren is a poet, novelist, and essayist from Uruguay. His latest volumes of poetry are: *Performance* (2000), *Casino Atlántico* (2004), *Centralasia* (2005), *El expreso entre el sueño y la vigilia* (2009), and *Ruido de fondo* (2010). His novels are *Ave roc* (2007), *El diablo en el pelo* (2005), *Yo era una brasa* (2009), and *La salud de los enfermos* (2010). His latest books of essays are: *Fuera de género: criaturas de la invención erótica* (2007) and *Arte andrógino: estilo versus moda* (2010). He has taught literature at the University of London, New York University, Centro Rojas of the University of Buenos Aires, and the Universidad de la República (Montevideo).

Gaston Franssen is Assistant Professor of Modern Dutch Literature at the University of Amsterdam, The Netherlands. In 2007, he contributed an article on modern poetry, impersonality, and life-writing to the collection *Stories and Portraits of the Self*, edited by H.C. Buescu and J.F. Duarte (Amsterdam: Rodopi); and in 2008 he published *Gerrit Kouwenaar en de politiek van het lezen* (Nijmegen: Vantilt), an analysis of the interpretive conventions at work in Dutch poetry criticism. His current research topics include contemporary Dutch literature, reception aesthetics, authorship, and popular celebrity. Recently, he contributed to the *Journal of Dutch Literature* 1.1 (October 2010) an article on these topics, entitled "Literary Celebrity and the Discourse on Authorship in Dutch Literature."

Irina Garbatzky holds a degree in Literature and Linguistics (Universidad Nacional de Rosario, Argentina), and works on Latin American poetry, performance art, activist art, theater, memory, and post-dictatorship poetry. She is currently writing her doctoral dissertation on "Orality, Poetry and Performance: Poetical Practices in the Río de la Plata Area in the Late 20th Century," with financial support from CONICET (Consejo Nacional de Investigaciones Científicas y Técnicas). She has published several academic and journalistic articles, and has contributed to the edited volume *Los límites de la literatura* (Rosario, UNR, 2010). Her poetic work is included in the anthology *El management envilece al mundo* (Clase Turista, Buenos Aires, 2010), and she has written the texts for the exhibition *Bajo la hierba. Territorios, ciudad y memoria* (Museo de la Memoria, Rosario, 2009).

Cornelia Gräbner is Lecturer in Hispanic Studies at Lancaster University, U.K. She holds an M.A. in Comparative Literature from the University of Bonn, Germany, and a Ph.D. from the Amsterdam School for Cultural Analysis. Her current research interests focus on contemporary European, Latin American, and North American literature, particularly poetry. Research projects explore the performance of poetry, poetry as a practice of resistance, literary engagements with the *dirty wars* in Latin America, and literary representations of and interventions in megacities.

Urayoán Noel is Assistant Professor of English at the University at Albany, SUNY, where he is affiliated with the Department of Latin American, Caribbean, and U.S. Latino Studies. His research focuses on U.S. Latino/a and hemispheric poetry and poetics, with an emphasis on questions of performance, translation, circulation, and the relationship between aesthetics and politics. He is currently completing a book-length manuscript on the cultural/body politics of Nuyorican poetry, on and off the page, since the 1960s. A contributing editor of *Mandorla*, Noel is also the author of various bilingual books of poetry and performance work, most recently *Boringkén* (Ediciones Callejón, Puerto Rico) – named of one of the ten Books of the Year for 2008 by El Nuevo Día – and the forthcoming *Hi-Density Politics* (BlazeVOX). His articles and reviews have appeared in *Contemporary Literature*; *Bomb*; *CENTRO*; and *Diasporic Avant-Gardes: Experimental Poetics and Cultural Displacement* (Palgrave, 2009).

Deirdre Osborne is a Senior Lecturer at Goldsmiths, University of London. She recently edited a Special Issue on Contemporary Black British Women's Writing for *Women: A Cultural Review* and has an AHRC Fellowship to complete her monograph *Critically Black: Contemporary Black British Dramatists and Theatre in the New Millennium* (Manchester UP). She has edited *Hidden Gems*, an anthology of Black British plays and critical essays (Oberon) and interviewed and published essays on Andrea Levy, Lemn Sissay, Valerie Mason-John, Roy Williams, Kwame Kwei-Armah, debbie tucker green, and Courttia Newland over the past decade. Her other published research includes work on Victorian motherhood and colonial ideology and female spies in WWII Occupied France.

Mercè Picornell Belenguer is Lecturer in Catalan Literature and Comparative Literature at the Universitat de les Illes Balears. She has published essays on testimonial and ethnographic writing, experimental literature, and Catalan contemporary culture. She is the author of *Discursos testimonials en la literatura catalana recent* (2002), and the editor of Catalan works of Gabriel Maura (*Pegaso arando. Obra completa de Gabriel Maura*, 2007), Pere d' Alcantara Penya (*Els brams de l'ase*, 2007), and Maria Mayol (*Delers i altres poemes*, 2008). Current research interests include the analysis of the cultural context of experimental literature. As a member of the LiCETC (Comparative Literature: Theoretical and Comparative Studies) research group she is coauthor of the books *Literatura i cultura: aproximacions comparatistes* (2009), *Poètiques de ruptura* (2008), and *Textualisme i subversió* (2007).

Jeffrey Manoel Pijpers studied Latin American Studies with a specialization in Literature at Leiden University, The Netherlands, with a minor in classical guitar at the Royal Conservatory in The Hague. Throughout his M.A. and M.Phil., he combined literary studies with music through the analysis of musical lyrics. His research focuses on identity and resistance in the song lyrics of marginal musicians, related to the concepts of hegemony and diaspora. His focus has shifted from post-Revolutionary Cuba during his M.A. thesis, to 1970s Brazil during his Research Master. He is currently undertaking a Ph.D. dissertation at ASCA (Amsterdam School for Cultural Analysis), University of Amsterdam, on marginal musicians in Cuba and Brazil. He has spent extended periods of time in La Habana and Rio de Janeiro for research purposes.

Margalida Pons is a Professor at the University of the Balearic Islands, where she has been teaching a wide range of courses on Catalan Literature, Literary Theory, and Comparative Literature since 1996. She has been visiting professor at Brown University. After obtaining her Ph.D. from the University of Barcelona (1993), she pursued further study and research in Comparative Literature at Indiana University, U.S.A. She has written a number of studies on twentieth-century poetry and experimental literature. Her publications include, among others, *Blai Bonet: maneres del color* (1993), *Els poetes insulars de postguerra* (1998), *Corrents de la poesia insular del segle XX* (2010), and, as an editor or co-editor, *(Des)aïllats: narrativa contemporània i insularitat a les Illes Balears* (2004), *Textualisme i subversió: formes i condicions de la narrativa experimental catalana (1970-1985)* (2007), *Poètiques de ruptura* (2008), and *Literatura i cultura. Aproximacions comparatistes* (2009). She leads the research group LiCETC (www.uib.es/depart/dfc/litecont/), which focuses on literary experimentation and interdiciplinarity.

María do Cebreiro Rábade Villar holds a doctorate in Literary Theory. She is a lecturer at the University of Santiago de Compostela. Her research focuses on contemporary Galician poetry, anthologies on the Spanish Peninsula, cultural processes that are linked to migration, and the relationship between literature and spectrality. Through various objects and foci of analysis, her research is related to the analysis of the relationship between literature and power, and phenomena of cultural resistance. She has published articles in several national and international journals. She is author of the monographs *As antoloxías de poesía en Galicia e Cataluña. Representación poética e ficción lóxica* (2004), which was awarded the Dámaso Alonso Prize for Filological Research, *As terceiras mulleres* (2005), and *Fogar impronunciable. Poesía e pantasma* (2010). Together with Fernando Cabo she has co-authored *Manual de teoría de la literatura* (2005).

Jonah Raskin teaches American literature, law, and critical thinking at Sonoma State University. He is the author of a dozen books, including *American Scream: Allen Ginsberg's 'Howl' and The Making of the Beat Generation*, and he is also a performance poet. His most recent book of poetry is *Auras*.

SuAndi, OBE is based in Manchester, U.K. but goes to family reunions in North America, across Europe, Brazil, and India. She has taken to the stage as a live artist, keynote speaker, panel contributor, and, in her best clothes, as the poet. She has been at the helm of the NBAA (previously Black Arts Alliance (www.blackartists.org.uk) since 1985 and sees herself as a proactive creator who uses the arts as a vehicle for learning, understanding, and experience across diverse communities. She has traveled such different routes across the arts that she can comfortably wear the attire of a curator of visual arts, a producer, and a director of community-based performances (alongside those of her fellow NBAA artists). SuAndi conceives of the arts as a means to help heal wounds and eradicate misconceptions that can develop into blatant racism; thus, the arts are for her a means of empowering individual self-worth. Her poetry draws on the power of laughter, the depth of wisdom, and a good piece of gossip. See http://www.lancs.ac.uk/fass/projects/writersgallery/content/SuAndi.html.

Zoë Skoulding's most recent collections of poems are *Remains of a Future City* (Seren, 2008), long-listed for Wales Book of the Year 2009, and *The Mirror Trade* (Seren, 2004).

Her collaborative work includes *Dark Wires*, with poet Ian Davidson (West House Books, 2007), *From Here*, with images by Simonetta Moro (Dusie, 2008), and *You Will Live in Your Own Cathedral*, with sound by Alan Holmes (LAF-Seren, 2009). She is a member of the group Parking Non-Stop, whose album *Species Corridor* was released by Klangbad in 2008. She holds an AHRC Research Fellowship at Bangor University, where she also runs part-time courses in literature and creative writing. She has been Editor of the international quarterly *Poetry Wales* since 2008.

Index

A

Abramović, Marina, 145, 161
Abuín González, Anxo, 11, 14, 279
Acconci, Vito, 152–54, 170, 172
ACG Vianen, 47
Adorno, Theodor, 87
Adyanthaya, Aravind, 106
Agamben, Giorgio, 58, 61, 67, 69, 139–40, 149
Aguirre, Soidade, 148–49
Aínsa, Fernando, 274, 277
Alcàntara Penya, Pere d', 280
Aldana, Rodrigo, 188
Aldao, Lucía, 126
Allen, Donald, 30
Allen, Gay Wilson, 32
Allen, Steve, 30
Altaió, Vicenç, 271, 274, 277
Álvarez Valle, Alana, 108
Amado Rodríguez, Teresa, 130
Anderson, Laurie, 87, 154, 158, 169–71
Andújar, Rey, 106
Angelou, Maya, 223
Angueira, Anxo, 123–26, 129
Antin, David, 155
Aptowicz, Cristin O'Keefe, 106, 108
Arana, R. Victoria, 198, 213, 215–17, 227
Arias, Xiana, 126–27
Aristotle, 119, 131
Armstrong, Charlie, 216
Artaud, Antonin, 38, 43, 50, 163, 169, 184
Aston, Elaine, 170

Attridge, Derek, 46–8, 51, 72, 76, 86–7
Auden, W.H., 27
Augé, Marc, 242, 244, 253, 261
Auslander, Philip, 96, 106, 108, 154, 170
Austin, John L., 118, 129–30
Aviram, Ammittai, 86–7
Ayala, Hermes, 97, 99–101, 108

B

Bach, Johann Sebastian, 25
Bachelard, Gaston, 266
Bacon, Francis, 259–61
Baker Houston Jr., A., 216
Bakhtin, Mikhail, 63–5, 69, 120, 163
Baljon, Sieger, 47
Banu, Georges, 160
Baraka, Amiri, 30, 87–8
Barbosa Sánchez, Alma Patricia, 188
Barker, Lewis, 213, 215
Barthes, Roland, 138, 149, 152, 170, 233
Basquiat, Jean Michel, 107
Batista, Antoni, 241, 244
Baudelaire, Charles, 273
Bauman, Zygmunt, 156, 166–67, 170
Beasley, Paul, 15, 86–7
Beat Poets, 12–3, 24, 30–2, 36, 54, 73, 86–7, 154, 281
Beatles, 29, 60
Beckett, Samuel, 119, 160, 167, 170, 213
Beets, Nicolaas, 38, 51
Bejerman, Gabriela, 193
Beneventi, Dominic, 258, 261

Benjamin, Walter, 124, 131, 148, 255, 261
Benveniste, Émile, 139
Berg, Wim van den, 37–8, 51
Bernstein, Charles, 9, 19, 86–8, 96, 105, 107–08, 172
Bhabha, Homi, 61–2, 64, 69
Biau, Christophe, 170
Biet, Christian, 159, 170
Billington, Michael, 213, 215
Black, Mary, 276
Blades, Rubén, 91
Blake, William, 28, 109
Blackmur, Richard P., 109
Blanchot, Maurice, 266
Blaser, Robin, 24
Blau, Herbert, 170
Blonk, Jaap, 48
Boal, Augusto, 226–27
Bollig, Ben, 279
Bolter, Jay David, 253, 261
Bonet, Blai, 281
Bonin-Rodríguez, Paul, 107–08
Bonney, Jo, 169–70
Bonney, Sean, 255, 261
Borges, Jorge Luis, 192, 243
Borrell, Pere Jaume — see Perejaume
Bourdieu, Pierre, 125
Bourriaud, Nicolas, 182, 188
Bowie, David, 175
Boykoff, Jules, 249, 261
Boyle, Mark, 269
Boyle Family, 269
Brand, Jo, 219, 227
Brassens, George, 235
Brathwaite, Edward Karnau, 12, 73, 75–6, 84, 86–7
Brecht, Bertolt, 161, 169, 187
Brel, Jacques, 235
Brems, Hugo, 34–6, 51
Brik, Osip, 86

Brossa, Joan, 270, 273–74
Bruinja, Tsead, 48
Brun, Jean-Paul, 270, 277
Bruno, Giordano, 152
Buarque, Chico, 57
Buell, Lawrence, 109
Buescu, Helena Carvalhão, 279
Bürger, Peter, 181, 186, 188
Burgos, Julia de, 94
Burke, Seán, 271, 277
Burroughs, William, 154, 238
Bustamante, Maris, 187
Butler, Judith, 98, 108, 113, 129–30, 178, 187–88, 252, 261

C

Cabo, Fernando, 281
Cage, John, 152, 154
Calderón, Tego, 91, 102
Calinescu, Matei, 234, 244
Calvet, Agustí — see Gaziel
Campos, Leo F., 124–27
Cangi, Adrián, 186, 188–89
Capel, Horacio, 264
Cara de Cavalo [Manoel Moreira], 57–8
Caravaggio, 142
Careri, Francesco, 276–77
Carrera, Arturo, 173
Casadesús, Alícia, 265
Casas, Arturo, 15, 129–30, 149, 279
Casasses, Enric, 265, 269, 278
Castaño, Yolanda, 122–23, 129–30
Castro, Rosalía de, 111, 125, 130, 139
Cauter, Lieven de, 243–44, 249, 251, 253, 261
Certeau, Michel de, 80, 198, 200, 202–04, 207, 213, 215, 237, 242, 244, 247, 261, 273, 277
Chacal, 54–5, 59
Champagne, Leonora, 169–70

284 | Index

Chang, Jeff, 109
Chaplin, Charles, 114
Château, Dominique, 277
Chateaubriand, 159
Chávarri, Jaime, 243
Christiansen, Bernhard, 48
Chtcheglov, Ivan, 256, 260
Clarke, John N., 214–15
Claudio, Karina, 17, 97–9, 101–08
Claus, Hugo, 51
Clemons, Leigh, 39, 51
Cochón, Iris, 149–50
Cocteau, Jean, 177
Coelho, Frederico, 56–7, 69
Cohn, Sergio, 54–7, 59, 63, 65–6, 70
Colectivo Ronseltz, 125
Coleridge, Samuel Taylor, 152
Colón, Carlitos, 99–100
Coltrane, John, 28, 83
Columbus, Christopher, 235
Conboy, Katie, 108
Conrad, Joseph, 192
Coogan, Steve, 219, 227
Coolbrith, Ina, 24
Cooper, Alice, 184
Cooper, Carolyn, 86–7
Copjec, Joan, 129–30
Corboz, André, 265, 272, 277
Cordal, Xabier, 129
Cornago, Óscar, 162, 164, 170
Cornejo Polar, Antonio, 232, 244
Coromines, Joan, 268
Corso, Gregory, 36
Cortés, Lurdes, 242
Costa, Lis, 264
Costa e Silva, Artur da, 56
Couttenier, Piet, 37–8, 51
Crane, Hart, 28
Crapranzano, Vincent, 118
Creus, Estevo, 129

Critcher, Chas, 214–15
Culler, Jonathan, 40–1, 51
Cunningham, Merce, 154
Curros Enríquez, Manuel, 111

D

Dalí, Salvador, 265, 270
Damon, Maria, 107
Danto, Arthur C., 181, 188
Darby, Ken, 117
Darío, Rubén, 186
Davidson, Ian, 282
Dávila, Arlene, 94, 106, 108
Dávila, Ángela María, 95
Dawes, Kwame, 198, 211, 215
Dean, Roger, 252–53, 261
Debord, Guy, 107, 238
Debroise, Oliver, 187–88
DeFeo, Jay, 23
Dehaene, Michiel, 243–44, 249, 251, 253, 261
Deleuze, Gilles, 93–4, 106, 108, 194
Delgado, Manuel, 237, 244, 464, 276–77
Delgado, Sergio, 189
Derrida, Jacques, 118, 129, 133, 150, 233
Díaz-Quiñones, Arcadio, 93–4, 108
Dickinson, Emily, 32
Diderot, Denis, 159
Didi de Paris, 47
Dieste, Rafael, 279
Dimock, Wai Chee, 109
Dios, Josechu de, 144
Dios, Xoán de, 144
Dollan, Jill, 98, 104, 107–08, 121–24, 130, 155, 170
Donne, John, 28
Doorn, Johnny van, 11, 13, 16, 36–9, 41–8, 51
Doors, 184
Dorleign, Gills, 40, 51

Doubrovsky, Serge, 159
Droog, Bart F.M., 34, 47
Duarte, João Ferreira, 279
Duchamp, Marcel, 115, 152, 177
Duijnhoven, Serge van, 33–4
Dunbar, Paul Laurence, 225, 227
Duncan, Robert, 24
Durall, Jordi, 232, 244
Dütting, Hans, 38, 42–3, 46, 51
Dylan, Bob, 29, 242

E

Eberhart, Richard, 29, 32
Echavarren, Roberto, 10–1, 13, 14, 16, 173–89, 191–92, 194, 279
Economou, George, 42, 51
Edwards, Justin, 261
Edwards, Viv, 12, 19
Ehrenberg, Felipe, 187
Eisenstein, Sergei, 163
Eliot, T.S., 26–8
Elrick, Laura, 249, 261
Emerson, Ralph Waldo, 27
Engen, Max van, 43, 51
Ensor, James, 267, 276
Epps, Brad, 242, 244
Escobedo, Helen, 187
Escoffet, Eduard, 264
Espina, Eduardo, 191
Esteirán, María, 117, 121, 128, 142–43
Etchells, Tim, 156, 158, 170

F

Fabre, Jan, 163
Fages de Climent, Carles, 265
Fegan, Kevin, 219, 227
Ferlinghetti, Lawrence, 26–7, 31
Fernández Rei, Francisco, 129
Fernández Sanmartín, Celso, 123–25, 129
Fernando Jr., S.H., 86–7

Ferrer, Esther, 142
Figueiredo, Luciano, 57
Finley, Karen, 169
Fish, Stanley, 40, 51
Fisher, Mark, 194
Fitzgerald, Ella, 25
Flores, Juan, 92, 94–5, 101, 105–08
Flores, Luis Vicente, 181
Foix, J.V., 270
Foley, John Miles, 12, 19
Foreman, Richard, 161
Foster, Hal, 182, 186, 188
Foucault, Michel, 15, 17, 143, 237, 239, 243–44, 247–49, 251, 254–55, 261
Franco, Francisco, 7, 111, 146, 229–32, 239–41, 244, 263, 270, 276
Franssen, Gaston, 10, 11, 13, 16–7, 34, 38, 47–8, 51, 86, 279
Fraser, Steve, 176–77, 179
Freschi, Romina, 193
Freud, Sigmund, 182

G

Gallego, 10, 91–7, 100, 102–04, 107–08, 129, 131
Gallop, Jane, 129, 131
Garbatzky, Irina, 10, 13–4, 279
García Canclini, Néstor, 232, 244
Garcia-Soler, Jordi, 234, 236, 244
Gasparini, Philippe, 159, 169–70
Gaudí, Antoni, 266
Gaziel, 265, 277
Geest, Dirk de, 35–6, 51
Gelman, Juan, 186
Gerbrandy, Piet, 33, 48, 51
Gil, Gilberto, 59, 61, 69
Gil de Biedma, Jaime, 235
Giles, Paul, 106, 108
Gimferrer, Pere, 271
Ginsberg, Allen, 13, 23–32, 36, 238–39, 281

Giorgio, Marosa di, 173, 191
Giorno, John, 154
Giralt-Miracle, Daniel, 277
Goedegebuure, Jaap, 36–7, 51
Gogh, Ruben van, 34, 51
Goldberg, RoseLee, 39, 51, 169–70
Golding, Sue, 248, 261
Gómez, Lupe, 129–30
González, José Raúl — see Gallego
Govan, Emma, 158, 170
Gräbner, Cornelia, 11–4, 16–7, 87, 207, 211–12, 215, 280
Graham, Helen, 243–44
Gray, Christopher, 249, 256, 262
Gray, Scott, 177
Gray, Spalding, 157, 161
green, debbie tucker, 280
Greham, Helena, 156, 171
Grosz, Elizabeth, 253, 255, 262
Grotowski, Jerzy, 154
Grusin, Richard, 253, 261
Guattari, Felix, 93–4, 106, 108
Gubern, Román, 153, 171
Guerra, Carles, 267, 269, 271, 277
Guillamon, Julià, 238, 243–44, 275, 277
Guillén, Claudio, 272, 277
Guimerà, Àngel, 265

H

Hac Mor, Carles, 264
Hall, Stuart, 214–15
Haller, Albrecht von, 272
Hamed, Amir, 174, 186, 188
Hanssen, Peter Holvoet, 47
Haraway, Donna, 253, 262
Harris, Geraldine, 170
Harryman, Carla, 262
Harte, Bret, 24
Harvey, Campbell R., 214
Harwood, Gwen, 209, 215, 217

Haynes, Todd, 175–189
Heddon, Deirdre, 156, 158, 171
Heizer, Michael, 270
Henry, Ianie, 227
Herberg, Ben, 43, 46, 51
Herbert, George, 201
Hernández, Lucienne, 107
Hernández Cruz, Víctor, 103
Heytze, Ingmar, 33, 47
Hicks, Philip, 29–30
Higgins, Dick, 152, 171
Hillis Miller, J., 118
Hintz, Suzanne S., 106, 109
Hodler, Ferdinand, 267, 276
Hölderlin, Friedrich, 134, 140, 149
Holman, Bob, 30–1
Holmes, Alan, 256–57, 262, 282
Holst, A. Roland, 36
Holt, Nancy, 270
Homer, 12, 19
Horkheimer, Max, 87
Howell, John, 154–55, 158, 171
Hubbard, Sue, 200, 216
Hughes, Holly, 155, 169
Huguet, Damià, 265
Huxley, Aldous, 237
Huyssen, Andreas, 177, 179, 186, 188
Hyde, Lewis, 32

I

Iggy Pop, 175
Indiana Hernández, Rita, 106
Innes, C.L., 214, 216
Ivison, Douglas, 261

J

Jakobson, Roman, 35, 49, 51, 115
James, C.L.R., 214
James, Henry, 103, 109
Jameson, Fredric, 115

Jansen, Tjitske, 33, 52
Jáuregui, Carlos A., 116, 131
Jefferson, Tony, 214–15
Jirku, Brigitte E., 114, 131
John, Gus, 214
Johnny the Selfkicker — see Johnny van Doorn
Johnson, Linton Kwesi, 11, 72
Jonas, Joan, 154
Joosten, Jos, 33, 40, 50, 52
Joseph, Marc Bamuthi, 106, 109
Juana Inés de la Cruz, 181
Jujol, Josep Maria, 266–67, 270, 278
Julien, Isaac, 199, 209, 216

K

Kafka, Franz, 108
Kalu, Pete, 210, 216
Kamenszain, Tamara, 183, 188
Kantor, Tadeusz, 159–60, 171
Kaprow, Allan, 161
Kay, Jackie, 225–27
Kaye, Nick, 156, 171
Kelso, Fiona, 242
Kent, Conrad, 242
Kerouac, Jack, 24–5, 28, 30, 238
Kirby, Michael, 152
Kitt, Eartha, 7, 219, 221–23, 225, 227
Koetter, Fred, 267, 278
Konstan, David, 116, 119, 131
Kosinsky, Jerzy, 169
Kouwenaar, Gerrit, 13, 36, 38, 279
Kozer, José, 180, 187–89
Krauss, Rosalind, 169, 171
Kristeva, Julia, 138, 233
Kurticz, Marcos, 187
Kwei-Armah, Kwame, 280

L

Labany, Jo, 243–44
Lacan, Jacques, 114–15
Laclau, Ernesto, 115
Lado, María, 126, 128, 130
Lamantia, Philip, 25
Lamborghini, Osvaldo, 173
Lanoye, Tom, 34
Larive, J.M., 37–8, 52
Lauwaert, Guido, 36
Lavoe, Héctor, 104
Le Gendre, Kevin, 210, 216
Le Roi Jones — see Amiri Baraka
LeCompte, Elizabeth, 157
Lee, Matt, 194
Lefebvre, Henri, 15, 17, 71–3, 76, 78–80, 85–6, 88, 247–49, 262, 266
Lehmann, Hans-Thies, 160, 163, 167, 171
Lennon, John, 29
Lévinas, Emmanuel, 167, 171
Levy, Andrea, 280
Lezama Lima, José, 173, 187, 194
Liceaga, Yara, 106
Liddell, Angélica, 7, 151, 161–71
Lindsay, Vachel, 28
Lira, Miguel de, 142
Llavina, Jordi, 274, 277
Lloréns Torres, Luis, 94
Lo Cascio, Paola, 243–44
London, Jack, 24
Longoni, Ana, 186, 188
López Roig, Cecilia, 114, 131
Lopo, Antón, 18, 114–16, 123, 128–29, 131, 145, 149
Love, Heathet, 131
Ludwig II of Bavaria, 266–67, 271–72, 278
Lulofs, B.H., 37, 51–2
Lussac, Olivier, 169, 171
Lyotard, Jean-François, 129, 131, 157, 169, 171

M

Macalé, Jards, 63, 69
Maderuelo, Javier, 272, 277
Maldonado, Adál, 96, 109
Maleczech, Ruth, 154, 171
Mallarmé, Stéphane, 134, 186
Maragall, Pasqual, 241, 243
Margolin, Deb, 155
Maria, Walter de, 270
Marmion, Patrick, 210, 216
Marsh, Hazel, 10, 15
Marín, Martí, 243–44
Martín Ramos, Ángel, 277
Mason-John, Valerie, 280
Massey, Doreen, 248
Massumi, Brian, 119, 129, 131
Matson, Vera, 117
Maura, Gabriel, 280
Mayol, Maria, 280
McClure, Michael, 25
McGobern, Timothy, 131
McNeil, Donald, 242
Medina, Nadia, 108
Melendes, Joserramón, 100
Melendres, Jaume, 234, 244
Meltzer, David, 30
Méndez Ferrín, X.L., 129–31, 139
Mercer, Kobena, 199, 209, 216
Meschonnic, Henri, 86, 88
Meseguer, Lluís Bartomeu, 236, 244
Mesquida, Biel, 233, 270, 277
Meyer, Ursula, 152, 171
Middleton, Peter, 12, 13, 15, 19, 38, 42, 47, 52
Milán, Eduardo, 173–74, 180, 186, 188
Miles, Barry, 32
Milling, Jane, 156, 171
Mills-Courts, Karen, 123, 131
Milton, John, 28
Minarelli, Enzo, 276
Mir, Joaquim, 267, 276
Miralda, Antoni, 235, 245, 277
Miró, Joan, 270, 274, 278
Mondrian, Piet, 268
Monet, Claude, 267, 276
Monk, Geraldine, 15, 247, 254–56, 260–62
Monk, Meredith, 154
Monk, Thelonius, 28
Montaigne, Michel de, 159
Montaner, Josep M., 242
Montoute, Carline, 221
Monzó, Quim, 233, 264
Mooney, Claire, 219, 227
Moore, Marianne, 75
Moro, Simonetta, 282
Morris, Adelaide, 9, 19
Morrison, Jim, 181, 184
Moure, Erín, 149–50, 259, 262
Mourits, Bertram, 35, 38, 47, 52
Muir, Richard, 272, 277
Mulder, Simon, 48
Mullen, Harryette, 198
Munch, Edvard, 267, 276
Muntaner, Maria, 244
Muxí, Zaida, 242

N

Nabokov, Vladimir, 192
Nagle, Marlene, 61, 70
Nagy, Gregory, 12, 19
Nakh Ab Ra, 193–94
Nascimento, Milton, 57
Nazario, 264
Negrón-Muntaner, Frances, 107, 109
Nel·lo, Oriol, 265, 277
Neto, Torquato, 59, 63, 65–6
Newland, Courttia, 280
Newton, John, 214
Ngai, Sianne, 119, 129, 131

Nicholson, Helen, 158, 171
Nicholson-Smith, Donald, 262
Noel, Urayoán, 13, 15, 17, 86, 109, 280
Nogué, Joan, 265, 275, 277–78
Nogueira, María Xesús, 129, 131
Noland, Carrie, 87–8
Nora, Pierre, 235
Normal, Henry, 219, 227
Normington, Katie, 158, 171
Novoneyra, Uxío, 125, 130–31, 279
Nuvem Cigana, 10, 14, 16, 53–9, 61–7, 70
Nuyorican Poets, 10, 15, 30, 73, 76, 91–7, 101–04, 106–07, 109, 280

O

Oakes, Chantal, 227
Ocaña, José P., 264
O'Hara, Frank, 104–05, 109, 262
Oiticica, Hélio, 57–62, 64, 67, 69–70
Okoro, Elaine, 221
Olsen, Redell, 250–51, 262
Olson, Charles, 12–3, 73–6, 84–8
Ong, Walter J., 12, 19, 197, 200, 202, 207, 212, 216
Opland, 37
Oppenheim, Denis, 269
Ortega Cantero, Nicolás, 277
Osborne, Deirdre, 10, 12, 14–6, 213–14, 216, 280
Ostaijen, Paul van, 38
Owusu, Kwame, 217

P

Paes, Tavinho, 65
Palau i Fabre, Josep, 274, 278
Palés Matos, Luis, 94
Palumbo-Liu, David, 103, 109
Parker, Charlie, 28
Parret, Herman, 277
Pastor, Mara, 106

Pato, Chus, 10–1, 15–6, 117, 121–22, 128, 133–35, 137, 139, 141–43, 145, 147, 149–50
Pavis, Patrice, 158, 171, 186, 188
Peacock, D. Keith, 213, 216
Peeren, Esther, 18
Peeters, Hagar, 47
Perdomo, Willie, 11, 17, 73, 76–80, 85–86, 88, 93, 102
Perejaume [Borrell, Pere Jaume], 10, 14, 263, 266–78
Perloff, Marjorie, 86, 88
Perlongher, Néstor, 173–74, 180, 187, 189
Perniola, Mario, 67
Pfeiler, Martina, 38, 42, 52
Picornell Belenguer, Mercè, 13, 15–7, 244, 276–77, 280
Pietrafesa, Renée, 191
Pietri, Pedro, 10, 91, 95–8, 103–04, 107, 109
Pijpers, Jeffrey Manoel, 13–4, 16, 280
Pinter, Harold, 160, 213, 216
Piñero, Miguel, 95, 101
Pla, Josep, 265
Pla, Maurici, 277
Poe, Edgar Allan, 208, 216
Poggi, Christine, 153, 172
Poggioli, Renato, 39, 52
Pollock, Della, 156, 172
Pondal, Eduardo, 111, 129–31
Pons, Agustí, 244, 265, 277
Pons, Margalida, 14–5, 233, 244, 281
Porrúa, Ana, 175, 186, 189
Prado, Ignacio, 177, 189
Prado, Iván, 114–16, 129, 131
Premat, Julio, 189
Presley, Elvis, 117, 174
Prima, Diane di, 30
Prosper-Sánchez, Gloria D., 100
Pryor, Jaclyn, 107–08
Pujol, Jordi, 243

R

Rábade Villar, María do Cebreiro, 10, 13–4, 16, 111, 281
Rafart, Susanna, 274, 278
Raimon, 240
Ramey, Lauri, 210, 213, 216
Raskin, Jonah, 10, 13, 32, 86, 281
Rebollo-Gil, Guillermo, 10, 94, 101–04, 107, 109
Redes Escarlata, 141, 143
Reddy, William M., 116, 118–19, 131
Reed, Lou, 175
Reeves, Marcus, 86, 88
Reixa, Antón, 125
Resina, Joan Ramon, 231, 244, 264, 266
Rexroth, Kenneth, 24
Reyes, Israel, 97, 107, 109
Reynés, Josep Antoni, 244
Riba, Pau, 238
Rijghard, Ron, 36, 52
Rimbaud, Arthur, 28, 87
Risco, Vicente, 129
Risques, Manel, 244
Rivero, Federico, 183, 189
Rivero, Marino, 191
Riviere, Joan, 127
Roberts, Brian, 214–15
Roig, Josep Ramon, 264–65, 269
Roger, Alain, 272, 278
Rojo Gama, Vicente, 187
Romaní, Ana, 114, 117, 123, 129, 131
Romeo, Anxos, 129
Ron, Xesús, 142
Rose, Tricia, 87–8
Rosenwein, Barbara H., 116, 131
Rossell, Benet, 264
Rosselló, Pedro, 98
Rousseau, Jean-Jacques, 159
Rowe, Colin, 267, 278
Ruído, María, 117, 121, 130, 141–42
Ruskin, John, 269
Russel, Mark, 169, 172

S

Sabater, Xavier, 264
Sala, Toni, 274
Salabert, Pere, 277
Salvat-Papasseit, Joan, 240, 243
Salzano, Juan, 194
Sánchez, José Antonio, 157–58, 172
Sand, Kaia, 249, 261
Sandburg, Carl, 28
Sandford, Mariellen R., 152, 172
Santos, Barbara, 226
Santos, Ronaldo, 57, 63–4
Santos Febres, Mayra, 93, 95, 107
Sardà, Zeneida, 269, 278
Sarduy, Severo, 173, 180, 187, 189
Saura, Emma, 242
Savran, David, 157, 172
Sayre, Henry, 153, 155, 172
Scalapino, Leslie, 262
Schechner, Richard, 160
Schneemann, Carolee, 136–37
Schroeter, Werner, 177
Schulze Schwarz, Herta, 114, 131
Schwitters, Kurt, 38
Scramim, Susana, 67, 70
Sedgwick, Eve Kosofski, 129, 131
Seeger, Pete, 242
Sefamí, Jacobo, 187–89
Segantini, Giovanni, 267, 276
Sell, Mike, 39–40, 52
Shakespeare, William, 192
Shange, Ntozake, 225, 227
Shaw, Lytle, 105, 109
Sienkewicz, Thomas J., 12, 19
Silliman, Ron, 158, 172
Sisa, Jaume, 10, 15, 17, 229–42, 244, 277

Sissay, Lemn, 10, 12, 15, 197–205, 207–17, 219, 221, 223, 227, 280
Skoulding, Zoë, 11, 15, 17, 257, 259, 262, 281
Smith, Anna Deavere, 155
Smith, Hazel, 247, 251–53, 255–56, 260–62
Smith, Linda, 219, 227
Smith, Patti, 87
Snyder, Gary, 25, 30
Solfa, Ricardo — see Jaume Sisa
Solomos, John, 214–16
Sontag, Susan, 234, 245
Sotomayor, Áurea María, 107, 109
Spence, Jo, 169, 172
Spicer, Jack, 24
Stalker Group, 273
Stanbury, Sarah, 108
Starr, Chicky, 99–101, 108
Stearns, Carol Z., 116
Stein, Gertrude, 155
Steiner, Peter, 86, 88
Stendhal, 159, 273
SuAndi, 10, 12, 15–6, 197–203, 205–17, 219, 221–22, 225–28, 281
Sunyol, Víctor, 265
Szondi, Peter, 159, 172

T

Tamsho, Tina, 221
Tàpies, Antoni, 270
Tarcisio, Eloy, 187
Tarrida, Joan, 267, 278
Taylor, Diana, 106
Templeton, Fiona, 10, 15, 169, 247, 249–52, 262
Terada, Rei, 129, 131
Thomas, Dylan, 28
Thomas, Lorenzo, 88, 107
Thurston, Scott, 261
Timmer, Nanne, 86, 88
Toczek, Nick, 219, 227
Todorov, Tzvetan, 86, 88, 103, 109
Tomaševskij, Boris, 86
Tomlin, Lily, 155
Tonkiss, Fran, 248, 262
Treece, David, 56, 60, 70
Triau, Christophe, 159
Trig, Stephanie, 209, 217
Trigo, Xosé Manuel, 149–50
Tropicália, 59–60, 62–63, 69
Tropicalistas, 56, 59–63, 69
Tutu, Desmond, 197
Tutu, Samera Owusu, 198, 211, 217
Twain, Mark, 24

U

Ubac, Ignasi, 233

V

Vaessens, Thomas, 34–5, 40, 47, 50, 52
Vanvuugt, Ewald, 36–9, 41, 49
Vega, Ana Lydia, 100
Velázquez, Diego, 144
Veloso, Caetano, 59–61, 63, 69–70
Velvet Underground, 126, 177
Venuti, Lawrence, 261–62
Verdaguer, Jacint, 265, 268–70, 272–73, 276, 278
Vergeer, Koen, 33–4, 48, 52
Verhagen, Hans, 37
Vianna Baptista, Josely, 180, 184, 189
Vicente, Joan, 265, 278
Vico, Giambattista, 148
Vilanova, Antonio, 277
Vilariño, Ignacio, 117, 141–42
Vilhena, Bernardo, 53–5, 66–7
Villa, Saúl, 180–81, 187–88, 192
Villora, Pedro Manuel, 163
Vinkenoog, Simon, 13, 36–7, 41, 51

Visocchi, Michael, 197, 201
Voltaire, 148

W

Walcott, Derek, 86
Waldman, Anne, 31
Warhol, Andy, 177
Warner, Michael, 107, 109
Weems, Carrie Mae, 223
Weigel, Sigrid, 129, 131
Wenders, Wim, 116
Whalen, Philip, 25
White, Greg, 253, 261
White, Kenneth, 266
Whitman, Walt, 23, 27–9, 32, 75
Wijndelts, Ward, 36, 52
Wilde, Oscar, 24, 175
Wilberforce, William, 205, 214
Williams, Raymond, 272, 278
Williams, Roy, 280
Williams, Saul, 11, 16–7, 73, 80, 82–8
Williams, William Carlos, 24, 153
Wilson, Michael, 172
Wilson, Robert, 154, 158, 161
Witte, Arjan, 34
Wittgenstein, Ludwig, 257, 262
Wolffer, Lorena, 188
Wout, Rob — see *Opland*
Wright, Beth Sarah, 198, 212, 217

Y

Yeats, William Butler, 28
Young, Lola, 213

Z

Zappa, Frank, 184
Zizek, Slavoj, 113, 131

RACE / ETHNICITY
Multidisciplinary Global Contexts

A peer-reviewed journal jointly-produced through The Kirwin Institute for the Study of Race and Ethnicity and the Office of Minority Affairs at Ohio State University

EDITED BY JOHN A. POWELL AND MAC A. STEWART

Race/Ethnicity offers a critical intervention in contemporary thinking on race and ethnicity by recognizing and responding to shared challenges. Through a multidisciplinary approach, a concern with race and ethnicity on the global scale, and a willingness simultaneously to engage theory, practice, and other forms of knowledge, the journal offers new ways for scholars, activists, and practitioners to exchange vital information, perspectives, and insights with each other.

Special Issue: Human Rights, Social Justice, and the Impact of Race, VOLUME 3, ISSUE 2

PUBLISHED SEMIANNUALLY
eISSN 1935-8562
pISSN 1935-8644

Available in electronic, combined electronic & print, and print formats

SUBSCRIBE http://www.jstor.org/r/iupress

For more information on Indiana University Press
http://www.iupress.indiana.edu

601 North Morton Street, Bloomington, Indiana 47404-3797 USA

Literatura y errabundia

(Javier Marías, Antonio Muñoz Molina y Rosa Montero)

Alexis Grohmann

En años relativamente recientes, el género de la novela ha ido experimentando cambios notables, abanderados por la realidad y su invasión del territorio de la ficción. En el presente estudio exhaustivo de tres obras españolas (de Javier Marías, Antonio Muñoz Molina y Rosa Montero), situadas en un amplio contexto literario europeo, Alexis Grohmann propone como clave de esas transformaciones el concepto de la digresión. La porosidad o errancia genérica de las obras, su divagación argumental o ausencia de trama, su digresividad estilística y la errabundia de los procesos de creación, además del disperso y heterogéneo material con el que se trabaja, hacen que la digresión se perfile no tanto como un recurso o simple figura retórica, cuanto como una verdadera *Weltanschauung*, una manera de contemplar el mundo.

Alexis Grohmann es Senior Lecturer in Hispanic Studies en la Universidad de Edimburgo. Es autor de *Coming into one's Own: The Novelistic Development of Javier Marías* (2002) y numerosos otros estudios sobre literatura española y europea, y ha editado varios libros de ensayos, entre ellos, con Caragh Wells, *Digressions in European Literature. From Cervantes to Sebald* (2011) y, con Maarten Steenmeijer, *Allí donde uno diría que ya no puede haber nada. Tu rostro mañana de Javier Marías* (2009) y *El columnismo de escritores españoles (1975–2005)* (2006).

Orders@rodopi.nl – www.rodopi.nl

rodopi

Amsterdam/New York, NY
2011. 292 pp. (Foro Hispánico 42)
Paper €59,-/US$86,-
E-Book €59,-/US$86,-
ISBN: 978-90-420-3334-4
ISBN: 978-94-012-0034-9

USA/Canada:
248 East 44th Street, 2nd floor,
New York, NY 10017, USA.
Call Toll-free (US only): T: 1-800-225-3998
F: 1-800-853-3881

All other countries:
Tijnmuiden 7, 1046 AK Amsterdam, The Netherlands
Tel. +31-20-611 48 21 Fax +31-20-447 29 79
Please note that the exchange rate is subject to fluctuations

The Dancing Word

An Embodied Approach to the Preparation of Performers and the Composition of Performances

Daniel Mroz

The product of over eighteen years of embodied research by the author, *The Dancing Word* presents a systemic and phenomenological description of a contemporary intercultural theatre practice. This volume offers a blueprint for both training and collaborative performance creation that integrates the best of western laboratory theatre with the practice and ontological underpinnings of Chinese martial (*Wushu*) and healing/self care (*Qigong*) arts. This is a book for theatre practitioners, students, scholars, and those interested in exploring transcultural methodologies.

Daniel Mroz is a theatre director and acting teacher specializing in the physical and vocal training of performers. He leads *Les Ateliers du corps*, a theatre training and performance studio in Ottawa, Canada. He is an Associate Professor in the Department of Theatre at the University of Ottawa.

Amsterdam/New York, NY
2011. 219 pp.
(Consciousness, Literature and the Arts 30)
Paper €44,-/US$64,-
E-Book €44,-/US$64,-
ISBN: 978-90-420-3330-6
ISBN: 978-94-012-0026-4

USA/Canada:
248 East 44th Street, 2nd floor,
New York, NY 10017, USA.
Call Toll-free (US only): T: 1-800-225-3998
F: 1-800-853-3881

All other countries:
Tijnmuiden 7, 1046 AK Amsterdam, The Netherlands
Tel. +31-20-611 48 21 Fax +31-20-447 29 79
Please note that the exchange rate is subject to fluctuations

Michon lu et relu

Etudes réunies par Jean Kaempfer

rodopi
Orders@rodopi.nl—www.rodopi.nl

Michon lu et relu : ce titre, en écho au *Balzac lu et relu* d'Albert Béguin, prend acte du fait qu'aujourd'hui, Pierre Michon est un « classique ». Un classique se reconnaît d'abord à cette évidence que l'on a affaire le lisant non seulement à une parole singulière, mais plus encore à une puissance d'énonciation qui s'impose absolument, nécessairement. Avant, il n'y a rien (ou le journal du matin) ; puis on lit : et dans l'énergie imparable des phrases qui se découvrent, un *fiat* s'affirme, fondateur d'une langue et d'un monde… Puis s'ajoute le consensus critique. Le désir de commenter Michon, depuis les études fondatrices de Jean-Pierre Richard, n'a pas connu de cesse : on verra qu'il poursuit dans ce volume sa carrière, au confluent nourricier de l'érudition et de l'admiration.

Amsterdam/New York, NY
2011. 245 pp. (CRIN 55)
Paper €49,-/US$71,-
E-Book €49,-/US$71,-
ISBN: 978-90-420-3331-3
ISBN: 978-94-012-0027-1

USA/Canada:
248 East 44th Street, 2nd floor,
New York, NY 10017, USA.
Call Toll-free (US only): T: 1-800-225-3998
F: 1-800-853-3881
All other countries:
Tijnmuiden 7, 1046 AK Amsterdam, The Netherlands
Tel. +31-20-611 48 21 Fax +31-20-447 29 79
Please note that the exchange rate is subject to fluctuations

Restoring the Mystery of the Rainbow

Literature's Refraction of Science

Edited by
Valeria Tinkler-Villani and
C.C. Barfoot

Keats' misgivings about science unweaving the rainbow and robbing Nature of its mystery were shared by many of contemporaries, and successive generations have been compelled to ask how this rapidly escalating knowledge of the universe would affect their understanding of themselves and the world they lived in. This is the concern of most of the essays in these two volumes: how are we to live with science and the issues scientific discoveries and propositions raise? And how has this relationship with science been explored and expressed in literary works? Yet even before science became such a challenge to the imagination, an awareness of how people interact with the natural world – in terms of sickness and health, medicine, mathematics – had already been a literary subject, also reflected in a number of articles in *Restoring the Mystery of the Rainbow: Literature's Refraction of Science*. In the twentieth century doubt became a crucial component of science as well as literature, and the relativism and uncertainty of quantum physics have proved fruitful to a wide range of dramatist, poets and novelists as many articles indicate. A systematic desire for objective criteria, verifiability, and conceptual frameworks has also increased the importance of methodology and of criticism: the many approaches adopted by the contributors to these volumes further point to the refraction of science in literature.

Amsterdam/New York, NY
2011. XI, 1.106 pp. Bound
in a 2 volume set (DQR
Studies in Literature 47)
Bound €220,-/US$319,-
E-Book €220,-/US$319,-
ISBN: 978-90-420-3325-2
ISBN: 978-94-012-0001-1

USA/Canada:
248 East 44th Street, 2nd floor,
New York, NY 10017, USA.
Call Toll-free (US only): T: 1-800-225-3998
F: 1-800-853-3881

All other countries:
Tijnmuiden 7, 1046 AK Amsterdam, The Netherlands
Tel. +31-20-611 48 21 Fax +31-20-447 29 79
Please note that the exchange rate is subject to fluctuations

Shift Linguals

Cut-Up Narratives from William S. Burroughs to the Present

Edward S. Robinson

Shift Linguals traces a history of the cut-up method, the experimental writing practice discovered by Brion Gysin and made famous by Beat author William S. Burroughs. From the groundbreaking works of Dada and Surrealism that paved the way for Burroughs' breakthrough, through the countercultural explosion of the 1960s, *Shift Linguals* explores the evolution of the cut-ups within the theoretical frameworks of postmodernism and the avant-garde to arrive at the present and the digital age.

Some 50 years on from the first 'discovery' of the cut-ups in 1959, it is only now that we are truly able to observe the method's impact, not only on literature, but on music and culture in a broader sense. The result of over nine years of research, this study represents the first sustained and detailed analysis of the cut-ups as a narrative form. With explorations of the works of Burroughs, Gysin, Kathy Acker, and John Giorno, it also contains the first critical writing on the works of Claude Pélieu and Carl Weissner in English, as well as the first in-depth discussion of the writing of Stewart Home to date.

Edward S. Robinson has published articles on William Burroughs, Stewart Home and Kathy Acker, and provided the introduction to Jürgen Ploog's cut-up novella, *Flesh Film*.

Amsterdam/New York, NY
2011. XIII, 289 pp.
(Postmodern Studies 46)
Paper €60,-/US$87,-
E-Book €60,-/US$87,-
ISBN: 978-90-420-3303-0
ISBN: 978-90-420-3304-7

USA/Canada:
248 East 44th Street, 2nd floor,
New York, NY 10017, USA.
Call Toll-free (US only): T: 1-800-225-3998
F: 1-800-853-3881

All other countries:
Tijnmuiden 7, 1046 AK Amsterdam, The Netherlands
Tel. +31-20-611 48 21 Fax +31-20-447 29 79
Please note that the exchange rate is subject to fluctuations

CPSIA information can be obtained at www.ICGtesting.com
Printed in the USA
LVOW051901220612

287097LV00002B/269/P